Cambridge Middle East Studies

Women and the political process in twentieth-century Iran

Cambridge Middle East Studies 1

Cambridge Middle East Studies has been established to publish books on the nineteenth- and twentieth-century Middle East and North Africa. The aim of the series is to provide new and original interpretations of aspects of Middle Eastern societies and their histories. To achieve disciplinary diversity, books will be solicited from authors writing in a wide range of fields including history, sociology, anthropology, political science and political economy. The emphasis will be on producing books offering an original approach along theoretical and empirical lines. The series is intended for students and academics, but the more accessible and wide-ranging studies will also appeal to the interested general reader.

In a comprehensive and original analysis of the role of women in the Iranian political process, Parvin Paidar considers the ways they have influenced and been influenced by the evolutionary and revolutionary transformations which have dominated twentieth-century Iran. In so doing, she demonstrates how political reorganisation has necessarily entailed a redefinition of the position of women. Challenging the views expressed by conventional scholarship, which emphasizes the marginalisation of Muslim women and defines their role in terms of Islamic precepts, the author asserts that gender issues are, in fact, situated right at the heart of the historical and political process of contemporary Iran. The implications of the study bear on the broader issues of women in the Middle East and in the developing countries generally.

Women and the political process in twentieth-century Iran

Parvin Paidar

CAMBRIDGE
UNIVERSITY PRESS

CAMBRIDGE UNIVERSITY PRESS
Cambridge, New York, Melbourne, Madrid, Cape Town, Singapore, São Paulo

Cambridge University Press
The Edinburgh Building, Cambridge CB2 2RU, UK

Published in the United States of America by Cambridge University Press, New York

www.cambridge.org
Information on this title: www.cambridge.org/9780521473408

First published 1995
First paperback edition published 1997

A catalogue record for this publication is available from the British Library

Library of Congress Cataloguing in Publication data
Paidar, Parvin.
Women and the political process in twentieth-century Iran / Parvin Paidar.
p. cm.–(Cambridge Middle East library)
Includes bibliographical references.
ISBN 0 521 47340 3
1. Women in politics – Iran. 2. Women – Iran – History.
3. Feminism – Iran. 4. Muslim women – Political activity. I. Title.
II. Series.
HQ1236.5.17P35 1995
305.42′0955–dc20 94-16062 CIP

ISBN-13 978-0-521-47340-8 hardback
ISBN-10 0-521-47340-3 hardback

ISBN-13 978-0-521-59572-8 paperback
ISBN-10 0-521-59572-X paperback

Transferred to digital printing 2005

Contents

Plates

Preface

The objectives of this book in providing detailed information and comprehensive analysis on women's formal position in the twentieth-century Iran are twofold: to challenge the marginalisation of gender issues within the mainstream Iranian studies, and to expose some of the prevalent mis-conceptions about the role and place of women in Iranian society.

The conceptual framework of the study is influenced by two bodies of feminist literature, the literature on Middle Eastern women, and western feminist literature of the last two decades – particularly as developed in Britain. These feminist trends have grown in conjunction with each other: the influence of Western feminist theories on the literature on Middle Eastern women has been considerable, and in turn Middle Eastern feminist movements have instigated challenge and stimulated debate within Western feminisms.

The history of Iranian women's movements demonstrates the contagious nature of feminism. Despite enormous differences in the development of feminist movements across and indeed within nations, and irrespective of the absence of a history of organised and systematic communication between them, women everywhere have sought to increase their opportunities and choices in the twentieth century. I will use the simple and broad framework of 'aiming to increase women's rights, opportunities and choices within any ideology or context' as my definition of the term feminism in this book, and describe a wide variety of women's activities in this direction in twentieth-century Iran as feminist activism. This broad definition of the term 'feminism' will accommodate many feminisms in many political or ideological frameworks in this book. The different feminisms that I will refer to include Western feminism, Middle Eastern feminism, Iranian feminism, radical feminism, socialist feminism, secular feminism, Islamic feminism, and so on.

This study is about the construction of women by political discourses, institutions and processes. It does not aim to be a general sociological study of women in Iran, nor does it claim to provide a comprehensive analysis of the effects of political change on women's lives in any of the historical periods it covers. These aims have not been followed for a number of reasons.

With regard to historical parts of this study, the volume and quality of historical materials available to me, particularly those pertaining to gender issues, were not adequate to allow proper historical sociology. I have had mainly secondary sources available to me for the historical parts, since in the 1980s access to original historical materials in Iran was very difficult indeed. This means that I have not been able to confirm or reject the reliability of some of the material that I have used in the historical parts, let alone base a historical sociology of women on them. This task will remain to be undertaken by scholars in the future.

As to contemporary parts of this study, material on the 1970s and 1980s periods was collected both in Iran and Britain and included primary and secondary written sources, interviews and discussions. Extensive use was also made of Iranian and Western newspaper reports on these periods. Two working visits were made to Iran, one during July-November 1979 and another June-September 1980. These concentrated on the post-revolutionary Islamic women's movement. Interviews with Muslim women activists and visits to Islamic women's organisations were made and written materials collected. Another study visit was made to France in 1982 for the purpose of interviewing exiled opposition leaders and collecting materials about the views and activities of opposition forces during and after the Revolution. My links with Iranians in exile and my involvement with the Iranian women's movement in exile provided an opportunity to understand the theoretical and political bases, and organisational forms of secular opposition to the Islamic Republic.

However, lack of subsequent access to field work in the Islamic Republic has limited the scope of this study. Indeed it was only possible to rely on primary and secondary published materials, discussions with prominent Iranians abroad, and the accounts provided by visitors from Iran to build a picture of post-revolutionary Islamisation policies and institutions and their effects on the lives of ordinary women. Because of these limitations, this study needs to be complemented by further sociological field work to provide a better understanding of how the lives of different categories of women have been affected by the institutions of the Islamic Republic.

A final word about the structure of the book. The Introduction will survey the relevant literature and expand on the conceptual framework and the main themes of this study. The rest of the chapters are organised around three broad political discourses that have dominated Iranian political life in the twentieth century. These discourses, which have been non-exclusive and overlapping but yet rather distinct, will be examined in three parts as follows. Part 1 will cover the discourse of modernity which dominated the long period of 1900–77 and included a number of political phases. These will be covered in chapters 1 to 5. Part 2 will cover the discourse of revolution which was dominant during 1977–79 in Iran. The different aspects of the discourse of revolution will be examined in chapters 6 and 7. Part Three will cover the discourse of Islamisation which has been dominant in Iran since the establishment of the Islamic Republic. This part will be covered in chapters 8 to 10. The conclusion will provide a summary of the main themes of the book.

Acknowledgements

This book is dedicated to my family in gratitude for their love and support.

I am indebted to a number of people for their assistance with this book: Soroush Javadi for his tremendous intellectual and practical support; Sami Zubaida for his valuable academic guidance; Deniz Kandiyoti, Joanna de Groot, Fred Halliday, Afsaneh Najmabadi for reading this long text and making valuable comments; Marigold Acland of the Cambridge University Press for co-ordinating the production of the book; Nasrollah Kasraian and Hamideh Zolfaghari for making their unpublished photographs available to me. I would also like to thank my colleagues at the World University Service (UK) for their support.

I have been inspired by many women throughout the years that I have worked on women's issues. To mention a few, I wish to thank Sudabeh Daghighi for her feminist inspirations from across the mountains. From the editorial board of *Nimeye-Digar*, an Iranian women's journal in exile, I am indebted to Afsaneh Najmabadi, Parvin Alizadeh, Shahran Tabari, Fathieh Yazdi, Sima Motamen, Haleh Afshar and Shahla Haeri for their intellectual stimulation, challenge and support. For influencing my formative feminism, I am grateful to Jennifer Sumerville, Parvin Adams, Beverley Brown and Maxine Molyneux.

Finally, I would like to acknowledge that I have previously published under the name of Nahid Yeganeh.

Transliteration and references

The arrangement followed for translation of Farsi (Persian) words in this book is as follows. Farsi common words, with some exceptions, have not been translated in the text and the reader needs to consult the Glossary for the meaning of these words. The exceptions are those common words which have only been mentioned once in which case their meaning is explained in the text. Other Farsi words translated in the text (always in parentheses) are speeches or names and titles of political parties, organisations, books and journals.

Transliteration of Farsi words follows a simple system without diacritic, and *a*, *o*, *e* are used for Farsi short vowels. For long vowels, long *a* is transliterated as *a*, long *e* as *i*, and long *o* as *u* or *ou* as appropriate. The plurals of familiar Farsi words are identified by adding an *s* such as *mollas* for *molla*, but in most cases the correct Farsi plural is used such as *fatavi* for *fatva*. The same transliteration system is used in quotations from cited works, but in the case of references the original transliteration is preserved. The reader will notice some discrepancies in transliteration, partly because of preserving the original transliterations in the references, but particularly in relation to the use of *gh* and *q*. This is because *gh* has been used as a norm here, but where usage of *q* has become customary in the literature, such as in the name Mosaddeq, it has been preserved.

In following this transliteration system, I have attempted to preserve the Farsi pronunciation of both Farsi and Arabic words. This is because the application of Arabic transliteration to Farsi tends to destroy the specificity of the Farsi language, which is an important aspect of the cultural context of this text and relevant to the political discourses discussed here. Where the transliteration system used here has resulted in difference of spelling from conventional usage both spellings are referred to in the Glossary.

In the section listing references, Farsi titles are translated into English in parentheses. These translations will not always be exact but sometimes just an abridged description. For Iranian newspapers, both Western calendar and Iranian solar dates are provided. To avoid overcrowding the text, footnotes are excluded and for books and articles only the author's surname and date of the work is mentioned in the text. For newspaper and magazines, reference numbers are given in the text and the full details are listed in the reference section.

Introduction Marginalisation of gender and approaches to women in Middle Eastern studies

The aim of this introductory chapter is to place the subject matter of the book, that is women in Iranian political discourses, within the wider context of the Middle Eastern and North African women's studies. A survey of relevant literature on women in these regions will be presented to help explain the conceptual framework and the main themes of this book.

The study of women that is before you is an interdisciplinary one, and one of the disciplines that it refers to is history. It would be useful, therefore, to adopt a historical approach in surveying the relevant interdisciplinary literature to present the academic context for each of the historical conjunctures that will be examined in the following chapters.

In surveying the literature on Middle Eastern and North African women, a critical approach will be adopted to clarify the conceptual framework and theoretical approach of this book. The following selective survey of the literature will identify some of the inadequacies of conventional Middle East studies, and examine the ways in which they have influenced the analysis of women in the Middle East. Two major issues will be at the heart of my criticism of the conventional Middle Eastern and North African studies (hereafter Middle Eastern studies for short). First, the marginalisation of gender and women's issues in the twentieth-century studies of the region. Second, the analyses of Muslim women within the framework of inadequate general theories.

Marginalisation of gender

One of the main shortcomings of the Middle Eastern studies has been the marginalisation of gender, that is the politics of male-female relations in the society. Until recently, marginalisation of gender relations was symptomatic of most areas of social sciences. But the field of Middle Eastern studies is still one of the less developed ones in relation to the integration of gender relations into the wider social studies. Despite the growing academic interest in the 1980s in the contemporary political history of the region, gender issues do not feature except marginally in scholarly works. The mainstream or rather 'malestream' Middle Eastern studies, as some feminists may prefer to describe it, has continued to adopt a gender-blind methodology. The position(s) occupied by women in the family and society at large are central to the definition(s) of gender relations in any society. In talking about marginalisation of gender relations, the emphasis in this book will be on the position(s) of women and issues of concern to women, while acknowledging the wider meanings and implications of gender relations for women, men and society as a whole.

A major symptom of gender marginalisation in studying the political history of the Middle East has been the persistence of certain assumptions about Muslim women and their roles in society. Such assumptions, it must be said, have been shared across the board by Western and Middle Eastern male and female scholars. One widespread assumption is that the only political and economic domains worth studying in Muslim societies are the formal ones, and Muslim women are unimportant or at best marginal to these domains because they have few formal political and economic rights and make a limited contribution to formal domains. Women's activities and contributions to national processes are thus ignored in a number of ways. On the one hand, the non-formal spheres of politics and economy in which women have traditionally been more active are undervalued (Tucker, 1983). On the other hand, women's existing roles within the formal domains of politics and economy are ignored (Beck & Keddie, 1978). Moreover, women's activities are seen as separate and at best complementary, but not as an integral constituent of the social system (Rassam, 1984, pp. 122–3).

The operation of these assumptions have no doubt adversely affected the development of the field of Middle Eastern political history. The quality of the literature is affected because of its failure to fully appreciate and establish the links between gender, politics and society. As will be demonstrated in the following chapters in relation to Iran, the question of women is far from an optional extra in analysing Iranian political history. On the contrary, the study of Iranian political discourses shows that gender relations and women's positions are situated at the heart of these discourses. Women's issues have not arisen in twentieth-century Iran merely because of the openmindedness and progressive policies of our revolutionaries and statesmen, as is often assumed. They have become the burning issues of this century in Iran because any discourse which has addressed the question of political and social reorganisation of Iranian society has necessarily entailed a redefinition of gender relations and as part of that the reorganisation of women's positions. To marginalise the relevance of women's issues to national processes is to misunderstand the political history of Iran and other Middle Eastern societies which have revolved around the question of development and change in this century (Kandiyoti, 1991a).

Another effect of the operation of inaccurate assumptions about women's activities manifests itself in the unevenness and quality of information and research on women. A vicious circle is created in the sense that the more gender issues are treated as isolated the less new information and data become available on women, which then prohibits development of further integrated research and analysis. Adoption of gender-blind methodology has prevented many mainstream scholars from recognising and utilising historical and contemporary material on gender relations when they come across them (Keddie, 1979). The unevenness of data and information has been further exacerbated by the resource-led nature of much of the gender research. Government and private funding agencies have tended to fund certain types of research as a result of their own particular misconceptions about Muslim women and their roles and activities. In relation to the Middle East, research on health and family planning have tended to have a higher profile than any other areas of women's involvement in Middle Eastern societies, especially in comparison with women's activities within the formal and non-formal spheres of politics and economy (Van Dusen, 1979; Baffoun, 1984).

The problem of marginalisation of women's issues has been responded to in recent years by a growing body of Middle Eastern women's studies. This recent development has been encouraged by the success of Western women's studies in establishing the point that women's absence in academic literature is not a true reflection of women's actual place in society, but a symptom of social researchers' misconceived assumptions about them. Recent studies of Middle Eastern women have argued that women constitute the backbone of social systems such as the family and the community and play an important role in sustaining and changing them (Fernea, 1985; Agarwal, 1988). Numerous research undertaken on women's history to remedy the undervaluing of women's traditional productive roles have also shown their important contributions to family subsistence and demonstrated the ways in which they have sustained the informal economic sector (Gran, 1977; Afshar, 1985; Tucker, 1986). Women have also participated in the formal economy as workers and professionals, where they have sustained the service sector, especially education, health and welfare (Hijab, 1988; Moghadam, 1990).

Women's contribution to the sphere of formal politics in Middle Eastern countries has also attracted increasing attention. The present study is an addition to the increasing volume of research and analysis on women's participation in national processes. Women have taken part in the complex process of the formation of the state and state policy as political actors and contributors to public opinion and popular culture. They have participated in nationalist movements, anti-colonial uprisings and armed conflicts and have formed pressure groups and women's movements for the advancement of their rights and interests (Fluer-Lobban, 1980; Jayawardena, 1986; Yuval-Davis & Anthias, 1989). In short, the Middle Eastern women's studies has begun to make the case for the centrality of gender relations to the political, economic and social organisation of these societies (Van Dusen, 1979). It has also acquired a political dimension by providing the conceptual tools for the development of Middle Eastern women's movements (Mernissi, 1988).

Approaches to women in Middle Eastern studies

Another major problem which was quite widespread within Middle Eastern studies until the early 1980s, was the adoption of general theories as a tool for the explanation of women's position. This problem was rooted in conventional Middle Eastern studies which was dominated by a variety of development theories for most of this century. These development theories were variations on the theme of 'modernity' as an evolutionary model of universal progress.

The terms 'modernity' or 'modern condition' have been used to define, broadly speaking, the global social and political forces unleashed in the post-Enlightenment era by the industrial revolution and the French revolution – these forces flourished in the nineteenth and early twentieth century and became institutionalised in the Europe and North America of post World War II (Berman, 1982). The process of modernisation entailed establishment of nation state, new forms of power and class structures, citizenship, democracy, civil society, individualism, economic development, industrialisation, world market urbanisation, population growth, new systems of communication, and so forth. The advent of modernity in the shape of capitalist industrialism in the West also relied upon a colonialist and imperialist expansion that subjugated large sections of the non-Western world.

The conviction was that societies move, albeit at a different pace, towards a common form of social and political existence, and modernity is the trajectory for this historical shift which has continued since the Enlightenment. The most powerful modern development theory conceptualised Western societies as the vanguard of modernity and hence universal development and progress, and all other societies were thought to eventually follow in the same direction (Harrison, 1988). The dominance of this development theory was rooted in several centuries of Christian expansionism and intrusion into non-Western societies on the basis of the desire to spread modern Western civilisation to all humanity.

In the field of Middle East studies, the universality of the Western model of development and modernity was represented in a variety of forms which included Orientalism, Islamism and the modernisation theory. These constituted the theoretical vehicle for the study of Muslim women within conventional Middle Eastern studies. With the development of feminism and the establishment of Middle Eastern women's studies as a field of enquiry in its own right, new approaches towards Muslim women appeared. Radical feminism, Marxist feminism and Islamic feminism all attempted to identify and analyse the factors which accounted for Muslim women's situation. But despite the search for new understanding, many of the underlying assumptions of conventional Middle East studies crept into the feminist analyses of Muslim women.

Orientalism

One of the most influential of conventional theoretical approaches to the Middle East was Orientalism, which has been subjected to frequent and vigorous criticism since the 1970s (Said, 1978). I will raise those aspects of Orientalism which were applied to women in the context of twentieth-century political processes in the Middle East. At the core of Orientalism as a theoretical approach lay a particular conception of Islam and its place in Middle Eastern societies. Orientalism believed in the essentiality of cultures and in the case of these societies considered Islam as the factor which distinguished it from the West. Orientalist scholars regarded Islam as the sole designator of Middle Eastern society and as such the main determinant of women's position. The Orientalist analysis of political change as it affected women was built upon the above premise and consisted of at least three dimensions. First, the notion of Muslim women as oppressed; second, the construction of oppositional dichotomies of tradition and modernity to explain political change; and third, essentialisation and reification of women's history.

Orientalism propagated the notion of Muslim women as slaves. An assortment of missionaries, travellers and scholars, sometimes all in one, set out to explore the conditions of Muslim societies and peoples around the turn of the century. In relation to women, the following plea made by Christian missionaries was typical: 'No one can study the tragic story of women under the Muslim faith without an earnest longing and prayer that something may be done by the united Church of Christ to meet this need. We think with pity and sorrow of the veiled women of Islam' (Zwemer & Zwemer, 1926, p. 5).

Similar accounts of women's lives in the Middle East were provided by Western women travellers. The writings of Isabella Bird, Lady Anne Blunt and Gertrude Bell portrayed misery, suffocation, lack of autonomy and powerlessness because they saw Muslim women being caught in a system of seclusion and polygamy (Baron, 1982, p. 31). These images were complemented by the obsessive attention paid to royal *harams* by Western explorers of Eastern cultures. Lack of access to the *haram* did not prevent male writers from describing it simultaneously as fascinating and revolting (Ahmed, 1982). The negative image of Muslim women was occasionally challenged in favour of more heterogeneous images which showed women's strengths as well as weaknesses (Baron, 1982). But whether uniform or heterogeneous, the image of the Muslim woman was engraved in a concept of society as synonymous with Islam and tradition.

Having constructed Muslim women as oppressed and Islam as their oppressor, Orientalist observers turned their attention to the possibility of change in the position of Muslim women (Rice, 1923). The early twentieth-century period was one of great political change and an unprecedented surge towards modernity in the Middle East. In Iran, the Revolution of 1905–11 established a constitutional monarchy and a limited form of parliamentary democracy. This was followed by the collapse of the Qajar dynasty and the establishment of the modernist and autocratic rule of Reza Shah Pahlavi. Other Middle Eastern societies experienced similar tremors. The political scene in Turkey was dominated by a nationalist movement which, having gone through different phases since the Tanzimat period of reform in the nineteenth century, resulted in the dissolution of the Ottoman empire after the First World War and the establishment of a republic under Mustafa Kemal Ataturk. In Egypt the movement for independence from British rule, which had been recurring since 1882, erupted into a revolution in 1919 and resulted in the Constitution of 1923 which established parliamentary democracy. In Afghanistan, Amanollah Khan's success in seizing the throne in 1919 ended decades of tribal feuds and foreign power rivalries between the British, Russians, Turks and Iranians.

The Orientalist understanding of these events and their implications for women, was based on the construction of the oppositional dichotomies of tradition and modernity. The clash between these dichotomies was considered as the motor of change in the Middle East, particularly so in relation to women. Muslim societies were depicted as inherently traditional, and traditionalism was associated with stagnation and backwardness. This was juxtaposed with modernity which was associated with dynamism and progress, and was considered to be Western in origin. Traditionalism, being defined as a static and indigenous condition, meant that Muslim women were seen to be doomed to an unchanging condition in the absence of a Western challenge to Islam (Tucker, 1983). The following excerpt is a good example of the application of the dichotomy of 'tradition versus modernity' to the Constitutional Revolution of 1905–11 in Iran:

> In nineteen hundred and five the Persian lay asleep by the wayside. It was no afternoon nap he was taking but the heavy sleep of centuries of stupid indifference. A closely woven mantle of traditions and customs was thrown over his head to keep out the light. It kept out the air too, but he only slept more soundly, all unconscious of the dogs fighting around his head or the donkeys and mules that nearly walked over his feet. One day something happened. The Idea of constitutional government came that way, saw the sleeping Persian, seized him, shook him, stood him on his feet, faced towards the light, and sped away. The Persian rubbed his eyes, dazed by the brightness, stretched himself and said, 'Ya Allah.' But he did not lie down again, the Idea had given him a too thorough shaking. Instead, he walked to the public square and made a speech. He did not know the meaning of all he said, but the words which most often came to his lips were, Constitution, Freedom, Progress, Education. When he went home he found the Idea had come into the *andarun* and the women were talking of the same great subjects, though they comprehended even less of what it all meant. From that day to this the Persian has never been the same . . . They [Persian women] are adopting our dress, they will get our education in a measure, perhaps our freedom to a certain extent. Shall they have our Christ? (Woodman Stocking, 1912, pp. 367, 372).

Having taken 'Islam' and 'society' as identical and having defined Islam as static, the changing position of women could only be explained in terms of the declining hold of Islam and the increasing impact of Christianity. In this scheme of things, men and women were no more than passive and confused victims of tradition and recipients of modernity.

The third dimension of the Orientalist analysis of political change was its essentialisation and reification of women's history. Orientalism resorted to Islamic doctrine to explain the position of women, taking what was prescribed in the *Qoran*, *hadith* and *shariat* as historical fact (Keddie, 1979). While the history of women in the West was regarded as the product of complex economic and social development, Middle Eastern women's history was considered to be the product of the 'traditional Muslim view' seen 'as an inherited given' (Tucker, 1983). As a result, the process of historical change was often bypassed by Orientalist observers and countless essays on 'women in Islam' did little to explain the development of women's positions in various Middle Eastern societies and the differences which existed in Muslim women's histories within the region.

In short, the Orientalist approach to the question of women and political change suffered from endemic essentialisation, ethnocentrism and stereotyping. Nevertheless, despite vigorous criticism of these inadequacies, the influence of Orientalism within the field was neither confined to the past nor specific to Western scholars (Sayigh, 1981). Its influence may have been more subtle and refined within the contemporary literature, but the field of Middle Eastern women's studies was yet to be totally liberated from it even in the 1970s (Hammam, 1981; Abu-Lughod, 1981). Orientalist assumptions infiltrated a wide variety of often opposing schools of thought, ranging from modernisation theory to feminism.

Modernisation theory

Western domination of the Middle East in the nineteenth and early twentieth centuries acquired many dimensions: the mission to 'civilise' Islamic societies through Christianity constituted its moral dimension; direct and indirect colonisation constituted its political and economic dimensions; and Orientalism constituted its social and cultural dimension. With the rise of nation states and independence movements in the Middle East in the early and mid-twentieth century, all three dimensions of Western domination evolved and changed. Islam developed and asserted itself as a political force and met the challenge of Christianity head on. Nationalist movements managed to change Western foreign policies from direct colonisation of the region to a more indirect protection of Western interests through modernisation of the region. Orientalism gave way to modernisation theory in the 1950s and 1960s as a new social science framework for the study of the region. The latter inherited many characteristics of the former.

The affinity between modernisation theory and Western foreign policy was as close, at least initially, as that between Orientalism and colonialism. With the replacement of Britain by the United States as the main foreign influence in the region, American political science gained analytical dominance within the field of Middle East studies. Modernisation theory associated 'modernism' with 'Westernism' and turned 'modernity' as a process into 'Westernisation' as the end result. This was based on the idea of 'the passing of traditional society' through state modernisation (Lerner, 1958; Halpern, 1963). With the consolidation of pro-Western states in some Middle Eastern countries such as Iran, the West found an indigenous ally in its battle for the salvation of Muslim societies from the stronghold of tradition and Islam. The effort of the modernising state to transform backward 'Muslim' society in the image of the modern West dominated the literature. The obsession with Islam as the 'cause' of society's backwardness and women's oppression was matched with a preoccupation with the state as the sole instrument and agent of social change. The main contradiction within Middle Eastern societies was now considered to be the resistance by traditional forces such as the Islamic clergy to state modernisation (Woodsmall, 1936).

The cornerstone of modernisation theory was the conviction that the implantation of Western institutions in backward countries would create the same effects there as in the West (Benard & Khalilzad, 1984, pp. 1–24). The state as the agent of modernisation, or Westernisation, was expected to introduce Western institutions in the Middle East, and by overcoming the forces of tradition reverse the state of backwardness and create a duplicate Western society in this region. What was being introduced as modernity entailed a number of processes such as secularisation, industrialisation, urbanisation, nuclearisation of the family, education, paid employment and so on. The success or failure of the modernisation process was gauged by the replacement of 'traditional' sources of identity such as ethnicity and religion with ones based on modern institutions. Modernisation theory conceptualised the position of women within these parameters. Women's oppression was firmly placed in the sphere of traditional Islam and their emancipation was defined in terms of their acquisition of appropriate roles within modern institutions. The transition from the former to the latter was supposed to be achieved through state policy. The state and its gender policies were conceptualised as unified, and modernisation was seen as a homogeneous and coherent process, affecting women's position in a total and consistent way (Patai, 1967).

The modernisation literature monitored women's transition from tradition to modernity and discussed the effects of modernisation on women. Ruth Woodsmall surveyed women's entry into education and employment and their participation in social and political affairs (Woodsmall, 1960). A growing volume of sociological and anthropological literature collected and tested data on whether modern institutions were changing women's position in conformity with Western patterns. Let us examine some of the literature on Iran, a country seen at the time to conform to the expected course of modernisation and to lead other Middle Eastern countries in this respect.

'Modernisation' was found to have contributed to the decline of polygamy in Iran (Momeni, 1975), changed the pattern of fertility of Shirazi women (Paydarfar & Sarram 1970) and altered the status of urban women in the same direction as in the West (Touba, 1972). Modernisation proved not to have had any influence on household size (Paydarfar, 1975), sex-role differentiation in the family (Touba, 1975) and the domestic environment of women in Esfahan (Gulick & Gulick, 1976 and 1978). Where such close proximity in the pattern of change in the position of women in Iran and the West did not occur, the difference was explained in relation to economic or cultural factors. Keller and Mandelson concluded that the family remained a relatively unchanged institution in Iran and found 'the basic difference between Iran and the West' in this respect in 'different levels of industrialisation' (Keller & Mandelson, 1971, p. 10). Sedghi and Ashraf regarded it as their 'main assumption' that 'modernisation of Iran has changed the position of women in society', but introduced the 'role of the Islamic culture' as 'the determining influence in the creation of an environment in which the role of male dominance has been tightly interwoven with social relations' (Sedghi & Ashraf, 1976, pp. 201–2). Behnaz Pakizegi pointed to the large gap between 'Westernised law on women' and 'social customs' (Pakizegi, 1978). Shahla Haeri concluded that 'Westernised legal code' did not achieve the intended reform because it 'bypassed the inner dynamics of [the Iranian] culture' (Haeri, 1981, p. 230). Michael Fischer defined the main underlying contradiction in Iranian society as a 'confrontation between conservative Muslim leaders and an aggressive modernising state' and introduced the concept of 'social value' and its correspondence to economic classes and political forces as the key to the understanding of the position of women (Fischer, 1978, p. 190).

What these studies established was that the modernisation route in Iran, as the leading modernist country in the Middle East, did not necessarily move in the anticipated direction. This was the beginning of the demise of modernisation theory because it proved to be inadequate within its own terms. The process of demise was accelerated because of the failure of modernisation theory to take into account social and historical processes which were being raised as important issues by other theories. Modernisation theory was criticised for ignoring the indigenous and exogenous political processes which played important roles in the formation of the nation state and secured its continuance (Sayigh, 1981). These processes were not problematised and defined in relation to the state, and in that sense the modernising state was assumed to be above the internal and international relations of its time. In the case of Iran, lack of interest by modernisation literature in the effects of internal political repression and Iran's position within international alliances, which tied it to some of the most reactionary regimes in the world, was raised as a criticism. This brought into question the political credibility of modernisation policy (Nirumand, 1969).

Furthermore, the conceptualisation of tradition and modernity as fixed oppositional categories, which modernisation theory inherited from

Orientalism, was rejected because it overlooked the constant redefinition and reconstruction of these categories within current political processes (Rassam, 1984, p. 10; Baykan, 1990). As a result, despite its claim to predict the course of the social and political development of the Middle East, modernisation theory failed to account for the changing circumstances in the region and the rise of Islamic populism in the 1970s. Moreover, the conceptualisation of women as the main beneficiaries of modernisation did not stand up to challenges presented by other discourses. The notion of class difference challenged the universality of modernisation gender policies (Beck & Keddie, 1978, p.12). The effectiveness of legal reform as the main vehicle for transformation of gender relations was questioned (Haeri, 1981). The process of the construction of state policy on women was challenged and the concept of state policy as the reflection of the will of the monarch was criticised (Afkhami, 1984). The concept of family as the site of the struggle between traditionalists and modernists for the salvation of women was challenged, on the one hand by a neo-Marxist linkage of the family to the needs of the capitalist state (National Union of Women, 1979a), and on the other by a radical construction of the family as an Islamic institution (Motahhari, 1978). These were some of the challenges which signalled the beginning of the end of modernisation theory as a dominant mode of analysis within Middle Eastern women's studies (Allaghi & Almana, 1984). The crisis of modernisation theory was accompanied by the rise of the new wave of feminism in the West which signalled the end of the illusion that modernity was going to deliver emancipation to women without a major struggle.

Three different theoretical and political responses to Orientalism and modernisation theory began to exert considerable influence within the literature in the 1970s. These were dependency theory (which made claim to socialist modernity as opposed to the prevailing capitalist one), the new Islamism (which proposed Islamic modernity as an alternative to Western modernity), and feminism (which aimed to challenge patriarchal modernism of capitalist, socialist and Islamic kinds). These challenges to the politics of Orientalism and modernisation theory, however, continued to carry some of their underlying assumptions with regard to Islam, its place in society and its role in female subordination.

Dependency theory

Many of the challenges to modernisation theory arose within neo-Marxist theories of development, or socialist modernity, in reaction to the former's theoretical inadequacies and pro-establishment politics. The application of modernisation theory in the 1950s and 1960s as the theoretical arm of US foreign policy coincided with a vigorous adoption of the neo-Marxist theory of development by the Soviet Union to secure its interests in the developing world. This was taking place in the context of the Cold War which divided the world into two camps, namely the Western and Eastern blocs. The increasing influence of Maoism as an anti-imperialist populist ideology, the success of the Cuban Revolution in establishing an anti-imperialist regime across the US borders, and Soviet support of the communist and nationalist liberation movements in the developing world, facilitated the appearance of a range of neo-Marxist theories of development in the late 1960s and 1970s.

The most influential neo-Marxist development theory during this period was the Latin American school of dependency. This model of analysis which exerted tremendous influence amongst the liberation movements in the developing world, including the Middle Eastern left, situated developing societies within a global system of capitalism which was created, according to this view, by the West to facilitate Western development and prosperity. This was argued to be tantamount to a process of underdevelopment of the former by the latter. While the periphery was impoverished and its development distorted, the metropolis prospered and developed. Dependency theory defined the relationship between the West and the developing world in terms of unequal exchange and advocated a break-up of the global capitalist system, which had subordinated and drained the developing world, as the only route for the satisfactory development of the disadvantaged regions (Amin, 1976; Baran, 1975; Frank, 1969; Wallerstein, 1979; Benard & Khalilzad, 1984).

The class structure of satellite societies was considered, in the last analysis, as the reflection of a wider economic structure. The state in the developing world was defined either as a directly administered colony, or a 'comparador' (dependent) agent government, which in each case ruled on behalf of the interests of Western capitalism and in doing so catered most for the rich and least for the masses (Baran, 1975). Women in the developing world, it was argued, were particularly exploited by the class system which was created in underdeveloped countries. Within the Middle Eastern Marxist literature, the concept of 'imperialism' replaced 'Islam' and 'tradition' as the cause of women's oppression. Women's liberation, therefore, was no longer sought in Westernisation but in a socialist break from the West. It was the 'dominance of Arab world by colonialist and imperialist powers', it was argued, which had necessitated the 'Arab ruling classes to "respect" Islamic tradition and to administer Islamic states' (Salman, 1978, p. 26). Middle Eastern women were acknowledged to be exposed to different forms of oppression 'national, class and sexual', nevertheless 'the original cause of their triple oppression' was not seen to be Islam, but rather the 'patriarchal class system which manifests itself internationally as world capitalism and imperialism and nationally in the feudal and capitalist classes of the Third World countries' (El Saadawi, 1982, p. 206).

The application of dependency theory to the case of Iran brought to the fore those features of modern Iran which modernisation theory had avoided or concealed: rural poverty, urban slums, unemployment, inflation, the growing gap between rich and poor, widespread corruption, dependence on food imports, wastage of oil revenue through high military spending, economic and political dependence on the US, CIA intervention in internal political processes, lack of political freedom and democracy and so on (Nirumand, 1969, p. 197). This, in particular, challenged the concept of the 'modernisation of women'. Iranian and other Middle Eastern women, it was argued, were victims of imperialist exploitation and not beneficiaries of modernisation. The policies of pro-Western states towards women, it was argued, had two main purposes. First, to 'utilize the cheap labour of women for the labour market of colonialism and dependent capitalism', and second, to 'transform women into fundamental consumers ... of the female-linked goods which are the products of economically important industries' (NUW, 1979a, pp. 147–48). Furthermore, it was argued that the legal reforms carried out on the position of women did not affect the position of lower-class women and only benefitted 'women from dependent bourgeoisie' (*ibid.*, p. 148). The question of women's rights, according to this view point, was irrelevant anyway because 'where people were fighting for the most elementary human rights, the problem of sex discrimination could not be posed' OWE 1980, p. 162). Women's 'double class and sexual oppression', it was emphasised, was rooted firstly in the 'infra-structural conditions and dominant mode of production', and secondly, in the 'cultural and superstructural effects caused by the dominant mode of production' (NUW, 1979a, p. 143). Therefore, 'no solution to the question of women's emancipation is possible' unless 'the women's movement fights alongside the movement of the masses against imperialism and for social liberation' (*Ibid.*, p. 167).

Similar arguments were presented in relation to other Middle Eastern countries regarding the link between imperialism and women's emancipation. In relation to North Africa, Baffoun argued that 'The state of economic dependence in particular, and the unequal terms of trade between the societies of North Africa and the developed and dominant countries, imbue every level of practical living in North African society with its characteristic historical flavour' (Baffoun, 1984, pp. 53–54). This, she argued, necessitated a critical rethinking of concepts such as women's liberation. Another writer in her discussion of the integration of Lebanon into the 'World Capitalist System' supported the view expressed at the UN conference in Nairobi (1986) that 'colonialism and new-colonialism, are at the heart of Third World women's exploitation. Colonialism did not bring civilisation; on the contrary, it forced degradation'. She conceded that some women did benefit from capitalism, namely 'women of the emerging comparador bourgeoisie', but believed that 'these spoilt daughters of the world capitalist system were partly responsible for the problems with which the indigenous poor Lebanese women had to struggle. . . . To them, women's liberation was a fashion they imported, as they did their perfume, to be worn occasionally to show off' (Sabban, 1988, pp. 125–6).

Despite its original success in exposing the inadequacies of modernisation theory, however, the application of dependency theory to Middle Eastern societies created a new set of political and theoretical problems. Dependency theory clearly suffered from economic reductionism, theoretical generalisation and political dogmatism. Three main criticisms of dependency theory are particularly relevant here. The first, which arose in relation to nationalism, concerned the inability of dependency theory to account for national variations. The generality of the reference to Marxist categories and the universality of the neo-Marxist theory of underdevelopment made national differences irrelevant in the last analysis. The application of dependency theory to individual countries tended to confirm the generality of the theory rather than the specificity of the situation. In this way, national and cultural processes and struggles played no significant role in the analysis.

Second, the particularly crude version of class analysis of society and state which dependency theory adhered to, came under severe criticism from within Marxism in the 1970s. Economic determinism, it was argued, was incapable of accounting for the specificity of ideology (Althusser, 1971). Dependency theory as applied to the Middle East was therefore accused of inability to explore 'the specificity of Islam, whether it appears in the form of local cultural practices justified in religious terms, as items of legislation derived from the *shariat* or as a more diffuse ideology about cultural authenticity' (Kandiyoti, 1991a). By replacing 'Islam' with 'imperialism' as the 'cause' of women's oppression, Islam was further essentialised as a set of ideas situated outside social relations (Yeganeh, 1982). The process of capitalist expansion in the Middle East and the specific ways in which it affected women were also reified. The criticism of the concept of 'world capitalist system' and its eventual deconstruction resulted in an emphasis on the variability and heterogeneity of the relationship between the West and developing nations, and the importance of political and ideological factors in shaping international relations.

Third, the feminist criticism of dependency theory attacked it for failing to recognise the specificity of women's oppression and for not accommodating the women's movement (Tabari, 1982). The economic reductionism of this position which tended to privilege global economic relations over all social, political and cultural processes and relations, did not allow for the relationship between women's oppression and social class to be problematised constructively. The proponents of dependency theory tended to devalue the gains women had made in formal rights and social participation under the 'dependent bourgeois' rule, and women's struggles were too readily subordinated to anti-imperialist struggles (Yeganeh, 1982). In advocating a universal path to socialist liberation which was seen to guarantee women's liberation, neo-Marxist theories of development were criticised for ignoring the operation of patriarchal relations within existing socialist societies (Molyneux, 1981). For feminist discourse, the Marxist theory of development proved as problematic as modernisation theory. The latter modelled women's emancipation after the ideal type image of North American woman, and the former sought women's salvation in following the path of the ideal type Soviet woman.

Political defence of Islam

Another influential theoretical and political response to Orientalism and modernisation theory in the 1970s and 1980s was political Islam. This was based on the conviction that neither Western modernity nor socialist modernisation had fulfilled their promises for the developing world. Islamism as a theoretical approach was of course as old as Orientalism. The defence of Islam in the face of Western challenge took many forms, but ultimately aimed to prove the 'progressive' nature of the *Qoran*, *hadith*, and the *shariat*, either by denying the 'low status' of women in Muslim countries, or by attributing it to pre-Islamic traditions and contemporary extra-Islamic factors (Al-Qazzaz, 1977). Islamism shared the basic tenets of Orientalism in its essentialist and ahistorical approach to both Islam and the West. Western Orientalism and Islamic Occidentalism were indeed two sides of the same coin (Abu-Lughod, 1981).

Islamism, as a serious theoretical and political approach to the analysis of women's position in the Middle East, had previously been overshadowed by modernisation and dependency theories, but it gained a new lease of life in the 1970s as a result of the rise of Islamic modernism. The political defence of Islam was not a return to 'tradition' in a pre-modern sense. On the contrary, it solicited reference to modern concepts and institutions, such as 'state' and 'people', and made a claim to modernity, independence and progress (Zubaida, 1989a). So far, modernists had been roughly divided between left and right, but in the 1970s the Islamists joined them as a third modernising political force. The new political defence of Islam shared its essentialised conception of Islam with the former theories, but differed from them in one way. While in modernisation and dependency theories Islam was a force to be overcome in the drive towards Western or socialist progress, the political defence of Islam considered the uniqueness of 'Islamic culture' as the reason for Middle Eastern societies to take a separate development route, that of Islamic modernity. It rejected the manifestations of Western development as alien, therefore at best irrelevant and at worst harmful to Islamic societies.

At the core of the newly emerging political Islam, which was facilitated by the Iranian Revolution of 1977–9, lay the belief that over a century of 'acquiring Western education, adjusting and adopting to Western political, cultural and intellectual domination, undergoing the transition to nationalist/secular identities and capitalist/ democratic philosophies' has destroyed the 'moral fabric of the human personality and society and has led to mortal conflicts at social, political, economic and international levels' (Siddiqui, 1980, Appendix, p.1). The quest for 'modernisation' and 'progress' through 'Westernisation of Muslim individuals and Muslim societies', according to this argument, 'was bound to fail and has done so at great cost to Muslim culture and the economic, social and political fabric of Muslim societies' (*ibid.*). In order to save their society and heritage, Muslims were seen to have only one choice, that is, 'to conceive and create social, economic and political systems which are fundamentally different from those now prevailing in Muslim societies throughout the world' (*ibid.*). The 'Muslim intelligentsia' was urged to reject the 'systems and structures of contemporary "advanced" civilizations as alien to the Muslim intellectual tradition and irrelevant to our needs', and instead to 'commit themselves to the historical role of recreating fully operational social, economic and political systems of Islam in all Muslim societies' (*ibid.*).

Within the framework of rejection of West and East and reconstruction of a new Islam relevant to the present world, a variety of Islamic movements set out to change the world for Muslims in the 1970s and 1980s. Some of these made a special contribution to the conceptual development of revolutionary Islam in Iran particularly in relation to gender (Yeganeh & Keddie, 1986, pp. 122–36). Similar models of Islamic gender analysis were presented within the Arab-Islamic literature (Abdel Kader, 1984). One of the architects of the revolutionisation of gender relations in the context of the Iranian Revolution of 1977–9, Ali Shariati, located the oppression of women in 'cultural imperialism' which he saw as the greatest conspiracy of humanity (Shariati, 1980). The aim of this 'Western conspiracy', in Shariati's view, was to deprive the developing nations of their character and traditional values and thus of any kind of resistance so that they could be economically exploited.

Woman, as the pillar of the family, he believed was the perfect target for Western conspirators. She was particularly targeted for exploitation through a double strategy by Western capitalism which turned her into a sex-object and an insatiable consumer (*ibid.* pp. 108–18). Women's liberation, therefore, was in their ability to break out of this mould and turn into committed Muslims. Shariati constructed an 'Islamic role model' for women to enable them to make this transition. In following her Islamic role model, the Muslim woman gained her freedom by wearing the Islamic *hejab* to shed the image of sex-object, and by changing her values from those of passive consumer to active participant in the Muslim community. The new Islam rejected Western criticism of Islam in relation to lack of equality of rights between Muslim men and women, on the grounds that the discourse of gender equality, far from being a universal principle, was a Western product and therefore irrelevant to Islam (Motahhari, 1978). Islamic gender relations, it was argued, were based on the 'innate differences' between men and women, and it was a different type of equality that Islam was interested in. This 'equality' was achieved through men and women performing their 'natural and biological' complementary and harmonious functions. What women (and men) gained from Islam, then, was acknowledgement of their 'natural rights and responsibilities' and the freedom to be 'real and natural beings' (*ibid.*). Islamic liberation of women released her from capitalist violation as a sex-object and communist violation as an eternal labourer. Islam placed her where she naturally belonged, that is, in the family (*ibid.*).

The political defence of Islam, however, encountered criticism from within and without after the realisation of the Islamic state in Iran. The discrepancies between Islamic ideals and the actual situation of women in the Islamic Republic gave credence to both secular and Islamic criticisms. A trend of Muslim feminism developed which sought equality of opportunity for men and women and fought for a system which 'would allow the Muslim woman to become a perfect woman, a multi-dimensional being by realising both her motherhood instinct and her need to participate in the liberation of her country' (Rahavand, 1979, p. 91). The Islamic Republic, with its encouragement of the polygamous family and male domination, it was argued, was failing to grant women their Islamic rights within the family and society (Hashemi, 1981a). The establishment of Islamic theocracy in Iran also attracted secular feminist criticism. The common feminist verdict on the post-revolutionary position of women was that the Islamic Republic not only did not restore the freedom and dignity that women had expected from the anti-Shah Revolution, but it also reversed the small legal and social gains they had made before the Revolution. But what was the analysis behind this feminist assertion?

Feminism

The repressive nature of the post-revolutionary state in Iran and its particularly rapid and forceful Islamisation of women's position, confirmed the age old theory of Islam as the cause of women's oppression in Middle Eastern society. It was after all an Islamic state 'modelled on the ordinance of the Koran and the early Islamic community of the time of the prophet and his successor', which was veiling and domesticating women in Iran (Nashat, 1980, p. 176). This conception inspired a wave of feminist opposition to Islam in the 1980s and revived some of the old arguments against the position of Muslim women.

The new feminist articulation of the conception of Islam as the 'cause' of women's oppression was based on an eclectic choice of concepts from within various discourses. The concept of patriarchy was a central one in this articulation. The theory of universal oppression of women by men, which originally appeared as part of the new wave of radical feminism in the late 1960s and 1970s, conceptualised 'patriarchy' as the source of women's oppression and by transferring it into the arena of personal relations gave it substantial political significance. This made classification of societies and cultures in terms of the degree of dominance of patriarchy a prevalent method of analysis. It was in this context that a new criticism of Islam as the most patriarchal religion and an understanding of 'Muslim women' as the most oppressed was constructed. This is where Orientalism and radical feminism converged.

The concept of patriarchy was grafted on to a variety of social theories to make them relevant to gender. Within Middle Eastern feminist movements, this concept was widely appropriated despite the almost universal rejection of its original theoretical and political context of radical feminist sexual politics (El Saadawi, 1982). Fatima Mernissi's study of the Islamic conception of female sexuality argued that there is a fundamental contradiction between Islam and the equality of the sexes (Mernissi, 1975, p. xv). It was also proposed that 'Muslim culture has a built-in ideological blindness to the economic dimension of women, who are ordinarily perceived, conceived and defined as exclusively sexual objects' (Sabbah, 1984, p. 16). Nadia Youssef explained the pattern of female employment in the Middle East with reference to Islam (Youssef, 1974). Beck and Keddie pointed out that the specificity of Islam in relation to women lay in 'the degree to which matters relating to women's status have either been legislated by the *Qoran*, or by subsequent legislation derived from interpretations of the *Qoran* and the traditional sayings of the prophet' (Beck & Keddie, 1978, p. 25). Azar Tabari considered Islam's all-encompassing nature as the main problem for women's emancipation in the Islamic community (Tabari, 1981). Farah Azari rejected the existence of variation within Islam and argued that Islamic bias against women was 'at the heart of the tradition of women's subjugation in Muslim societies' (Azari, 1983, p. 3). Another writer supported the view that 'Islam and feminism are incompatible' (Ghoussoub, 1987, p. 17).

Feminist criticism of Islam defined women's oppression in terms of Islam and saw women's liberation in opposition to it. It was argued that 'any struggle against women's oppression . . . will have to take on the task of opposing Islamic legislations in this area, openly and unambiguously' (Tabari, 1982, p. 24). Guity Nashat wondered whether women would continue to 'accept the concept of womanhood thrust upon them by the leaders of the Islamic Republic of Iran (Nashat, 1980, p. 190). In defining how victory against Islam could be achieved, some women argued for the formation of an 'international and unitary [feminist] ideology to cut across national and cultural barriers, to go beyond political systems and economic divisions' (Sanasarian, 1982, p. 155). But the counter-argument which rejected the essentialisation of Islam and its view of women was also present within this literature. Some women argued that in reality the religious systems of no two Islamic communities were identical, and pointed out that the position of Muslim women could not be understood without a thorough appreciation of the contexts in which they live (Beck, 1980).

Others explained the existence of variation within individual Muslim communities in terms of 'the forces of tribal and family custom' (Fernea & Bezirgan, 1977, p. xix; Kandiyoti, 1991b). The possibility of different interpretations of Islamic principles on women 'according to the political and social climate of the time' was pointed to (Benard, 1980, p. 22). It was also argued that 'the essentialisation of ideas and practices present in a so-called Muslim society as Islamic obscured the specific ways in which Islamic doctrine influenced women' (Yeganeh, 1982, p. 53; 1992). A scholar pointed to variations in the role and status of women both within and between Middle Eastern societies and explained the sources of social divisions amongst women (Van Dusen, 1979). Another scholar attempted to refute Western ethnocentrism by presenting an alternative perception of seclusion, veiling and *haram* in the Middle East (Ahmed, 1982). It was also argued that it is the ideology of male supremacy rather than Islam which affects women's lives in the Middle East (Afshar, 1985).

To counteract the 'idealist bias' in feminism, some scholars turned to 'feminist materialism' to explain women's subordination in Middle Eastern societies. Judith Gran analysed the historical differences in the value system of the 'upper middle class liberal segment in which women are relatively liberated socially and a petit bourgeois or lower middle class segment which cling to Islamic, conservative values in family life and sexual behaviour' in Egypt, with reference to the impact of the world market on urban society in Egypt (Gran, 1977, p. 3). Judith Tucker argued that there were 'four interlocking determinants of women's position and power in order to evaluate change in women's roles and status within the family and larger society' (Tucker, 1985, p. 328). These were women's access to property, her position in the family unit, her participation in social production and the prevailing ideological definitions of women's roles. She situated these determinants against the backbone of 'economic and social changes arising, in part, from the ongoing integration of Egypt into an economic system dominated by the West' (*ibid.*). It was also proposed that the ideological shifts in relation to women in turn of the century Egypt reflected class change (Cole, 1981). Beck and Keddie argued that the role of intellectuals in pushing for increased women's rights was not based on imitation of the West, 'but had indigenous bases in the needs of capitalism' (Beck & Keddie, 1978, p. 11).

The 'idealist bias' in feminism was also challenged by the undeniable diversity of Islamic positions on women. Feminist analysis of Islam was confronted with a variety of often opposing Islamic views on women within the Islamic Republic and other Middle Eastern societies. Feminism also had to explain why women's subordination ran across both Islamic and secular political ideologies. Furthermore, the heterogeneous nature of the Islamic state in Iran and the complex revolutionary process which it resulted from, were raised as important issues. How could these be accommodated in a single conception of women's oppression by Islam? These questions effectively reduced the importance of Islam in the analysis of women's oppression in Iran. The doctrinal effect of Islam became one factor amongst others for consideration. This meant that specific examinations of the various contexts within which Islam operated, and analyses of factors which supported specific Islamic and non-Islamic conceptions of women gained a new priority (Beck, 1980).

The debate on 'idealism' versus 'materialism', however, created many dualities: is political change caused as a result of contact with Western ideas or because of the integration of Middle Eastern economies into the Western capitalist system? Is it the indigenous or exogenous ideas and forces which should be referred to in explaining political change? Should the standpoints adopted and the divisions present in 'Muslim' countries on the question of women be explained in terms of ideological struggle between a modern pro-Western secular intelligentsia and traditional clerics, or should their roots be sought in class differences?

These dualities obscured the fact that the process of political change is a complex process which cannot be reduced to a simple equation of cause and effect. Indeed, neither of the 'idealist' and 'materialist' approaches applied satisfactorily to the case of Iran, where it was more useful to identify the multiplicity of the causes of change and the ways in which indigenous and exogenous factors, both cultural and economic, acted in a combined and complex manner to bring about change and transformation (Yeganeh, 1993a and 1993c). Such processes were present during both the Constitutional Revolution of 1905–11 and the anti-monarchy Revolution of 1977–9 in Iran. Despite the differing circumstances, the constitutions of 1906 and 1979 turned out to be the end products of processes of internal political debate and the social articulations of Iran's changing relations with the West. In both instances the new political systems that emerged were neither a mere duplication of Western political systems, nor a reflection of global economic relations. Each, on the contrary, reflected the specific configuration of social forces, economic interests and political ideas of their particular conjuncture.

Towards a specific analysis of Iranian women

To summarise the preceding survey of the literature, it was demonstrated that until the 1980s, the study of Middle Eastern women was dominated by the application of general theories. Orientalism defined Islam as the essence of these societies and analysed women's position as the reflection of Islamic doctrine. Modernisation theory conceptualised their political history, particularly in relation to women, in terms of the battle between the forces of 'tradition', represented by an essentialised Islam, and the forces of 'modernity', represented by a reified state. Dependency theory defined the process of development of the 'Muslim' regions as an ahistorical instance of the operation of world capitalism which entailed a pre-determined definition of women's oppression and liberation. In essentialising and reifying the process of historical development, none of the general theories were able to account for different courses and patterns of development in different Middle Eastern countries. None could theorise on the specificities of each political history in relation to women.

However, the above survey also demonstrated that the literature contains the seeds of the deconstruction of the general theories as well. Development theories, cultural relativism and feminist universalism, among other general theories, began to give way in the 1980s to specific analyses of Middle Eastern societies. This coincided with a new theoretical and political criticism of 'the archaeology of modernity' associated with 'poststructuralism' (Smart, 1990). The crisis of modernist projects, both capitalist and socialist kinds, and problems of modern social and political institutions, provided a crucial context for the rejection of 'metanarratives' of modernity on the basis of the heterogeneity, fragmentation and pragmatic nature of social development (Boyne and Rattansi, 1990).

The 'specific' approach that has developed in relation to Muslim women begins, as it has been argued, 'not with Arab "difference", nor with Islam, but with social and economic forces that shape them' (Sayigh, 1981, p. 266). Instead of Islam, global capitalism or patriarchy, an understanding of the position of Middle Eastern women is now being sought in both historical and contemporary social relations and political processes (Keddie and Baron, 1991). One of the determining factors in shaping the position of women in the twentieth-century Middle East has been considered to be the process of nation building. It has been argued that despite their differing political systems, Middle Eastern societies have all had to grapple with the problems of establishing modern nation states and forging new notions of citizenship, and that 'the degree of formal emancipation they [women] are able to achieve, the modalities of their participation in economic life and the nature of the social movements through which they are able to articulate their gender interests are intimately linked to state building processes and are responsive to their transformations' (Kandiyoti, 1991a, pp. 2–3).

The role of the state in establishing and maintaining the link between gender issues and national projects has, too, received attention. It has been demonstrated that state policies are not gender-neutral but construct men and women differently. This proposition has been well-documented in relation to state policies in a variety of Middle Eastern and other societies (Yuval-Davis & Anthias, 1989). Women are, on the one hand, constructed like men as citizens. But they are also treated as a special category in relation to various roles they play in society. These include reproductive and symbolic ones. Women are assigned status as mothers and revered as symbols of national and communal identity (*ibid.*, pp. 6–11).

The claim in recent decades by cultural nationalism and Islamic populism in the Middle East over women's reproductive and symbolic roles has illustrated the inadequacy of essentialising Islam in relation to women, and further established the multiplicity and complexity of factors and processes affecting Muslim women. Alongside the development of Islamic modernism and Muslim feminism, the world has witnessed a new Islamic zeal developing in relation to women. The family and women have become the subject of a power struggle in the battle between the Western intervening powers and indigenous resisting forces. In this setting, women have become the bastions of Muslim identity and preservers of cultural authenticity (Ghoussoub, 1987; Kandiyoti, 1991a). Many instances have been documented in the history of the Middle East's encounter with the West of resort to Islamic traditions in the face of overwhelming interventions by Western powers (Cole, 1981; Tucker, 1983). In this context, the nature of Middle Eastern contact with the West has proved more important in instigating 'indigenous' Islamic stances towards women than has following of the *Qoran* and *hadith*. The role played by women themselves in the political processes of the twentieth-century Middle East have also helped to bring into question the fallacy inherent in general theories of Muslim women that women are no more than passive victims of Islam, global capitalism or patriarchy. Many aspects of women's participation in national processes and their sources of power and authority within the family, community and nation have now been recognised within the field of Middle Eastern women's studies (Hijab, 1988; Yeganeh, 1993b).

This study of women in Iran aims to make a further contribution to the deconstruction of the general theories of Muslim women. I will present a specific analysis of the links between gender and political processes in twentieth-century Iran. These links will be established and analysed by tracing the development of the position of women through the evolutionary and revolutionary transformation of political discourses which have dominated Iranian society in this century.

Political discourse is used here as the broad political framework within which the state, political parties, social movements and civil society communicate, relate to each other, negotiate power and control, and take action. It has been argued that the specific analysis of Middle Eastern societies, as opposed to an essentialist one, entails showing, 'how, for any given social formation, a series of historical conjunctures, each with its own patterns of socio-political processes, have led to a distinctive configuration' (Zubaida, 1989a, pp. 129–30). The political history of women in Iran can indeed be analysed in terms of specific political discourses which have governed historical conjunctures in this century.

I have identified three broad, overlapping, non-exclusive but rather distinct political discourses which have dominated twentieth-century politics in Iran. These include the discourse of modernity, the discourse of revolution and the discourse of Islamisation. Since the turn of the century, 'modernity' has been and continues to be a central issue in Iranian history. My identification of one of the three discourses as modernity is not intended to mean that the other two discourses represent a clean break with modernity. Indeed, as will be demonstrated, the discourses of revolution and Islamisation are in different ways engaged with the issue of modernity. Modernity was broadly defined in the context of early twentieth-century Iran as a socio-political process which promised the establishment of economic prosperity, social and technological progress, social justice, political freedom and national independence. This 'vague', 'idealist' and 'ultimate' view of modernity as the road to the salvation of the Iranian nation, has remained strong up to the present day and provided the impetus for a century of political struggles.

These struggles, however, have resulted in a periodic revision and reconstruction of the concepts and processes associated with modernity. The distinctions between the three political discourses under consideration arise from these periodic reconstructions of modernity. From the turn of the century to the 1970s, the concept of modernity was associated with Westernisation. As the discourse of modernity evolved, modernisation, as a synonym of Westernisation, became dominant in Iran. During the late 1970s a revolutionary discourse emerged which redefined the concept of modernity. Once again modernity became associated with its idealistic meaning of the turn of the century and a number of secular and Islamic political ideologies strove towards the attainment of economic prosperity, social justice, political freedom and national independence. The transitional discourse of revolution gave way to another dominant discourse, that of Islamisation, which aimed to separate modernity from Western-style modernisation and associate it with Islamic-style modernisation.

The political discourses under consideration are neither manifestations of a fixed cultural and historical Islamic or Iranian essence. Nor are they products of global relations. Political discourses on gender are rather produced and reproduced at every historical period in relation to different situations and issues (*ibid.*). In a sense, the political history of gender in Iran can be read as the history of political discourses on gender.

Part 1

The discourse of modernity

Part 1 will concentrate on the discourse of modernity and how it has constructed women. The discourse of modernity made an impact in Iran in the late nineteenth century. It set the terms for political debate and determined the shape of the social and political institutions in Iran until the late 1970s. The discourse of modernity was not a monolithic entity and did not have a fixed content. On the contrary, it evolved and changed over time and went through different phases. In all of its phases, the concept of modernity was also associated completely with Western civilisation. The West was seen as the originator of modernity, and modernity was defined in terms of Western institutions and practices.

The discourse of modernity went through three rather distinct phases. The early phase of the discourse of modernity was manifested in the movement for constitutionalism at the turn of the century. Chapters 1 and 2 will cover this historically crucial period. Chapter 1 will set the background for the emergence of the concept of modernity and Chapter 2 will concentrate on the debate on modernity in the era of constitutionalism as it related to women. This will include examining women's participation in the turn of the century revolutionary process, how it gave rise to new definitions of women's oppression and emancipation, and what links were created between the concepts of 'women's emancipation' and 'national progress'.

The concept of modernity existed in its most vague and idealistic sense during this period. Modernity was about the attainment of economic prosperity, social progress and justice, and political freedom and independence. These ideals suggested different meanings to different political forces, and not all aspects of modernity were accepted or admired by everyone. But, on the whole, the concept of modernity encompassed technological progress, secularism, the rule of law, women's emancipation, and a monogamous family system. Another rather distinct phase of the discourse of modernity came to the fore during the period from the 1920s to the early 1940s as the era of nation building. This was when the transition of state power from the Qajar dynasty to the Pahlavi dynasty occurred. Chapter 3 will discuss the process of establishing a modern nation state in Iran and analyse its implications for women. During the phase of nation building, the concept of modernity became more precise, and came to be understood as the establishment of a central state and the creation of a unified nation in Iran. This involved the establishment of national sovereignty, social and economic infrastructures, a single language and religion, and a nationally binding legal and social position for women. Modernity continued to be associated with the West, but during the process of nation building certain aspects of modernity that had been important in the early phase lost their priority. These included political freedom and the rule of law. As the process of nation building developed, political manipulation and control by the state increased and the new Constitution (1906) was contravened. In the same way, certain aspects of modernity in relation to women, such as the desegregation of public space, were adopted and others, such as legal enforcement of monogamy, were rejected.

The third phase of the discourse of modernity, which came to the fore in the 1940s and continued until the mid-1960s, was characterised by the domination of nationalist politics in Iran. Chapter 4 will discuss the transformation of state nationalism, which was dominant in the nation-building stage, into liberal nationalism and cultural nationalism as new political challenges to the state. The implications of this process for women will also be explored. During the period 1940s–60s, the concept of modernity evolved again. This time, the state's definition of modernity was criticised by new interpretations of the original ideals of modernity. The state's national priorities were challenged by liberal nationalism which demanded political freedom and the observance of the Constitution; by cultural nationalism which demanded that the process of social reform should not bypass national culture and traditions; and by the pro-Soviet left who demanded the establishment of socialist modernity in Iran. As a result of these challenges, the earlier total and complete association between modernity and the West began to crumble. The concept of modernity became much more heterogeneous and incorporated contradictory meanings.

The final phase of the discourse of modernity was established during the 1960s–70s, an era which became characterised by the state's double strategy of political repression and aggressive modernisation. Chapter 5 will focus on this particular phase of state modernisation and examine the ways in which it affected women. The process of diversification of the discourse of modernity accelerated in the late 1960s and the 1970s. The state's Westernisation policy reached a dimension which was regarded to be unacceptable for a number of reasons. This was partly because

American foreign policy was strongly behind the state's modernisation drive and the Western media loudly applauded it. But it was also because the visible signs of Westernisation included importing materialistic and vulgar features of life in the West. The state channelled the oil revenue into the reconstruction of 'The Great Civilisation' of ancient Iran by undertaking grandiose projects while the reality of Iranian society included massive poverty, repression and injustice.

Moreover, as state modernisation moved in the above direction, the opposition movements which had come into existence earlier in the 1950s and 1960s developed their capacity for presenting serious socio-political alternatives to Westernisation. By the late 1970s, the Islamic forces had modernised and radicalised their opposition movement; nationalist criticism regarding lack of political freedom and individual rights was stronger; the left was waging a guerrilla warfare against the state; and women were objecting to negative images of women presented by the state and reflected in the mass media. These opposition alternatives were proposing different routes towards the achievement of modern values such as political freedom, gender equality, economic development and social justice, despite the fact that they each defined these values differently. Furthermore, new values such as radicalism and populism were being introduced and supported by both secular and Islamic opposition, to replace discredited ones such as modernisation and Westernisation.

The discourse of modernity, therefore, which dominated the terms of the political debate in Iran for the greater part of the century, started in the late nineteenth century with a broad vision and pro-Western values, and had developed into an anti-Western political discourse by the late 1970s. This discourse included a variety of different and sometimes contradictory conceptions of modernity.

1 Social diversity on women's issues in nineteenth-century Iran

Contrary to common assumptions about the universal seclusion and oppression of women in traditional Middle Eastern societies, nineteenth-century Iranian society contained a variety of conceptions and positions of women. These were heterogenous and even contradictory at the concrete level, but were unified broadly by being situated within a patriarchal framework. The sources of social diversity for women were multiple and included historical and religio-cultural differences, geographical and economic divisions, and various influences resulting from contact with outside economies and cultures. These differences often cut across each other and created a complex picture of the position of women in society which has remained little understood and much under-researched. The description which follows is no more than a tentative and general sketch of the sources of unity and diversity on women's position in turn of the century Iran.

Life in nineteenth-century Iran revolved around communities. Due to prevailing social and geographical factors, communities retained a fair degree of isolation and self-sufficiency, and mobility from one to the other was minimal (Abrahamian, 1982, p. 18). The existence of a central state apparatus did not have a unifying effect on the social structure of the society. Under the Qajar state (1796–1925), communities remained culturally and socially autonomous. The Qajar Court was only one community amongst many others and hence was unable to dictate social and cultural norms for other communities. However, it manipulated other communities politically and economically.

Social factors such as history, religion, ethnicity and language were some of the main sources of differential treatment for women. The Muslim population of Iran was divided into many branches and ethnicities. The majority religion was Shiism. The minority Sunni Muslims were mainly composed of tribal, nomadic and ethnic minorities such as the Kurds, Torkamans, Arabs and Baluchis. Other branches of Shiism such as Ismailism, Sufism, Alavism, Sheykhism and Babism were active but experienced various degrees of persecution. The non-Muslim population of Iran consisted of adherents of Zoroastrianism, Armenian and Assyrian Christians, and a Jewish community. The official language was Farsi (Persian), but many other languages were spoken. The dominant rules and regulations which women lived under were predominantly communal ones. Women played a full role in the productive and reproductive life of their communities (Keddie, 1981, p.34). They were the sustaining force within these communities and their familial position, behaviour and clothing constituted the markers of communal identity and difference.

Minority communities

The limited, and often unreliable, information which is available on minority communities indicates that they experienced prejudice and social bigotry (Rice, 1923, p. 25). They lived in distinct quarters and did not intermarry with other religious-ethnic groups. Communal rivalry and conflict were features of Iranian society in the nineteenth century. Zoroastrians, one of the main minority communities, dated back to the Persian Empire before the Islamic conquest in 651 AD. In the nineteenth century, Zoroastrians (Parsis) followed their own particular traditions, and marriage with next of kin and polygamy were unknown amongst them. The position of women in the Zoroastrian civilization of ancient Iran was a source of pride for this community and to others who attributed society's ills to Islam. Zoroastrianism in ancient Iran was in favour of monarchy and social hierarchy, and held patriarchal views about women and the family. The family was considered by Zoroastrianism as the basic unit of society and was ruled by men (Dhalla, 1922, pp. 297–301).

Zoroastrianism was interpreted differently in different historical periods and women's positions varied in practice within the old Persian Empire. It has been argued that Kianian writers held women 'in high esteem', while Pahlavi writers considered them inferior. Under the Sassanian, women owned property and acted as guardians of the family in the absence of a living male. Women were also raised to the throne and upper-class women engaged in sports (*ibid.*, p. 300). Veiling and seclusion existed among elite Sassanian women (Nashat, 1983, pp. 8–11). During the late Sassanian period between the fifth and sixth centuries AD various new Zoroastrian social movements rose which spread new messages about women. Mazdakism rose in reaction to prevalent inequalities and injustices perpetuated by the Zoroastrian clergy. It was an offshoot of an earlier religious revolt, Manichaeism, which had been heavily persecuted. Mazdak preached against inequality and believed that worldly goods and privileges should be shared by everyone. Mazdak's teachings are often referred to as an early form of communism, and most historians of Ancient Iran have attributed an idea of 'communality of women' to him. This, however, could be no more than an exaggeration of Mazdak's opposition to the treatment of women in those times.

The Christian communities, too, followed their own tradition and religion. Armenian women traditionally wore headscarves and did not cover their faces (Ravandi, 1978, III, p. 217). The Armenians lived in urban quarters and villages, and were generally able to follow the teachings of their religion in marriage, divorce and other social matters. They arranged marriages and required women to be modest and obedient. Social tolerance was relatively greater towards Armenians and Assyrians (the latter were mainly based in the northern town of Orumiyeh). Many Armenians became wealthy merchants, and others were employed in government offices. Some Armenian women became nurses and teachers in missionary hospitals and schools (*ibid.*, p. 31).

The Jewish minority, too, lived in distinct localities, and traditionally followed trades such as moneylending which were forbidden in Islam (Bahrami, 1965, p. 72). Jewish women wore veils outside the home, but did not cover their faces and enjoyed more freedom in going out and walking in the streets than their Muslim counterparts. Some of them were educated and taught French and English in *andaruns*. Many others functioned as marriage brokers and messengers for upper-class Muslim families (Bamdad, 1977, p. 13). Illiteracy was widespread amongst lower-class women from religious-ethnic minorities but less so amongst upper-class women who were the first women to be educated formally. In 1835 American missionaries opened the first girls' school in Iran. This school was opened in the Christian dominated town of Orumiyeh (later Rezaiyeh) and Armenian and Assyrian girls attended it. The same missionaries opened another school in Tehran in 1875, which later in 1888, accepted Zoroastrian and Jewish girls.

Islamic diversity

Another main source of diversity of theory and practice on women's position was Islam itself. After the advent of Islam in Iran, three different interpretations of Islam existed in parallel: Sunnism, Twelver Shiism, and esoteric Shiism which included Sufism and Ismailism. Sunnism was originally the majority religion, but various forms of Shiism managed to become influential among minorities and gave expression to social grievances of these communities. In early and medieval Islam, social developments such as expansion of urban centres and cultural contacts arising from wars, invasions and change of ruling dynasties resulted in differing norms for women, some of which became incorporated into Islamic law (Nashat, 1983, pp. 11–13). It was not until the sixteenth century that Twelver Shiism became the dominant religion in Iran. The twelve Shii *emaman* were a chain of descendants of the Prophet through his only child Fatemeh and his cousin and son-in-law Ali. Fatemeh was accorded equal, if not higher, status with her descendants the *emaman*. This is often stated by Shiis as the source of Shii high esteem for women. According to Shiis, the twelfth *emam*, Mehdi, went into occultation to return in an unspecified future to fill the world with justice. In the absence of Mehdi, Shii *olama* systematised and codified the collected accounts of the words and deeds of the Prophet and Shii *emaman*, known as *hadith*, to provide practical moral guidance for the Shii community. Until the sixteenth century these *olama* remained as mere scholars and had little contact with the public.

During the Safavid period (1501–1736) Twelver Shiism (hereafter Shiism) became the status of the state religion in Iran. This was based on the suppression of Sunnism and other branches of Shiism, in particular Sufism and Ismailism. The institution of Shiism acquired features which became quite specific in comparison with the position of Islam in other Middle Eastern societies. The specificity of Shiism was reflected in a number of aspects. First, the institution of Shiism became economically independent from the state by setting up mechanisms for acquiring donations and endowment land (*vaghf*) from the public. Second, by the establishment of the practice of *ejtehad*, a process by which a *mojtahed* used his own reasoning in addition to the *Qoran* and *hadith* to arrive at legal decisions and issued religious instructions to his followers in the form of *fatva*. In the late eighteenth century *ejtehad* was implemented for the first time (Momen, 1985, p. 186). Third, the Shii faithful were required to follow the religious instructions and judgements, *fatva*, of a living *mojtahed* on all aspects of social life. Fourth, the Shii clergy took over the secular judicial system of the pre-Safavid period. These courts, which had government-appointed judges, were gradually replaced by *shariat* courts and Shii clergy gained the power to make judicial decisions and even administer punishment. Fifth, a 'dry, formal, dogmatic, legalistic style of Shiism' developed which was reflected both in scholarly works and in more mundane religious instructions to the faithful (Momen, 1985, pp. 116, 191).

One Shii clergyman was instrumental in achieving all this. This was Mohammad Bagher Majlesi, one of the most influential *olama* of the Safavid period, who was also largely responsible for the adoption of the Farsi language by Shii *olama*, which facilitated ordinary people's understanding of the Shii *feqh* (*ibid.*, p. 116).

Shii and Sunni jurisprudence developed different laws regarding women, particularly in relation to marriage and inheritance. Three Shii deviations from Sunnism have been singled out as the most important ones: temporary marriage or *sigheh*; restriction of a husband's right to discretionary repudiation of wife (*talagh*); and improvement of women's inheritance rights. In other matters regarding women, Sunni and Shii laws differed very little (Madelung, 1979). The main differences on women's rights regarding property, inheritance and marriage arose from local and cultural differences as opposed to the strictly doctrinal. Shii *feqh* developed its own particular style of argument and reasoning in relation to women during the Safavid period. Majlesi's many volumes of writings on Shii *hadith*, the most important of which was *Bahar ol-Anwar* in fourteen volumes, were instrumental in this. His *hadith* collections in Farsi included the influential *Helliyat ol-Mottaghin* [The Ornament of the Pious] which examined the most intimate aspects of personal life down to eating, sleeping, washing, defecating and sexual intercourse (Ferdows & Ferdows, 1983). Under each of these headings, Majlesi cited various *hadith* from the Prophet and Shii *emaman* to show the different treatment of men and women (Majlesi, 1951). On 'The Rights of Husband and Wife towards Each Other', Majlesi made 'the approved qualities of women' a matter of 'the rights of the husband over his wives'. Men had the right to have virtuous, obedient and submissive wives. Women were not allowed to leave the house or spend their own wealth without their husbands' permission unless it was spent for religious purposes or given to their own parents. The wife's religious activity was also brought under the husbands' control. Women were not allowed to fast without their husbands' permission, a woman's prayer was not acceptable to God if she wore scent for men other than her husband, and she was cursed by angels all night if her delay in responding to her husband's wish for intercourse resulted in him falling asleep. But a wife had the right to be fed, clothed and forgiven for her wrong doings. To emphasize the significance of the inequality of rights between husband and wife, Majlesi cited a *hadith* from *emam* Jafar Sadegh in response to a woman's enquiry about marital rights. After hearing the *emam*'s response, the woman was quoted as saying 'I do not have as many rights over my husband as he has over me. I swear to God not to ever marry' (*ibid.*, p. 77).

Majlesi's style of dogmatic reasoning was dominant during the eighteenth century. By the early nineteenth century, then, Shiism with anti-esoteric and pro-*ejtehad* features had fully established itself. But although Shii tradition in the nineteenth century was largely based on the teachings of Majlesi, the practice of *marjae taghlid* made the institution of Shiism a heterogenous and lively one. The clergy was not a unified category in the

Qajar period. The Shii clergy expressed different and at times conflicting responses on the question of reform and modernisation. The edicts issued by *mojtahedin* were often far from pure expressions of Shii *shariat*. Instead, they were engrained in the politics and power relationships of the moment. The clergy were also somewhat divided on the position of women. Some Shii *mojtahedin* even argued for the principle of equality and justice for all women. An exceptional sixteenth-century Shii text was produced at the turn of the century which expressed reformist intentions regarding women. This was a text that had been started in the early Safavid period by Sheykh Bahai, a prominent Shii scholar, but remained unfinished because of his death. Sheykh Bahai managed to write only five chapters of his book *Jamee Abbasi*; the last fifteen chapters, which discussed the position of women, was completed by Nizam ibn Hussain Savaji in 1905. This text recommended that women could become judges and pass judicial verdicts on condition that 'the witness is a trusted one' (Sheykh Bahai, 1905, p. 350). This indicated that the idea of women engaging in judicial activities existed in nineteenth and twentieth-century Shiism. In another chapter of the same book, the number of *sigheh* wives allowed for a Shii man was limited to four (*ibid.*, p. 263). This was an unusual idea since Shii texts did not normally put any limit on the number of temporary wives. Shiism also included a category of female *mojtahedin* and *mollas*. But the general consensus among male *mojtahedin* was that, while women could reach the level of learning and accomplishment necessary to become a *mojtahed*, they should not issue binding religious edicts and have followers (Keddie, 1981, p. 32). A directory of learned Shii women dated women's scholarship in Shiism back to early Islam (Mahallati, 1955). Female *mollas*, enjoyed freedom to act as private tutors or reciters of *rowzeh* in women's gatherings. The institution of female *mojtahedin* continued during the nineteenth century and beyond, and women carried on writing exegeses on the *Qoran* (Kamarehi, 1941).

Mainstream Shiism was not very tolerant towards other religious movements, however, and conflict between various forms of Shiism was a feature of Iranian history. Its main conceptual rival, esoteric Shiism, avoided involvement in *shariat* matters and concentrated on philosophy, ethics and poetry. Esoteric Shiism believed in a direct relationship between the individual and his or her God. Esoterism considered intermediaries such as the clergy redundant and attempted to reach an inner meaning (*baten*) of things instead of concentrating on the appearance of things (*zaher*) as the Twelver Shiis allegedly did. Sufism which was an extreme form of esoteric Shiism allowed women to participate in religious activities and many women reached the status of sainthood within it (Nurbakhsh, 1983; Schimmel, 1982).

Moreover, women reportedly enjoyed higher status among the Shii Fatemids and especially the radical Shii Qarmatians, rulers associated with Ismailism (Yeganeh & Keddie, 1986, p.117). In the late nineteenth and early twentieth century new off-shoots of esoteric Shiism developed and presented a challenge to the official conceptions of women. These movements responded to changing social conditions and reflected social discontent, including dissatisfaction with the position of women. The main off-shoots of esoteric Shiism in the nineteenth century were the Sheykhi and Sufi movements. The Sheykhi movement, which spread in Iran in the late eighteenth century, criticised the authority of the *mojtahed*, and denounced *taghlid* as contrary to the teachings of Shii *emaman*. It defended the ability of human beings to progress rationally and lead worthy and fulfilling lives in this world (Bayat-Philipp, 1981, pp. 40–3). The Sheykhi movement considered polygamy as highly improper and disapproved of it. They apparently believed in equality of intellectual capacity in both men and women (Fazai, n.d., p. 75). Nineteenth-century Sufism, which appeared in many different forms, banned polygamy amongst its followers and apparently did not prescribe strict veiling and seclusion for women (Nahid, 1981, p. 10). Other Shii 'heresies', including the movements of Ahl Hagh and Ali Allahi, also allowed greater freedom for women in ritual and in daily life (Yeganeh & Keddie, 1986, p.118). Images of women as presented in diverse Islamic movements can be found in abundance in post-Islamic art and literature in Iran (Javadi, 1985).

But the most far-reaching social criticism attempted by religious movements in this era came from the Babi movement (Amanat, 1989). Seyyed Ali Mohammad, the founder of the Babi movement, attacked the Shii clergy for their worldly corruption, spiritual ignorance, and abuse of ideological power, and proclaimed himself as the awaited twelfth *emam*. He also claimed to be the supreme authority on earth, overriding the authority of the Shahs (Bayat-Philipp, 1981, pp. 44–5). Babism was a peaceful and this-worldly religion, which advocated social change here and now. Its founder restricted polygamy, and allowed Muslims two wives instead of four as permitted by mainstream Shiism. The second wife was only allowed in Babism if the first wife was sterile and was prepared to give her consent (*ibid.*, p. 44). The Babi movement considered men and women to be spiritually and intellectually equal, at least in theory. It was also strictly against women's seclusion and veiling. Seyyed Bab emphasised, in a letter to his female disciple Qorrat ol-Eyn, that 'Women have been permitted to come out of their houses dressed and made up like angels [*huri*] of paradise and to mix with men and sit on chairs unveiled' (Fazai, n.d., p. 165).

Adultery by men and women did not carry a heavy penalty in Babism. The fact that adulterers of Babi faith could go free after paying a fine outraged the Shii clergy. Another thing which outraged Shiis was the activities of Seyyed Bab's female disciple Tahereh Qorrat ol-Eyn, who was an extraordinary woman who acquired a high position within the Babi movement. She was from a Shii clerical family and had abandoned her husband and children to devote herself to the cause of Babism. Unveiled, Tahereh preached Babism and caused an uproar (Milani, 1992). Her learning and knowledge of Shiism and Persian literature brought her admiration from friends and enemies (*Nimeye Digar*, 1, pp. 92–104). Babism suffered particularly severe persecution by the government of Naser od-Din Shah and the Shii clergy of the time. Seyyed Ali Mohammad was executed in 1850, and two years later Tahereh Qorrat ol-Eyn was arrested and killed on the Shah's direct order (Bayat-Philipp, 1978, p. 296).

Socio-economic diversity

In most Muslim communities in nineteenth-century Iran, there was a tremendous gap between the Islamic ideals on women and women's actual living conditions. Iranian society was divided into urban, rural and tribal communities. Ethnicity, religion and linguistic diversity coincided with geographical and economic ones. Tribal and nomadic societies, it has been argued, allowed women to mix with men to a certain extent and some tribes considered polygamy and temporary marriage undesirable (Ravandi, 1978, vol. III, pp. 715, 723). Child marriage was prevalent amongst tribes. In many tribes, including Qashqai, Boir Ahmadi and Mamsani, women were given in marriage before the age of puberty (*ibid.*, pp. 280, 282). In most tribes, women did not inherit and had no economic rights but they played an important productive role. As a result of the dominance of local traditions, tribes often did not adopt Islamic laws and this applied to property and inheritance rights. The relative laxity on veiling and seclusion of women did not necessarily secure a high status for tribal women.

In rural areas, too, the treatment of women could differ. In some regions, such as rice growing regions of Gilan and Mazandaran around the Caspian Sea in the north, women wore colourful clothes and worked in rolled-up trousers in rice plantations where they laughed and sang loudly (*ibid.*, pp. 713, 727). They mixed with men to an extent not allowed in many other regions. In other rural areas, women wore thick veils over their headscarves and led a secluded life, mainly engaged in carpet weaving (*ibid.*, pp. 186, 200). As was the case with tribes, villages too were hierarchical communities and women of different status and age enjoyed different powers and privileges. Unlike women from the lower strata of the rural sector, women from the upper strata of both rural and urban sectors practised strict veiling and seclusion. The application of *shariat* laws to women was likewise subject to variation. *Sigheh* seemed to be widespread amongst all classes in rural and urban settings, that is, amongst lower-class women and upper-class men, as is mentioned frequently in historical monographs, but social historians often associated it with economic need and social norms rather than with strict adherence to Islamic *shariat*. Polygamy seemed to be more popular amongst the better-off. Inheritance and property rights for women often varied among localities, communities, and modes of production, often differing substantially from *shariat* instructions.

The urban community in Qajar society was divided roughly into the social categories of nobility and large landowners, state officials and bureaucrats, merchants, traders, clergy and various lower strata. In a census of the population of Tehran which was carried out under Naser od-Din Shah Qajar (1848–96), Tehrani women were likewise ranked in the order of social prestige into categories of royal women, respectable women, wives of merchants, wives of shopkeepers, nannies, maids and black concubines (Ravandi, 1978, III, p. 4). Each of these categories of women lived according to the rules and regulations of their sub-communities set in the context of existing economic and social conditions. The Qajar state was in theory the central political power which had a small army and a small bureaucracy. Its revenues came from tribal and rural land and cattle tax and urban properties. The effectiveness of the Qajar state in asserting its political, military and economic power, however, differed from period to period. In this segmentary political system there existed a relatively decentralised political structure in which several different groups such as the *olama*, tribal leaders, landlords and merchants shared power with the Shah (Keddie, 1978). The relationship between society and state in the nineteenth century was such that the former was expected to serve the latter and not vice versa. The Qajar state was synonymous with the royal Court. The state did not have programmes for public services and a significant part of its revenue was spent on maintaining the royal households.

'Royal women' and 'respectable women' of the landed aristocracy and merchants who maintained households in the city, lived their lives within *harams* and *andaruns*. Qajar Shahs and princes maintained large *harams* of at times up to eighty-odd wives and large numbers of concubines and female members of the family and their in-laws. Women in Qajar *harams* lived their lives in seclusion. They travelled rarely and, if at all, in total seclusion. Marriages in the royal family were arranged and took place in childhood and adolescence. Royal children were brought up by nannies and educated by private tutors. The smaller *andaruns* of the landed aristocracy and high merchant class were often kept as rigorously secluded as *harams* of the Qajar Shahs. A document gives an example of the ways in which an *andarun* was preserved from 'wicked eyes' (Nategh, 1979; Gurney, 1983). Women from this strata were only allowed to go out for a socially approved reason which included women-only religious gatherings and ceremonies related to the life cycle of birth, marriage and death. Other socially acceptable reasons for going out included regular visits to public baths, and occasionally shopping in bazaars. When they went out, women had to cover themselves from head to toe in a veil and use a separate pavement from men.

Images projected by *haram* women, however, were not homogeneous. Alongside the image of passive consumers and sex-objects, *haram* women were also seen to be active, shrewd, domineering and intellectual. Fath Ali Shah, the second Qajar ruler (1794–1834) benefited from the assistance of his daughters Khazen od-Douleh, Anis od-Douleh and Zia ol-Saltaneh as trusted secretaries and advisors (Nashat, 1983, p. 16). Mahde oliya, Mohammad Ali Shah's wife (1834–48) and Naser od-Din Shah's mother used her influence to remove and murder Amir Kabir, the prominent and popular minister. She was a shrewd politician and a strong-willed woman who practically ran the country during her husband's illness (*ibid.*, pp. 16–17). Fatemeh, better known as Anis od-Douleh who was the favourite wife of Naser od-Din Shah (1848–96), exerted a lot of influence over the Shah and within the court and indirectly influenced the running of the country. These women were highly educated for their time and their education consisted of religious studies, literature and sometimes music (Khaleghi, 1974, pp. 465–86), which were taught by private tutors or more often by their fathers and husbands (Bamdad, 1977, p. 19). A number of women from Qajar *harams* were also known to follow intellectual pursuits and study literature, philosophy and languages and learn to play musical instruments. Taj ol-Saltaneh and Fakhr od-Douleh, Naser od-Din Shah's daughters were both famous. The latter translated and wrote fiction and the former became a social critic and joined the anti-Qajar constitutional movement. But the most important emphasis in women's education centred on running a household and raising children. Well-to-do women were expected to be as hard working as lower-class women, and idleness was considered a handicap for a woman. Women were trained to administer and manage the day-to-day running of busy extended households, and taught to work collectively with other women. Many well-to-do women did not take male domination for granted, and strove to increase their power and influence over their menfolk. Some women used their personal wealth and influence to set up welfare and educational institutions.

The relationship between the state and the religious establishment was another important aspect of Qajar society. Since power and authority was vested in both the king and the *mojtahed*, a relationship of mutual inter dependence was maintained between the state and the Shii *olama* despite occasional conflicts of interest. The state needed the support of the religious establishment for legitimacy, and the clergy needed the support of the state to strengthen their social position. The specific features of Shiism further developed during this period. Under the Qajars, contact between the clergy and ordinary people increased through a more thorough practice of the institution of *marjae taghlid.* Contemporary developments influencing the institution of Shiism were brought about by Sheykh Morteza Ansari (d. 1864), the sole *marjae taghlid* of his time, and provided the opportunity for the Shii clergy to issue more frequent *fatva* on a wider range of issues than was possible before (Momen, 1985, p. 187). Historically, the clergy had controlled education, but they now became involved in social affairs such as marriage, death and inheritance transactions and provided advice to people on day-to-day aspects of life. The clergy also increased their ideological hold over the population through ritualistic celebrations of the birth and martyrdom of Shii *emaman* and sessions of *rowzeh.* They also surrounded themselves with private armies of religious students (*tollab*) and local thugs (*luti*) (*ibid.*, pp. 143, 199).

In nineteenth-century Iran, the bazaar was the economic and social heart of the city: 'It was there that landowners sold their crops, craftsmen manufactured their wares, traders marketed their goods, those in need of money raised loans, and it was there that businessmen built and financed mosques and schools' (Abrahamian, 1982, p. 192). Merchants, traders, craftsmen, and many others in the urban middle strata conducted their businesses through the bazaar and coordinated their political activities through bazaar guilds. The higher ranks of the bazaar were traditionally influential and respected and the guilds played an important political role in urban society. Data is not available on women's participation in trade and trade guilds in Iran. But it has been shown in relation to Egypt that 'women bought, sold, traded and made their husbands' fortune' (Al-Sayyid Marsot, 1978). Despite their participation in the economic and social life of the city, Egyptian women did not play a documented role in guilds. Although women appeared in guild processions in nineteenth-century Egypt, nevertheless the membership seemed to be exclusively male (Tucker, 1978). Whether this was the case in Iran and the extent to which women from families associated with the bazaar participated in family trades and businesses needs to be researched. Gender-specific businesses, however, such as running women's public baths and selling goods in houses obviously existed. Women from the urban lower classes led a different style of life. The lower classes in the nineteenth century suffered from many social ills. Illiteracy was widespread in urban centres and there was no state provision for social welfare. One estimate was that 'three in a thousand' women were literate (Rice, 1923, p. 102). Poverty created an army of urban beggars and prostitutes and prompted many families to send their womenfolk to work.

Lower-class women worked at home as seamstresses, spinners and weavers, or went to work in other women's homes as maids, nannies, midwives, healers, preachers, matchmakers and sales women (Ravandi, 1978, III, p. 403). Some women worked in public baths and mortuaries and others played music, sang and danced in women-only and mixed bands. Prostitution was quite widespread and existed side-by-side with child marriage and *sigheh*. Veiling was not as strict among lower-class women who on the whole tended to be more mobile. Girls of nine years of age (which is the *Shariat* maturity age for women) were sold or given in *sigheh* to older men for a lump sum of money. One of the main sources of income for *mollas* was through contracts with poor families who were paid to rent their daughters to be given in *sigheh*; for this exchange the *mollas* were paid a commission. The urban lower classes were traditionally lax about formal religion and unlike the middle strata associated with the bazaar, did not observe strict religious duties. Nevertheless, owing to the social hold exerted by the clergy and widespread religious awe and superstition, the lower classes often constituted a faithful crowd for clergy-led protests and demonstrations. Lower-class women also showed a readiness to participate in economically motivated riots. Shortages and price rises of staple foods frequently brought crowds of lower-class women into the streets, damaging shops and punishing hoarders.

Diversity arising from contact with the West

Another source of diversity on women's position in turn of the century society related to the differing effects of Iran's relationship with the West. These acquired a variety of economic, ideological and political dimensions during this period.

Iran's contact with the West in the nineteenth century came about through Russian territorial intrusions. Russia's territorial wars with Iran began during Fath Ali Shah Qajar's reign (1797–1833). Between 1800 and 1828, Russia attacked Iranian borders in the north a few times and annexed several northern provinces. Finally in 1828 the Torkamanchay Treaty was signed between Russia and Iran which not only finalised the annexation of the northern ports by Russia but also granted far-reaching commercial and political concessions to it. Britain, too, started to send envoys to Fath Ali Shah's court as early as 1801 and succeeded in signing advantageous political and commercial treaties with him. These treaties amounted to capitulations by Iran to Russia and Britain which enabled both powers 'to open consular and commercial offices anywhere they wished and exempted their merchants not only from the high import duties but also from internal tariffs, local travel restrictions, and the jurisdiction of *shariat* law courts' (Abrahamian, 1982, p. 51). The military, economic and political superiority of Russia and Britain, therefore, affected the lives of different urban sectors and became a significant cause for concern among various strata of Iranian society.

Qajar states on the whole reacted to Western powers by hurried attempts to modernise, but these remained superficial and insignificant. The Shahs, surrounded in their courts by corruption and political intrigue, remained complacent and lacked initiative when facing Russian and British envoys. Naser od-Din Shah travelled to Europe three times, and after each trip introduced new customs, manners and styles of dress in his Court. He even attempted to introduce Iran's first cabinet of six ministers headed by the prime minister, Moshir od-Douleh, and established a public complaint box. His efforts, however, quickly became entangled in Court intrigues and came to nothing (Arasteh, 1964b, p. 100). Some attempts to modernise the army and the bureaucracy were made by prime ministers and state officials. During Fath Ali Shah's reign, Crown Prince Abbas Mirza and his minister Ghaem Magham tried to reorganise the army. Later on during Naser od-Din Shah's reign (1848–96), his first prime minister, Amir Kabir, continued Abbas Mirza's efforts to reorganise the army by establishing a polytechnic (Dar ol-Fonun) (1851) and by sending students and guild leaders abroad to learn new techniques. These efforts were continued by other prime ministers and state officials, who also became enmeshed in court intrigues; many of the reformers lost their jobs or lives as a result of internal and external machinations.

Western encroachments in the late nineteenth and early twentieth centuries affected various economic strata of the society. The agricultural sector witnessed a shift from family subsistence to cash crops for export. There was also a shift from small private landownership and state-owned lands to large-scale private holdings by landlords who lived in cities and ran their estates by appointees. The effects of these changes on the family as a production unit and women in particular remain to be studied. It has been argued, however, that as agriculture was commercialised and trade expanded, the living standard of the peasantry on the whole declined and the position of women deteriorated (Foran, 1989, p. 31). Rural and tribal women were also affected as producers of textiles and rugs by the rising demand for export of these commodities (Nashat, 1983, p. 16). Again, the positive and negative aspects of this development remain to be assessed.

The urban economy was equally affected by Western economic intervention. The institution of the bazaar was deeply affected by Western treaties with Iran. Western competition ruined some businesses, and caused others to prosper. But overall, the losses outweighed the gains and Iranian merchants and manufacturers who were witnessing the decline of native industries began to protest against uncontrolled European imports as early as the 1830s (Keddie, 1981, pp. 45, 58). The shift from cottage production to factory production also changed the labour process. Women moved from home-based carpet weaving to producing carpets in commercial workshops as demand for export rose substantially. Working conditions for these women have been described as atrocious (Foran, 1989, p. 40). Other factory-based production which also involved women relied on the urban poor and on peasant migrants as their labour force. Many unemployed traders and crafts people migrated to Russia for work (*ibid.*, p. 44). All of these must have had a deep and lasting effect on the family's productive and reproductive roles and female participation in wage labour.

Another influential strata of urban society to be affected both economically and ideologically were the Shii clergy, who had traditional ties with the bazaar. The economic grievances of the clergy revolved around the state imposition of taxation, which affected the bazaar and hence its donations to the clergy, and their dependence on financial contributions from sources which were under the control of the Shah and other wealthy laymen (Martin, 1989). Indeed, it has been argued that the defining feature of the clergy's political behaviour was not so much their attitude towards constitutionalism, but their economic interest. The clergy found themselves in increasing competition with each other over the chief sources of funds which included religious foundations, income from endowment (*vaghf*), donations from their followers, fees for judicial services, salaries and pensions. This was one of the main sources of division amongst the clergy in the constitutional period (*ibid.*, pp. 195–200).

Contact with the West acquired a cultural-ideological dimension in addition to the above mentioned economic one. Western ideas were accessible during this period through merchants and state officials who travelled abroad and conducted business in the neighbouring Ottoman

Empire, Egypt and Russia. Western missionaries, diplomats, administrators and travellers, too, disseminated Western thoughts and concepts in Iran. Some Iranians travelled abroad and wrote essays about European life and published critical newspapers demanding social and political reforms at home. Others created circles of debate and delivered speeches on the necessity for social and political reform. Reformist views, which had always existed as minority views in Iran, gained strength from world movements. The French Revolution with its slogan of liberty, equality and fraternity was followed in the nineteenth century by a flourishing of liberalism in Britain and of socialism across Europe. The separation of church and state and secularisation of society in Europe made an important impact on the thinking of the intelligentsia in Iran and in most other non-Western countries. The freedom that European women had in mixing with men and choosing their own spouse, their participation in society and their freedom from such social restrictions as seclusion and veiling, too, left a deep impression on those Iranians who observed them or heard about them. The suffragette movement with its determination and violent tactics inspired Iranian women who learned about it. The family in Europe, portrayed in an idealised fashion by Christian missionaries, presented images of romantic love, happiness, stability, mutual support and absence of divorce. This contrasted in the eyes of the Iranian intelligentsia with the image of family life in Iran based on arranged marriage, polygamy, suppression and exploitation of women, incompatibility between spouses, and easy divorce. Reforms in other Middle Eastern societies such as Turkey and Egypt were also inspirational and contagious. In short, the flourishing of the movement of modernity in Europe began to make a deep impact on Iranian social and political thought.

Moreover, the process of absorbing exogenous ideas and movements occurred alongside a revival of interest in positive virtues of an indigenous distant and independent past. The pre-Islamic past indeed proved to be a source of inspiration and a point of reference in reformers' quest for modernity. At times of social and political crises, many movements looked back on the Persian Empire and propagated ancient images of women to legitimise their contemporary point of view (Bayat-Philipp, 1981, p. 35). Many drew upon both indigenous and Western ideas in their prescription for overcoming the weaknesses of Iranian society. In doing so, they rejected certain views and practices as traditional and backward and accepted certain others as modern and progressive.

The above process of redefinition gave rise to a diversity of indigenous views on the future direction of Iranian society and the position of women within it. On the one hand, it created ideological resistance on the part of some Shii clerics. The clergy traditionally considered non-Muslim foreigners as unclean (*najes*) and suspected them because they drank alcohol and kept their women unveiled. Foreign envoys who were in a powerful position inside Iran sometimes inflamed native suspicions by adopting a lax attitude towards local traditions. A particularly striking example of this was demonstrated by the so-called Griboyedov affair. In 1829, a Russian mission was sent to Iran headed by Griboyedov to force the Iranian government to pay its debt to Russia. The mission, however, did not limit itself to its specific task and attempted to rescue a number of Christian women who, according to rumour, had been forcibly converted to Islam and kept in the *harams* of wealthy Iranians (Nafisi, 1952, II, p. 195). The news of Russian Cossacks forcing their way into *harams* and taking these women out insulted national honour and prompted the clergy to issue a *fatva* declaring it a religious duty to rescue Muslim women from the unbelievers. As a result, a crowd of Iranian men attacked the Griboyedov mission and killed all of them (Keddie, 1981, p. 46). The clergy, then, were fearful that foreign powers might not stop at taking over Iranian commerce, mining, banking and construction, but also put their hands on 'wheat plantations and Muslim women' (Adamiyat, 1978, p. 28).

On the other hand, contact with Western ideas and movements was responded to by the rise of indigenous Islamic and secular reformist movements. In the late nineteenth century, the Arab Middle East was witnessing an upsurge of Islamic reformism on the question of women. In Egypt, Muhammad Abdu and Qasim Amin were revolutionising Islamic thinking on women. Qasim Amin's *The Liberation of Women* and *The New Woman* argued for the emancipation of women on the basis of a new interpretation of the *Qoran* (Baraka, 1988). Their aim was to bring Islamic theory into line with modern social relations while maintaining its authority as a religious system. Such Islamic reformism did not take place in Iran. This was partly because of the historical development of the institution of Shiism, its place within Iranian society and links with the state. But this was also partly due to the fact that Islam was an imported religion in Iran, and reformist movements in Iran had traditionally sought reference to either pre-Islamic ideas or anti-establishment Islamic concepts. Nevertheless, the Islamic reformist movement in the Middle East did influence many nineteenth-century reformers in Iran and helped them to find a legitimate space for expressing discontent with the position of women. Jamal od-Din Afghani [Asadabadi] (1834–97) who associated with Muhammad Abdu, was one of these reformers. Afghani's pan-Islamic movement criticised traditional Islamic practices and argued for the introduction of modern science and technology into Iranian society.

He was an ardent anti-imperialist who considered the adoption of Western science and technology in Muslim countries as an instrument for waging an effective opposition against imperialist advances (Keddie, 1968). Afghani's movement exerted tremendous influence amongst successive generations of Islamic and secularist Iranian intellectuals.

Another indigenous response was secular reformism. Alongside Babism, Sufism and Sheykhism, new prophets with new religions emerged in turn of the century Iran. These were the intellectuals who propagated the secular ideology of 'humanity', 'freedom' and 'emancipation'. Some rejected Islam, others compromised with it. But all sought Iran's salvation in secular universal ideals. To secularist reformers, women's emancipation was part of the universal movement to reach human ideals. Three nineteenth-century intellectuals were particularly known for their secularist views and their defence of women's emancipation. Mirza Fath Ali Akhundzadeh (1812–78), who was a professed atheist, declared polygamy a social ill and argued for women's right to education (Abadi, 1993). Akhundzadeh was a nationalist who expressed a deep admiration for pre-Islamic Iran. He set a precedent for successive generations of Iranian intellectuals who looked back on the Persian Empire as the glorious age of Persian society and expressed disdain for the Islamic conquest as the origin of contemporary social evils (Adamiyat, 1970). His glorification of Zoroastrian Iran, however, had little to do with the 'reality' of women's position in ancient Iran. On the contrary, such a presentation of the past was a construction relevant to the existing socio-political situation. Akhundzadeh praised those who believed in women's education, emancipation, unveiling and in the monogamous family. He reminded Iranians that in some contemporary societies women were even involved in politics and that Iran, too, had queens before the Arab invasion (*ibid.*, pp. 223–5). Mirza Agha Khan Kermani was another reformist who published the first opposition Iranian newspaper abroad. *Akhtar* (The Star) was published in Istanbul in 1875. Kermani, who was a Babi, was deeply influenced by liberal and socialist ideas and preached liberty, equality and fraternity. For him, liberty could only exist where there was freedom of thought, expression, religion, work, dress, marriage, property and citizenship. Equality, in his belief, was not complete without equality of rights between men and women. He believed that the prerequisite for reaching a state of 'perfect fraternity' was full equality for men and women (Adamiyat, 1967, p. 242). In promoting equality for men and women, Kermani strongly attacked the institutions of polygamy, temporary marriage and seclusion (Kermani, 1990). He, and others, argued that the present status of women in Iran was a degradation of their former status in ancient Iran:

In ancient Iran women were equal with men in life. Men and women mixed freely, travelled together, and shared everything except rulership and government. Since the Arab invasion, Iranian women have been buried alive under *hejab*, and have become interned and locked-away in seclusion. *Hejab* has deafened and blinded women. Spiritual vision and wisdom can only be attained through seeing and hearing, and since women have been deprived of their sight and hearing, they cannot develop those qualities. Seclusion has prevented women from associating with men; participating in art, trade, industry; learning, knowledge, techniques and rules of civilisation; acquiring skills for earning a living; and learning the fundamentals of childrearing and household management. Women are bound members of society. Blind marriage is another social ill. Lack of freedom in the choice of a husband and unfamiliarity with the personality of her husband-to-be, makes cooperation between husband and wife impossible and gives rise to social corruption. Polygamy is another cause of the destruction of the Iranian nation, for the spread of which we should thank Shiism. Polygamy turns the pleasures between man and wife into discord and enmity, and drives families into poverty and distress. Polygamy promotes desperation and prostitution and spreads contagious disease. (*Ibid.*, p. 195)

Malkom Khan was yet another reformist who criticised the status quo (Nourai, 1973). He was Iran's ambassador to Britain under Naser od-Din Shah, but was dismissed from his post owing to disagreements with the Shah. After his dismissal Malkom Khan remained in London and published a newspaper by the name of *Ghanun* [Law]. Malkom Khan was a passionate proponent of secular law and attributed the backwardness of Iran to lack of a constitution and codified law (Nategh, 1976, Introduction). Malkom Khan, who had converted from Christianity to Islam, did not attack Islam as such and avoided controversial discussion of women's rights. Throughout the year-long publication of his paper (1889–90), he often mentioned women in relation to the 'Movement of Humanity'. For him, the rule of law was the sign of humanity, and women were the 'angels promoting humanity'.

Half of every nation is constituted by women. No social programme can proceed without the cooperation of women. Iranian women should be the angels promoting humanity. They should be highly regarded. A responsible woman can promote humanity more than a hundred wise men. At this moment in time, women are promoting humanity in Tehran and a few other provinces. Now that many Iranian men have turned into females, it is high time that women taught them manliness. (*Ghanun*, 1, p. 3)

The last decade of the nineteenth century witnessed the proliferation of secularist newspapers. Mirza Mohammad Ali Khan Kashani (known as Parvaresh) published *Soraya* in Cairo (1898–1900), which was followed by *Parvaresh* during 1900–2. These newspapers were followed at the turn of the century by *Habl ol-Matin* which was published by Moayed ol-Eslam. *Parvaresh* published a series of articles on the position of women.

In these, women's positions in the past and present were compared and the conclusion reached was that although Iranian history had produced many creative women in literary fields, the present situation of women had degenerated and it stifled women's creativity. In the present ignorant society, it was argued, women were considered to be devoid of human attributes. The belief that literacy and acquisition of knowledge would endanger women's chastity was criticised. The articles argued that 'there is no natural law which proves women have less capability and talent than men' (Mansur, 1984, p. 16). *Habl ol-Matin* also ran a series of articles under the title of 'Women's Rights and Freedoms'. These articles pointed to the link between social progress and women's emancipation and begged Iranian men and women to awaken to the necessity of reform. The editor of the newspaper, Moayed ol-Eslam, regretted the fact that 'women have been deprived of their rights for centuries and are considered as mentally deranged and devoid of will power. Talent in women is attributed to trickery and deceit or is regarded as accidental. Christian women can at least take refuge in their church; our women do not even have that' (*ibid.*, p. 18).

Secular reformist views in the nineteenth century were not the monopoly of men. Some women took their place in criticising the status quo and demanding reform on the position of women. Indeed, a most interesting piece of writing on women was produced by a woman who adopted a satirical style to express her discontent. Bibi Khanum, a woman from a lower-class background, wrote an essay in 1896 in reply to the degrading views of a male writer towards women and entitled her essay *Maayeb ol-Rejal* [The Vices of Men]. This was a response to an essay written by a man titled *Tadib ol-Nesvan* [The Chastisement of Women]. The latter essay argued that women's religious duty was to work at home and stated that making bread and spinning would increase women's value before God, and housework would secure women's virtue. Women were threatened that anger and disobedience towards their husbands would send them to hell. The consolation he offered to women was that if their hard work, patience, slavery, obedience, and total physical, spiritual and financial submission to their husbands did not bring them personal happiness in this world, they would certainly secure it in the other world (Adamiyat & Nategh, 1978, pp. 20–7; Najmabadi, 1992). Bibi Khanum pointed out in her satirical reply that men needed chastisement more than women and went on to count the flaws of character in men. She warned women not to take heed of such offensive advice since it was meant to perpetuate the superiority of men over women. She believed that if women were left alone by men they would quickly acquire knowledge and become competent as Western women had done already. Who is to be blamed, she asked, for the backwardness and corruption of this country? Certainly not women, she answered; how could they, when they did not have political power. The creators of the misfortunes of this society were men. The least they could do, therefore, was to stop going around advising women. Instead, men should spend their time seeking a remedy for their own corruption (Najmabadi, 1992).

The above economic and cultural-ideological responses to Western economic and cultural penetration of Iran can be summed up in short as paradoxical. On the one hand, the British and Russian intrusions and manipulations of Iran's resources were detested for their adverse economic effects. On the other hand, Western superiority which was a direct result of economic, technological, military, social and political progress created an awareness of an alternative model of society to aspire to. Each social strata developed its own formula for counteracting the detested aspects of Western influence and for gaining power and strength to enable Iran to challenge the West. The paradoxical position that at once admired Western progress and opposed Western domination prompted a reappraisal of the indigenous concepts. The result was a new definition of tradition and modernity, backwardness and progress. This was made possible within a context of new conflicts of interest and differences of thought on the position of women, brought about by political events of the turn-of-the-century, which will be discussed in chapter 2.

2 Women and the era of constitutionalism

The early phase of the discourse of modernity manifested itself in the movement for constitutionalism. This crucial movement revolved around the debate on the relevance of modernity to Iranian society.

During the last two decades of the nineteenth century, economic interference by and cultural contact with the West became channelled into a concrete anti-Qajar movement. This movement incorporated most sections of urban society, and brought about new alliances as well as new divisions. The constitutional movement was a response to a changing world which created new threats as well as promises for Iranian society. The movement gathered force and resulted in a revolution through an alliance of various socio-political strata in the face of a domineering foreign power and a weak state. The Constitutional Revolution accelerated the pace of political change and determined its direction. It also brought about a major shift in women's contribution to mass politics. It provided a space for the articulation of new ideas on women and the reappraisal of old ones, created an opportunity for women to experience political participation, and facilitated the formation of a woman's movement in Iran. Despite considerable historical interest in the Constitutional Revolution, relatively little is known about the extent and nature of women's participation in it. It would be useful, therefore, to use the existing accounts to draw a picture, even if a scant one, of where women featured in the chronicle of events of this crucial historical period.

The demand for a constitution

The first signs of the emergence of the new political alliances in the late nineteenth century, came about in 1890 as a result of an economic concession given to a British company by Naser od-Din Shah. The concession for curing and selling tobacco was criticised by Iranian newspapers published abroad and gave rise to massive protests which were led by clerics and with merchants as allies. In December 1891, the prominent Shii *mojtahed* Haji Hasan Shirazi issued a religious edict which forbade the use of tobacco. The *fatva* resulted in a nationwide boycott of tobacco. Government attempts to break the boycott and suppress the protest led to further unrest. Naser od-Din Shah warned Mirza Mohammad Hosein Ashtiani, one of the leaders of the protest, that either he had to smoke tobacco in public or leave town. He chose the latter and prepared to leave Tehran. The news of his exile spread and prompted numerous groups of men and women to assemble in front of his house. On their way, groups of women attacked shops which had not closed in protest and forced them to do so. They also shouted insults at the Shah calling him 'the female with a moustache', 'scarf wearer' and 'unbeliever'. Kamran Mirza, the Shah's third son, tried to calm women protestors by promising them that the Shah was planning to expel all foreigners from Iran and would not exile any of the clergy. But he was soon attacked by angry women and fled. The efforts of a pro-state cleric did not calm women protestors, and he too had to escape from their attacks. Eventually, the Shah ordered his cossacks to shoot at the crowd and many were killed (Teymouri, 1982, pp. 151–3).

Women observed the boycott as strictly as men (Nahavandian, 1978, pp. 96–100). Smoking was popular amongst women in those days. Even the Shah's wives refused to smoke tobacco and when Naser od-Din Shah tried to break the boycott in his own *haram* his wives resisted and told him in protest that 'tobacco has been boycotted by those who have married us to you' (Teymouri, 1982, pp. 106–8). Mass protests and the successful boycott of tobacco forced Naser od-Din Shah to cancel the tobacco concession in 1892. After the tobacco protest, a shortage of food provoked riots in many parts of the country. Women participated in these riots and even led some of them. The famous Tabrizi heroine, Zeinab Pasha, led many riots against the governor and merchants who hoarded foodstuffs and caused shortages and rising prices. In Tehran, women rampaged in the streets and demanded justice (Nahid, 1981, pp. 43–54; Adamiyat, 1980, pp. 78–9; Adamiyat & Nategh, 1978, pp. 394–5). Whilst the opposition was becoming more organised, Naser od-Din Shah was assassinated by Mirza Reza Kermani and Mozaffar od-Din Shah succeeded him (1896–1906).

The era of Mozaffar od-Din Shah was marked not only by unpopular economic policies, but also by a degree of relaxation of political repression (Abrahamian, 1982, p. 75). This was an opportunity for opposition views against the Qajar state to spread among a wider public. Critical newspapers published abroad were read aloud publicly in mosques and tea houses, and by 1905 discontent with the state assumed some degree of organisation through the formation of 'secret societies'. These organisations played an important role in directing the anti-Qajar movement towards a popular, constitutional movement. The Secret Centre (Markaz Gheybi) and The Secret Society (Anjoman Makhfi) were established in Tabriz. The former established close ties with the Social Democratic Party (Hezb Ejtemaiyun Ammiyun) which was formed in 1904 in Baku to work within the ranks of thousands of Iranian migrant workers in Russia (Abrahamian, 1982, p. 77; Adamiyat, 1975). In Tehran, The Society of Humanity (Jameeh Adamiyat) and The Revolutionary Committee (Komiteh Enghelabi) resumed activity. Despite their different socialist and liberal ideologies, these societies shared basic convictions about the need for public welfare, public education, a house of justice (Edalat Khaneh), equality, protection of life and property and liberty through secular law, and the establishment of parliamentary democracy.

By 1905, these demands were increasingly incorporated into the single concept of constitutionalism, first mentioned by Malkom Khan in *Ghanun*. The concept of constitutionalism gradually became accepted among wider circles including such clerics as Seyyed Abdollah Behbahani and Seyyed Mohammad Tabatabai and many merchants who were members of various secret societies. There was a general consensus amongst the supporters of constitutionalism that the parliamentary rule by people's representatives was the only way to curtail the excesses of the Qajar Shahs and to pave the way for progress. It was believed that constitutional rule did not contradict Islam and many clerics such as Naini argued that it was the best type of rule in the absence of the messianic twelfth *emam* (Hairi, 1977). Moreover, to many clerics constitutionalism entailed the promise of political power which they were interested in having in addition to their ideological power (Fischer, 1980, p. 149). Merchants, too, hoped to benefit from constitutional rule through participating in the making of commercial laws which would protect and secure their property and trade interests. The fact that constitutionalism was defined and debated in the broadest of terms helped to make it acceptable to an even broader audience, and enabled various sections of the population to read into the concept their own meaning.

Women, too, joined in the quest for a constitution. They turned their traditional social and religious gatherings into political meetings. Women learned about the latest political events at mosques and *rowzeh*, and discussed them in their secret societies (Bamdad, 1977, pp. 13–14, 34). Women's political activities in this period ranged from circulating information, spreading news, acting as informers and messengers, participating in demonstrations, and taking up arms in protest. Malkom Khan praised women's participation in the 'movement of humanity' in his newspaper *Ghanun*. He wrote 'The rush of women to participate in the movement of humanity is surprising. The state of affairs is such that many of our noble women have gone ahead of men [in promoting humanity]. Women have understood the meaning and advantages of humanity much better than men, or rather non-men' (*Ghanun*, 2, p. 2). In a later issue of *Ghanun*, a woman confirmed Malkom Khan's enthusiasm about women's role in spreading the message of humanity:

Do not be disappointed by Iranian women. We have not yet become as unmanly as our husbands and the young people of our time by spending our life in idleness. In this conjuncture of humanity, we know our duty very well. The defeat of the agora of unmanliness and dishonour depends on us. We did not know what to do. But the light of law has opened our eyes and hearts. The torch of humanity is in our hands. Now that we have set ourselves on this path, you will witness how women will set alight a flaming fire in this country with the torch of humanity. (*Ghanun*, 3, p. 4)

From June 1905 to August 1906, a series of public protests about internal and external matters dealt a final blow to the resistance of the Qajar state against constitutionalists. The deteriorating economic situation, the shortage of sugar and punishment of a respectable merchant for allegedly hoarding sugar, the failure of the Shah to convene a House of Justice, and the granting of trade concessions to a Belgian, which left the country in great debt, all led to three important public protests by men and women (Abrahamian, 1982, p. 81). In June 1905, the first group of public protestors led a peaceful procession and demanded the dismissal of Monsieur Naus, the Belgian customs administrator. Some clerics included the dismissal of women workers from factories amongst their demands (Nategh, 1983b, p. 9). Mozaffar od-Din Shah promised to dismiss Monsieur Naus and left the country for a European trip. In December 1905, a large group of clerics and merchants occupied the shrine of Shahzadeh Abdolazim in protest against the government's punishment of a prominent merchant for allegedly hoarding sugar and demanded the convening of a House of Justice. Women participated in this protest alongside men. While the shrine was surrounded by soldiers women climbed to the rooftops carrying stones to throw at them (Doulatabadi, 1947, p. 26). Near the royal palace, a group of women surrounded the Shah's carriage and demanded respect for the clergy:

We want the masters and leaders of our religion! We are Muslims and believe in obeying their commands! The masters have taken care of our properties! All our affairs are in the masters' hands! How could we accept your banishing them to exile? O, King of the Muslims, respect the command of the Muslim leaders. O, King of Islam, if Russia and England come to your support, upon the masters' command, millions of Iranians will declare *jahad*. (Bayat-Philipp, 1978, p. 298)

Women also sent threatening letters to the Shah. A letter from a 'Women's Revolutionary Committee' which carried a letterhead showing a red hand holding a pistol, threatened the Shah with death if he ignored the people's demand for a House of Justice (Malekzadeh, 1949, II, pp. 61–4). Mozaffar od-Din Shah eventually gave in to this demand and the occupation ended in January 1906. Although Tehran remained the major scene of opposition to the government, discontent had also developed in other main provincial towns. In Esfahan the rise in the price of copper created riots. Many merchants and craftsmen encouraged their wives to attack the British Consulate and the telegraph office as they would not be recognised under their heavy veils (Ravandi, 1978, III, p. 727). The final mass protest in this period came about when it became obvious that the Shah had no intention of convening a House of Justice. In July 1906, criticism of the government by radical preachers received a violent response from the state. The shooting of a young *molla* by government forces created hysteria amongst men and women alike (Kasravi, 1978, I, p. 97). Crowds gathered in mosques and the preacher's body was carried by a group of men and women. Women wore shrouds and marched in the bazaar, mourning his death and cursing the soldiers (Moaser, 1973, p. 81). Demonstrations continued for a few days (Kasravi, 1978, I, pp. 95–6), and concluded in a crowd of more than 12,000 occupying the British Legation. The sit-in lasted for three weeks and resulted in the demand for a constituent assembly and a constitution. During the occupation, merchants formed an administrative committee and intellectuals gave speeches on the advantages of adopting a European-style constitution. Women attempted to join in but were prevented from doing so by the administrative committee. The British Ambassador sent a note to the government informing that, 'The number of occupiers has reached five thousand. . . . I have also been informed that a few thousand women are intending to join in the occupation. I will do my best to persuade those presently involved in the occupation to oppose women's participation' (Rain, 1975, p. 99).

Women, however, were encouraged by the administrative committee to hold demonstrations outside the Legation and royal palace (Abrahamian, 1982, p. 84). Many women supported the sit-in financially and otherwise (Kermani, 1982, I, p. 539). Mozaffar od-Din Shah finally dismissed his prime minister and accepted the need to convene a Constituent Assembly three weeks after the start of the sit-in. The Constituent Assembly was convened in August 1906 to formulate an electoral law for the forthcoming National Assembly (hereafter Majles). The electorate was divided into princes and Qajars, Shii clergy, landowners, rich merchants, shopkeepers, and high craftsmen and tradesmen. There was no mention of women, and lower-class and illiterate men were likewise excluded from the electoral register. The Constituent

Assembly was immediately followed by elections for the first Majles which opened in October 1906. The Majles took as its first task the drafting of a Fundamental Law which was basically a translation of the Belgian Constitution. The Fundamental Law limited the Shah's power and granted the Majles extensive powers as the representative of the Iranian nation. The Fundamental Law was ratified by Mozaffar od-Din Shah a few days before his death and by his successor Mohammad Ali Shah in December 1906.

The Majles set out to draft a Supplementary Fundamental Law. As time passed, the initial consensus on the broad definition of constitutionalism and what it entailed began to crumble. As a result, it took the Majles more than a year to succeed in writing a compromise draft. While various factions within the Majles, including Moderates, Libertarians and Royalists, fought over every issue, people waited impatiently for the Supplementary Fundamental Law. A woman wrote to *Habl ol-Matin* in December 1906 and asked the editor to explain 'Why is it that the Constitution has prevented women from gaining their rights?' Women, she continued, 'did not take part in the Revolution to have their rights trampled upon' (Mansur, 1984, p. 23). *Nedaye Vatan* (The Voice of the Homeland) published a long letter from the Women's Secret Union (Ettehadiyeh Gheybi Nesvan) which asked Majles deputies to end the existing chaos by drafting the Supplementary Fundamental Law as soon as possible:

> Fourteen months have passed since the advent of the Constitution. During this period we have spent our time reading the newspapers to find out what is being done in the Majles . . . . All we have heard is, God willing, it will be finished the day after tomorrow. . . . When will this day after tomorrow come? . . . If we wanted the Shah and his ministers to govern, why did we bother with this game . . . Where is your Law? Where is your Senate? Where is your House of Justice? (*Ibid.*, pp. 64–8)

Another woman writer challenged the Majles to let women run the country for a trial period: 'We shall elect the deputies, we shall elect the ministers . . . we will amend the laws, we will put the city police in order, we will assign the governors, we will send legal guidelines to the provinces, we will uproot oppression and autocracy' (Najmabadi, 1993). *Anjoman*, the organ of a Tabriz secret society published a letter which was addressed to representatives of Azarbayjan in the Majles. The letter explained that 'The atmosphere in the city is inexplicable. The people of the city even women holding their babies have assembled in the mosques. Impatience is running high, and it is not possible to calm it' (Rafii, 1983, p.118).

A group of women assembled in front of the Majles and demanded the

Supplementary Fundamental Law (Nahid, 1981, p. 64). They were turned away on the ground of provocation, and Sani od-Douleh, the head of the Majles, used this incident as an excuse to resign. On another occasion, the widows of the late Naser od-Din Shah began a sit-in the Majles to protest against the discontinuation of their pensions (Navai, 1976, p. 32). Women, nonetheless, supported the Majles for its nationalist aims. In 1906, the Majles rejected the government's intention to request a loan from Russia and Britain to pay its debts. People supported the Majles by offering donations to set up a national bank. Women offered to sell their jewellery. A woman said in a mosque gathering: 'Why should the government borrow money from foreigners? Are we dead? I am a laundress and can contribute my share of one tuman. Other women are ready to contribute too' (Kasravi, 1978, I, pp. 180–2). Another woman wrote to the Majles on behalf of herself and other women from Qazvin and offered to buy shares in the National Bank (Kermani, 1982, II, pp. 92–3). The Supplementary Fundamental Law was eventually drafted in 1907.

The civil war

The foregoing developments strengthened the conviction of many of the anti-constitutionalists about the anti-Islamic nature of the Constitution and converted many pro-constitutionalists to their cause. Anti-constitutionalists gained much support from Mozaffar od-Din Shah's successor Mohammad Ali Shah and his Royalist supporters. Mohammad Ali Shah who was an ardent anti-constitutionalist had already made his position clear by refusing to ratify the Supplementary Fundamental Law. But he had been forced eventually to give in to mass protests and put his seal of approval on it. But this time, after strengthening his support amongst clerics such as Sheykh Fazlollah Nuri, he struck harder by first organising violent anti-constitutionalist demonstrations and then bombing the Majles in June 1909. The resistance put up by armed constitutionalists was broken and with the announcement of martial law many prominent reformers were arrested, killed or exiled.

People reorganised and fought back, and the civil war spread to many provincial towns. The resistance of constitutionalists in Tabriz was particularly heroic. Mohammad Ali Shah's forces surrounded the city. The Shah wrote a letter to the clergy in Tabriz requesting their support. In his letter, the Shah attacked constitutionalist ideas of social equality as being against Islam and the monarchy and warned the clergy, who, in the guise of rejecting superstition and backwardness, had prompted women to establish women's societies and talk about emancipation (Nategh, 1983b, p. 13). Despite this, Tabriz remained fairly united in defending the Constitution. Government forces killed, burned and ruined many areas of Azarbayjan. The suppression was particularly harsh in Maku and Gharadagh which created enormous sympathy all over the country. *Habl ol-Matin* reported that 500 women assembled in the main square in Tehran in support of the Azarbayjani people and shouted anti-despotism slogans (Nahid, 1981, p. 69). In Esfahan, women collected jewellery, carpets and furniture to sell for donations to the people of Azarbayjan. In Shiraz, women received a letter requesting help from Tabrizi women and set out to demonstrate and assemble in the telegraph office. The Women's Committee in Tabriz sent a telegram to the Iranian Women's Committee in Istanbul and asked for support in informing world public opinion about the danger that was threatening their city. Iranian women in Istanbul subsequently sent telegrams to European governments, including the British government, and pleaded for their help in restraining Mohammad Ali Shah. The British government replied by informing them that Britain and Russia were cooperating to bring about order in Iran (*ibid.*, pp. 70, 81–3).

During the eleven-month seige of Tabriz by the Royalist forces, men and women fought side-by-side. The Tabriz Society (Anjoman Tabriz) gained national fame. *Anjoman*, the organ of the Tabriz Society, regularly reported the fight between constitutionalists and Royalists. One report stated: 'According to reliable sources, a number of valiant women are dressed in disguise and are fighting the forces of the enemy. These women have occupied a strategically important part of the city and are showering the enemy with their ammunition'. Another report stated that armed women had been found killed in the battlefield of Amirkhiz Square and their corpses lay amongst the martyrs of freedom (Rafii, 1983, p. 117). Many other women remained behind the front lines to cook, wash and attend to the wounded. These women too, however, did not hesitate to take up arms when their camps were invaded by the Royalist forces (Nahid, 1981, p.84). *Anjoman* also reported women's riots against hoarding and shortages of staple foods (Rafii, 1983, p. 117). In one incident, a group of women came across a wealthy merchant who was known as a hoarder of food. Women attacked Haji Ghasem Ardabili, hitting him all over; he was rescued by a group of men and taken to the telegram office. Women followed them to get hold of him again and the crowd eventually hanged and castrated him (Kasravi, 1978, I, p. 355). Women also set up committees which collected money and jewellery for the families of constitutionalists (*ibid.*, II, p. 610). *Anjoman* printed a letter by a group of women from Tabriz to Prime Minister Eyn od-Douleh. The letter reminded him of his opposition to the Shah in the past and told him that he was wrong if he thought he could 'prevent the nation from wanting a constitution by imposing starvation'. The letter continued, 'We have enough food to last for a few months and after that we will survive on leaves, vegetables, fruit, and dogs and cats. We will resist the Shah until we are drowned in our own blood.' The letter concluded by warning him to 'think about escaping abroad as there can be no safety for a wrongdoer like you here' (Rafii, 1983, p. 119).

In Tehran, women were seen demonstrating in the streets and giving refuge to deputies and hiding volunteer soldiers in their homes (Kasravi, 1978, II, p. 646). They carried pistols under their veils and in one incident a women shot and killed an anti-constitutionalist preacher addressing a crowd in the central square in Tehran. She herself was immediately killed by the crowd (Malekzadeh, 1949, vol. 3, p. 145). The occupation of the streets of Tehran by the cossacks prompted women to send telegrams abroad in protest against Russian intervention in Iran. On 15 September 1908, the London *Times* published a reply by Sir Edward Grey (Bayat-Philipp, 1978, p. 299). He stated that the Queen had received the telegram and that England and Russia would take all necessary steps to restore order in Iran. The civil war was finally won by the constitutionalists. Majles deputies met and acted as a constituent body. Mohammad Ali Shah was deposed and his son Ahmad Shah was crowned. A few outspoken opponents of the Constitution, including Sheykh Fazlollah Nuri, were executed.

The Russian ultimatum

The second Majles convened in 1909, and in 1911 employed an American by the name of Morgan Shuster to put the country's finances in order. The fact that he was American caused the Russians to worry about American influence in Iran and they issued an ultimatum. The Majles was given the option of dismissing Shuster and undertaking not to employ more Americans or else face occupation by the Russians. The ultimatum caused an outrage in the country. Shopkeepers closed their shops, schools were closed, and men and women poured into the streets in protest. It was reported that on one occasion 300 women in heavy veils went to meet the head of the Majles threatening the deputies with death if they wavered 'in their duties to uphold the liberty and dignity of the Persian people and nation' (Shuster, 1968, p. 198). It was also reported that these women carried pistols under their veils (Malekzadeh, 1949, VII, pp. 93–4). *Anjoman* reported that thousands of women wore shrouds and demonstrated against the Russian ultimatum (Rafii, 1983, p. 118). As in 1906, when women offered money and jewellery to the Majles for the purposes of establishing a National Bank, this time too women collected money and jewellery to help the government pay off its debts to Russia (Bamdad, 1977, p. 37).

Some women chose this moment to wage a war against women's veiling. A group of women appeared in the streets of Tehran shouting pro-constitutional slogans and demanding their freedom from the veil. The sight of these women removing their *chador* created a public outcry not least from their constitutionalist sisters who dissociated themselves from the actions of 'a bunch of prostitutes' (Bayat-Philipp, 1978, p. 302). The majority of pro-constitutionalist women preferred to concentrate on nationalist activities. The National Ladies' Society (Anjoman Mokhaddarat Vatan) wrote to the Women's Suffragette Committee of London asking for help in quelling the demand by the Russian government 'to surrender our independence' (Bayat-Philipp, 1978, p. 299). In December 1911, the Majles held a session to discuss the forty-eight-hour ultimatum given by the Russians. The National Ladies' Society organised a public meeting outside the Majles in which women 'made fervent speeches in defence of the constitutional regime and in favour of national independence and social justice' (Bamdad, 1977, p. 35). The London *Times* reported in December 1911:

> The patriotic demonstrations continue. A curious feature is the prominent part taken in them by women. At a large meeting of women held in the great mosque of Sepah Salar, addresses were delivered by female orators; it is said that they were very eloquent. One lady announced that, although the law of Islam forbade it, the women would nevertheless take part in a holy war. (Bayat-Philipp, 1978, p. 303)

The next day a group of women went to the telegraph office and sent telegrams to foreign governments complaining about the Russian ultimatum. They then went to the house of the prominent constitutionalist, Sardar Asad Bakhtiar, held a meeting and delivered patriotic speeches demanding Iran's 'independence and dignity' (Bamdad, 1977, pp. 36–7). A few days later in December 1911, the National Ladies' Society sent a telegram to the Majles reminding the deputies of their duty 'to determine the nation's laws, to keep watch on the policies of the ministers, and to supervise the activities of the government's agents' (*ibid*., pp. 37–8). The efforts of the National Ladies' Society to oppose the ultimatum must have been taken seriously by the Russians. In December 1911, the Russian Legation issued a circular trying to undermine the confidence of activist women. It said:

> To the respected Ladies of Iran, long may they thrive! Since the present status of women in Iran is such that they cannot freely express political opinions on behalf of the general public, the ladies are respectfully requested to go to the trouble of answering the following questions:

Has the principle of constitutional government in Iran in any way changed the status of Iranian women? If it has caused a change, what is the nature of the change? If it has not caused a change, what is the reason? Do the women of Iran prefer constitutional government to the previous system? Is so, why do they prefer it, and if not, why not? Are Iranian women content with their present status and position, and if not, why not? Do they consider the status of European women preferable to their own position, and if so, why? By what means and in what form do they hope to see their worth and dignity improved? Ladies who desire that their names shall not be disclosed are requested to indicate this, instead of signing at the bottom of the form. (Bamdad, 1977, pp. 38–9)

The National Ladies' Society replied point by point in an uncompromising tone:

1 Being strong or weak obviously produces effects. In sofar as the constitutional regime in Iran has lacked strength, it has to that extent failed to open many girls' schools or offer much scope to women who prefer civilization and education to lack of skills and idleness.
2 Every person who has a sound conscience prefers justice and legality to autocracy and arbitrary rule. This attitude is shared by men and women alike.
3 We are not content with our status and position. We are the victims of unruliness and lack of law.
4 We consider the position of European women preferable because they possess skills, but not for any other reasons.
5 We hope that our position will be improved through the enactment of a code of equality, because human worth and dignity are secured by the spread of law and in no other way. (*Ibid.*, p. 39)

The Russian ultimatum, however, was successful. The Majles dismissed Shuster and three weeks after the ultimatum the head of the Majles, Naser ol-Molk, closed the Majles and exiled the Social Democrat and the Moderate leaders to Qom. The closure of the Majles was a serious setback for constitutionalists and put the country back under the rule of the Qajar monarch. Ahmad Shah, however, did not reach the age of majority until 1914 and meanwhile Naser ol-Molk ruled over the country for few years with much repression (Bahar, 1944).

The debate on women in the National Assembly

The fluid and transitory political situation in the constitutional era included a debate on the position of women in Iranian society. In discussing this debate, it is important to emphasise that the constitutional movement was a diverse one only unified broadly by a quest for social and political reform. The composition of political forces changed may times during the Constitutional Revolution. As pointed out earlier, pro-constitutionalists were initially a broad alliance of social groups mobilised around a vague demand for 'a constitution'. As time passed and opportunities arose for dialogue and debate, the issues at stake became clearer and alliances and groupings changed accordingly. By the time the first Majles was convened, in October 1906, political differences had become more distinctly marked.

The first Majles was composed of three loose but distinct political groups. The Royalists (Mostabedin) were few in number but enjoyed the support of the Court and of clerics such as Sheykh Fazlollah Nuri. The Libertarians (Azadikhahan) constituted the largest minority and enjoyed support amongst intellectuals. They were led by prominent reformers such as Taqizadeh and Eskandari, a Qajar prince. This group published *Iran now* [New Iran] in Tehran, *Shafagh* [Sunrise] in Tabriz, and *Now Bahar* [New Spring] in Mashad. The Moderates (Motadelin) were the largest group and their support came from wealthy merchants. Their leaders included high ranking clerics such as Ayatollahs Tabatabai and Behbahani.

The Supplementary Fundamental Law which was drafted by Majles deputies reflected the fact that the balance of power in the Majles favoured the combined forces of the Moderates and Royalists. The Supplementary Fundamental Law gave important powers to the Shii clergy. Article 2 appointed a 'Supreme Committee' consisting of five leading *mojtahedin*, to check and assess the compatibility of parliamentary laws with the *shariat*. Article 71 defined the judiciary as the exclusive domain of the Shii clergy. The press was prohibited from expressing anti-Islamic opinions (Article 20), and those scientific and technological subjects which 'contradicted Islam' were forbidden in schools (Article 18). Articles 19 and 13 gave Iranian citizens the right to public education and equality before the law, but women were not specifically mentioned in any of the articles and the law addressed men. However, the article on public education was used ten years later to establish public education for women. The occasional debates which took place in the Majles on women's issues reflected the power of the conservative forces. What follows is a collection of views expressed by Majles deputies on women's issues:

AGHA SEYYED MEHDI: In this country, constitutionalism has been taken to mean freedom of expression and women's emancipation. Some people are spreading corruption in the guise of constitutionalism.

EMAM JOMEH: Today nothing is more dangerous for the Majles than these newspapers. ... *shariat* has not made people equal and God has not created women free.

MIRZA MORTEZAGHOLI KHAN: It is obvious that our country is Islamic and according to the Constitution all laws should be compatible with Islam. We are also obliged to correct people's ethics. I have come across a [entrance] ticket which I will read out to you to see whether it is correct according to the *shariat* or not? [The ticket was read out and was related to a function organised by a women's society.]

AGHA MIRZA MAHMUD: This is not a matter for discussion in the Majles. The Ministry of Internal Affairs should be written to, to ban such a society.

VAKIL OL-ROAYA: First of all it should be made clear whether or not the assembling of women in one place has been banned by the *shariat* since the advent of Islam. The word *anjoman* [society or association] is a recently adopted name, but what is wrong with a group of women getting together and learning correct behaviour from each other? Of course if they commit actions which are against Islam, they should be prevented from doing so. Otherwise it [*anjoman*] is not basically a bad thing.

AGHA SEYYED ALI NAGHI: This issue is like the issue of some newspapers which the Minister of Internal Affairs is unable to control. It is a matter related to belief and should be prevented.

AGHA SEYYED HOSEIN TAQIZADEH: There are no objections on *shariat* grounds to women gathering in one place, and in Islam women have always been able to assemble. There is also no objection set against it in the Constitution. When the Constitution grants Iranian people the right to assemble, it means freedom of assembly for both men and women. As long as these assemblies are not for the purpose of rejecting Islam they are not prohibited.

AGHA MIRZA MAHMUD: I said at the beginning that this is not a matter to be discussed here. But since the discussion has taken place, I will give the opinion that there is nothing wrong with women getting together and learning about dress-making and other industries and discussing the boycott of foreign fabrics.

VAKIL OL-TOJJAR: As Mr. Taqizadeh said, these societies are not harmful as long as they do not act against Islam.

AGHA MIRZA FAZLALI AGHA: The principle of assembly is not contrary to the *shariat*, but I believe no respectable woman would want to involve herself in this kind of thing, and suspect that some people are setting up these societies to commit corruption through them. Therefore, these societies should not be allowed and future corruption should be prevented.

AGHA MIRZA MORTEZAGHOLI KHAN: Discussing this matter here is necessary because this issue is talked about outside. Some people say it is contrary to the *shariat* and some say it is correct. This matter should be clarified in the Majles, and then referred to the Minister of Internal Affairs.

AGHA SHEYKH MOHAMMAD ALI: '. . . this debate should not take place in the Majles. The duty of the Majles is to make laws and it should concentrate on building up the country'.

HOSEINGHOLI KHAN NAVAB: I am surprised to hear that women should not assemble. But as to the appropriateness of this debate, I agree that this is not a matter to be discussed here. The discussion should take place in newspapers. I would like to write an article about this and my opinion is that it is in accordance with the *shariat*, but for some other reasons, they should not take place.

EMAM JOMEH: The opinion of the majority that this matter should not be discussed here is correct. But other opinions expressed here are wrong. It is true that women can go out and assemble with the permission of their husbands. But the problem arises because of what is said in these assemblies. I don't want further discussion on this in the Majles, and what has been said is enough. (*Parliamentary Proceedings of First Majles*, 1946, pp. 217, 255, 266, 484)

Despite choosing compromise inside the Majles, the Libertarians did not restrain the words and deeds of their supporters outside. Their newspapers ridiculed those parts of the Supplementary Fundamental Law which confirmed the power of the clergy and demanded the separation of politics from religion. *Sur Esrafil*, which was edited by Mirza Jahangir Khan, published many provocative articles and was closed down many times. In an article in its July 1907 issue, a woman criticised the attitudes of both pro-constitutionalist clerics such as Tabatabai and Behbahani and anti-constitutionalist clerics such as Sheykh Fazlollah Nuri, who branded the liberal-minded people as 'anti-Islamic' and 'Babi'. She wondered why so many men gave in to such blackmail and were intimidated by such nonsense, and regretted that she was not a man so as to be able to say what she really wanted (Nategh, 1983b, p. 10). Dehkhoda, another Libertarian who was a frequent contributor to *Sur Esrafil* encouraged women to reject traditional practices and embark on learning new matters. He cited the example of Western women 'who have founded organisations, and attracted the attention of Western newspapers to their speeches and essays, and have written multiple books to establish the righteousness of their cause of enfranchisement'. Dehkhoda urged women to get together, open schools, establish organisations, become educated, break their ever-dirty pots and pans behind them and drive backward-looking *mollas* out of their lives (*ibid.*, pp. 10–11).

Iran Now [New Iran], which was edited by Malek ol-Shoara-e Bahar seemed to have a woman reporter called Tahereh who contributed to the journal regularly. Tahereh often complained about 'the Islamic culture'. She believed that although religion had done wrong to women, they (women) should take some of the blame for their own backwardness. Women, she argued, should take responsibility for changing their own situation. They should get together and support each other. They should organise and take action 'since no one else can fight our battles for us' (*ibid.*; *Nimeye Digar*, 2, pp. 104–14). Tahereh criticised men for being bound by 'rotten rules'. Instead of pioneering women's education, she argued, men cared only about multiplying their wives and falling for women's physical beauty. She asked, if polygamy is desirable and useful why is it only for men? If it's good, she argued, it should be good for everyone and if bad no one should practise it; why the double standard? (*ibid.*). In another issue of *Iran Now* another writer, Mazandarani, complained about those who regarded women's education as contrary to Islam and deprived women of their human rights and blocked all roads to their progress: yet these 'ignorants' and 'weaklings' were expected to raise the children of the nation. True progress for women, Mazandarani argued, could only be found in the West 'where men and women are considered as two halves of the same mould and complementary to each other'. Mazandarani believed that unless men and women were viewed as equals and complementary to each other the institution of the family could not be established on the right premises (*Nimeye Digar*, 2, pp. 104–14).

Edalat (1906–9) and *Molla Nasr od-Din* (1908) were other provocative newspapers published in Tabriz. They reflected the views of Azarbayjani Social Democrats and published many provocative articles by Seyyed Hosein Edalat and Jalil Gholizadeh. The latter believed that women's emancipation was not possible without their liberation from Islam. He cited the example of Soviet Central Asia where, despite the growth of class struggle, Muslim women clung to their 'ignorance' and 'superstition' and did not progress side-by-side with their menfolk. Gholizadeh wrote many plays showing the misery of women's life in Iran (Nategh, 1983b, p. 12). In addition to newspaper articles, many essays were also written on equality of rights between men and women. A manuscript by an anonymous author argued that the essence of nature lay in liberty and equality. Men and women, the manuscript argued, had different attributes but should possess equal rights. All members of society had equal rights and social progress depended upon the degree of women's emancipation (Adamiyat, 1978, pp. 326–9).

Contrary to the Libertarians, the position adopted by the Moderates inside and outside the first Majles was one of reform within the confines of Islam. While they allied themselves with the Libertarians on general reforms, they preferred caution on the question of women. *Davat Eslam* [Islam's Call] which was published in Bombay in 1907 by Agha Mirza Mohammad Amin ol-Tojjar, a supporter of the Moderates, attacked 'anti-Islamic and Babi propaganda' but gave qualified support to women's education. In an article in the July 1907 issue, Amin ol-Tojjar expressed his opposition to women's unveiling and considered their education desirable only if it was done in accordance with Islamic strictures. Girls' schools, he argued, should only have women teachers and the curriculum should be limited to subjects of particular use to women. Women's education, he believed, was necessary because it enabled women to earn an honest living when experiencing hardship instead of turning to prostitution (Mansur, 1984, pp. 15, 19). Tabatabai, the constitutionalist cleric who led the Moderates, expressed his disapproval of women's societies in a letter to his daughter:

> It appears from what is said in the Majles that Babism and Naturism have dawned on us and are strengthening. Recently, women have set up a society in a place opposite the house of Seyyed Reyhanollah. The head of this society is the sister of Gol-o-Bolbol ... and two other members of this society are the wives of Mirza Hasan Roshdiyeh and Bibi Khanum. All these women are known Babis. (Kasravi, 1978, I, p. 289)

As to the Royalists, they expressed strong objections when issues of women's education, women's societies and the anti-clerical articles of some newspapers were discussed in the Majles. One Royalist deputy warned that the law regarding public education should be interpreted to prevent girls and 'pretty boys' from going to school (Nategh, 1983a, p. 47). Another deputy demanded the banning of *Sur Esrafil* and *Habl ol-Matin* and the arrest of their editors and journalists, particularly Dehkhoda (*ibid.*). But amongst the Royalist clerics, the most fanatical objection to the activities of Libertarians was put forward by Sheykh Fazlollah Nuri. This anti-constitutionalist cleric argued that the spirit of the Constitution was contrary to Islam. In his view, Islam treated 'the social minor and the social major, the sane and the insane, the healthy and the sick, the husband and the wife, the rich and the poor, the *mojtahed* and the layman, the Muslim and the non-Muslim' differently and held different injunctions for each category (Torkman, 1983, pp. 107–8). Fazlollah Nuri was frightened by the upsurge of liberalism and anti-Islamic sentiments amongst pro-constitutionalists. In a letter entitled 'For the Awareness of Muslim Brothers', he talked about the conspiracy by the advocates of modernity to 'spread consumption of alcoholic drinks, promote prostitution, open schools for women, redirect the money that should be spent on religious projects into building of factories, roads, railways and other foreign projects in Iran' (*ibid.*, p. 262). In another letter, he warned against those who 'interpret the sacred *Qoranic* verse of *hejab* in a devious way'. This was a reference to the argument put forward by the Libertarians that the *Qoran* rejected women's strict veiling (*ibid.*, pp. 299–300). Nuri also issued *fatva* against the opening of schools for girls (Malekzadeh, 1949, III, pp. 179–80).

The second Majles convened in 1909 after the collapse of the Royalist forces in the civil war. This time, two groups, the Democrats (former Libertarians) and Moderates, occupied the Majles. The two groups put forward programmes. The Democrats called for the extension of the vote to all adult males; free, direct and secret ballots; the equality of all citizens irrespective of religion and birth; the separation of politics from religion; free education for all, including women; the abolition of capitulations; industrialisation; and the distribution of land among those who worked on it (Abrahamian, 1982, p. 106). A document published in Rasht in 1910 by the Social Democrats also asked for public education for children of both sexes (*Historical Documents*, 1976, VI, p. 8). The programme of the Moderates included protecting family life and private property; enforcing the *shariat*; defending society against anarchism, atheism and Marxism (Abrahamian, 1982, p. 106). The second Majles got down to amending the electoral law immediately and the new electoral law included more categories of men, but excluded from voting illiterate men, women, minors, lunatics, criminals, bankrupts, murderers and offenders against the *shariat* (Bamdad, 1977, p. 29). The open conflict between the Moderates and the Democrats continued in the second Majles and resulted in the exile of Taqizadeh, the Democrat leader, who was alleged to have assassinated the Moderate leader Tabatabai. In 1911, women's enfranchisement became once again the subject of debate in the Majles. The London *Times* published the following report in August 1911 which was modified in a later issue:

> Women's rights in Persia: Appeal for the suffrage in the Majles . . . a champion of the woman's cause has been found in the Persian Majles. This is none other than Hadji Vakil ol-Roaya, Deputy for Hamedan, who, on August 3, astonished the House by an impassioned defence of women's rights. The Majles was quietly discussing the Bill for the next election, which takes place in the autumn, and had reached the clause that no woman shall vote. Discussion on a proposition so obvious seemed unnecessary and the House shivered when the Vakil ol-Roaya mounted the tribune, and declared roundly that women possessed souls and rights, and should possess votes. Now Vakil ol-Roaya has hitherto been a serious politician, and the House listened to his harangue in dead silence, unable to decide whether it was an ill-timed joke or a serious statement. The orator called upon the *olama* to support him, but support failed him. The *mojtahed*, whom he invoked by name, rose in his place, and solemnly declared that he had never in a life of misfortune had his ears assailed by such an impious utterance. Nervously and excitedly, he denied to women either souls or rights, and declared that such doctrine would mean the downfall of Islam. To hear it uttered in the Parliament of the nation had made his hair stand on end. The cleric sat down, and the Majles shifted uncomfortably in its seats. The President put the clause in its original form, and asked the official reporters to make no record in the journals of the House of this unfortunate incident. The Majles applauded his suggestion and turned with relief to the discussion of subjects less disturbing than the contemplation of the possibility that women had souls. (Bayat-Philipp, 1978, pp. 303–4)

The *mojtahed* mentioned in the above report was Modarressi, who argued passionately that 'in our religion, Islam, they [women] are under supervision, and men are in charge of women ... they [women] will have absolutely no right to elect. Others [men] should protect the rights of women' (Najmabadi, 1993). Some of the constitutionalist clerics, however, seemed less vehement in their opposition to women's right to elect. Tabatabai replied to a letter from a woman on this matter, that he agreed with women's education and learning 'domestic sciences', but 'for the time being women's involvement in politics is not necessary' (Afari, 1993). Some secular deputies, too, expressed the same reservation about the timing of the issue of women's right to vote. Zuka ol-Molk stated that although many deputies, including himself, would have wished to see women's political rights improved, he had to admit that at present it was not possible to grant this (Najmabadi, 1993).

Clerical opposition to women's emancipation, however, was not all based on the *shariat*, but also on fear of adultery and loss of female chastity and male honour. For them, there could be only one motivation behind women's emancipation, and that was the conspiracy of 'morally corrupt' Westernised intellectuals to create easy sexual access to women. This argument, of course, was not specific to Sheykh Fazlollah Nuri. Mohammad Ali Shah, who was far from an exemplary Muslim himself also used it. The fear of loss of 'male honour' resulting from women's emancipation was also widespread among Moderate clerics such as Tabatabai and Behbahani. But Tabatabai allowed his daughter to learn to read and write and, therefore, did not dismiss the whole idea of women's emancipation.

Women's issues were the most sensitive of all for both anti-constitutionalists and pro-constitutionalists. During the constitutional period, despite having opposing views on national issues, social conservatives from both groups allied with each other to reject reforms relating to the position of women in society. Moreover, their opposition to women's emancipation was defensive rather than offensive. There were no coherent arguments or Islamic apology put forward by the defenders of the status quo on women. Contrary to other countries in the Middle East, this kind of Islamic apologia which aimed to justify the lowly status of women developed several decades later in Iran.

Establishment of women's societies and schools

Women's societies proliferated in the course of the Constitutional Revolution. The idea of women's societies first came from Libertarian men. Some of them saw the need for the sexes to mix and began to set up mixed gatherings for men and women. In 1907, The Women's Freedom Society (Anjoman Horriat Vatan) was founded. This was a mixed society which had sixty female members. Its objective was to provide a setting in which men and women could meet and familiarise themselves with cross-gender political debate and discussion. Special emphasis was put on helping women to overcome shyness and embarrassment. Members were required to be accompanied by a relative from the opposite sex and the presence of unaccompanied men and women was forbidden. Some of the female members of this society, such as Sedigheh Doulatabadi, acquired a lasting interest in women's issues (Sanati, 1993).

The society, however, did not manage to continue its work for long. After a few sessions it had to dissolve owing to mob attacks (Bamdad, 1977, pp. 29–31). Despite the problems, women continued to sow the seeds of their movement for emancipation. Two of Naser od-Din Shah's daughters became well-known constitutionalists. Malekeh Iran, who was a Sufi, attended the meetings of Okhovvat (Brotherhood), a constitutionalist secret society which was headed by her husband Zahir od-Douleh (Ghaemmaghami, 1967). She appeared at meetings unveiled and spoke often (Bamdad, 1977, pp. 31–2). Taj ol-Saltaneh, a Qajar princess who had divorced her husband, founded a literary society (Anjoman Adabi) and wrote in praise of socialism that 'today there is no ideal more free and progressive than socialism' (Nategh, 1983b, p. 13). In her book of memoirs she wrote about her personal experience of being brought up as a woman in a Qajar *haram*. Taj ol-Saltaneh criticised polygamy, veiling and seclusion for women, and prescribed education, political activity and participation in productive labour for women (Ettehadiyeh, 1982).

Women also established women-only organisations. The Women's Society (Anjoman Nesvan) attracted 150 members who pledged themselves to the struggle against reactionary and backward-looking views. One of the organisers of this society was Agha Beygom, daughter of the prominent pro-constitutionalist cleric Sheykh Hadi Najmabadi who was detested by the Royalist clergy for his pro-Republican views. In a speech delivered at a meeting of the society she talked about the importance of women's education for achieving patriotic unity and appealed to Majles deputies to stop pursuing personal rivalries and to concentrate on building a future for their daughters (Nategh, 1983a, p. 13). In Tabriz, too, women's societies flourished. A women's group was organised by Hajiyeh Alaviyeh Khanum. She advocated a boycott of foreign goods on the grounds that 'our money should not go into the pockets of the foreigners' (Nahid, 1981, p. 100). *Anjoman* reported that 'A group of respectable women in Tabriz are getting together to talk about the kind of clothes they and their families should wear. They have decided to stop depending upon foreign textiles and to be content with their old clothes until the time when fabrics can be produced indigenously' (Rafii, 1983, p. 117).

In 1910, The Women's Society reappeared under the name of The National Ladies' Society (Anjoman Mokhaddarat Vatan). The Executive Committee consisted of Agha Beygom, Agha Shahzadeh Amin and Sedigheh Doulatabadi. The members consisted of women from prominent constitutionalist families such as Malek ol-Motakalemin, Rashti, Jahangir, Meykadeh, Khajehnuri, Mahmudi and Tonekaboni. The Society gave itself over to nationalist issues. They opposed the acceptance of loans from foreign countries and foreign interference in Iran's internal affairs. Members of the Society waged a campaign for indigenous fabrics and founded an orphanage which was run by an Armenian woman (Bamdad, 1977, pp. 33–40). In the same year women held a conference in Tehran, to discuss and plan for women's education, which was reported in the *Times* of London (Bayat-Philipp, 1978, p. 300).

The turn of the century also witnessed an upsurge of educational establishments for women. In Tehran and other provincial towns girls' schools began to flourish. In Bushehr, the first Muslim girls' school was opened in 1899. This school, which was named Saadat [Prosperity], continued to function until the mid-1960s (Sheykholeslami, 1972, p. 171). Muslim girls began to attend schools run by religious minorities (Nahid, 1981, p. 18). The American missionary school in Orumiyeh allowed Muslim girls to enrol in 1906 (Nashat, 1983, p. 23). In the same year, Yousof Khan, a French convert to Islam, opened the Ecole Franco-Persan for Muslim girls in Tehran (*ibid.*). This was followed by another French school, Jandark [Joan of Arc] which was opened by two French sisters (Arasteh, 1969, p. 177). Effatiyeh [The House of Chastity] girls' school was opened in 1907 by Mrs Safiyeh Yazdi who was married to Sheykh Mohammad Yazdi, a high-ranking cleric (Nashat, 1983, p. 23). Namus [Honour] was opened by Mrs Tuba Azemudeh who came from a military family; this school soon opened several other branches in Tehran (Bamdad, 1977, pp. 42–3). Omm ol-Madares [Mother of Schools] was opened by Mrs Dorrat ol-Maali in Tehran (Nategh, 1983b, p. 11). The main social activities of liberal men and women were channelled into the field of education. Women's enthusiasm about education was enormous. They often provided both the staff and the budget of the schools themselves (Bayat-Philipp, 1978, p. 299).

The support of men was equally great. Hasan Roshdiyeh, a well-known educationalist, helped Mrs Azemudeh in running her school and many other men followed his example (Nahid, 1981, p. 24). These schools were opened against a background of resistance by an influential section of the clergy. A girls' school which was established in a traditionally conservative area of Tehran caused an outrage in the neighbourhood and prompted Sheykh Fazlollah Nuri to issue a *fatva* that 'the founding of girls' schools is against the Islamic *shariat*' (Bayat-Philipp, 1978, p. 300). Seyyed Ali Shushtari, another cleric, staged a sit-in the foyer of the Shah Abdolazim shrine and distributed a handout which said 'Shame on a country in which girls' schools are founded.' The handout was rapidly sold out and later appeared on the black market (Nahid, 1981, p. 19). *Maaref* [Knowledge] (1907) wrote an article about the opening of the Tavassol school in Qazvin and reported that Agha Mirza Hasan Sheykh ol-Eslam, a Qazvini cleric, had threatened to send a group of women to destroy the school and expel its founders from Qazvin. After the threat materialised, the author of the article, who preferred to remain anonymous, asked for the readers' help.

Girls' schools continued to grow, however, despite the opposition of hardline clerics. In 1910, the first group of women graduated from the American School in Tehran which now had 120 Muslim students. Tarraghi [Progress] School was founded (1910) by Mahrokh Goharshenas who came from a strict Shii family. Her husband's disapproval did not stop her from running the school secretly. This school apparently admitted boys to junior classes and employed male teachers to teach in the girls' secondary school classes. Despite this, the school managed to have a good reputation, so much so that the prominent cleric Sheykh Khalili Eraghi sent his daughter there (Bamdad, 1977, pp. 45–7).

Summary

Contrary to the conventional association of traditional Middle Eastern society with Islam as its sole designator and the main cause of women's oppression, nineteenth-century Iranian society contained a variety of conceptions and positions of women. These were based on a complex range of social factors, including historical, religious, economic and political ones. Moreover, the political transformation of nineteenth-century Iran further affected and diversified the position of various categories of women.

The constitutional movement, which gathered force in the latter part of the nineteenth century and grew into a fully fledged revolution during the period 1905–11, inspired the existing society to change and drew upon both indigenous and Western ideas to conceive of the future political order and women's place in it. In doing so, a new domain of political struggle was created at the turn of the century. This domain entailed ideals such as emancipation, freedom, justice, economic prosperity and technological progress as the key to Iran's strength, which was considered as a prerequisite for national independence. The pro-active and reactive response to these ideals, which were seen as the hallmarks of modernity, did not necessarily run along the secular–Islamic division. The Shii clergy shared the leadership of the constitutional movement with secularists. Modernity and national prosperity was what most political ideologies wanted for Iran. The battle was not so much tradition versus modernity, but what form this modernity should take. The central concern of the movement was a redefinition of Iran's relationships with Russia and Britain which had hitherto been based on domination and exploitation by the latter powers. The redefinition of this relationship involved an appreciation of the contradictory nature of contact with the West. For, although contact with the West resulted in the manipulation of the Iranian economy and polity, it also generated enthusiasm for Western technological progress and military strength. The dilemma became how to preserve independence in the face of such superior and domineering powers. It was around this question that various positions in the debate on constitutionalism were upheld and the issue of gender was raised. The constitutional monarchy which was finally established was the specific product of the discourse of modernity in this phase. It neither duplicated Western political systems, nor reflected global economic relations. It was not 'essentially' Islamic either.

Women's emancipation and national progress

Women's participation in the Constitutional Revolution established women as fellow participants in the national struggle. This was an aspect of a wider definition of 'women's emancipation' and its relation to 'national progress' within the discourse of modernity. The concepts of nation and national sovereignty entered into Iranian political vocabulary in the nineteenth century with the institutionalisation of the 'modern condition' in the West. The ideas of nationhood and nation state which originated from the European history of modernity proved highly diffusible in the nineteenth and twentieth centuries. The nation state, based on the ideas of citizenship, constitution, law and a definition of the state as the expression of popular will, became the model of statehood to follow for dependent and colonised countries seeking independence (Zubaida, 1989a, pp. 121–3). Nationalism became the main trajectory for political struggle in most Middle Eastern countries (Kandiyoti, 1991a). As was the case in Europe, the rise of modern nation states in the Middle East, too, was associated with the rise of capitalism. In this case, however, the catalyst was European economic penetration, political domination and cultural influence. As a result of Iran's incorporation into the modern international system of sovereign states, a new notion of the state as an 'impersonal organisation in charge of the Commonwealth of the nation' became prevalent in this period (Arjomand, 1988, pp. 28–9). This definition of the state was complementary to the notions of nation and national sovereignty and was underpinned by structural and institutional transformations such as urbanisation, weakening of primary communities, emergence of individualised labour market, spread of education and development of printed communication (*ibid.*, p. 146).

The concept of nation was essential to the theoretical and political standpoint of reformists because it allowed them to create their own political space and develop a constituency of their own. Islam was the territory of the Shii clergy, and other religious, tribal and ethnic communities had historically created their own constituencies. Nationhood, associated with modernity and progress, became the political space occupied and propagated by an urban intelligentsia which arose from the ranks of merchants, traders, nobility, clerics, and other upper and middle classes. Nationhood was the basis on which these social groups united against the mismanagement of the patrimonial state and the domination of foreign powers. Although during the earlier stages of protest against foreign economic intrusions the clergy assumed the dominant leadership, during the Constitutional Revolution religious forces shared the leadership with secular reformists and spoke the same language of nationhood and constitutional state. Secular nationalists, however, aimed to create a secular 'Iranian' culture to counteract the Islamic cultural influence. To construct a new Iranian nation, many referred to ancient Iran as a point of origin. As in other emerging nations, here too, the 'foundational fiction' of the Iranian nation was created (Bhabha, 1990).

The language of nationhood revolved around the notions of national progress as the highest aim and national interest as the paramount objective. It defined women's position in terms of national interest and saw it as one of the elements on which the nation depended. Women were linked to the nation in a way different from men. Nation was automatically taken to include men and the interests of the two merged inseparably. The link between women and nation/men, however, had to be specified. Malcom Khan invited men to support women in 'promoting humanity' since 'women are the educators of children and hence the creators of our nation' (*Ghanun*, 4, p. 4). Taqizadeh, another reformer, argued that 'Women are the carriers of national traditions and customs. Women function as the main pillars and the firm foundations of ethnicity, religion, language, culture and the national heritage. Women can exert enormous influence in the education of the new generation' (Afshar, 1977, p.163). Moreover, in linking women to the nation the constitutional movement established 'a discursive association ... between sexual and national honour' (Najmabadi, 1993). Many injustices committed against families, particularly women and children, by the Qajar state and its representatives in towns and villages were invoked within the constitutional movement to appeal to the traditional sense of male honour. Men were urged by the leaders of the movement 'to stand up, to protect and to take possession of their wealth and of their women and children' (*ibid.*).

Women, then, were considered as significant to the nation because of their role as biological reproducers of the nation, educators of children, transmitters of culture and participants in national life. Their position in any society, it followed, was central to the definition of that society. A social and political redefinition of Iranian society, therefore, had to entail a reorganisation of women's position. It was for this reason that women's issues remained on the agenda of pro-constitutionalists and anti-constitutionalists alike. It was within this context that women's participation in the Constitutional Revolution and the resulting growth of the women's movement took place. Certain aspects of these developments merit further analysis and summing up. First, the social composition, organisational forms, and demands of the women's movement; and second, the link between the women's movement and the national struggle.

Formation of the women's movement

To sum up the observations made in the previous section, it can be stated that women's participation in the constitutional movement took a variety of forms. The limited evidence available indicated that, as was the case with men, women from lower and middle classes took part in street demonstrations and riots and gave enthusiastic support to the clergy, an enthusiasm which was tinged with superstition. Since the clergy were divided in political outlook, both constitutionalist and Royalist clerics enjoyed a following amongst the ranks of women from various strata. In contrast, upper-class women concentrated on educational activities and followed their menfolk in founding and joining secret societies and writing and delivering speeches on constitutionalism and women's emancipation. Their support for the clergy was more tactical and circumstantial. Many of them spoke out against the clergy's approval of oppressive practices towards women and criticised the widespread and religiously encouraged problem of superstition amongst women.

The difference in the pattern of participation of lower and upper-class women became more of an issue after the convocation of the Majles and also during and after the Civil War. As a result of political polarisation, more lower-class women tended to support the Royalist and anti-constitutionalist clergy while affluent women generally tended to side with constitutionalists. This was the period in which lower-class women came into face-to-face conflict with pro-constitutionalist women. There is evidence of such conflict when a group of women, who demonstrated against the Russian ultimatum and boycotted foreign goods, experienced the wrath of lower-class women at first hand. The former group wore a special emblem, a ring engraved with two clasped hands, and had taken an oath not to give up their struggle for women's rights until death. Members of this group faced constant insult and abuse from lower-class women and on one occasion a member of this group, Mahrokh Goharshenas, was thrown into a pool by a group of lower-class women (Bamdad, 1977, pp. 45–6). But despite its reactionary message, women's collective action in support of the clergy had a positive side to it. The very act of collective political action irrespective of its support for the clergy or the secular reformists was beneficial to the women's movement because it provided a space and opportunity for women to learn to organise themselves. It also changed the social image of women from private beings to public participants and in that sense was no small achievement (Yeganeh, 1984).

In some respects women's collective actions during the Constitutional Revolution were consistent with previous patterns and in other respects they represented a break with the past. Women's public protests during the tobacco crisis and the Constitutional Revolution were a break with the past only in content and not so much in form. Women had a history of public protest because their total seclusion in fulfilment of the instructions of spiritual leaders had never been fully achieved. Economic constraints and heterogeneity of ethnic and local practices made total seclusion of the majority of women impossible. Women had been able in the past to express their collective protest through riots over the shortage and high cost of food. But during the tobacco crisis and the advent of the constitutional struggle some important shifts occurred. The emphasis in women's riots changed from an expression of economic to political demands. As men turned to political protest women followed suit. This was partly possible because of the clergy's approval; since women's participation added extra weight to the clergy's cause. Moreover, women's public protests, at first spontaneous, gradually became more organised and militant. They developed in various forms, including protests waged by groups of armed women.

The same analysis applies to the activities of women from upper strata as writers, educators and organisers of women's societies. Some of these activities were not new as such. Women had written and taught for centuries in the seclusion of their homes and, exceptionally in public forums. Some women had even become prominent as literary figures in previous centuries. But what was new in the context of the Constitutional Revolution was the upsurge of these activities, their public nature and the message that was conveyed through them. Women began to construct their own language of political struggle. While the male language in the constitutional movement talked about protecting 'women of the nation', the female political language talked about citizenship and being part of the nation (Najmabadi, 1993).

Furthermore, women were now opening schools for girls, they were writing in journals, and were putting forward nationalist and feminist demands. Women had begun to transfer their skills from domestic settings to social ones. The most important break with the past was women's participation in secret societies. There is little information available on the structure and membership of these societies or on how they were organised. But it certainly was a novelty for women to gather in one place to discuss politics and women's emancipation. Once this step was taken, women's political standing changed for the better.

The women's movement and national struggle

The demands raised by women through participation in the Constitutional Revolution is another aspect to touch upon. It has already been pointed out that the link between nationalism and feminism created the framework for the definition of 'women's emancipation'. Since the very idea of women's emancipation was grounded in the need for national progress, those aspects of women's position that enhanced the country's development and progress were given priority within the constitutional movement. Women's education was the absolute first priority and was mentioned and demanded by men and women alike more than anything else. It also gained a wider political support than other women's issues. The early age of marriage for women and the influence of superstition amongst them, both of which were seen as impediments to their education, were widely scorned and criticised by the supporters of women's emancipation. The next important areas of reform constituted veiling and polygamy. However, these practices were not so much publicly denounced as privately complained about. Articles against the practice of veiling, seclusion and polygamy could result in the banning of the newspaper which published them, while complaints regarding women's education and early age of marriage were generally tolerated. Resolution of these problems was seen as necessary to national development and progress. It was often argued that Western progress had resulted from the absence of such practices.

In the constitutional movement differences of opinion on women's emancipation did not run along gender lines. A minority of women tended to include women's emancipation in their definition of constitutionalism in contrast to their menfolk. But it was uncommon for men who favoured women's emancipation to face anti-feminist opposition from their womenfolk. During the periods of disagreement and debate amongst various groups of pro-constitutionalists, the majority of women took sides with their men while a minority exerted their independence of opinion by favouring the side that argued for women's emancipation. Taj ol-Saltaneh, for example, divorced her husband for not sharing her nationalist and feminist ideas and feelings. Moreover, there is evidence that some women from upper-class families opened girls' schools or participated in women's societies without the knowledge of their disapproving husbands or fathers. The Libertarians/Democrats included women's emancipation in their definition of constitutionalism, grounding it in the demand for equality and justice for all citizens. But this was not necessarily the case for all Moderates.

It is not, therefore, possible to generalise about male–female differences of opinion on female emancipation. The women's movement did not have a separate identity from the constitutional movement at this stage. The Libertarians/Democrats and some of the Moderates were very much part and parcel of the movement of women's emancipation in this period. This was, of course, owing to the nature of the constitutional movement and the inseparability of nationalist and feminist issues. While it was possible for nationalists to be non-feminists, it was not tolerated or possible for feminists to be non-nationalists. One can cite here the example given above of the demonstration held by unveiled women during the Russian ultimatum. The negative reaction to this event by nationalist women is a good example of intolerance towards purely feminist gestures. The movement for women's emancipation in the constitutional period was very much a mixed movement. The first women's society had mixed membership and throughout this period Libertarian/Democratic men constituted the backbone of the movement.

To conclude, it must be emphasised that only a minority of Iranian women (and men) participated in the Constitutional Revolution. Nevertheless, the pioneering nature of women's participation made that minority a significant one. Women's contribution to the Constitutional Revolution was the beginning of a new era for women in Iran. It legitimised the integration of women and men in the society, established the necessity of women's education, raised sensitive issues such as family and veiling as a public and national concern, and created the opportunity for women to organise and establish a women's movement with the long-term aim of women's emancipation. The pattern of women's participation in the Constitutional Revolution and the variety of forms it assumed established the pioneering nature of women's activities during this period. Moreover, the link postulated between women and the nation constituted the bedrock of the gender issues raised, and determined the integrated nature of participation. These indicated the existence of a women's movement with its own specific features.

3 Women and the era of nation building

The second phase of the discourse of modernity came to the fore during the 1920s to 1940s as the era of nation building. During this phase, the discourse of modernity went through a distinct shift of emphasis as a result of post-constitutional developments.

The constitutional movement crystallised the desire for freedom and independence in the demand for nationhood. The transformation of Iran from a dependent backward society to a modern independent nation state became a major political preoccupation for the constitutionalists. But although the Constitutional Revolution achieved its goal of political reform by creating a system of parliamentary democracy, this was not followed in the immediate post-constitutional decades by complementary social and economic reforms. This situation arose because despite the creation of a powerful and independent Majles as the legislator, the Qajar state remained weak, corrupt and vulnerable to political manipulation by Western powers. Therefore, there did not exist an equally powerful executive power to initiate and implement social reforms advocated by the Majles. This facilitated the transformation from the era of constitutionalism to the era of nation building. The nationalist state which was established by Reza Shah Pahlavi (1925–41) after the dissolution of the Qajar dynasty, seemed to fulfil the demand for a strong state capable of overcoming Iran's economic, technological and military weaknesses. This entailed a change of emphasis in the discourse of modernity from idealist concepts of economic prosperity, political freedom and social justice, to the more specific and pragmatic programme of establishing a nation state. As part of this development, a shift occurred in the direction of nationalism from a domain of independent political action to a domain of state leadership, and action, that is, a state nationalism.

The post-constitutional period (1911–25) witnessed the emergence of a strong centralised state capable of initiating deep and long lasting reforms. This entailed the dissolution of the Qajar dynasty and the establishment of Pahlavi rule in 1925. A number of factors contributed to this process (Arjomand, 1988). To begin with, the political developments of the post-constitutional period demonstrated the successes and failures of the Constitutional Revolution, and these determined the direction of future political change. During this period, the Majles continued to operate whenever political events allowed it to do so. The third, fourth and fifth Majles convened in 1914, 1921 and 1923 respectively but each time had to close prematurely due to political pressures. The country was in turmoil during this period and the adolescent Qajar king and his ineffective prime ministers were unable to control events. In November 1915 Russian troops occupied northern Iran and a year later British troops moved to southern Iran. The Majles elected a Government of National Defence which was destroyed by the British and its members exiled (Abrahamian, 1982, p. 11). Trouble also developed in the northern provinces of Azarbayjan and Gilan, where in the latter Mirza Kuchak Khan Jangali established a socialist republic. Regional governments were formed in other parts of the country and tribal rebellions struck more blows against the central authority. In short, chaos and disintegration seriously threatened the central government for over a decade.

These events demonstrated that although the Majles had retained and even strengthened its position within the state as legislator, its operation had been crippled seriously by the absence of an equally strong executive power. Moreover, not only did the Majles not receive adequate protection from the king against foreign intrusion and internal chaos, but, most of its legislated reforms remained unimplemented by the weak and disorganised executive. This created public disillusionment with the Majles and changed its image as the embodiment of the nation's desire for democracy to a mere talking shop. Moreover, the advent of the 1917 Bolshevik Revolution in Russia resulted in British support for the call for a strong executive power in Iran (Arjomand, 1988). This was followed by the Bolshevik seizure of power which brought about the unexpected withdrawal of Russian troops from Iran. This was greeted with celebrations all over Iran. The era of Russian military influence ended and a cultural relationship between the two countries replaced it. In 1923 Iran and the Soviet Union signed a peace treaty and Soviet schools and cultural centres replaced Russian military bases in Iran. The Bolshevik Revolution was considered by many as a mixed blessing since although it removed Russian military influence it also created a new threat, that of the spread of communist ideology in Iran. With the communist inspired uprisings in Gilan and Azarbayjan and the mushrooming of socialist parties on the political scene, anti-communist forces in Iran became extremely nervous. The clergy, the non-socialist Majles deputies and the British, all supported the idea of a strong state to quell the spread of socialist ideology in Iran.

The state as an instrument of social reform

It was within this political atmosphere that Reza Khan of Mazandaran, a military officer from an ordinary background, seized the moment to establish a strong centralised state. He rose to power through a *coup d'état* in February 1921 with the support of Seyyed Zia od-Din Tabatabai who then became prime minister and appointed him war minister. Reza Khan began to build a strong army in a vigorous fashion and to put down socialist revolts in Gilan and Azarbayjan. Tribal rebellions, too, were brought under control. His military successes won the support of the Majles and silenced criticisms of the unconstitutional expansion of his political power. In 1923 as a result of an alliance with the Revival Party in the fifth Majles, Reza Khan became prime minister. Reza Khan's political outlook was secular and pro-military and his programme focused on the creation of a strong modern central state in Iran. Many of his proposed reforms had been contemplated and attempted before by the Majles (*ibid.*, p. 63). He was a strong leader with a clear political programme; something that had been lacking in the Iranian political scene. Most political forces supported him for alleviating their anxiety over the fate of the country.

Moreover, at this initial stage of his ascendance to power, he was willing to ally himself with conservatives and Islamic forces. His initial conciliatory approach towards the clergy was demonstrated on many occasions. An incident during his premiership in which Reza Khan came into conflict with lower-class women was indicative of this. In 1924, a bread shortage occurred and a rumour spread that Reza Khan was responsible for it. A few thousand women led a procession to the Majles shouting and demanding bread. Some of these women came from an area of Tehran called *Chaleh Meydan* which was famous for its 'bold and assertive' women (Maki, 1979, III, pp. 370–1). Demonstrators gathered in front of the houses of leading clerics and requested their support. But the clergy refrained from supporting them against Reza Khan and refused to march to the Majles. When the crowd of demonstrators reached there women shouted insults and threats at Majles deputies. The gates of the Majles were closed and guards aimed their guns at the crowd. Sheykh Hasan Modarres, a prominent moderate clerical deputy came out of the Majles and asked the crowd to disperse. Demonstrations continued for three days. On the last day, Modarres was heckled by the crowd which was by now shouting pro-Qajar slogans and demanding the removal of Reza Khan. This resulted in Reza Khan's intervention to order the guards to fire at the crowd. Martial law was announced and the riots were brought to an end after many arrests and much bloodshed (*ibid.*, pp. 372–4).

Reza Khan's attempt to create a strong centralised state promised what the Majles had wanted for a long time, that is, the protection of a strong state and the implementation of social reforms by a powerful executive. Reza Khan, who by now was a very powerful prime minister enlisted the support of many Majles deputies to declare a republic but this intention never materialized. The secular direction of the newly formed Turkish Republic under Mustafa Kemal frightened the Iranian clergy and prompted strong clerical opposition to republicanism. Reza Khan, who still needed the support of the clergy (for reasons which will be explained in the section on the subjugation of the Shii establishment later in this chapter) dropped the idea. He subsequently announced that he would ban gambling and called on women to uphold the 'national honour' (Abrahamian, 1982, p. 135). In 1925, the Revival Party introduced a bill to depose the Qajar dynasty and entrust the throne to Reza Khan. Support for the bill was overwhelming. Dr Mohammad Mosaddeq of the Revival Party pointed to the danger of dictatorship by Reza Khan, and Soleyman Eskandari argued that it was against his socialist principles to vote for another monarchy (*ibid.*, p. 135). But almost all other deputies voted in favour of the bill. The Constituent Assembly was convened and the Qajar dynasty was deposed. Reza Shah was named as the founder of the Pahlavi dynasty.

The era of nation building entailed a redefinition of the role of the state in society. The state was constructed as the central focus of society. The *raison d'étre* of the new state came from its coercive power. A national army was built which then became the core of the state (Najmabadi, 1991). As the army succeeded in establishing central authority in the country, the state rose in power and authority above all social groups and soon became the most powerful institution in Iran. The state used its economic and political power to initiate and implement reforms within the society. Although the idea of the state as instigator of reform had existed in Qajar society the new state was breaking ground in the extent, depth and pace of its reforms. The state also assumed responsibility for the welfare of the population, particularly in health, education and transport. State bureaucracy increased substantially and the state became a major employer. It soon extended its control over most aspects of social and political life.

The state as the embodiment of society undertook the construction of a nation state in Iran. The new nation state was conceived on the basis of a particular definition of modernity and progress which included the imitation of certain aspects of Western societies and the exclusion of others. The main features of this model were a central state, a unified nation, a single language and religion, the secularisation of society and national sovereignty, technological progress, economic development and the emancipation of women. In all this, the state selected what to include and what to exclude from Western models to make up the Iranian model of a nation state, and amongst the items excluded were democracy and individual rights.

National unification

The first and foremost programme of the state was national unification. The aim was to turn multicultural Iran into a unified state with one nation, one language, one culture and one central political authority. This was attempted by means of the social, cultural and political repression of tribal and ethnic diversities which made up the old Iran. Reza Shah started what was to become the Pahlavi legacy of associating progress with uniformity and despotism. Indigenous social resources and ethnic and cultural traditions were crushed or pushed aside. The heterogeneous society of Iran was made socially, politically and ideologically a hierarchical society with a small circle of upper-class urban elite at the top of the social pyramid. The way of life of the urban upper classes was promoted officially and other ways of life such as tribal and ethnic ones were considered a hindrance to progress. Reza Shah ordered the population to abandon its local costumes and turn to a uniform way of dressing, that is, in the style of the West. Uniformity of appearance was regarded as an important aspect of becoming a nation, and the government imported large quantities of European made clothes and sold them cheaply. Civil servants were given one month's extra salary to enable them to buy new Western clothes for themselves and their families (Arasteh, 1969, p. 184). On the political front, too, opposition points of view and independent thought were stifled in the interest of unification and progress.

Reza Shah implemented an effective censorship which meant that 'only official nationalism, stressing national homogeneity, anti-clericalism, and a modernity and strength that were read into the pre-Islamic past, could flourish' (Keddie, 1981, p. 94). It was this statist nationalism which replaced the independent, heterogeneous and anti-colonialist nationalism of the constitutional era. The new nationalism went together with a new national identity which sought its roots in a 'national culture' as opposed to religious or communal allegiance. For the first time the state reached out from the capital into towns and villages to create national awareness. The process of 'imagining the nation as a community', which has been described as the basis of nationalism and the nation state (Anderson, 1983, p. 40), was accelerated by such state policies as mass conscription, compulsory birth certification, uniform style of clothing, country-wide systems of transport, communication and press, and a central administrative bureaucracy and security system.

An important aspect of all this was the construction of a nationally binding legal and social position for women. The state policy of national unification had far-reaching implications for women. For the first time the Iranian state was in a position to engineer a specific position for women and impose it on society. Although the state's gender policies may not have penetrated deep enough and affected all categories of women, nevertheless, the theoretical power of the state to intervene on the position of women challenged patriarchal, communal and religious authority over women. It struck a blow at the idea placing women in the realm of the 'private' which was prevalent in the nineteenth century (Vielle, 1988). There is little information available on how various tribal, rural and urban communities and ethnic and religious minorities reacted to the state challenge on women. But, no doubt, state policies must have led to both intended and unintended consequences for women and mixed reactions by communities. As has been shown in relation to other Middle Eastern societies, this may have resulted in the intensification of communal and religious control over women in some instances and the erosion of exclusive control of the family over women in others (Tucker, 1978).

Subjugation of Shii establishment

The second fundamental aim of the state was the reorganisation of the hitherto existing relationship between the state and the Shii establishment. Under the Qajars, power and authority were invested in both the king and the *mojtahed*, and the state and the religious establishment maintained a relationship of mutual interdependence. During the Constitutional Revolution the clergy's influence in political affairs increased. With the establishment of parliamentary democracy, the clergy consolidated its role in politics by taking up seats in the Majles as people's representatives. The Shii establishment had throughout the post-constitutional period exerted tremendous power and influence in the affairs of state, nation and individual. It had, on the other hand, lost control over education after the establishment of a national education system in 1918.

The establishment of the Pahlavi state accelerated the clergy's loss of control over the education system and added the judiciary as another area of de-clericalisation. State intervention in education and the judiciary was intended to increase state control over the socialisation and punishment of its citizens. The education system was ideologically geared to the training of modern citizens and the propagation of statist nationalism. Banning the teaching of the *Qoran* and *shariat* in schools and the promotion of pre-Islamic Iranian nationalism decreased the cultural influence of the clergy. The reform of the judiciary, which was since the Safavid period an exclusive domain of the clergy through the operation of a system of religious courts and independent religious judges, struck an even harder blow at the Shii establishment. The Ministry of Justice took over the control of the judiciary. Religious courts and judges were replaced by secular ones in all spheres of the law except that of the family. The establishment of public notary offices to register deeds as well as births, deaths, marriages and divorce further reduced the role of the clergy. To the dismay of the clergy, the new civil and penal laws, except in relation to the family, were drawn from Western laws. The religious establishment was also weakened by the state's control over endowment (*vaghf*) of property, as a result of which the clergy was forced to turn to independent sources of income such as religious taxes (Arjomand, 1988, p. 83). Other privileges lost by the clergy included immunity from conscription into the army which created unrest amongst religious students in Shii seminaries. More serious was the state imposition of a curriculum for religious schools which was considered an insult to the scholarly integrity of the Shii establishment. The religious establishment was also brought under control through political repression and personal degradation of the clergy. The imprisonment of Sheykh Hasan Modarres, an ardent constitutionalist, in 1929, and his execution in 1937 was an example.

These reforms had the effect of reducing the clergy's political role and cultural influence. Interdependence between the state and the Shii establishment was reduced by enforcing a separation between politics and religion. The emphasis put, in the process of nation building, on national culture as opposed to Islamic heritage in creating a new national identity for citizens, resulted for the first time in a relative symbolic and ideological separation of nationalism and Islam. The clergy were pushed to the background in the political sphere and their officially legitimate field of influence was reduced to the spiritual, personal and familial affairs of the citizen. The grounding of family law in the Islamic *shariat* when most other areas of law were derived from Western laws, had the effect of situating the family within the ideological sphere of Islam as opposed to secular nationalism. All future attempts by secular states to reform family law along secular lines attracted strong protests from the clergy who aimed to retain their legal control over the family and women.

National sovereignty

The third foundation of the new state was built upon the concept of national sovereignty which implied the transformation of Iran's existing relationships with the West. In this respect, the result of the state's economic and foreign policies can be summed up as the removal of outright signs of foreign intervention and control, but the continuation, albeit in a more indirect form, of Iran's economic dependency on the West. The state's attempts to assert national sovereignty included the annulment of the nineteenth-century capitulation rule which excluded foreign nationals from the jurisdiction of Iranian laws, and the takeover of some state functions from the British and Belgian officials. These included printing money, administration of the telegraph system and collection of customs (Abrahamian, 1982, p. 143). The state also prohibited the management of schools by foreigners and in particular by missionaries (*ibid.*, p. 144).

But as one scholar has argued, 'For all his nationalist talk , he [Reza Shah] did not end Iran's dependence on the West or undermine foreign interests in Iran, although he acted with considerable independence' (Keddie, 1981, p. 109). During this period, Britain continued to be the major Western power in Iran. Reza Shah also turned to the United States for technical advice, reorganisation of state finances and loans and investment for modernisation on the pretext of preventing the threat of communism (*ibid.*, p. 89). Reza Shah did not reduce the influence of the Anglo-Iranian oil company and British investments in the oil fields overshadowed all other foreign involvements in trade and industry. Germany too, took the lead in Iran's foreign trade and played a large role in trans-Iranian railroads. The Germans came to be favoured over the British because of old bitterness against the latter, and Reza Shah promoted Nazi ideology and methods. In return the Germans declared Iran a pure Aryan Country. Overall, Western influence during this period resulted in a negative balance of trade for Iran (*ibid.*, pp. 98, 110).

Economic development

Closely associated with the notion of national sovereignty was that of economic development. The latter constituted the fourth fundamental aim of the new state. State initiatives resulted in the growth of industry, development of trade and commerce, building of roads and railways, urban construction, and development of education and welfare services. All this had a major impact on the social structure of Iranian society. Nevertheless, it has been argued that the state's policy of modernisation did not result in the kind of fundamental socio-economic reform which could have led in the long run to economic self-determination for Iran (*ibid.*, p. 110). On the contrary, the state's economic programmes, intentionally and unintentionally, benefitted certain categories in the upper and middle strata at the expense of the lower strata who remained impoverished.

In the rural sector, state policy favoured enhancement of private property and strengthening of the economic and political powers of the landlords (Arjomand, 1988, pp. 70–1). The agrarian picture in the 1930s was one in which 90 per cent of the land was owned by private landlords and the state, and 95 to 98 per cent of the agricultural population were reportedly landless (Keddie, 1981, p. 103). As to the condition of peasants, traditional exploitation continued and new pressures were brought to bear on them. So much so that it has been argued that 'landlordism and declining ruling standards were the weakest point of Reza Shah's modernisation' (*ibid.*, p. 105). The forcible settlement of migrating tribes, who were generally better off and more independent than peasants, reduced their living standard to the level of peasants. The tribal population of Iran dropped from 25 per cent of the total population at the beginning of the century to about 8 per cent in the 1930s (Arjomand, 1988, p. 69). This was done in the interest of national unification and suppression of tribal powers. Yet 'no alternative way of making a living was provided ... and tribes were settled at the cost of impoverishing nomads' (Keddie, 1981, p. 97). All this must have affected rural households and women's living conditions. Yet there is little information available on how peasant and tribal households adjusted to these changes. This is particularly unsatisfactory because the overwhelming majority of the working population worked in the rural sector with women making a significant contribution and being particularly exposed to exploitation both in the fields and in the carpet and textile workshops.

The main economic development of this period occurred in the urban sector and here too state policy privileged a relatively small upper and middle strata over the majority of the urban population. The upper strata was strengthened by the growth of industry, the development of trade and commerce and urban construction. Contrary to past opposition by Russia and Britain to the expansion of transport in Iran, during this period Western and Iranian interests coincided and an extensive programme of road and railway building facilitated for the first time the growth of industry and trade on a nationwide scale. New industry was dominated by the state through state sole or part ownership and state financing, and developed in the 1930s to include hundreds of large and small modern factories which produced textile, soap, tobacco, vegetable oil and sugar, and which cleaned, milled and processed agricultural products. Modern industry excluded heavy industry and mining in which Iran remained dependent on the West (*ibid.*, pp. 100–1). The oil industry remained the monopoly of the British government and 'there were more workers employed in the oil fields than in all other industries combined' (*ibid.*, p. 109). The state also sponsored and invested in trade and commerce. It created a number of trade monopolies, which had exclusive control of foreign trade and guaranteed high profits to these monopolies. State investment in trade and commerce was greater than in all other sectors: 'merchant capital with strong Western ties continued to be the dominant form of capital' (*ibid.*, p. 107). The expansion and strengthening of the economic power of aristocrats, industrialists and entrepreneurs was intertwined with their political manipulation and control. A policy of dividing, coopting and suppressing the upper strata ensured that their increasing economic power did not threaten Reza Shah's monopoly of political power (Abrahamian, 1982, pp. 149–50).

The effects of economic development and state policy on the urban middle strata were rather mixed. On the one hand, land ownership, trade and industrial monopolies, and the resulting concentration of wealth in the hands of a few obstructed the development of small businesses and produced discontent in the bazaar community (*ibid.*, pp. 151–2). On the other hand, the expansion of education and state bureaucracy created new opportunities for a substantial development of the professional middle class. The privileged middle strata included army officers, government employees, doctors, lawyers, teachers, engineers, journalists, writers and students. This strata grew to constitute 7 per cent of the country's workforce (*ibid.*, p.145). The new middle strata was the bedrock of social reform and political opposition. Many state reforms had their basis in the independent ideas of the urban intelligentsia and the leadership of the opposition movements normally came from this group. The intellectual development of the intelligentsia, however, was strongly contained and controlled by state suppression of freedom of speech. Despite their support of the state's social reforms, the intelligentsia did not form a political link with the state because Reza Shah preferred to base his rule on the army rather that on a political party. But the main beneficiaries of the state's social reforms were no doubt the upper and middle classes. Although the legal reform of the family was limited in nature, there may have been a decline in polygamy and temporary marriage during this period (Keddie, 1981, p. 109). Women of these classes were the main beneficiaries of the state's gender policies including unveiling, education, desegregation and employment.

The urban lower strata, too, were a growing body but with fewer rights and benefits. Since economic development and state expansion were urban based, mostly centred in and around the capital, Tehran, the population of urban centres grew as a result of labour-force migration. The new urban workers who were drawn from rural and tribal regions and who worked in the oil industry, railway, factories and plants made up 4 per cent of the total workforce (Abrahamian, 1982, p. 147). These workers often worked under appalling conditions and the 1938 labour law which set standards for work conditions was largely ignored. Low wages, unhygienic work atmosphere, long hours, lack of safety and lack of compensation were the norm. Women, who had worked in workshops and factories since the turn of the century, were amongst the most exploited. Child labour was also a feature of working-class living conditions in this period. The state's labour legislation did not regulate the employment of women and children in the factories (Elwell-Sutton, 1941, p. 127). It did not propose special treatment for women in relation to night shifts or heavy work, nor did it address the special needs of pregnant women and mothers. Young children often under the age of 10 who commonly worked in textile and carpet factories, too, did not receive special treatment. The state simply hoped that child labour would decrease with a more effective enforcement of compulsory education (*ibid.*).

The only change seriously enforced as a result of the 1938 labour law was the outlawing of strikes and workers' unions. The state's suppression of any demand for better working conditions, together with urban unemployment and rising costs helped keep the urban working classes impoverished. To this was added the burden of taxes levied on items of mass consumption to finance the state's programme of road, rail and urban construction. There is no comprehensive study of the urban lower strata in this period. In particular, there is little detail available on how these households and the women within them were affected by economic changes which were taking place. However, it is clear that lack of measures to improve the living and working conditions of the poor hindered fundamental economic change (*ibid.*, p. 105).

Finally, the new nation state was also based on two other important premises. The emergence of the state as an instrument of change resulted in the imposition of social reform at the price of political autocracy and the contravention of the constitution. The twin processes of social change and political suppression constructed a specific conception of women in the era of nation building and shaped the development of an independent women's movement. The last two premises of the new nation state were political autocracy and the position of women.

Post-constitutional political proliferation and control

The post-constitutional era started with an unprecedented flourishing of political parties and the rapid expansion of an independent women's movement. This was partly due to the internal political situation where the lack of strong government and the existence of relative freedom of expression allowed women to build upon the momentum of the constitutional movement and to set up journals and organisations for themselves. But it was also due to the influence of post-World War I developments in the position of women in Britain and the Soviet Union where in the latter the success of the Bolshevik Revolution enhanced the prospect of women's emancipation (Sanasarian, 1982, p. 38). The post-constitutional era, however, ended with political autocracy, state control and the stifling of independent political action. The consolidation of statist nationalist ideology was instrumental in bringing this development about.

Post-constitutional political parties

One the main political developments of this period was the spread of socialist ideology amongst Iranian reformers which resulted from the radicalising effect of the Bolshevik Revolution of 1917. In 1920, the Communist and Socialist Parties of Iran were established. The First Congress of the Communist Party of Iran took place in the northern town of Anzali. The Congress called for 'compulsory free education for all children until the age of fifteen', but did not mention women specifically (*Historical Documents*, 1976, VI, p. 108). Democratic rights in the context of a bourgeois state were rejected as superficial and inconsequential, and the dictatorship of the proletariat was praised as the only system within which 'true rights' could be achieved (*ibid.*, p. 99). The Socialist Party of Iran (Fergheye Socialisti Iran) asked for the 'emancipation of women'; 'equality of rights before the law for male and female Iranians irrespective of race, religion and ethnicity'; and 'the right to elect and be elected for all Iranians without any restrictions' (*ibid.*, p. 74).

In the same year, the Jangali Movement announced the establishment of a socialist republic in Gilan together with the Communist Party and in cooperation with the Red Army. The Jangali movement, which gained its name by using the thick forests of Gilan to wage guerrilla warfare, contained both religious and secular left tendencies. Its programme called for the 'protection of Islam' (Abrahamian, 1982, pp. 111, 116), as well as for the abolishion of all titles and privileges; equality of treatment before the law irrespective of race and religion; freedom of thought, opinion, assembly, press, and the right to work; a pension after the age of sixty; and equality of rights for men and women (*Historical Documents*, 1974, I, p. 85). There is also evidence that women participated in the Jangali Movement (*Marxists and Women's Question*, 1975, p. 3). Another socialist movement of this period took root in Azarbayjan where a prominent Democrat, Khiabani, founded the Democratic Party of Azarbayjan.

Other political parties, too, flourished in the post-constitutional decades. During the period 1914–22, parliamentary political activity was limited. The opening of the Third Majles became possible in 1914 and the main piece of legislation passed was the amendment of the electoral law to include universal male suffrage. Women's suffrage was not discussed and women were left out of the voting lists. The Majles, however, had to be abandoned after a few months. The Fourth Majles was convened in June 1921. This time four political parties dominated the Majles. The Reformists (the Moderates in the previous three Majles), who were led by Modarres the reformist cleric, gained the majority of seats; the Revival Party, which believed in modest reform, came second; the Socialist Party and the Communist Party also gained some seats and formed a small minority. Those once known as the Democrats now joined either the Revival Party or the Socialist Party. The Revival Party proposed a programme of separating politics from religion and expanding educational facilities for all including women (Abrahamian, 1982, p. 123). The attitudes of the Revival Party were reflected in two Iranian newspapers published in West Germany under the names of *Kaveh* and *Iranshahr*.

The Socialist Party, which was led by Eskandari, called in its programme for the establishment of an egalitarian society; equal justice for all citizens irrespective of birth and nationality; freedom of speech, press, thought and assembly; the right to organise unions and strikes; compulsory public education; education for women; a ban on child labour and an eight-hour working day (*ibid.*, p. 128). The Communist Party, which worked closely with the Socialist Party, opened branches in major provincial towns and published about six newspapers. The party organised special sections for women, youth and Armenians, and assumed a leadership role in many workers' unions.

As in previous Majles, the Reformist (Moderate) deputies remained uninterested and at times hostile towards the reform of the position of women. The Revivalists and the Socialists, on the other hand, continued to relate the question of national progress to women's position. The Communists did not opt so much for nationalism as for the necessity of establishing working-class rule as a precondition for women's true emancipation. During the 1920s, each of these parties established links with and promoted various women's groups and newspapers.

The post-constitutional women's movement

The post-constitutional period was the era of the development of a spontaneous women's movement and independent political action. The seeds of women's activities which were sown during the Constitutional Revolution matured in the post-constitutional era to give rise to a small but vocal women's movement. Women's activities became more structured and organised and women took responsibility for their movement to a greater extent. Although men continued to play a paternalistic and pioneering role, nevertheless, women managed to become the primary representatives of their own movement. This development was reflected in the changing relationship between women's organisations and political parties.

During the constitutional period there was no clear separation between the women's movement and political parties. The movement for women's emancipation was an integrated part of the constitutional movement. Post-constitutional political events, however, brought about the separation of women's organisations from political parties. The latter were now much more distinctly structured. The loose political groupings of the constitutional period developed into distinct political parties in the 1920s. Having achieved some degree of separation and independence, women's organisations and political parties began to forge alliances and to create mutual support networks. Various women's groups obtained their support from the Socialists, the Communists and the Revivalists.

The relative independence of women's organisations from political parties and the heterogeneity of political views amongst women, however, did not create a confrontational feminism. Women's groups and sympathetic political parties continued to share a similar view of women's emancipation, and raised similar demands on women's rights. Education, veiling, seclusion, child marriage and polygamy continued to be the main areas of campaign and struggle for women's organisations and sympathetic political parties. Women's emancipation continued to be seen in the context of national development and progress by both women's groups and political parties. Women's education constituted the main area of progress for women in the first post-constitutional decade. By 1914, the Namus girls' school opened five branches in Tehran and taught 3,473 students (Sheykholeslami, 1972, p. 86). In 1915, Shams ol-Madares was the latest secondary school that joined the list (Bamdad, 1977, p. 57). A correspondent of *Moslem World*, who visited Iran in 1911, gave the following picture of the changing attitude of affluent Tehrani women towards their daughters in the post-constitutional period:

> In her home the New Woman receives you as graciously as ever, prepares less elaborate refreshments than formerly, does not force you to eat as much as in old days, and offers cigarettes instead of the water-pipe. Her guests are seated on chairs instead of the floor, and drink their tea from cups as tea-glasses have gone out of style . . . Yet she still speaks with sadness of her own childhood, 'There were no schools for girls in our day; we had no opportunity.' Or she tells how she was married at the age of ten or twelve, and how good it is that times have changed.

The fact that her own daughter of fourteen or fifteen is still at school gives the mother a feeling of self-respect. If a girl is sixteen and unmarried, the mother is a little nervous about it, for their old-fashioned neighbours will talk; or, perhaps, no one will want to marry a girl so old, and not to marry at all would be monstrous misfortune. The mother speaks of her daughters with as much pride as of her sons, and is keenly interested in their progress. A few weeks ago I was congratulating a young mother on her first-born, and added, 'I suppose you are sorry the baby is not a boy.' To my amazement she replied, 'What better service could I render my fatherland than to bring up girls, for until there are good mothers the country will make no progress.' A few years ago this girl was in school, and with her best friend one day remarked, 'Every time we hear of the death of an old man we are downright happy, for it means the removal of one more obstacle from the path of women's progress. We can grow up with new ideas but the old folks cannot change'. This year the American School has enrolled more than one hundred and sixty Persian girls alone, and there are said to be seventy girls' schools in the city, with a total enrolment of five thousand. Abandoning the veil is still a cherished dream of Persian women, but they have come to realise that it is not time yet for this radical change. (*Moslem World*, 1911, p. 367)

An important development in women's activities came about in 1910. Women had been contributing to progressive journals yet they had never had a newspaper of their own. The first women's newspaper *Danesh* [Knowledge] was published by Mrs. Kahal eighty-eight years after the publication of the first Iranian newspaper (Sheykholeslami, 1972, pp. 76, 82–3). *Danesh*, which was published on a weekly basis in eight pages, wrote on most aspects of the woman question with an emphasis on women's social habits. In l913, Mrs. Maryam Amid Mozayen ol-Saltaneh founded *Shokufeh* [Blossom] newspaper. Soon after she founded a women's organisation as well. This organisation was known as the Iranian Women's Society (Anjoman Khavatin Irani) (Golbon, 1975, p. 35). The objectives of the above society were stated in *Shokufeh* as 'promotion of Iranian goods, promotion of art and industry amongst women, and promotion of education, science and art amongst women' (Sheykholeslami, 1972, p. 87). The membership of the Iranian Women's Society reached 5,000 a few weeks after its foundation (*ibid.*). *Shokufeh*, which continued to come out until Mrs. Mozayan ol-saltaneh's death in 1919, published articles mainly on women's issues. Literature, education, superstitious attitudes amongst women, child marriage, housekeeping, childraising, and 'elevating women's moral standards' constituted the subjects of the articles of this journal. After the establishment of the Iranian Women's Society, *Shokufeh* acquired a strong political tone and published mainly on nationalist issues of independence and struggle against foreign influence, reminding women of their nationalist duties and calling on them to unite against foreign influence (*ibid.*, pp. 84, 87).

The influence of Bolshevism created a radical political atmosphere in

Iran which resulted in an upsurge of feminism, socialism and communism. One of the concrete effects of the new radical atmosphere in relation to women was the promotion of women's education through a liberal interpretation of Article 19 of the Supplementary Fundamental Law. In 1918, Prime Minister Vosugh od-Douleh took up the challenge to extend public education to women. Naser od-Douleh, the Cabinet Minister for Cultural Affairs, announced the decision to open public (state) schools for girls for the first time. Ten public schools were opened and a Department of Public Instruction for Women was established. This was immediately followed by the opening of the first teachers' training college for women. This move met with opposition from some clergy who denounced it vehemently. Nevertheless, the opening of public schools for women spread rapidly throughout Tehran. Women's newspapers and organisations, too, grew rapidly. During the 1911–17 period of political repression women had managed to take the leadership of their movement firmly into their own hands. The long period of Majles closure, the suppression and exile of its political leaders, and the foreign occupation of the country created other priorities for men and situated women in the forefront of their movement. Women's growing organisational skills and experiences gained in the preceding years helped them to take good advantage of the new radical atmosphere in 1917. From 1917 to 1927 many new newspapers and organisations were set up by women (Sadr-Hashemi, 1984).

The new era of women's feminist and nationalist activities was opened up by an Esfahani woman. Sedigheh Doulatabadi was a remarkable woman who started her political activities by affiliating to the National Ladies' Society in 1911, and carried on working for reforms for women until her death in 1961. She was born into a strict family and was married off to an elderly man at a young age against her will. Family prejudices did not allow her to run the school she herself had founded in Esfahan and her friend Badr ol-Doja Derakhshan became its headmistress. However, the school came under attack by mobs and had to close down within three months. The headmistress was imprisoned for three months and Doulatabadi was beaten up. But this was not the end of her feminist activities. Doulatabadi set up the Esfahan Ladies' Company (Sherkat Khavatin Esfahan) and a women's newspaper called *Women's Language* (*Zaban Zanan*). This time, too, her women's organisation and newspaper were banned and she was exiled from Esfahan. The ban was issued by the Esfahan Chief of Police who told Doulatabadi, 'You have been born a hundred years too early.' She replied 'I have been born a hundred years too late, otherwise I would have not let women to become so enchained by men today' (Sheykholeslami, 1972, p. 97). After her exile from Esfahan, Doulatabadi went to live in Tehran. The capital was more tolerant towards women's activism and she was soon able to resume the publication of her newspaper. *Women's Language* was published for two years and had a circulation of 2,000. Doulatabadi wrote controversial editorials in her newspaper. Issues such as the Anglo-Iranian Treaty of 1919 were taken up and criticised. One of her editorials brought about the second ban for her newspaper in 1921. A year later Doulatabadi went to France to study psychology. While in France, she represented Iranian women in international women's congresses and wrote articles on Iranian women for French journals. In 1927 Sedigheh Doulatabadi came back to Iran after obtaining a degree in psychology from an adult education college in Paris. She refused to veil herself and appeared in the streets of Tehran in European clothes and hat (*ibid.*, p. 98). In 1920, another woman attempted to establish a newspaper for women in Tehran. Shahnaz Azad founded and edited *Women's Letter* (*Nameye Banovan*). In the first issue of the newspaper it was stated that 'The misfortune of an individual or a society is due to the ignorance and foolishness of that individual or society. To struggle against women's ignorance, this newspaper will only publish for women' (Sheykholeslami, 1972, p. 99).

Women's Letter published articles both on politics and issues specific to women. The paper carried the slogan 'women are men's first teachers' (*ibid.*, p. 100). *Women's Letter* was published for one year and it was banned when it argued for the abolition of the veil. Two more women's newspapers were founded in 1921. Fakhr Afagh Parsa founded *Women's World* (*Jahan Zanan*) in Mashad. She, too, came from a strict clerical family and her education was kept secret from her father. Her husband, however, happened to be open-minded and supported her interest in women's issues. *Women's World* tried to refrain from offending the clergy but the publication of a letter from a Kermani woman brought about the banning of the paper. The letter implied that the clergy had a vested interest in keeping women ignorant. Mrs Parsa was exiled to Tehran where she started publishing her paper for the second time round. But the publication of one issue was sufficient to create an uproar in Tehran. Mrs Parsa and her family were exiled to the city of Arak and from there to Qom. She was allowed eventually to return to Tehran. Mrs Parsa was prohibited from publishing *Women's World* until the late 1920s when she started a third edition. *Women's Universe* (*Alam Nesvan*) was founded in 1921 by the Association of the Graduates of the American Girls' School. This magazine was forty pages in length and was one of the rare Iranian publications to be edited by an editorial board. The objectives of the journal were explained as:

> Assisting the elevation and progress of women; encouraging them to serve their country and family, and improve their education. [This journal] does not aim to publish political news and will concentrate on six areas of importance for women:

1 Medical issues ...
2 Instructions on nursing and training children ...
3 Instructions on correct and hygienic methods of housekeeping and cooking ...
4 Fashion ...
5 News of women's progress in the world and in Iran ...
6 Literature and poetry ...
(*Ibid.*, p. 125)

During its thirteen years of publication *Women's Universe* printed many articles on the backward position of women in Iran and the harm caused by seclusion and veiling, and campaigned for the improvement of women's rights through theoretical discussions as well as literature and poetry. Another woman activist, Zandokht Shirazi, who was also an outstanding poet, founded The Society of Women's Revolution (Majmae Enghelab Nesvan) in 1927 in Shiraz. The name of the organisation was later changed to The Society of Women's Movement. Zandokht explained the reason behind the name change: 'By the word "revolution" I meant social revolution. But since this word created misunderstanding among people, it was changed to "movement"' (Basari, 1967, p. 22). The Society of Women's Revolution set out its objectives as 'to gain the freedom of women, to struggle against veiling, and to gain equal rights with men' (Sheykholeslami, 1972, p. 177).

Zandokht was eighteen years old when she founded this society. She had been given in marriage when she was ten years old, but she obtained a divorce and spent the rest of her short life writing poetry and struggling for women's rights. She was an extremely sensitive woman and her vulnerability drove her into depression and death at the age of twenty-eight. The Society of Women's Revolution was banned after nine months of activity and Zandokht moved to Tehran. There, she started a newspaper entitled *Dokhtaran Iran* [Daughters of Iran]. This was an illustrated newspaper and its aim was to write about 'social issues and women's progress' (Sheykholeslami, 1972, p. 174). Zandokht's main contribution to the women's movement lay in her passionate and moving poetry which drew on her own personal experiences (Basari, 1967). But the most far-reaching development within the women's movement in this period was the establishment of socialist and communist women's organisations. These organisations maintained close relationship with one or other of the Socialist or Communist Parties. The largest and best established of these women's organisations was the Patriotic Women's League (Anjoman Nesvan Vatankhah) which was set up in 1922 by Mohtaram Eskandari, a Qajar princess who was married to Soleyman Eskandari the prominent socialist leader. This organisation associated itself with the Socialist Party. The objectives of The Patriotic Women's League were:

To emphasise continuing respect for the laws and rituals of Islam; to promote the education and moral upbringing of girls; to encourage national industries; to spread literacy among adult women; to provide care for orphaned girls; to set up hospitals for poor women; to organise co-operatives as a means of developing national industries; and to give material and moral support to the defenders of the country in the event of war. (Bamdad, 1977, p. 64)

The executive committee of the League consisted of Nurolhoda Manganeh, Fakhr ol-Ozma Arghun, Mastureh Afshar and Safiyeh Eskandari. Later on, other prominent women activists such as Sedigheh Doulatabadi and Fakhr Afagh Parsa joined the executive committee. Together these women established one of the most active and enthusiastic women's organisations in Iranian history. During the three odd years of the campaign for women's rights, members of the Patriotic Women's League faced many attacks from religiously inspired men and women. They, however, continued to take their campaigns into the classrooms and targeted female students as the main audience for their speeches and writings on women's rights (*ibid.*, p. 64; Sheykholeslami, 1972, p. 152). To attract attention to women's needs, members of the League waged a campaign by setting fire to reactionary publications. One of these daring campaigns took place in the central square of Toopkhaneh in Tehran. Members of the League assembled in the square and set fire to a pile of anti-woman literature. They were immediately arrested. Members of the League also attended the court hearing of a male writer who had been charged for criticising women's veiling (Bamdad, 1977, p. 76). The League also set up literacy classes for adult women, published books and organised plays.

The leader of the League Mohtaram Eskandari died in 1925 as a result of an operation on her spine. After her death Mastureh Afshar became the leader (*ibid.*, p. 65). The League continued to operate until 1932. *Patriotic Women* (*Nesvan Vatankhah*) was the title of the journal published by the League. Mohtaram Eskandari was the chief editor but the journal was run by a cooperative of a few other women. The importance assumed by the League and its journal attracted contributions from many women. Sedigheh Doulatabadi and Fakhr Afagh Parsa who had run their own newspapers contributed to this journal when their newspapers were banned. *Patriotic Women* allocated one section of the journal to politics and another to religion. The rest of the journal focused on matters 'which were of general use to women' and consisted of articles on social reform, women's rights, girls' education and poetry and literature (Sheykholeslami, 1972, p. 146).

Pro-Communist women took up activities within the Communist Party and formed adjacent women's organisations. The Communist Party increased its female membership, emphasised the mobilisation of women and allowed women members to participate in the activities of independent women's organisations (Kambakhsh, 1972, p. 34). Soltanzadeh, a prominent Communist leader, wrote the first Communist statement on the position of women in Iran (*Historical Documents*, 1974, IV, pp. 105–6). Communist women established correspondence with Soviet women's newspapers and journals such as *Eastern Woman* (*Zan Shargh*). In 1921 this journal published a report about the first celebration of International Women's Day by Iranian women in the northern town of Anzali. According to this report about fifty women took part in the celebration (Nahid, 1981, p. 106). A group of Iranian women known as 'freedom seeking women' wrote in a letter to Soviet women that 'We consider you as our friends and guardians and ask with ringing voices for your help. Do not forget the oppressed women of Iran . . . Long live women's emancipation! Long live the October Revolution, a revolution which will be the basis for the revolution of the whole world' (*ibid.*, p. 107).

Another letter from Iranian women asked Soviet women to 'send the red flag of your revolution to the East' (*ibid.*, p. 107). The Communist Party encouraged women members to take part in the activities of the Patriotic Women's League. But those who did found the League less radical than they wished and broke away to found the more militant Women's Awakening (Bidari Zanan) in 1923. During its three years of activity, Women's Awakening set up adult education and literacy classes, organised plays and celebrated International Women's Day (Kambakhsh, 1972, p. 31). The Second Congress of the Communist Party took place in 1927 in Orumiyeh. The agenda of the Congress included 'work among women' (*Historical Documents*, 1974, IV, p. 116). The resolutions of the Congress which included detailed items on economic and social matters concentrated on the condition of working-class women. The Congress asked for the abolition of night shifts for women and children and demanded paid maternity leave for the working woman (*ibid.*, II, p. 107). *Red Star* (*Setareh Sorkh*), the organ of the Communist Party of Iran, wrote in 1927 that in order to attract the majority of the working classes, the Communist Party should pay special attention to the female masses (*ibid.*, 1976, VI, p. 232).

In 1927, another pro-Communist women's organisation was founded in Rasht. The Messenger of Women's Prosperity (Jamiyat Peyk Saadat Nesvan) was founded by Roshanak Nowdoust who was a headmistress in Saadat (Prosperity) school. She also edited the organ of the above organisation which carried the same name. The organisation's newspaper was published with the assistance of the pro-Soviet Iranian Cultural Society in Rasht (Kambakhsh, 1972, pp. 30–1). The organisation set out as its objective the expansion of literacy and social awareness among women (Sanasarian, 1982, p. 35). It organised literacy classes for women and set up discussion seminars for its members. The Messenger of Women's Prosperity celebrated International Women's Day on 8 March 1927 by putting up pictures of Clara Zetkin, the international communist leader (*Historical Documents*, 1974, I, p. 118).

The link between political parties and women's groups was not limited to socialists and communists. The Revival Party, too, forged its own links with feminists. These links were mainly made through pro-Revivalist newspapers such as *Kaveh* and *Iranshahr*. The Revival Party was not interested in the mobilisation of women as a priority but the party contained many longstanding reformists who were interested in women's emancipation. Taqizadeh, the editor of *Kaveh*, was one such reformist who first argued for the right of women to establish their own organisations in the first Majles in 1907. Taqizadeh was a firm believer in mass literacy and his concept of mass education included both sexes. He believed that unless women were educated and able to enjoy human rights, Muslim countries could not progress to the level of Western societies. He praised the efforts of the Islamic reformers such as Qasim Amin to change 'the pathetic position of Muslim women' (*Kaveh*, 1, pp. 1–2). Taqizadeh strongly believed in the Westernisation of Iran (Vatandoust, 1977). His statement in one of his editorials that 'Iran should be Westernised inwardly and outwardly, physically and spiritually' demonstrated his belief in the West (*Kaveh*, 2, p. 2). Taqizadeh was treated by the women's movement as a supporter and an advisor. He was invited to social gatherings and graduation ceremonies to deliver speeches on the objectives of women's emancipation (Afshar, 1972). During his long years of exile in Berlin he continued to play the role of the patron of the women's movement. Taqizadeh followed the nationalist argument about the necessity of women's emancipation and set certain duties and responsibilities for the women's movement in Iran. He believed that society was a complex machine each part of which performed a specific role. The machinery could not function without any one of its parts. Taqizadeh explained what the role of women within the machinery of society was:

> Women are the bastions of civility, chastity and patience. With the growth of women's emancipation men are increasingly influenced by women's chastity, courtesy and purity of words and deeds ... Women are also the prime sources of cleanliness and good health. In a society where women do not exert influence people are ignorant of cleanliness and hygiene ... Women are educators of men and can influence the best aspects of the human personality ... Women are the carriers of national traditions and customs. Women function as the main pillars and the firm foundations of ethnicity, religion, language, culture and the national heritage. Women can exert enormous influence in the education of a new

generation who often express a disregard for their traditions ... Women are the main link within the proximity, clan and lineage. (Afshar, 1972, pp. 159–63)

The role of women within the machinery of society, according to him, created certain rights and duties for women. Taqizadeh thought these to be the following:

Women have grave social duties. Since woman is the manifestation of fine emotions and natural sentiments, her social responsibility is to reproduce and raise children. It is women's social duty to campaign on matters related to children's health and well being. The question of health and hygiene of the poor should also be taken up by women. Charities, orphanages and hospitals should be set up by women and the question of drugs and welfare of drug addicts should also be tackled by them. Women should fight against moral decay and ethical frailty. But above all, woman's first and foremost duty lies in the enlightening of her sisters. It is woman's heavy responsibility to take her pioneering work among the under-privileged and ignorant women and assist their development. (Afshar, 1972, pp. 163–6)

Taqizadeh's newspaper published articles on women and reported on the progress of women's education in Iran. The longest article on women in *Kaveh* was one written by the European wife of the great writer Mohammad Ali Jamalzadeh. In this article she challenged the belief in the physical and mental inferiority of women by making reference to the latest debates in the West. The article quoted the German Socialist, Bebel, and asked for a 'social revolution on the position of women in Iran' (*Kaveh*, 3, pp. 6–7). *Kaveh* often reported on developments in Iran in the field of women's education. One report indicated that the number of women's schools continued to rise. According to this report, there were 58 girls' schools in Tehran in 1920 which provided education for more than 3,000 girls. About another 1,000 girls were said to be receiving education in public schools (*Kaveh*, 4, p. 27). The picture was, according to another report, different in the provinces where religious opposition often prevented the opening of girls' schools (*Kaveh*, 5, p. 2). In 1922, *Kaveh* was followed by another newspaper in exile. *Iranshahr* was published by another longstanding pro-Revival Party reformist, Hosein Kazemzadeh Iranshahr. *Iranshahr* followed the same kind of approach towards the question of women in Iran:

In the civilised world women have acquired social and political rights, and are participating in social affairs. But in our country, women are living under unbelievable conditions. These unfortunates are the lowest of the low and are exposed to medieval treatment. It would not be an exaggeration to say that no other strata in the world is more deprived than Iranian women. (*Iranshahr (Berlin)*, 1, p. 370)

In reply to a letter by an Iranian woman who complained about the attitudes of Shii clergy towards women, Kazemzadeh said 'An ignorant, prejudiced and savage *molla* would, of course, want to keep women as animals, that is, in his own rank' (*Iranshahr (Berlin)*, 2, p. 426). But women, Kazemzadeh argued, should struggle against ignorant clergy. Women should organise and take the following tasks on board:

Women should set up meetings at least once a week, to talk about child care, the health of pregnant women, the advantages of cleanliness and hygiene, the fundamentals of house-keeping, and relations between husband and wife, a woman's duties towards her husband and children, how to reform the improper aspects of betrothal and marriage ceremonies, and what to accept and what to reject from the West . . . These meetings should take place in members' houses in turn. The meetings should be free from extravagant hospitalities. Even tea and sweets should not be offered so that lower class women could participate . . . Women who are good speakers should deliver speeches to illiterate and underprivileged women on topics that are discussed in women's meetings . . . Women's groups should organise literacy classes on a voluntary basis and teach illiterate women to read and write. These classes should be set up in women's houses to save money that would otherwise be spent on rent . . . Women's groups should encourage women to give up jewellery and make-up and teach them how to economise. Women pioneers should set an example by throwing away their jewellery and fancy trinkets and by refraining from taking annual trips abroad . . . Women's groups should set up schools to teach lower-class women skills such as dressmaking, knitting, cooking, housekeeping, and child care . . . Women's groups should collect donations from well-to-do families to assist poor women in setting up businesses, and also to fund orphanages and schools . . . Women's groups should publish women's journals to propagate their cause and to advise women on various matters in simple language. (*Iranshahr (Berlin)*, 2, pp. 426–9)

Iranshahr published a wide range of articles on women's issues. It also initiated a debate on whether or not Iranian men should marry foreign women. Sedigheh Doulatabadi participated in this debate and criticised those Iranian men who preferred to marry foreign women (*Iranshahr (Berlin)*, 3, pp. 702–8). Both *Kaveh* and *Iranshahr* exchanged letters with Zandokht Shirazi who founded The Society of Women's Revolution.

Political parties and the women's movement during this period continued to be sustained by the urban upper and middle classes, but the rise of the labour movement resulted in some working-class political participation too. Studies of the social background of the leading members of the Communist and Socialist Parties showed that they were overwhelmingly drawn from the urban professional middle class (Abrahamian, 1982, pp. 132–3, 158–61). Another study of the women's movement in this period demonstrated a similar pattern, where twelve leaders/founders of women's organisations and magazines came from upper and middle classes. They were all educated and had educated fathers and husbands (Sanasarian, 1982, pp. 40–4). The general membership of the left parties and organisations, too, was drawn from the educated strata. According to

British documents, most of the 2,500 members of the Socialist Party were educated people (Abrahamian, 1982, p. 128).

The entry of the expanding skilled working class into politics was facilitated by the formation of trade unions throughout Iran. The Communist and Socialist Parties created the central Council of Federated Trade Unions (Shoraye Motahed Ettehadieh Kargaran) which obtained affiliation from such varied unions as the oil workers, printers, pharmacists, shoemakers, bath attendants, bakery assistants, municipal employees, teachers, tailors, textile workers and carpet weavers, and whose membership grew to over 8,000 in the 1920s (*ibid.*, p. 129). Many of these groups such as the bath attendants, textile and other factory workers, carpet weavers, cooks, domestic servants, and professionals such as teachers, included women. But the extent of women's participation and contribution to the post-war labour movement has not yet been studied. Women's contribution to the newly set up welfare, health and education systems is also understudied.

Nation state and independent political action

Reza Shah's creation of a strong executive power did indeed provide the Majles with protection against internal chaos and external interference, and ensured the effective implementation of social reforms. But it also affected the very character of the Majles as a powerful and independent legislator. Post-constitutional political history has witnessed a long and unequal power struggle between the Majles and the executive. This tension continued throughout the reign of the Pahlavi Shahs and was only resolved by the Iranian Revolution of 1977–9. The constitutional precept of the separation of executive, legislative and judiciary powers did not work well in reality due to the tendency of the executive power to manipulate the other two. The Majles and judiciary could only assert independence during odd periods of weakness in the position of the monarch in power.

This political autocracy had an important effect on the development of the women's movement and political parties in this historical conjuncture. After Reza Shah became monarch in 1927 with the help of a wide cross-section of political groups, he began a crusade against the spread of socialism in Iran. In 1931 Reza Shah forced the passage of a law through the Majles to declare communist and anti-monarchical activities illegal and to ban opposition political parties. The Socialist Party was dissolved after its leader Eskandari was forced into retirement. The Communist Party was banned and its leaders were either killed or exiled. But political repression was not aimed solely at socialists and communists.

Reza Shah considered democracy and independent political action a hinderance to rapid modernisation. He interpreted the popularity of his reform programme as a mandate for despotism. Even his own support group amongst the intelligentsia did not escape repression. The Revival Party was banned and its leaders, such as Mosaddeq and Taqizadeh, were isolated and silenced. The Majles was gradually stripped of its power and independence and assumed a mere ceremonial role confined to rubber-stamping Reza Shah's programmes. Elections were stage-managed and the twenty-year tradition of independent political campaigning was brought to an end. The press and media were also censored extensively. Many left-wing and pro-democracy newspapers and magazines were banned and state control grew over what was published.

The fate of women's organisations was no better. The spontaneous nature of the women's movement was altered and women's activities were brought under state control. The Patriotic Women's League which was associated with the Socialist Party was finished off by enticing a crowd of fanatics to destroy its premises and burn its publications while the police looked on (Abrahamian, 1982, p. 139). In Rasht, the pro-communist Messengers for Women's Prosperity was banned and two of its founding members, Jamileh Sedighi and Shokat Roosta, were arrested and sent to a women's prison in Tehran (Nahid, 1981, p. 113). The Awakening of Women, another pro-communist women's organisation, was also banned (Kambakhsh, 1972, p. 31). In Qazvin, the Women's Society was crushed and twenty-four of its members were imprisoned for holding pro-communist views. Even the non-communist women's newspapers did not escape. *Women of Iran* was forced to stop publication and its founder Shahnaz Azad was imprisoned for criticising Reza Shah (Soltanzadeh, 1922, pp. 105–6). *Women's Universe*, which had been running for thirteen years and enjoyed great popularity among women was banned (*ibid.*, p. 105). Reza Shah acted against any independent and spontaneous political and feminist activity. By 1935 when he set up an official women's organisation, there was virtually no sign of the vocal independent women's movement which had flourished during the previous two decades. Even the pro-Reza Shah poet, Zandokht Shirazi, was not allowed to maintain her own women's organisation and magazine.

The last semi-independent activity undertaken by women before the establishment of the state-initiated women's organisation took place in the Congress of Oriental Women which was organised in Tehran in 1932. Although some of the speeches delivered by women began by praising Reza Shah, on the whole a spirit of independence was preserved. The conference paid its respects to Mohtaram Eskandari, the deceased founder of The Patriotic Women's League which had borne the brunt of

Reza Shah's repression (Nategh, 1983b, p. 14). Mrs Iran Arani, a socialist, made an influential speech about the position of women in Iran and proposed socialist remedies for the problems faced by women. Iran Arani criticised the existing system 'which treated women like animals' and pointed out that 'the emancipation of women can only be attained by women themselves' (*ibid.*, p. 16). This would only be possible, she argued, if women achieved economic independence through participation in production:

> Some say that women's work is in the home. This is true. But home is not the four-walled residence of a family any more ... Today, a woman's home is the world, and her role is to participate in world affairs ... The women's movement is a social movement and does not strive to replace the rule of one class by another. On the contrary, the fruits of the women's movement will benefit the whole of society ... When one talks about equality of rights between men and women, one means the equality of human rights ... Although men have joined in this movement, nevertheless, women should be the leaders of their movement. (*Ibid.*, pp. 16–17)

Mrs. Arani's speech did not fit into either the policies of the Communist Party nor those of Reza Shah. She adopted an independent stance and considered the objectives of the women's movement to be 'to attain equality of rights and then to work side-by-side with men to drive society forward (*ibid.*, p. 17). The priority given by the Communist Party to the objectives of the women's movement world-wide were the reverse: women should first work side-by-side with men to achieve socialism and male and female equality would follow. Reza Shah, too, could not agree with Mrs. Arani's view that 'the emancipation of women could only be attained by women themselves'. Neither would he go along with a call for 'equality of rights between men and women'. The former aim opposed his intention to be regarded by history as the champion of women's emancipation in Iran and the latter contradicted his deepest beliefs regarding the legal position of women. The content of the laws passed by Reza Shah concerning the position of women and the manner in which social reforms were enforced reflected this.

Women's emancipation and national progress

However, women's emancipation was another important premise on which the emergence of the nation state was based. The era of state building consolidated the link hitherto made between gender equality and national progress and transformed some of the gender demands of the constitutional movement into state policy. For the first time women became a focus of state policy. Women's emancipation was considered an important aspect of national progress. The existing gender relation had to be replaced by a 'modern' one to allow for women's participation in national projects (Sadeghipour, 1968, pp. 137–9).

The state, now strong enough to initiate and implement reforms, was expected to intervene to bring about women's integration into national processes. The state policy defined what was considered as modern in relation to gender and which categories of women were to be targeted. The state's gender programme touched upon two broad areas: women's social participation and the family. Its main aims were: first, women's integration into social life as this was considered to be the hallmark of modernity and essential for progress in the country; second, the creation of educated mothers to improve the prospects of the future generations; third, preservation of the patriarchal family system despite the fact that this did not go hand in hand with the other two aims. To implement these policies, the state needed to complete the process of control and manipulation of the independent women's organisations and leaders. This was achieved with the formation of an official women's centre. In 1934 Reza Shah visited Turkey and was very impressed with the social reforms that were being carried out in that country by Mustafa Kemal. Women were participating in education and employment in an unprecedented fashion, a ban was proposed on women's veiling but it did not result in legal sanctions, and women were also participating in local elections and granted the right to elect and be elected in 1934, and the Turkish Civil Code abolished polygamy and granted women divorce rights in 1926 (Shaw & Shaw, 1977). After his return from Turkey, Reza Shah invited the students of the women's teacher training college and some other active women to a reception organised by the government on 12 May 1935. These women were chosen on the basis of their education, activism in women's rights, and pro-Reza Shah allegiances of their husbands or fathers. In this gathering, the idea of establishing a 'Ladies Centre' (Kanun Banovan) under the honourary presidency of his daughter Princess Shams Pahlavi was proposed and the aims and objectives of the centre were discussed. These were summed up in the charter inaugurating the centre:

> The Ladies' Centre of Iran is instituted under the honourary presidency of H.I.H. Princess Shams Pahlavi and the patronage and supervision of the Ministry of Education, for the purpose of achieving the undermentioned objectives:
>
> 1 To provide adult women with mental and moral education, and with instruction in housekeeping and child rearing on a scientific basis, by means of lectures, publications, adult classes, etc.
> 2 To promote physical training through appropriate sports in accordance with the principles of health preservation.
> 3 To create charitable institutions for the support of indigent mothers and children having no parent or guardian.

4 To encourage simplicity of life-style and use of Iran-made goods.
5 This centre has legal personality in accordance with article 587 of the Commerce Code, and its president is the legal representative of the centre. (Bamdad, 1977, pp. 93–4)

The main objective in founding the Ladies' Centre was to prepare the ground for women's unveiling (*kashf hejab*). The Centre organised lectures on unveiling and their success was 'so much so that at every lecture, session or meeting held by the centre more unveiled women could be seen at the back of the audience behind the school-mistresses who sat in front' (*ibid.*, p. 94). The lectures covered subjects such as 'ethical duties of women in society', 'women's education and social duties', 'health of mothers and babies', 'women and the professions', 'women and the economy', 'some famous women in history', 'women in Turkey' and 'women and art'. These lectures were quite unified in their overall understanding of women's role in society. They covered subjects like women's chastity and virtue; women's role as wife and mother; women's education and participation in society and the social harms of veiling, seclusion, ignorance and superstition; the importance of health care and hygiene for women; and the importance of following a simple and non-extravagant life style (*ibid.*). Apart from these lectures, the Ladies' Centre also conducted debates on the position of women. In one of these sessions the subject of the debate was 'women's participation in social affairs' and a number of men and women talked about the pros and cons of this. Women taking part in the debate pointed out that 'women's psychological attributes such as patience, realism, kindness, and tolerance would benefit society if she could take part in social affairs.' Men taking part in the debate pointed out that ' women's psychological attributes and their physical and mental weakness prevented them from taking part in social affairs and therefore the best duty for women was to stay at home and raise children' (*Kanun Banovan*, 1935, pp. 162–84).

Although the establishment of the Ladies' Centre signalled the end of an era of women's independent activities, nevertheless it provided a much needed security to the movement of women's emancipation. It was financially secure, well-protected against the harassment of the fanatics and was respected by the authorities. It provided the first taste of legitimacy to women activists and indeed many chose to continue their struggle for women's emancipation within its framework. On the whole, a combination of factors including Reza Shah's repressive measures which prevented oppositional feminist activity, his intolerance of spontaneous and independent political action, and his programme of emancipation for women, proved a powerful incentive for women activists to become the propagators of the state policy on women (Sanasarian, 1982; Najmabadi, 1991).

Women's social participation

The policy on women's social participation was an articulation of the changes demanded by reformers since the Constitutional Revolution. It was therefore widely popular amongst reformers of all persuasion. The state made it official policy to integrate women, albeit in a limited sense, into society and Reza Shah mobilised the resources of the state to implement it.

The prerequisite for women's wider participation in national programmes was seen to be unveiling. This demand had been raised for decades by male and female reformists. Since the late 1920s educated women had challenged the practice of veiling in different ways. Some wore untraditional colours and styles of *chador* which outraged the local community (Bamdad, 1977, p. 85). Others, mostly in Tehran, refused to wear it after returning from abroad and began to appear in public unveiled despite facing abuse (Boyce, 1930). The state did not discourage women from appearing unveiled in public and the police sometimes even protected them. In 1928, after the visit of Afghanistan's reformist King Amanollah and his unveiled queen, rumours spread that women's unveiling would be made legal by Reza Shah. But the overthrow of King Amanollah in Afghanistan by conservative forces spoilt the momentum for women's unveiling in Iran. A Western woman observer anticipated 'that emancipation [from the veil] will take place in the not far distant future, no one seems to doubt . . . When unveiling does come, it will not be compulsory, and doubtless many of the older generation will never change their costume' (*ibid.*, 1930, p. 266).

The unveiling of women eventually came about in 1936, and contrary to this optimism, it turned out to be compulsory. In January, Reza Shah who had recently returned from a visit to Turkey, issued a decree outlawing the veil. He appeared at an educational function accompanied by unveiled female members of his family and delivered a speech to a preselected audience of unveiled teachers and wives of civil servants:

> I am extremely delighted to see that women have become aware of their rights and entitlement ... Women of this country not only could not [before unveiling] demonstrate their talents and inherent qualities because of being separated from society, but also could not pay their dues to their homeland and serve and make sacrifices for their country. Now women are on their way to gain other rights in addition to the great privilege of motherhood. We should not forget that half of our active force was laid idle. Women should consider today a great day and use the opportunities available to them to work for the progress of the country. I believe that we must all work sincerely for the progress and happiness of this country. ... Future prosperity is in your hands [because you] train the future generation. You can be good teachers to train good individuals. My expectation is

that now that you learned ladies are becoming aware of your rights and duties towards your country, you should be wise in life, work hard, become accustomed to frugality, and avoid extravagance and overspending. (Sadeghipour, 1968, pp. 135–9)

Reza Shah's decree forbade women to appear on the streets in *chador* and scarf, and ordered the police to remove these from any woman wearing them. A European wife of an Iranian man witnessed the police on the streets of Tehran 'tearing scarves from the women's heads and handing them back in ribbons to their owners' (Suratgar, 1951, p. 132). The compulsory unveiling was backed by a series of measures. Reza Shah issued an order to the owners of public places such as restaurants, theatres and hotels to prevent veiled women from entering (Abrahamian, 1982, p. 144). The first use of the new decree was made by the chief of police who took his unveiled wife to a cafe (*Moslem World*, No. 20, July 1930, p. 269).

Although this was a tremendous blow to the clergy's ideological authority, the clergy's opposition to unveiling remained ineffective. Reza Shah's readiness to take repressive measures against the clergy and the popularity of his social reforms amongst the urban upper and middle classes were major factors in explaining the clergy's quietism. When a *molla* condemned Reza Shah for allowing his family to appear unveiled in public, the *molla* was publicly insulted by the removal of his turban and shaving of his head and beard (A. Pahlavi, 1980, p.25). Another incident that took place in the shrine city of Qom is a good example of Reza Shah's determination to push through the unveiling of women. The queen and her daughters accompanied by a few other women from the court attended the shrine of Hazrat Masumeh in Qom dressed in European hats and clothes. The *mollas* present in the shrine felt insulted and were determined to exert their ideological authority in their traditionally independent domain of the mosque and shrine. They confronted the Shah's family and asked them either to put on the veil or leave. The queen and her company left the shrine but stayed in the vicinity and sent a message to the Shah explaining what had happened. A few hours later Reza Shah arrived in person and stormed into the shrine, cursing and beating any *molla* in his way. The arrival of the Shah himself, his disregard for the customs associated with the shrine such as entering it barefoot, and his insulting violent behaviour towards the clerics within, proved too daring a challenge for the religious establishment. The next day after the arrest of the *mollas* who had asked the Queen to leave, Sheykh Abdolkarim Haeri, a respected cleric who anticipated riots in Qom against the Shah, issued a decree and banned any discussion of the incident in public: 'the decree was like water poured over fire, and prevented the outbreak of public riots which would have led to killing and looting' (Maki, 1979, IV, pp. 282–5). Faced with state suppression and tremendous middle and upper-class social support for unveiling and other state reforms, the most important religious figure of this period Mirza Rezagholi Shariat-Sanglaji, made a plea to the *olama* to abandon their reactionary and superstitious attitudes and to use the tool of *ejtehad* to reinterpret and modernise Islam (Momen, 1985, p. 251).

The compulsory unveiling was accompanied by a series of measures to increase women's education and employment opportunities. A Ministry of Education was set up in accordance with Article 19 of the Supplementary Fundamental Law to administer a national system of public education. The new system rationalised and expanded the limited public schooling which had come into existence since 1911 for boys and 1918 for girls. Private schools and traditional *maktabkhaneh* run by the clergy continued to increase alongside. In 1934, a number of teacher training colleges were established. The University of Tehran was opened in 1935 and students were also sent abroad for specialisation. The budget allocated to education was 2 to 5 per cent of the national budget during the period 1927–41, which amongst other things catered for over a quarter of a million children in primary schools and 30,000 in secondary schools. In addition, 37,000 pupils were learning to read and write in *maktabkhaneh* (Arjomand, 1988, p. 68).

The education of boys, however, developed faster and was more of a priority as the limited statistics available on girls' education demonstrated. In 1930, the number of state schools for girls in the whole country was 73 and private schools were numbered at 145. A total of 16,328 girls were being educated in schools and 9,732 were learning to read and write in *maktabkhaneh* (Boyce, 1930). The Ministry of Education required women to enrol in physical education classes and school girls marched *en masse* in public parades. The government also set up a national Girl's Scout organisation (Arasteh, 1964a, p. 197). A small number of women entered the University of Tehran in 1936 and a few were privately educated abroad (Bamdad, 1977, p. 20). Women were not included in the quota of students sent abroad each year by the government. A woman activist complained that 'girls are clamouring for the right to be included in the quota [of students going abroad] . . . but as yet the government is not willing to grant this request' (*ibid.*, p. 268).

After compulsory unveiling, the civil service (but not the judiciary) was opened to women (Bagley, 1971, p. 49). Women's employment was concentrated mainly in teaching and midwifery. The newly set up Ministry of Health rationalised the practice of midwifery and set up a three-year training course in midwifery in the newly established government hospital under the charge of a French woman physician (*ibid.*). The new teacher training college trained women teachers for girls' schools. But women teachers were paid half as much as men (Elwell-Sutton, 1941, p. 126). Some women gained access to new middle-class professions. A handful of women who had been educated abroad returned home to practice medicine or lecture in the University of Tehran. Foreign companies were amongst the first to employ women as clerks and typists, a trend which was taken up by other firms and government departments (*ibid.*).

But at this early stage, public education for girls did not result in a substantial change in the pattern and extent of employment amongst women. Moreover, women's entry into education and employment was not followed by participation in politics. The state did not introduce any changes in the electoral law of 1907 and women were not granted the right to elect and be elected.

Women's legal status in the family

The state policy of women's integration into society stopped short of a substantial reform of the family to create the right conditions for women's wider participation in national programmes. The secularisation of the judiciary did not include secularisation of family law and the *shariat* continued to be applied to the family. While most other areas of social life were covered by new secular laws drawn from French law the secularisation of the family was limited to a codification of *shariat* precepts and prevalent customs and practices, and while secular courts and judges were put in place for all other areas of the law, the family remained the preserve of the *shariat* courts and religious judges. The new Civil Code which was completed in 1931 contained 1,335 articles of which 100 were devoted to the family. These articles dealt with wills, marriage and divorce, legitimacy and custody, guardianship and child maintenance (Emami, 1960).

In relation to marriage, the Civil Code specified a number of rules within the framework of the polygamous family. Article 1091 related to women's dowries: a woman's social worth was assessed by her family background, status, personal qualities and the local traditions in which she was raised. The minimum age of marriage was specified as fifteen for women and eighteen for men. Article 1062 required both parties to give their consent to marriage. Articles 1042–1043 required the woman to obtain her father's or grandfather's permission before contracting her first marriage. Article 1040 gave the right to either of the marriage partners to demand a medical certificate from the other. Articles 1059–1060 forbade Muslim women from marrying non-Muslim men and made marriage of women with other nationals conditional on government permission. Article 1105 pronounced the husband as the head of the household and put responsibility for the wife's maintenance on his shoulders. Articles 1075–1077 on *sigheh* marriage, allowed the man to take an unlimited number of temporary wives, each for a period of one hour to ninety-nine years.

In matters related to the dissolution of marriage, Article 1133 considered divorce as the right of the husband. Article 1134 specified that the husband could divorce his wife at will without having to give a reason. Divorce could take place either in the presence of two male witnesses or by proxy. The woman was not required to be present when divorce was taking place or have any knowledge of it. Article 1139 specified that the husband could renounce the unexpired period of his *sigheh*. Articles 1121–1132 gave the reasons under which women could ask for a divorce. These included the husband's failure to maintain his wife and perform his (unspecified) duties towards her, and his insanity. If the husband suffered from a venereal disease, the wife could not ask for a divorce but had the right to refuse to have intercourse with him (Article 1127). Articles 1146–1147 specified the ways in which a woman could buy a divorce from her husband by forfeiting her *mehrieh*. Article 119 empowered both parties in the marriage to stipulate other conditions under which a divorce could take place. However, the woman's request for a divorce, irrespective of the reason, had always to be made 'on behalf of her husband', as the right to divorce inherently belonged to the man. Articles 1150–1157 specified the period of *eddeh* for permanent and *sigheh* wives to be three menstrual cycles or until the birth of a child if the woman was pregnant.

In relation to child custody, guardianship and maintenance, Article 1169 stated that the custody of a child belonged to the father after a daughter had reached the age of seven and a son the age of two, until which time the mother was allowed to look after them on behalf of the father. Articles 1199–1203 gave financial responsibility for children at all times to the father or paternal grandfather and uncles. Article 860 specified that if the father or paternal grandfather and uncles died, the custody of children would be given to a guardian appointed by them. Article 1170 stated that if a mother remarried during the time she was allowed to look after them, custody of the children would be transferred to the father. In relation to inheritance, the Civil Code specified that daughters should inherit half of what sons did (Article 907), mothers would inherit one-third of their child's estate and fathers two-thirds (Article 906). Article 940 forbade a *sigheh* wife to inheriting from her husband, but her children had the same rights as the children of a permanent wife. Articles 927–938 stated that a permanent wife received one-eighth of the husband's estate if she was the only wife and had children. But if she had no children, she only received a quarter of the one-eighth. Co-wives received a proportion of one-eighth if they had children and a quarter if they did not. Articles 1197–1200 created an obligation for the offspring to maintain the parents in need.

On other matters, Article 1117 forbade women to travel and take employment without their husband's consent. Article 1005 specified that a woman's place of residence was where her husband resided, and in order to have a different place of residence the woman was required to have permission from her husband or the court. Article 976 defined citizenship as belonging to those born inside or outside the country from an Iranian father. The mother did not need to be Iranian. Foreign women who married Iranian men were considered Iranian nationals. Articles 963–964 specified that if a married couple did not hold the same nationality, their private and financial affairs and their relationship with their children would be governed by the laws of the country to which the husband belonged.

The Civil Code's articles on the family were supplemented in 1937 by the Marriage Act of Iran. Some of the provisions of this Act were repetitions of the rules already contained in the Civil Code, and some others were rather insignificant positive or negative amendments to it. The most significant aspect of the Marriage Act was that it made registration of all marriages, divorces and deaths in the state notary offices compulsory, a function which had traditionally been performed by the Shii clergy. It also provided punishment for those who failed to observe the minimum age of marriage for women (Naqvi, 1967, p. 131). In 1933, an act was passed to enable religious minorities to apply their own personal laws concerning the family and personal issues. Women from religious minorities, then, were not obliged to observe the rules governing gender in the above Acts. In 1940, the Assembly passed a Penal Law which was a replica of the Italian penal law except on a few matters. One of the exceptions was Article 179 which permitted a man to kill his wife if he caught her in the act of adultery or in circumstances leading to adultery. A man who killed his mother or sister under the same conditions received three months imprisonment.

State policy on the family, then, consisted of the codification of existing patriarchal relations. The state assumed responsibility for the nation and encouraged women to participate in education and employment. The family, in contrast, was left under the control of the clergy. This, as we will see later, created a permanent tension between the Pahlavi state and the Shii establishment over women.

Patriarchal consensus in the era of nation building

State policy on women's social participation and their position within the family was based on a particular definition of modernity and national progress which constituted the core of the process of nation building. The main elements of modern gender relations were considered to be the desegregation of the sexes, the education of women, and a secularised patriarchal family system which was considered essential for the upholding of national honour. National progress was seen to be achieved through, amongst other things, the legal construction of women as social participants, educated mothers and subservient wives. This means that the new Iranian nation state combined both 'modern' and 'traditional' elements to create social institutions and gender relations specific to Iran. In the context of women's social participation coexisting with the patriarchal family, the oppositional categories of 'modern' and 'traditional' were not analytically relevant or applicable.

The compulsory acts of unveiling and desegregation of public space were the most far-reaching aspects of state modernisation with regard to gender relations. Reza Shah believed that women's work was needed for national progress (Sadeghipour, 1968, pp. 135–9). But more than that, it was important for the state to open up the public sphere to women to strengthen the image of modern nationhood. Women were also defined as the bearers and nurturers of the nation's children, that is, its future citizens. Education of mothers was considered essential for the well being of the future generations. This was reflected in the family law. The Civil Code and Marriage Act ensured that women could not be legally prevented from attending school by early marriage. The age of marriage was increased to fifteen for women and it was made a criminal offence not to observe the age condition. Moreover, marriage could not take place without a woman's consent. Women's subservient status within the family was another aspect of the prescribed gender relations. The Civil Code and Marriage Act constructed women as dependent and dominated beings, and considered women's subservience in the family a matter of national honour. The new legal codes secularised patriarchal family relations by moving family law from the domain of the *Shariat* to the domain of the secular state. But since the content of the law remained the same, the family continued to represent the main site of struggle for the women's movement.

The adoption of *shariat* as the basis of family law has been interpreted as a caution exercised by Reza Shah in the face of a reactionary Shii clergy. But the Shah's fear of the clergy could not have been the real reason for this. After all, Reza Shah had not feared provoking the wrath of the clergy on other sensitive questions such as unveiling and desegregation of the sexes. Moreover, these reforms did not necessarily mean that he held deeply felt emancipatory views on women, particularly women in his own family. On the contrary, as his daughter Ashraf explained:

> To Reza Shah, as to any Persian man, anything concerning his wife and family was a private matter ... At home my father was very much a man of an earlier generation ... But as a King, he was prepared to put aside his personal feelings in the interest of bringing progress to his country ... Though I never felt he was willing to relax his strict control over us at home, he did make the historic decision to present the Queen, my sister and me unveiled to the population of Tehran. (A. Pahlavi, 1980)

Indeed, far from fearing the clergy and their fanatical followers, Reza Shah sought opportunities to further subjugate the clergy. Therefore, it could not have been inherently more dangerous for his popularity or security to abolish *sigheh* and polygamy, establish same age of marriage for men and women, and insist on similar familial rights for men and women, than it was to abolish the veil and segregation of the sexes, which he did with such determination and zeal. The main reason behind his lack of interest in such reforms was the fact that Reza Shah neither personally believed in, nor was he encouraged by, his supporters to seek these measures. The particular conception of women which Reza Shah put forward demonstrated this:

> Reza Shah never advocated a complete break with the past, for always he assumed that our girls could find their best fulfilment in marriage and in the nurture of superior children. But he was convinced that a girl could be a better wife and mother, as well as a better citizen, if she received an education and perhaps worked outside the home long enough to gain a sense of civic functions and responsibilities. (H.R.S. Pahlavi, 1960, p. 231)

Contrary to the myth that Reza Shah was a lone moderniser in the struggle against a traditional and hostile environment, he was no more above the social relations of his time than any other Iranian. Reza Shah was neither the originator of the idea of women's emancipation, nor was he above the social and political alliances of his day. He represented a certain sociopolitical point of view that had grown in Iranian society and he carried out a series of social reforms that had been demanded by generations of Iranian reformists. Reza Shah fell short of introducing comprehensive legal rights for women not because he feared the clergy, but because he faced consensus in preserving the fundamental aspects of patriarchy rather than its overthrow. The project followed by Reza Shah, as representative of similarly minded sections of the Iranian elite, was to bring modernity to Iran through the establishment of a secular nation state based on 'Iranian culture' rather than Islam. Within this project, the familial position of women as advocated in the 'Iranian culture' and 'Islam' happened to be more or less the same. Social conservatism coincided perfectly with the Shii *shariat*.

Despite his repressive measures, Reza Shah's views and policies on women were widely popular amongst reformist men and women. This popularity spread across opposition and non-opposition reformists. Taqizadeh, Bahar and Kasravi were among those intellectuals who, despite being dismissed by Reza Shah, supported his policies. Reza Shah's reforms on the position of women and the basic conceptions and philosophy behind these struck a chord with these intellectuals. They all shared a basic concept regarding the role of men and women in society. The women's emancipation movement had been part and parcel of the constitutional movement and the position of women had since the Constitutional Revolution moved along the lines of slow but gradual reform. By the 1930s, when Reza Shah presented his reform programmes, the areas of education, marriage age, veiling and segregation of the sexes had experienced changes for the better (Boyce, 1930, pp. 265–9). What Reza Shah did was to strike a tremendous blow against the inertia in which the reformists were trapped and the resistance which was exercised by the Shii clergy.

The principle of male domination was the point where Reza Shah's philosophy on the position of women united with that of independent reformists. This came across clearly in the writings of these intellectuals. Ahmad Kasravi, a well-known historian and social critic who was an ardent anti-cleric and whose views led to his assassination by religious fanatics in 1945, wrote essays on various questions related to the position of women (Kasravi, 1974). In these essays, Kasravi criticised the practices of veiling and seclusion, the low age of marriage for women and the high level of illiteracy among them. He praised Reza Shah's attempts to stamp out clerical resistance against changing the position of women. Contrary to Reza Shah, who did not criticise polygamy and himself took three wives, Kasravi criticised polygamy and *sigheh*, and considered monogamy as the right family system for Iranian society. For Kasravi, however, changes in the familial and social position of women were only desirable if they did not alter the 'natural' role of men and women within the family and the function of the family as the 'natural' place for sex and reproduction.

Kasravi was extremely suspicious and bitter towards those 'European educated men' who advocated European-style liberation for women, in his view in order to be able to 'deceive innocent girls into intercourse' without taking responsibility for setting up a family. Kasravi was a great believer in family life and advised women not to overstep familial principles in their quest for emancipation. Women, he believed, should protect their chastity and simplicity. They should always choose feminine professions if they had to work at all. Marriage, Kasravi argued, 'should result in children' and men and women should settle into their 'natural' roles within the family. Women's 'natural' role, he maintained, was to look after the house and raise children. Man's 'natural' role was to earn a living and 'run parliament, the courts, and the army'. It was not a woman's job to seek political office and 'lack of political rights does not belittle women'. Political responsibilities for him required 'farsightedness, confidentiality, coolness and calmness, patience, and physical strength'. Women, he believed, lacked these traits and their physical weakness and mental vulnerability made them unsuitable for serious social responsibilities (*ibid.*, pp. 16–20, 21–2, 23, 32–6).

Taqizadeh, too, despite being a firm believer in the Westernisation of Iran and a follower of Western champions of women's liberation such as John Stuart Mill, did not move very far from a socially conservative model of women's emancipation proposed by the policies of Reza Shah and contained in Kasravi's essays. Taqizadeh, of course, was not bound by statements on female physical and mental inferiority nor by obsession with the necessity of marriage and reproduction. His defence of women's rights was much more sophisticated and comprehensive. Nevertheless, he shared basic patriarchal conceptions about the family and women's role within it. Taqizadeh, while praising the West for providing women with freedom of choice in marriage and divorce and for allowing them to become scientists or politicians, retained the prevalent conception among Iranian intellectuals that women's 'main social responsibility' was 'the reproduction and raising of children' (Afshar, 1972, p. 160). Throughout his years of campaigning for women's rights, Taqizadeh applied double standards towards the issue of the place of women and men in society. Women were 'bastions of chastity' and 'the main link in the chain of ancestry' (*ibid.*, p. 161). For him, women were 'manifestations of fine emotions and natural sentiments' and had a special contribution to make towards the physical and moral health and purity of society. In short, he attributed special psychological and moral characteristics to women as part of their 'nature' and then loaded them with special social and familial responsibilities which did not apply to men. Similar assumptions were made in the writings of another great writer and social reformer Mohammad Ali Jamalzadeh (Jamalzadeh, 1978).

The place of the ideology of male dominance in the era of nation building was such that even socialists and communists did not escape it. Nor were feminists able to step outside their patriarchal cultural heritage. Despite the presence of a dream of full equality between men and women in the minds of socialists, communists and feminists, their demands remained within acceptable patriarchal boundaries. Women had no hesitation in identifying totally and completely with the nation – a symbolic example of this was the adoption of 'Iran' as a female name. But they could not and did not go as far in identifying with feminist causes. Reza Shah's patriarchal style of compulsory reforms on women did not raise many objections amongst these reformers. The forceful unveiling of women and the dictatorial way in which change was imposed did not create much controversy among socialists and communists. The Bolshevik state, which was then the ideal type of state in the eyes of Iranian communists, had itself chosen and carried out a similar draconian imposition of change within the Muslim population of Soviet Central Asia which led to much brutality and bloodshed (Massell, 1974). Feminists, too, in the interest of women's collective rights did not raise much objection to state infringements of the right of individual women to choose their own clothing, and went for forceful unveiling at any price.

As to the socialist challenge of patriarchy,the Communist and Socialist Parties, as noted in previous chapters, left many aspects of women's position in Iran unchallenged. The Socialist Party preferred to provide back-up support for certain sections of the women's movement and let women leaders do the writing and talking. The Communist Party was interested in the mobilisation of women as part of its general strategy to mobilise the working class and the middle strata of society. The Socialist Party did not include anything other than the issue of women's education in their programmes, and communist references to equality of rights for men and women and to working women was infrequent and lacked rigour and determination. The feminist movement made brave attempts to raise women's awareness about their position as well as to increase literacy and skills among women. On the whole, they aspired to have the right to be full citizens.

To summarise, the reforms on women's personal and familial status remained limited during this stage of the construction of the nation state in Iran. The main progress on women's position was made on the social front through unveiling, desegregation and opening up education and employment to women. The discrepancy between reforms on the personal and social status of women associated nationalism and secularism with women's social participation, on the one hand, and identified women's familial position with the Islamic *shariat*, on the other. This dichotomy became a permanent feature of the political debate on women in twentieth-century Iran. Although the link between national progress and women's participation in society was strongly made during this period, the state was not solely or even primarily concerned with the release of female labour for capitalist expansion in Iran (Najmabadi, 1991, p. 54).

The discourse of modernity in the era of nation building defined women's emancipation as a wider project and linked it to the notion of the modern nation state. Women were placed at the heart of the attempt to create a more unified and viable nation; a modern nation with a healthier, better educated and more productive population; and one with a family system which not only preserved the national honour but also produced better mothers, civilised partners and responsible members of society (Jayawardena, 1986, pp. 8–23; Kandiyoti, 1991a, pp. 10–11).

4 Women and the era of nationalism

The transformation of the era of nation building into the era of nationalism, as the third phase of the discourse of modernism, was characterised by three major developments in the 1940s and early 1950s.

First, it resulted in the separation of nationalism from the state and the rise of independent oppositional nationalism. Second, it changed the blind faith in the modern state. The process of nation building was one in which the initial idealism of the constitutionalists regarding freedom, independence and social progress was turned into political realism. The problem was not, any more, lack of a strong executive power to implement social reform. It was the existence of an all-powerful state which combined social reform with an unprecedented level of political repression. The terms of the political debate had to be changed to accommodate this. The central concern of post Reza Shah political debate became the state's observance of the Constitution of 1906.

Third, another important political development that occurred was the role of foreign powers in Iran during and after the Second World War. The Allies' occupation of Iran in 1941 demonstrated the fragile nature of the country's sovereignty. This was a response to Reza Shah's sympathy with Nazi Germany and led to his forced abdication and exile. Mohammad Reza Pahlavi (hereafter the Shah) replaced his father as head of state. Iran was once again divided into different zones of influence by Britain and the Soviet Union, only this time the United States also became a key influence. While the British and the Soviets concentrated on the South and the North respectively, the Americans placed advisers in key government departments and in the military. Each power tried to influence Iranian politics to its own advantage (Keddie, 1981, p. 118). The Allies, being eager to gain public support for the removal of Reza Shah from power, broadcast criticism of his abuses of power and mismanagement of the economy. The British reported that the people of Iran welcomed being saved from Reza Shah's tyranny more than they disliked the invasion of their country (Abrahamian, 1982, p. 165). The Allied occupation coupled with a number of other factors led to further developments.

The above developments resulted in the emergence of competing concepts of modernity around the issues of political freedom, national independence and cultural integrity, which facilitated another shift of emphasis in the discourse of modernity.

Social diversification and economic depression

The immediate post-Reza Shah period witnessed a reversal of the process of national unification so vigorously implemented by him. The Shah inherited the new social and political order established by his father. But since the unified model of a nation state in Iran had been established by means of repression, Reza Shah's abdication brought to the surface many religious, ethnic and language-based diversities. The Shah had neither the experience nor the strength of his father to bring indigenous conflict and dissent under control through further repression. He therefore compromised and adopted conciliatory policies towards political organisations and social groups. The Shah transferred some of his inherited land to its previous owners to build up support in the rural sector. The peasant family, however, suffered extreme poverty during and after the war since more severe war-time conditions increased debts, rents and taxes so much that 'the social and health conditions of the peasantry [in Iran in this period] were among the worst in the world' (Keddie, 1981, pp. 123–4). The post-Reza Shah period witnessed the return of many tribes to nomadism but since the previous policy of forced settlement had destroyed their livestock and disrupted their organisation, on the whole tribes remained as impoverished as peasants. Some tribes, however, were still capable of political rebellion (*ibid.*, p. 125).

In the urban sector, too, economic problems were evident. War and occupation disrupted internal trade, the prices of staple foods rose and a bad harvest in 1942 brought famine. The government's industrial and commercial activities were inefficient and the process of economic development was undermined. The bazaar benefitted from disruption of foreign trade during the war, but the post-war breakdown of government regulation of foreign trade due to foreign influence resulted in large imports of goods and shrank their share of the profit (*ibid.*, pp. 126–7). There was also little expansion in education, health and welfare services during and after the war. Despite these factors, the war stimulated further expansion in the urban sector and the trend towards the growth of the business and professional middle strata continued. The result was unemployment among intellectuals and social dissatisfaction: 'the demand, as distinct from the need, for professionals and scholars in Iran was outstripped by the supply. There was intellectual unemployment, and both students and mature intellectuals tended to identify their troubles with those of the Iranian nation'. Both the professional and business middle strata, for example, civil servants, artisans and shopkeepers, were a focal point of social and nationalist discontent and protest during this period (*ibid.*, p. 123).

The industrial working class, too, gained opportunity to regroup and form new trade unions and lead several major strikes in the post-war period. Many women from urban lower, middle and upper classes who had been affected by strict police monitoring of unveiling went back to using the veil again. But strict veiling, especially total covering of the face, was not resumed widely and became confined to women from clerical and merchant families and other devout Muslims. The new state went along with these developments during and after the war. The Shah gained the loyalty of the army, released political prisoners, returned endowment lands to the clergy, transferred much of his inherited land to its previous owners, and refrained from interfering in the affairs of the Majles (Abrahamian, 1982, pp. 176–7).

Post-dictatorship proliferation of political parties

The lead given by the Allies in criticising Pahlavi policies, the support provided by each of the Allied forces to those political parties whose aims coincided with their interests, and the conciliatory policies of the Shah, all encouraged the revitalisation of civil society and proliferation of political parties and women's groups. The decade of the 1940s was dominated by parliamentary politics and expansion of the activities of newly formed political parties. Some of these political parties gained enough ground during this period to exert a long-lasting influence on Iranian politics. Women's activities in this period regained independence and previously existing tendencies of nationalism and socialism within the movement continued alongside monarchism. On the religious front, some of the clergy, such as Ayatollah Khomeini, came to the fore and criticised Reza Shah's policies and a new fanatical Islamic group by the name of Fadaiyan Eslam (Crusaders of Islam) was formed. In the nationalist ranks, Dr Mohammad Mosaddeq founded the National Front, which was a coalition of diverse nationalist and socialist groups. Within the royalist camp, the People's Party (Hezb Mardom) was established and dominated the Majles for the next thirty years. As to the pro-Soviet left, the Tudeh Party of Iran was founded by a group of Marxists who were released from Reza Shah's prisons. Let us consider the political opposition and the women's movement in this period in more detail.

Shii opposition

The Shii establishment responded in various ways to the post-Reza Shah era. During the reign of Reza Shah the shrine city of Qom had become the centre of Shii scholarship. Sheykh Abdolkarim Haeri, the pre-Second World War Shii *marjae taghlid*, decided to move to Qom to fulfil the prediction of a *hadith* from the sixth Shii *emam* that one day knowledge would arise in Qom and be distributed from there to the rest of the world (Algar, 1980, p. 19). Haeri's successor Ayatollah Borujerdi continued his quietist scholarly work in Qom. Ayatollah Borujerdi was the sole Shii *marjae taghlid* during the period 1941–61 in which new trends developed within Shiism. The Shii clergy and laymen adopted rationalist methods in their writings and employed logic and reasoning in their arguments. Ruhollah Khomeini, a young cleric, provided a good example of this new trend in his book of polemics against anti-clerical reformists and Shii modernists such as Ahmad Kasravi and Shariat-Sanglaji. But Khomeini was also an anomaly among the Shii clergy in the post-war period because he took up a political stance in opposition to the reforms undertaken by Reza Shah. In his *Revealing of Secrets* (*Kashf ol-Asrar*) Khomeini announced that the orders issued by Reza Shah and the laws passed by his Majles had no value and should be scrapped. Khomeini criticised Reza Shah and Ataturk as 'idiotic dictators' who implemented their programmes forcibly and prevented 'real progress of the country' from taking place by 'suppressing the clergy', spreading 'the means of pleasure', and by 'preoccupying people with unveiling, European clothes, cinema, theatre, music and dance' (Khomeini, n.d.a, p. 331). He believed that:

> The dishonourable act of unveiling, or better call it, the movement of bayonets, inflicted moral and material damage on our country and is forbidden by the law of God and the Prophet ... The co-educational schools which have destroyed the chastity of girls and the masculine powers of boys are forbidden by God. ... The wine shops and drug businesses which exhausted the minds of our youth and damaged the health and sanity of the masses are against the *shariat*. ... Music which encourages the spirit of passion and love among the youth is forbidden in the *shariat* and should be taken out of school programmes. (*Ibid.*, pp. 313–14)

Another important development within Shiism during the 1940s was the founding of Fadaiyan Eslam in 1946 by Navab Safavi, a student of theology at Tehran University. This was a clear departure from the post-constitutional clergy-led political opposition. Fadaiyan Eslam presented the first systematic cultural defence of Islam and was the first Islamic political organisation with a comprehensive political programme for Iran.

The fanatical Fadaiyan Eslam pledged itself to uproot irreligious attitudes in society and in demonstrating its determination to do so assassinated Ahmad Kasravi as its first political action. Fadaiyan Eslam expressed an obsessive concern with 'moral decadence' and 'the rise of passion' in Iranian society. Their criticism of the position of women in society was conducted within the above framework. In relation to education, Fadaiyan Eslam believed that women should receive the kind of education that would be appropriate for their responsibilities within the family and rejected the idea of coeducational schools (Fadaiyan Eslam, 1950, p. 56). As to unveiling, they expressed concern that the 'flames of passion' that 'rise from the naked bodies of immoral women' would 'burn humanity into ashes':

> Day and night, men and women face each other in the streets, offices, schools and in other public places and their senses are stimulated at all times without control. The continual stimulation of the sexual sense gradually paralyses the nervous system and weakens the other senses of the people . . . and gradually all the organs of society get paralysed and society's affairs remain unattended to . . . Yes, yes, passion kills the wisdom and culture of society and when it is stimulated in a man by all these naked women around him, he becomes inattentive to his own family and divorce and separation between husbands and wives take place and increase every day. (*Ibid.*, pp. 9–11)

Fadaiyan Eslam disapproved of working women except those 'who for one reason or another, are responsible for leading the family and rearing children and need jobs' (*ibid.*, pp. 82–3). Fadaiyan Eslam asked:

> Do women want to stop legal and moral sexual relationships with their husbands and cease to menstruate and bear children, so that they can share social duties with men? In that case, fifty years from now, when this generation is dead, there won't be any more people in existence . . . or [do women want] the men to menstruate and become pregnant and bear children so that they can share in those responsibilities with women? Damn the logic and wisdom which presents this idea. . . . The best thing for a woman is to be the manager of the house and a mother and wife who will be the producer and the teacher of children at home. Is there any more basic duty than this for women in the world? (*Ibid.*, pp. 11–12)

On marriage and divorce, their belief was that: 'Girls who arrive at physical and mental maturity must be given in marriage by their parents in an effort to reduce the number of unmarried girls and boys as much as possible' (*ibid.*, pp. 36–7). *Sigheh* marriage was approved of and considered 'a holy bond between Muslims' and 'superior to that of a permanent one'. It was argued that *sigheh* has 'multiple eternal rewards' and its attainment should be made easy for Shiis through the setting up of 'special office' in towns and villages to deal with *sigheh* contracts (*ibid.*, pp. 41–3). Fadaiyan Eslam believed that if their prescribed rules were implemented 'Iran would become the paradise of the world' (*ibid.*, p. 87). The ideas of the Fadaiyan Eslam were the first articulation of a polemic with the West and Westernised Iranians produced by a group of modern fanatics. These ideas were revitalised four decades later in the Islamic Republic of Iran.

Pro-Soviet left

The decades after Reza Shah witnessed the proliferation of a pro-Soviet political tendency. In 1945, the newly established Democratic Party in Kurdistan set up an autonomous Democratic Republic there. A similar republic was created in Azarbayjan. The Democratic Party of Azarbayjan (DPA) demanded autonomy for Azarbayjan within Iran, elected a provincial government and took over military positions in Azarbayjan. The DPA formed its own women's section under the name of Women's Organisation of Azarbayjan and organised a conference in Tabriz in 1946 in which 300 women participated. A resolution of the conference stated: 'We swear by the sacred soil of our homeland Azarbayjan that we will fight until the last breath, side-by-side with our brothers to preserve our liberation. . . . We will struggle until the last breath for the emancipation of the oppressed women of Iran who live under the chains of injustice and captivity' (Sadigh, 1973, p. 57).

The Provisional Government of Azarbayjan allowed women to participate in elections for the first time in Iran. It also established equal pay for equal work for men and women and paid maternity leave to women workers (Ebrahimi, 1967, p. 322). The Tudeh Party, a pro-Soviet communist organisation, was also founded by a group of Marxists jailed by Reza Shah who were known as the 'Fifty Three'. The Tudeh Party published its provisional programme which included the protection of the Constitution, civil liberties and human rights of all citizens especially the working class (Abrahamian, 1982, p. 282). The programme excluded specific communist and feminist demands in the interest of forming an alliance with all sections of society (including the clergy) against fascism, which was in line with official Soviet policy at the time.

A year later, the Tudeh Party convened a conference and proposed a more detailed programme which addressed the peasants, workers, women and the middle class (*ibid.*, p. 284). Women, in this programme, were promised political rights and working women were specifically promised equal pay for equal work as well as welfare assistance. The conference approved the creation of special sections in the party for women and youth and also the building of an extensive trade union movement. The Tudeh Party soon expanded into the provinces and made significant inroads into the trade unions, including women's unions such as the 500–strong union of women carpet-weavers (*ibid.*, p. 292). In the 1940s, membership in the Tudeh Party was estimated to be 25,000 and trade unions enjoyed a membership of 400,000 (Halliday, 1979, p. 228).

In August 1944, the first Tudeh Congress took place. The Congress drew the attention of the future Central Committee to the necessity of mobilising and uniting women against 'reactionary provocations' (Kambakhsh, 1972, p. 71). Tudeh work amongst women was given special emphasis. In 1944 the Central Committee set up a special section for women under the title of the Association of Women (Tashkilat Zanan) in order to attract pioneer women and through their efforts in local branches of the party to mobilise women from various social strata. Although working-class women were the likeliest target for Tudeh Party propaganda, women of all other classes were also addressed. The position of working women was analysed and lack of paid maternity leave, nurseries, equal pay, and welfare rights for working mothers was criticised. The party appealed to 'Working women, intellectual women, and all women who have had enough of captivity' to eradicate their misfortunes by 'taking manly steps ... hand-in-hand with men' (*Historical Documents*, No. 1, 1974, p. 252). The article also pointed to the importance of economic independence for women (*ibid.*, p. 263). The Association of Women of the Tudeh Party demanded total equality of rights between men and women, improvements in the financial situation of working women, equal pay for equal work, social insurance and the combatting of prostitution. The organisation was under separate leadership and published a bi-monthly women's magazine by the name of *Our Awakening* (*Bidari Ma*) which was edited by Zahra Eskandari-Bayat. The journal carried the slogan 'We, too, have rights in this country' and published articles on social, political, literary, and scientific matters. *Our Awakening* strongly criticised the Pahlavi Shahs and rejected legislation introduced by Reza Shah, particularly the Civil Code and the Penal Law, as oppressive to women (Kambakhsh, 1972, p. 56). According to a Soviet woman writer:

> From the day of its foundation, this organisation was active over a large field. Under its leadership, hundreds of women took part in mass demonstrations and protests. It did great work preparing for each universal women's congress, and even more valuable was its work after these congresses. Throughout the country there were conferences of working women, peasant women and housewives, at which all the most urgent and vital problems were the subject of lively discussion. (Yankachena,1959, 74–83)

The Tudeh Association of Women became a member of the International Democratic Federation of Women in 1947 and was represented in international conferences in Budapest (1948) and Peking (1949). The Association was outlawed in 1949. But two years later, the Tudeh Party managed to replace it with the Democratic Association of Women (Tashkilat Democratic Zanan). The Democratic Association of Women (DAW) organised a celebration on the forty-fifth anniversary of the Constitution by demanding the right to vote and criticising the government for its reluctance to extend the franchise (Abrahamian, 1982, p. 322). Article 6 of the constitution of the Tudeh Party was adopted as the declaration of aims and objectives of the DAW. According to this, the new association set the following objectives for itself:

1 To struggle towards the attainment of social and political rights for women via conferences and speeches.
2 Cultural development – the struggle against illiteracy.
3 Mobilisation of women.
4 The struggle against prostitution and moral decadence.
5 The struggle against the exploitation of women and young girls in factories – the establishment of working hours for women workers – the right to paid leave on weekends and public and annual holidays – equality of pay for men and women workers.
6 Prohibition of work for children below the age of fourteen.
7 Paid maternity leave of at least two months for women workers and servants.
8 Free kindergartens for the children of women workers and servants.
9 The establishment of training workshops for young girls from poor families.
10 The establishment of clubs, reading centres and libraries for women.
11 The establishment of women's newspapers and journals. (Mohebbi, 1946, p. 102)

The Women's movement

As to post-Reza Shah women's movement, the relative freedom of expression and the existence of a radical nationalist atmosphere resulted in the resurfacing of women's organisations in the 1940s and 1950s alongside a more independent but still pro-establishment Ladies Centre (set up by Reza Shah).

The Ladies Centre later became a training centre for women who could not afford to go into further education. Sedigheh Doulatabadi continued her work in the Ladies Centre but also renewed publication of her independent journal *Women's Language* (*Zaban Zanan*) in 1942. The first issue of the journal concentrated on issues such as housekeeping, child-rearing, health and education. The second issue carried an editorial on 'women and the bread shop' which protested at the shortage of bread and reported women's riots against it. The journal was banned by the government but Doulatabadi managed to get the ban revoked and continued publishing for a further ten issues. The next political article to appear in the journal invited the Allies to leave Iran, as a result of which the paper was closed down (Sheykholeslami, 1972, p. 94). Doulatabadi, however, was a pro-monarchy nationalist and remained faithful to the values of the constitutional and post-constitutional movement on women's emancipation. She opposed the values of womanhood espoused by communism and believed that Iranian women would gain more from reforms carried out within the established order (*Zaban Zanan*, 1945).

A large number of women's magazines were published in the late 1940s and early 1950s. These often carried radical names and published materials on social and political matters. *Zanan Pishrow* [Progressive Women] was a weekly magazine published by Sedigheh Ganjeh in 1949, which considered its aim to defend social justice and women's rights (Sheykholeslami, 1972). *Ghiyam Zanan* [Women's Revolt] was published in 1949 by Soghra Aliabadi, and covered social issues and literature. *Hoghugh Zanan* [Women's Rights] was published by Ebtehaj Mostahaq in 1951; *Azadi Zanan* [The Emancipation of Women] by Zafardokht Ardalan and *Zan Mobarez* [Militant Woman] (by Kobra Saremi, were all published in 1951. *Alam Zanan* [Women's Universe] which was published in 1944 by the British Embassy in Tehran, lasted a year and totalled fourteen issues. In the first issue *Women's Universe* published an interview with Dr Fatemeh Sayyah to introduce prominent women in Iran. *Women's Universe* reported on progress with regard to the position of women in other countries, and in particular, compared the position of women in Turkey with Iran (Golbon, 1975, pp. 351–7). *Banu* [The Lady] was published by Mrs. Nayereh Saidi from 1944 to 1947. This magazine took up the question of women's suffrage and proposed a debate among women on 'what will you do if you are elected to the Majles?' (*ibid.*, pp. 148–50). *Banuye Iran* [Iran's Lady] was published by Malekeh Etezadi, a royalist activist.

In 1942, the Iranian Women's League (Jamiyat Zanan Iran) was founded by Mrs. Badrulmoluk Bamdad who also edited a women's magazine by the name of *Zan Emruz* [Today's Woman]. In the same year Safiyeh Firuz founded the Iranian Women's Party (Hezb Zanan Iran) and Fatemeh Sayyah became its secretary. The party's constitution specified the aims of the party to be preservation of women's social status and education and awareness raising among women (Mohebbi, 1946, p. 101). *Zanan Iran* [Iran's Women] was the organ of this party which was edited by Fatemeh Sayyah and received contributions from Zahra Khanlari, Forugh Hekmat, Simin Daneshvar, a future prominent writer, and Jaleh, a poet. The Iranian Women's Party was particularly vocal about the issue of women's suffrage. In 1944, when the issue of electoral reform was raised in the Majles, the Women's Party lobbied sympathetic deputies to support women's suffrage in the Majles. The Women's Party criticised the opponents of women's suffrage for their 'medieval views'. The secretary of the party, Fatemeh Sayyah, rejected the idea that women's essential duties were towards the family and argued that, 'Where there are no rights there are no duties' (Golbon, 1975, p. 146). She stated that, 'The equality of rights in marriage and divorce is the first thing that women demand from the Majles, the government and society' (*ibid.*). She believed that equality of rights within the family was a necessary precondition for the fulfilment of the responsibility of motherhood undertaken by women and protested that: 'I ask you, how is it possible for a woman to perform the duties of motherhood ... when her husband can divorce her at will and take away her children from her and leave their upbringing in someone else's hands? (*ibid.*, p. 146).

The Women's Party was also interested in the condition of women prisoners. In 1944, the party gained permission from the Ministry of Justice to investigate the situation of women in prison. The Women's Party also proposed remedies for the economic and political instability in Iran at the time of the formation of separatist movements in Azarbayjan and Kurdistan. Fatemeh Sayyah wrote that:

> Our party strives towards equality of rights for men and women. The experience has proved to us that unless there is a genuine democracy in the country, there will be no stability .... A genuine political democracy should be based on genuine economic democracy .... The government should follow a rigorous programme of agricultural reform and distribution of land. (*Ibid.*, pp. 369–70).

In 1946, the Party of Iranian Women was transformed into a council to permit wider affiliation of women with different political views (Mohebbi, 1946, p. 101). The National Council of Women was founded under the same presidency and covered the bulk of the activities of independent women's organisations in this period. The objective of the organisation was 'to establish equality between men and women, prohibit polygamy, safeguard mothers' health, raise the educational standard of women, teach child care' (Woodsmall, 1960, pp. 80–3). The Women's Council, too, was most vigorous in its campaign for political equality. It had a large membership which was mobilized whenever required. The first Iranian woman lawyer, Mehrangiz Manuchehrian, was the council's legal adviser. Fatemeh Sayyah and Safiyeh Firuz were educated women with pro-Soviet views but they preferred to work independently. Dr Fatemeh Sayyah was born in the Soviet Union of Iranian parents and was invited back to Iran to occupy the post of lecturer in literature in the University of Tehran. She was keenly aware of women's subordination in Iran and wrote and lectured extensively on the subject (Golbon, 1975). Fatemeh Sayyah and Safiyeh Firuz represented the National Council of

Women in many international gatherings including Women and Peace Conference in Paris (1945), the International Women's Assembly in New York (1946), Asian Women's Congress in Delhi (1947), The Women's Rights Commission in Beirut (1949) and Geneva (1953).

Another women's organisation campaigned actively for women's enfranchisement. The New Path (Rah Now) was founded by Dr Mehrangiz Doulatshahi and worked on issues such as prison reform, encouraging research, and providing leadership training for young women. This organisation had a minority of male members since it believed that 'men can help in numerous ways to secure the vote for women' (Woodsmall, 1960, pp. 74–5).

Women also began to organise in professional and religious/ethnic associations. The Iranian Women's Medical Association was founded in 1953 to promote the interests of women physicians, and it maintained a relationship with women physicians in other countries, and educated the public on health matters. In the same year, the Association of Iranian Nurses was founded with the aim of raising the standard of nursing and promoting cooperation among nurses. Many of these professional associations affiliated themselves to international associations of their respective professions (Woodsmall, 1960, pp. 80–3). The Iranian Jewish Ladies' Organisation was founded in 1947 to carry out welfare services in general and raise the standard of health and education of women and children. The Armenian Women's Charity Organisation which was founded in 1927 continued its activities (*ibid.*). Other independent organisations of this period included: The Ladies' Association of Municipal Aid (1945) which aimed to assist municipal agencies in welfare activities; The Women's Art Committee (1950), which tried to promote art and industry among women and youth; The International Women's Club of Iran, which aimed to establish friendship, sympathy and understanding between women of all nations represented in Iran, and to reach the poor and help them to a better life (*ibid.*). The main charity organisation of this period was The Charity Association of Soraya Pahlavi (1952) which aimed to improve the health and education of the poor.

Transition from state nationalism to liberal nationalism

Foreign occupation, social diversification and political proliferation constituted the background for the separation of nationalism from the state. Reza Shah's state had fulfilled the post-constitutional demand for a strong executive power which could implement social reform and turn the country into a modern nation state. However, this was achieved at the expense of power and prestige by the Majles. The executive violated the Constitution and infringed the independence and integrity of the legislator in the process of the construction of a nation state in Iran. In the post-Reza Shah period, the demand for constitutional rule was raised and addressed to the autocratic state. Once again the state became the target of demands by constitutionalists. In the atmosphere of foreign custody and a humiliated and demoralised executive, the new generation of constitutionalists were able to reclaim nationalism and move the Majles once again to political centre-stage and to re-establish it as the embodiment of the nation's desire for political freedom and participation. Nationalism once again became the domain of independent political action.

In 1949, the National Front (Jebheye Melli) was established as a broad coalition of a number of socialist, secular nationalist and religious parties which had been active in the forties, to articulate the newly revived nationalist sentiments of the urban middle strata. Under the leadership of Dr Mohammad Mosaddeq, a lawyer and social reformer, the National Front featured prominently on the political centre-stage in the early 1950s. The main social base for liberal nationalism was the urban middle strata including government employees and other professionals, and business people including bazaar merchants, artisans, shopkeepers, students and intellectuals. The movement, however, had some following amongst the lower strata and some of its leaders came from the upper strata.

The National Front adopted the pro-independence and anti-despotic slogans of the constitutional movement. It proposed a programme which included social justice, implementation of the Constitution, freedom of political opinion, and improvement of economic conditions (Abrahamian, 1982, p. 253). The emphasis by the nationalist movement on individual freedoms and anti-despotism, and its independent nature, as opposed to state nationalism, placed it in the category of liberal nationalism (Siavoshi, 1990, pp. 2–3). The nationalist aspect of this movement, however, was often prioritised over its liberal aspects and the political outlook of some of the organisations which affiliated to the National Front was far from liberal (Ramazani, 1988, pp. 311–14). Nevertheless, one of the main distinguishing factors of the nationalist movement of this period was the belief that individual liberties and freedoms of expression, belief, press and association are essential ingredients of an independent and strong modern nation state. This set a precedent for similar arguments to be made by future nationalist movements. For the first time since the Constitutional Revolution, the ideals of nationalism and liberalism were distinguished from that of state modernisation. While the state became obsessed with social reform, the nationalist movement preoccupied itself with the question of democracy. This became one of the important characteristics of the era of nationalism.

The rise and fall of nationalist government

The post-Reza Shah context of broken sovereignty, revived nationalism and freedom of expression brought back parliamentary politics. Once again political opposition played a major role in the independent Majles, and the Shah's power and responsibilities were confined to constitutional ones. But this time, too, the end result of this process was a power struggle between the Majles and the executive power.

The period between the convocation of the Fourteenth and Seventeenth Majles (March 1944–April 1952) was an unstable one. The Fourteenth Majles included seven caucuses and the shifting alliances between them transformed it into 'a complex maze of political bargaining, and produced in the course of two years as many as 7 premiers, 9 cabinets and 110 cabinet ministers' (Abrahamian, 1982, p. 200). The same situation prevailed in the next three Majles. The causes of governmental instability were both internal and external. Parliamentary caucuses differed on major constitutional and social issues and foreign intervention in the country's affairs added to the difficulties. During this period, a major source of instability was rivalry between the British, the Americans and the Russians for influence over political events, and for trade concessions and monopolies. At this time, the main internal and external issues in the Majles included the constitutional place of the monarch and his powers in relation to the armed forces, the government and the Majles; electoral reform; the army budget; tribal strife and independence movements in a number of provinces, including Azarbayjan and Kurdistan, and foreign policy and oil concessions to the Soviets and the British.

Among numerous prime ministers who emerged in the 1940s and early 1950s, two made a particular impact on the resolution of these issues and the course of events. The first was Ahmad Ghavam, a constitutionalist who had been exiled by Reza Shah. He formed the Democratic Party which was moderate but willing to make alliances with the left. The programme of the party called for extensive economic and social reforms including women's suffrage. Ghavam included three Tudeh ministers in his Cabinet, ordered the closing of the Shii paper *Flag of Islam* (*Parcham Eslam*) for inciting demonstrations against unveiled women and arrested Ayatollah Kashani, a leading political cleric, for organising bazaar protests against the government (*ibid.*, pp. 233–4). During Ghavam's premiership, the Shah, who was bitter about the constitutional limitations imposed on him and unhappy with Ghavam's drift towards the

Tudeh Party, used an assassination attempt against his life as an excuse and forced Ghavam out of office. The Shah also convened the Constituent Assembly to amend the Fundamental Law to create a Senate, half of whose members were to be nominated by the Shah, and granted himself the power to dissolve the Majles (*ibid*., p. 250).

The advantages gained by the Shah after Ghavam's fall from power were, however, brushed aside by the second strong premier of this period, Mohammad Mosaddeq. He and his National Front supporters in the Majles argued that the Shah's power was excessive and that there was no government control over the country's national resources. The National Front denounced the revised agreement with the Anglo-Iranian Oil Company as a sell-out and demanded nationalisation of the oil company (*ibid*., p. 263). A series of power struggles developed between Mosaddeq and the Shah in which Mosaddeq frequently appealed to the public for support. In July 1952, the Shah refused to accept Mosaddeq's nomination for the position of war minister. Mosaddeq resigned and made a direct appeal to the public. The appeal, which was also supported by the Tudeh Party, received an enthusiastic response from the public who poured into the streets and staged strikes in his support (*ibid*., p.271). A week later the Shah gave in and asked Mosaddeq to form a new government. Mosaddeq continued his policy of restraining the Shah's extra-constitutional powers and also instructed the ministers to bring about thorough reforms of the judiciary, electoral practices and education. When the reforms were opposed by other political parties, Mosaddeq called a referendum which he won.

However, the Majles approval of the nationalisation of oil in March 1951 prompted the British to bring their naval fleet into the Persian Gulf and complain to the United Nations. In October 1951, Mosaddeq went to New York to defend Iran against the British claim to Iranian oil. In January 1952 British officials were expelled from Iran and in May Mosaddeq presented the Iranian case at the International Court at the Hague. The court's ruling in favour of Iran prompted the British to place major restrictions on Iranian trade with Britain. The Americans initially supported the nationalisation of oil because of their own rivalries with the British government but later became alarmed by the Tudeh support for Mosaddeq and allied themselves with the British.

The combined British and American frustration over the popularity of Mosaddeq's government and its uncompromising stand on the issue of nationalisation of oil prompted them to attempt to remove Mosaddeq by a *coup d'état*. By August 1953 the Tudeh Party's support for Mosaddeq had weakened and the pro-Kashani section of the National Front had defected as well. The diverse Shii opposition which was initially united in rejecting foreign domination and demanding the rule of the Constitution joined the National Front in an atmosphere of revived nationalism. But later, when it came to choose between supporting the anti-constitutionalist monarch supported by the West and the secular nationalist movement supported by the left, the Shii opposition chose the former. Western intelligence services, moreover, funded the bazaar and the clergy to lead an anti-Mosaddeq march in the streets of Tehran which was supported by the army. The Tudeh Party refused to support Mosaddeq and did not call out its masses of followers to counter-demonstrate. The army removed Mosaddeq from the office of premiership and the Shah, who had fled Iran, was reinstated. Mosaddeq was tried and imprisoned. After getting rid of the most powerful and independent prime minister in the Pahlavi era, the Shah dissolved the Seventeenth Majles and began an extensive crack-down on political parties.

Women and the nationalist government

The decade of parliamentary politics did not produce many legal reforms for women. In fact Majles legislation affecting women was limited to Ghavam's new labour law which tightened governmental control over child labour and proposed twelve weeks of maternity leave with full pay for women workers (Keddie, 1981, p. 121). But women's issues, including enfranchisement, were raised a number of times without bearing positive results in the shape of legislation. In 1944, the Tudeh deputies set up a fraction inside the Majles to press for Tudeh programmes including reforms of the labour and electoral laws, land reform and equality of rights for women (Kambakhsh, 1972, p. 69). The Tudeh fraction introduced a bill on the extension of the vote to women which was not fully debated. The bill was attacked by one of the deputies as 'against Islam and *Qoran*' (Tudeh Party, 1944, p. 834).

In 1949, Mosaddeq attempted to draft an electoral bill and proposed to include female enfranchisement on the grounds that the constitution specified equality of all citizens before the law. Women's organisations lobbied sympathetic deputies to support women's suffrage in the Majles. The religious section of the National Front however objected by claiming that Islam limited the vote to men. A clerical deputy argued that the existing laws adequately protected women and warned that any change would 'encourage political instability, religious decay and social anarchy' (*ibid.*, p. 276). Ayatollah Kashani wrote an article in a leading magazine, asking the government to prevent women from voting so that they would stay at home and perform their true task of rearing children (*ibid.*, p. 276). The clergy also organised demonstrations against women's enfranchisement. In Qom one person was killed and ten injured when religious students (*tollab*) poured into the streets in protest (*ibid.*, p. 276). In the end, the electoral bill that was drafted ignored women. Opposition to female enfranchisement was not limited to the clergy. Hasan Nazih, a secular politician, who played an important oppositional role against the Islamic Republic three decades later, argued that:

> As we know, women do not have any psychological capacity for holding political status. . . . Woman more than man is the slave of fanciful wishes. The feelings of ambition, jealousy and pride are found more in women than in men. Now, if she is allowed to participate in elections an incredible chaos will be created in a woman's world. She will want to attract men as well as wanting to prove her superiority. You will even get schoolgirls dreaming of becoming Majles deputies. The natural duties of women, such as motherhood and other family tasks, will be either totally ignored or seen as insignificant. (Golbon, 1975, p. 144)

Unlike the Tudeh Party, the National Front did not present a united front and a systematic programme of reform on women. Nor did it make any systematic effort to mobilise women. Indeed, the very nature of the Front as a coalition of various political ideologies made that extremely difficult. Although National Front allies would have agreed on general principles such as social justice, freedom of expression and adherence to the Constitution, it would have been highly unlikely for its religious wing to present a joint programme with the socialist wing on women's emancipation. At one extreme pole of the National Front there was the Iran Party which called for a socialist society with full equality for all citizens including women (*ibid.*, p. 256); this party organised a special section for women and was apparently popular among educated women (*ibid.*, p. 253). At the other extreme was the Society of Warriors of Islam (Mojahedin Eslam), connected to Ayatollah Kashani, which called for the implementation of the *shariat* and the reimposition of the veil (*ibid.*, pp. 256, 258). Middle of the way parties in the National Front did not make women's rights a priority. Mosaddeq, as a lawyer, did not himself say much on the question of women's legal position. The only available piece of writing by him on the issue of rights within the family was a description of the Islamic *shariat* on the family, but he gave no additional commentary of his own on this question (Afshar, 1979, 97). In his prime ministerial capacity, he prioritised nationalism over the issues of individual rights and social reforms. He argued retrospectively that 'Due to the struggle on the foreign front, I did not think it would be wise to launch internal [socio-economic] reforms that would cause great tension. [I did not want] to impose war on the Iranian people on two fronts. That is why I tried as much as possible to maintain the status quo in internal affairs' (Siavoshi, 1990, p. 57).

The strength of clerical and secular opposition within and outside the National Front which prevented the draft electoral bill from extending the right to vote to women contrasted sharply with women's heightened political activism. During the period of nationalist struggle, women were active in both public political protest and the women's rights campaign. For the second time since the constitutional period women found an opportunity to reassert their interest and involvement in politics. Women were now participating in street protests as members of mixed political parties. The struggle for nationalisation of oil brought thousands of banner-carrying women into the streets of Tehran and other major cities (*Women and Struggle in Iran*, 1, pp. 12–14). The Tudeh Party organised mass demonstrations that included women (Kambakhsh, 1972, p. 65). The Tudeh-led strikes involved thousands of working women. In the oil fields of Khuzestan, women went on strike and were wounded and killed in clashes with the army (Sadigh, 1973, p. 37). In Nain, a public demonstration was called by the Tudeh Party in which women from surrounding villages took part (*ibid.*, p. 59). Royalist women also actively campaigned for their political convictions and set up campaigns for the preservation of monarchy in Iran. Malekeh Etezadi, for example, initiated demonstrations in support of the Shah and founded a royalist party named Zolfaghar. It is said that she even rallied the support of prominent politicians and religious figures such as Ayatollah Kashani; he is said to have promised to support her efforts to preserve the monarchy (Mojahedin Khalgh, 1981, p. 12).

In short, a decade of post-Reza Shah parliamentary democracy in Iran did not result in major reforms on the position of women. The nationalist movement did not put forward an agenda on women different from that of the state. Indeed, it separated nationalism from modernisation and abandoned the latter to the Pahlavi state. This situation was similar to the post-constitutional period in the 1910s and 1920s where lack of strong executive power enabled parliamentary democracy to be exercised but the Majles failed to produce positive gender legislation. The future was to hold other examples of this, as will be demonstrated in relation to the nationalist led Provisional Government after the Revolution of 1977–79 (see chapter 7). In all these instances women's enthusiasm and participation in the national cause far exceeded the ability or willingness of the independent nationalist leadership to tackle issues related to women's rights and liberties.

Consolidation of the modernising state

The 1950s and 1960s were characterised by the consolidation of the modernising state and the rise of cultural nationalism as a major political challenge to the state. The post-*coup d'état* witnessed a substantial consolidation of the Shah's personal power. The process of consolidation included constitutional change, political repression, pro-American foreign policy, economic development and co-optation of the women's movement. The Shah's initiation of further constitutional amendments increased his tight control over the elections and strengthened his position in relation to the Majles. The Eighteenth Majles and those following were packed by royalist parties. Two of these were particularly dominant, the People's Party (Hezb Mardom) led by Asadollah Alam and the Party of Nationalists (Hezb Melliyun) led by Dr Manouchehr Eghbal. Although the Shah personally appointed his prime ministers, they enjoyed some degree of independence and authority at this stage. This was reflected in the economic plans and social programmes of this decade. The clergy, having supported the Shah against the National Front and the Tudeh Party, accommodated the Shah and adopted a conciliatory policy towards him for a decade (Arjomand, 1988, p. 85). Ayatollah Kashani was briefly imprisoned in 1956 but was released after publicly dissociating himself from the Fadaiyan Eslam's fanatical criticism of the Shah (Abrahamian, 1982, p. 421). Political parties were also suppressed. The Tudeh Party was outlawed immediately after the 1953 coup and its leaders were either executed or fled into exile in Soviet Union and Eastern Europe. Radical parties in the National Front were also banned. The Iran Party was outlawed in 1957 and many of the National Front leaders were arrested. Fadaiyan Eslam was also crushed and its leader Navab Safavi was executed in 1956. The secret police known as SAVAK (Sazeman Amniyat va Ettelaat Keshvar) was established in 1957 with the help of the CIA and later the Israeli secret service MOSAD.

In foreign policy, the Shah accommodated British interests but moved towards the United States as its main Western benefactor and ally. The United States was happy to become the dominant foreign power in Iran because of concern about Soviet intentions in Iran and the economic opportunities this presented. The Shah resumed diplomatic relations with Britain and settled the oil dispute. Although oil was nationalised in theory, real control remained with an international consortium. Moreover, the Mosaddeq policy of refusal and boycott of foreign aid was reversed. The Shah adopted a more aggressive policy of economic development based on foreign loans and direct aid from the West. Relying on increasing oil revenues and considerable financial aid and technical assistance from the United States, the Shah strengthened the army and embarked on a series of development plans in the 1950s and 1960s which pumped money into agriculture, industry, mining and transport. The Gross National Product began to increase rapidly. Money was also spent on health, education and welfare and during the 1950s and 1960s the number of hospitals and health clinics increased, the standard of health care improved and the infant mortality rate was substantially lowered. The number of schools, technical colleges and universities increased and the ranks of the student population inside the country and abroad swelled rapidly (Ahmadi, 1964). Development planning of the post-Mosaddeq era culminated in a six-point reform programme which included land reform, nationalisation of forests, sale of state factories to private entrepreneurs, profit-sharing for industrial workers, the establishment of a rural literacy corps, and the extension of the vote to women.

Women's activities, too, were subjected to political repression and government planning but did not stop altogether. The government paid attention to the question of social welfare, and women's activities were channelled mainly into welfare services. In 1956, the Ministry of Labour founded the Welfare Council for Women and Children. Thirty-five women representatives were appointed to run the council. The function of the council was to provide assistance to women workers and act as a general advisory body for women working in the industry. The council's objective was to improve labour conditions for women and children through the avenues of law, social welfare and health (Woodsmall, 1960, p. 72). In the same year, the government asked the United Nations to assist in training welfare personnel. The first trained Iranian social worker was Mrs Farman Farmaian whose work on women's welfare continued into the 1970s (Farman Farmaian, 1992). Most welfare work was done through government-sponsored and foreign-aid funded projects. With enormous enthusiasm and zeal, women took part in various urban, rural and tribal projects on health, literacy, midwifery, community development, agriculture, industry, home economics, child-rearing, dressmaking and handicrafts. Woodsmall described the activities and social backgrounds of these women as follows:

> The composition of women's organised activity in Iran, especially in Tehran, represents a considerable amount of social services rendered by volunteers. There are two main types of volunteer: a fairly large number of women of the leisured, well-to-do upper class, mostly over fifty years of age, without special training, pioneer leaders in women's rights and in the government aid programs. The bulk of the remedial service and direct social service program in Tehran is carried out by this group of volunteers; a body of younger women between thirty and forty-five, mostly in the professions, well educated, a number with Anglo-Saxon educational backgrounds, university graduates and some with training abroad. They are primarily concerned with preventive programs, social research and social education, and youth programs. Their interests and services are specialized and are based on study of the actual situation with the program planned accordingly. In general, these two types of volunteer workers, because of differences in their primary interests, backgrounds and age carry on independently but with sympathetic understanding. (*Ibid.*, pp. 76–7)

Women's publications continued to be produced, but these were mainly pro-royalist journals which followed the government line on the question of women's emancipation. *Women's Information* (*Ettelaat Banovan*) was published on a weekly basis and soon turned into the main officially approved women's magazine in Iran, enjoying a high circulation. *Women's Call* (*Nedaye Zanan*), *Iran's Lady* (*Banuye Iran*) and *Women of Iran* (*Zanan Iran*) were less significant magazines published in the late 1950s. The latter was edited by Touba Khan-Khani who was a committed royalist who wanted her journal to become the official voice of the party of the Shah's Crusaders (Fadaiyan Shah). Furthermore, women's professional interests were represented by various associations which were formed by women employees and professionals including teachers, civil servants, doctors, nurses and working women (Binder, 1962, pp. 195–7).

However, there still was a legitimate channel through which radical women could direct their feminist activities. The highlight of women's activities in the late 1950s and early 1960s was the campaign for women's votes. This campaign was conducted at this time by independent women's organisations, operating with the general consent of the government. The New Path League (Jamiyat Rah Now) was founded by Mehrangiz Doulatabadi in 1955 with the objective of raising the status of women. In 1956 the League of Women Supporters of the Declaration of Human Rights which was previously known as the Iranian Women's League, joined the campaign for the vote for women (Bamdad, 1977, p. 110). The third organisation to join was the Association of Women Lawyers which was founded by the first woman lawyer in Iran, Mehrangiz Manuchehrian. The Association demanded political rights for women, equality of rights in employment, referral of divorce cases to courts, abolition of polygamy and *sigheh*, and reforms on other aspects of the legal position of women. Such explicit and provocative demands were made by the Association in the same year that Sedigheh Doulatabadi, the pioneer of the women's movement in Iran, died at the age of eighty. These organisations got together and formed an independent Federation of Iranian Women's Organisations, which acted as a coordinating body for fourteen member organisations. The representatives of these organisations sat as a board of directors, which proposed 'to coordinate the activities of the member organisations and promote cooperation in carrying out their common goals' and 'to raise the standard of culture and education and improve the social, economic and health conditions of women (Woodsmall, 1960, p. 83). Membership of these women's organisations and the background of their leaders have been described as follows:

> The women leaders are all from influential families, but they do not have the access of their male relatives. Their numbers are small, the total membership of all the organisations having been estimated from 3,000 to 5,000. Nor are the women very aggressive in demanding equal rights. Their social position largely determines their loyalty to the regime, though some high born women are known to have been stanch Tudeh members. These women do not try to reach out for mass support, but are mainly preoccupied with winning favours from the government by supplication. (Binder, 1962, p. 198)

Another organisation of women that joined the federation was the Women's Council which had survived the censorship of the post-1953 era. The Women's Council became actively involved in the campaign for women's rights and even received an audience with the Shah in 1956 to submit a request by women for political rights (Woodsmall, 1960, p. 74). The list of demands put to the Shah included:

> reform of laws regarding the status of children and the implementation of divorce; banning polygamy; banning temporary marriage; removing all inequalities between men and women under the civil law; granting women the right to vote in Majles and Senate elections; granting women equal opportunities for government employment; removing all traditional or customary inequalities in regard to such employment; eliminating provisions of the penal code which permit husbands, fathers or brothers to kill their daughters, wives, or sisters; enacting a labour law which more nearly equalizes the condition of men and women; establishing social insurance for women as well as men; in educational work, recognition of the equality of women in administrative, technical, and teaching work; where women are qualified, to put them in charge of girls' schools; inviting women to participate in the high council on education; giving women supervisory positions in social welfare projects; and more vigorous protection of the legal right of women to vote in municipal elections. (Binder, 1962, p. 198)

The rise of cultural nationalism

The period 1960–3 was marked by a serious economic crisis, renewed urban instability and limited liberalisation. This was caused by the combined effects of the government's unpopular austerity measures and political liberalisation. In response to the Shah's request for further US aid, the Kennedy administration forced the Shah to conduct comparatively free elections, give liberal politicians cabinet posts and implement land reform. These measures were regarded as safeguards against the spread of communism in Iran (Abrahamian, 1982, p. 422).

During the early 1960s several strikes took place in Tehran, notably by civil servants demanding pay rises. Protests against the rigged elections of June 1960 which excluded pro-Mosaddeq or ex-Tudeh candidates were quite vocal. The Shah distanced himself from the elections and ordered new elections. The second round of elections in January 1961 produced some independent Majles deputies including some previous National Front leaders. The Shah appointed Dr Ali Amini, a pro-American liberal reformer, as prime minister. Amini dissolved the Twentieth Majles, exiled General Bakhtiar the head of SAVAK and gave ministerial positions to reformers who had criticised the Shah in the past (*ibid.*, p. 423). Hasan Arsanjani who was the minister of agriculture in Amini's Cabinet initiated a programme of land reform in 1962. But Amini's spell in office did not last long as he came into conflict with the Shah. His reforms proved too controversial for the Shah and the US government and agreement was reached to put him aside (Abrahamian, 1982, p. 424). In July 1962, Assadollah Alam became the new prime minister and his government amended Arsanjani's original land reform proposal. The Shah added other reforms to the programme and aimed to create an image of popularity by putting his six-point programme to a plebiscite. Dissatisfaction with both the content of the reform programme, which increased the state's share of land and industry and commerce, and the manner of its formulation by royal decree rather than debate in a free Majles, led to public protests. A religiously led uprising unfolded which was crushed violently with the help of the army; many people were killed and its leaders, including Ayatollah Khomeini, imprisoned or exiled.

One of the most important aspects of liberalisation during 1960–3 was the resurfacing of nationalist and religious opposition to the Pahlavi state. The leaders of the National Front, some of whom had just been released from prison, managed to put the pieces of the shattered National Front together and renewed their activities under the Second National Front. The Shii opposition was also revived after Ayatollah Borujerdi's death and opposition clerics such as Ayatollah Khomeini became vocal against the Shah. The main objectives of the second National Front were stated to be restoration of 'basic individual and social rights of the Iranian people guaranteed by the 1906 Constitution', establishment of 'legal government through free public elections' and adherence to an 'independent foreign policy which, although in accord with the United Nations Charter, would give priority to Iran's national interests' (Siavoshi, 1990, p. 90).

Although these political goals were overtly secular and nationalist, nevertheless the Second National Front was governed by a religious undertone which differentiated it from the first National Front. If the latter represented liberal nationalism, the former can be defined to represent cultural nationalism. The change of emphasis was facilitated by a decade of clandestine existence under political repression. The disintegration of the first National Front and strict state surveillance of its remaining leaders affected secular membership more than religious ones. The institutional autonomy of Shiism (as described in chapter 1) enabled prominent religious members to maintain a clandestine existence under the cover of religious activities. Furthermore, the dominance of the policy of modernisation and its zealous defence by the autocratic state forced the institution of Shiism to undergo modernisation itself.

The clandestine process of reconstruction of the Second National Front, therefore, became intertwined with a process of construction of a new Shiism which adapted religion to the requirements of modern life, and sought to provide contemporary solutions for contemporary problems (*ibid.*, pp. 88–9). The construction of the new cultural nationalism relied on the combination of the two strands of 'modernity' and 'tradition' in Iranian society. This was a combining of commitment to the ideals of modernity (which included economic prosperity, political freedom, national independence and social justice), acceptance of modern institutions such as the secular state, urbanisation, education, technology and so forth, and demand for the application of indigenous culture and tradition in relation to women and the family.

The Liberation Movement of Iran (Nehzat Azadi Iran), a most important new cultural nationalist organisation, reflected the new trend within the Second National Front. Founded by Mehdi Bazargan and Hojatoleslam Mahmud Taleghani, both of whom later played important roles in the Islamic Republic, the Liberation Movement aimed to present to the younger generation the 'true Islam' which was considered to be the source of inspiration for fighting internal despotism and foreign domination. Its main objective was, therefore, to bridge the gap between Islam and politics in order to establish a just and culturally authentic society (Chehabi, 1990). Shii modernism, particularly in relation to women, will be examined more closely in chapter 5. To conclude here, the coming together of an autonomous Shii institution and a reconstructed nationalism gave rise to cultural nationalism which further heterogenised the concept of modernity.

Women's political rights

As explained, women's activities in the post-Mosaddeq era revolved around the campaign for suffrage. In 1959, the issue of women's enfranchisement was brought up in the Nineteenth Majles. The clergy objected strongly to the idea. Abdolghasem Falsafi, a famous preacher, denounced women's right to vote and Ayatollah Borujerdi received Prime Minister Eghbal in Qom and vetoed the government's plan to hold a women's day parade in Tehran (Akhavi, 1980, p. 95). Instead, women were asked by the government to place wreaths on the grave of Reza Shah under the auspices of the People's Party (Binder, 1962, p. 198). The cancellation of the street march which had been requested by the Federation of Women's

Organisations was reflected in the press by an exchange of letters written by two leading clerics and the Women's Council about this event (*ibid.*). The issue of women's political rights was dropped from the Majles debate but it did not go away for long.

During the 1960–3 period of relative political liberalisation, the issue of women's votes became once again a point of contention between the state and the opposition with the women's movement playing an important role in pushing the issue forward. To start with the state policy on female enfranchisement, at least three different sets of interests were at play: those of the Shah, women, and the prime minister. During Amini's premiership these interests did not coincide. While women were lobbying for enfranchisement, the Shah was undecided and the prime minister was publicly opposed to it. Amini's stance was due to his policy of wooing the nationalist and religious opposition. Despite coming from a constitutionalist family and having liberal nationalist credentials, Amini was not very popular with the opposition because of his pro-American position and his acceptance of government posts in the past (Keddie, 1981, p. 155). He did not have the cooperation of the National Front but needed it to make his premiership viable. He preferred not to alienate religious and nationalist opposition further by advocating women's vote. In April 1962, Amini told a group of American reporters that 'Iranian women should devote their attention and efforts to social and charity activities' (*Iran Almanac*, 1963, p. 410). In May 1962, Amini spoke against women's suffrage again at a graduation ceremony held by the social work college:

> We have many government employees who have become corrupt and dishonest as a result of pressure from their wives who have tried to keep up with the Joneses. ... If Iranian women do not insist only on political rights, and turn to their social rights, they will get political rights, which are of secondary importance anyway, in time. ... In the United States, where women wear trousers, men are so hard-pressed by their wives that their life expectancy has become shorter and husbands die sooner ... In Iran, the situation is not much different ... I myself suffer from it. (*Ibid.*, 1963, pp. 410–11)

In the same month an Esfahani woman named Mrs. Hakimi took advantage of the new municipal Electoral Law which had been passed recently by the Majles and did not directly prohibit women and non-Muslims from participating, and prepared to run in the local elections for Esfahan Town Council. The High Council of Women's Organisations wrote to Amini requesting him to order the relevant officials to ensure that every facility was made available to Mrs Hakimi in her municipal electoral campaign. The letter emphasised that 'The new municipal Electoral Law does not specifically prohibit the participation of women in elections because a town is like one big family in whose cleaning and other material and moral affairs women have a bigger share than men ... These are precisely the type of social services to which your Excellency has repeatedly referred in your speeches' (*ibid.*).

The Shah, on the other hand, was motivated to allow women to participate in politics as this seemed in line with his modernism and was the logical conclusion of women's participation in society. Nevertheless, he was unhappy about pushing it because he was not at this stage in the same position of control over the women's movement as his father was when he initiated the unveiling and other gender policies. The Pahlavi method of gender reform was firmly based on a patriarchal model of the family, where the father assumed total control and initiative over the rights and responsibilities of the women in the family. The two Pahlavi Shahs saw themselves in the same light: as father of the nation who had to have total control over the women of the nation. As was the case in relation to women in the family, women of the nation, too, were not allowed to act independently and take initiatives for fear of what the unknown might bring about (Najmabadi, 1991, p. 61). The prerequisite for reform on women's political rights, then, was the Shah's control over the women's movement. The Federation of Iranian Women's Organisations was dissolved in 1961 and the High Council of Women's Organisations of Iran (Shoraye Aliye Jamiyat Zanan Iran) was set up in its place under the presidency of the Shah's twin sister, Princess Ashraf. Once the women's movement was brought under the royal wing and the independent-minded prime minister, Ali Amini, was removed from his post, state policy became more unified and the Shah was able to take the initiative and the credit for women's political rights.

A series of developments which resulted in violent suppression of the opposition finally led to women's enfranchisement. It was started by the new prime minister, Asadollah Alam, who followed Amini in July 1962, announcing that local elections would be held under the new law which did not ban women from taking part. The clergy stepped up its criticism of the state (SJR, 1978, pp. 316, 319–24). Ayatollah Khomeini sent a long telegram to Alam warning him against ignoring the advice of the clergy and advising him that:

> your illegal bill [on local elections] is contrary to Islamic Law, the Constitution and the laws of the Majles. The *olama* have publicly stated that the franchise for women and the abrogation of the condition that one must be a Muslim in order to be allowed to vote or to run in an election is contrary to Islam and the Constitution. If you think you can replace the Holy *Qoran* by the Zoroastrian *Avesta*, the Bible, and other misguided books, you are mistaken. If you think that you can weaken the Constitution, which is the security for the country's sovereignty and independence, with your illegal bill, then you are wrong. (Floor, 1983, p. 85)

Khomeini's supporters spread rumours in order to arouse public opinion against the electoral bill, claiming that women would be called up for military service and that young girls had already been taken to the barracks (*ibid.*, p. 84). Ayatollah Khansari declared himself against 'women's interference in social matters since this will involve women in corruption and is against the will of God ...' (*ibid.*, p. 89). Clerical opposition to the new electoral law was supported by the Second National Front who renewed its opposition to the Shah by asking for free and fair elections and objected to the drafting of an electoral law prior to free elections for the Majles. But some sections of the National Front also gave qualifying support to the clergy's opposition to women's enfranchisement. The Liberation Movement issued a circular in support of the clergy's opposition to the electoral bill. This circular had the double aim of inviting the clergy to act moderately on the question of women's enfranchisement and at the same time trying to protect the opposition to the Shah from the charges of fanaticism and backwardness. The Liberation Movement argued that government propaganda against the clergy had created a misunderstanding about the position the clergy had taken on women's enfranchisement, and tried to clarify the misunderstanding:

The Liberation Movement of Iran is compelled to provide the following explanation regarding the misunderstandings caused by the government, the opponent of *shariat* and independence, in the minds of Iranian youth and women and in the minds of foreigners:

1 What the *olama* and the majority of the Muslim nation want is not the prevention of the freedom and rights of everyone in the nation including men and women. What we all want is a parliamentary regime, lawful government and the preservation of lawful and rational rights and freedoms.
2 Islam and the Islamic *olama* are not against the rights and value of women. Islam was the first religion to give women economic rights and considers men and women equal and complementary.
3 It is unlikely that the *olama* consider women the inferiors and slaves of men. On the contrary, women have the right to preside over their own economic affairs. But the *olama* are aware that it is not in the nature of this government to serve any social group, let alone women. The *olama* are opposed to the hidden intentions of the government. The *olama* are worried that the aim of the government is to break the framework set by Islam and the Constitution; that by pulling women into the chaos of politics and its immodesty and slandering, the government aims to prevent women from performing their natural duties, and allow conflict to enter into the pure and warm nest of the family. Otherwise, if it could be confidently assumed that the government's intention were to eradicate corruption and immorality, who would want to prevent Muslim sisters from having the right to express and defend, as well as perform those natural duties that have been bestowed on them by the *shariat*, reason, and by nature? (Liberation Movement of Iran, 1983, pp. 177–8)

After a series of clergy-led demonstrations, in December 1962 Alam announced the cancellation of the new Electoral Law (Pazargad, 1966, p. 309). On 10 December 1962, the Association of Women Lawyers issued a statement on Human Rights Day, complaining about the government's retreat:

Whenever there is talk of progress in this country, there are certain circles which try to make sure that this progress does not apply to one half of the population – the women.... We pride ourselves on being Muslims. Islam is the religion of logic and reason. In the Muslim world today, many Islamic countries have given suffrage to their women and none has been ex-communicated for it.... The policy of demagogy should not force the government to act against the interests of the country by withdrawing the Local Electoral Law. ... The Government, to compensate for its improper act, should not only reiterate the Law, but should also repeal Section 1 of Article 10 and Section 2 of Article 13 of the Majles Election Law which prohibits women from participating in the elections.... The government's action in approving the Local Electoral Law was not an unprecedented act which might have justified its cancellation. In fact, the act was a traditional one but the withdrawal was an unprecedented act which will be condemned by posterity. Is the Government not ashamed of sacrificing one half of the population of the country for the sake of political expediency? (*Iran Almanac*, 1963, p. 411)

On 7 January 1963, members of the High Council of Women's Organisations, boycotted the celebration of the anniversary of the compulsory unveiling ruling of 1935 and instead staged a sit-in in the prime ministerial Palace to protest against the government's withdrawal of the new Electoral Law. A notice was presented to the prime minister saying 'In view of the continuing denial of the legitimate rights of women, and in particular the government's failure to hold local elections in which the right to vote would have been given to women, The Women's Associations of Iran advise the male and female public that as a sign of protest the usual joyous celebration on 7 January will not now be held' (Bamdad, 1977, p. 117).

On 9 January, the Shah launched a six-point programme of reforms which included extension of the vote to women. The six-point programme was announced by the Shah in the Congress of Peasants, at which 35,000 peasants from all over Iran took part including, for the first time, a Kurdish woman named Mahsoltan (Pazargad, 1966, pp. 310–11). It was also announced that the six-point programme, named as the White Revolution (Enghelab Sefid), would be put to a referendum. On 22 January a major demonstration was held by the opposition against the six-point programme. The clergy denounced it and considered the referendum unconstitutional and irrelevant as an alternative to the *shariat*. Ayatollah Khomeini reminded the people that 'The Islamic *olama* had previously felt the same danger to Islam, *Qoran* and the country when the government took measures to change the local elections. Now it seems that the enemies of Islam are trying to achieve the same things through fooling people [into a referendum].' (Tabari, 1983, p. 69). A one-day strike on 23 January was announced by women teachers and headmistresses, who spent the day distributing in girls' schools tracts and flyers which asked women to stand up and support votes for women and demanded that women should not be grouped with aliens and criminals as those not having the right to vote (Pazargad, 1966, pp. 312–13). The next day the daily paper *Ettelaat* reported:

> Secretaries, nurses, air hostesses, receptionists, typists, teachers, doctors, telegraph operators, and all other women government employees and office workers, yesterday obeyed their organisations' call for a strike to prove the value of women in modern society. Their strike was orderly in most offices except in hospitals and the Ministry of Post, where their strike would have paralysed essential services, and hence, was not carried out. At schools, women teachers refused to deal with their lessons and instead lectured their classes on women's rights. (*Iran Almanac*, 1963, p. 411)

On 24 January, the Shah went to Qom to distribute his lands. He made a speech in the Shrine of Hazrat Masumeh in which he said: 'Today, the masks have been removed and the true faces of black reaction and red destruction are showing. . . . I hold in disdain this black reaction whose ideal is the regime of Nasser in Egypt with 15,000 political prisoners and no Majles' (Pazargad, 1966, p. 313). The same day, twenty-two leaders of the National Front, three clerics and a few students were arrested. The referendum finally took place on 26 January and women were allowed to take part in the voting. In February, the regime announced a large majority in favour of the White Revolution. Members of women's associations marched to Marmar Palace and the Shah made a speech, stating that 'Our Revolution was not complete without women's full emancipation, and with this Revolution we have now made a huge leap from terrible backwardness into the ranks of the civilised societies of the twentieth century. By granting women the right to vote, we have washed away the last stigma from our society and smashed the last chain' (*ibid.*). On 3 March 1963 the government issued a decree which made the right of women to vote official and announced that Article 13 of the Electoral Law which barred women from voting was annulled and that the word 'male' would be deleted from Article 6 and Article 9 of the electoral law to bring it into line with the spirit of the Constitution (Bamdad, 1977, p. 120).

Later in the month of March, The Association of Women Lawyers demanded that the government should pledge itself to securing equal rights for women in relation to land reform (Bagley, 1971, p. 53). On 25 March the minister of agriculture announced that women had equal property rights (Pazargad, 1966, p. 315). Moreover, the minister of justice told a reporter of the daily *Ettelaat* that as women had achieved political rights, 'I can say that there is no longer any impediment to women becoming judges in this country' (*Iran Almanac*, 1963, p. 413). The judiciary, however, did not become open to women until 1968. The tension between the government and the opposition subsided at this point. But in June 1963, during the Islamic holy month of *moharram*, thousands of clergy, shopkeepers, office workers, teachers and students poured into the streets in response to a call from Ayatollah Khomeini to denounce the White Revolution. Khomeini made a speech on 3 June attacking the Shah for undermining Islamic beliefs, capitulating to foreigners, spreading corruption, and violating the Constitution. On 5 June his arrest led to further demonstrations and violent clashes with the riot police. After three days of demonstrations involving many deaths and injuries, the government finally gained control and arrested the leaders of the National Front and later exiled Khomeini to Turkey from where he went on to live in Iraq until 1978.

The elections for the Twenty-first Majles ultimately took place in September 1963. For the first time women took part in the voting and stood for election. Six women were elected to the Majles and two women were appointed by the Shah to the Senate. Once again in the case of women's rights, what elected liberal and nationalist governments did not undertake was achieved by arbitrary action of an autocratic ruler.

5 Women and the era of modernisation

The post-1963 period had a number of features. It witnessed state modernisation and a drive towards the image of 'The Great Civilisation', an image reconstructed by the state with reference to the ancient Persian Empire. This process of modernisation was accompanied by political repression. State modernisation was also closely associated with Westernisation, and strongly supported by American foreign policy and the Western mass media. Modernisation of gender relations was a heterogenous process which affected women in unpredictable and contradictory ways. The modernisation process gave rise to further separation of state from society, alienation and radicalisation of secular opposition, and a growing Shii modernist movement.

All this facilitated the establishment of the final phase of the discourse of modernity, during the 1960s and 1970s, which was characterised by a rapid process of diversification and disintegration.

State and society in 'The Great Civilisation'

The Pahlavi state had always suffered from a degree of externality to society, which had its basis in the fact that neither of the Pahlavi Shahs gained the throne on the basis of a social movement and each managed to alienate most sections of society as a result of ruling through a combination of authoritarianism, favouritism and patronage. This externality, however, gained new dimensions in the 1960s and 1970s with the growth of oil revenues and near-complete control by the state over civil society (Vielle, 1988; Zubaida, 1989a, pp. 162–3). The steady increase in oil production from the 1950s to the early 1970s brought a steady increase in income. A steep increase in income then resulted from OPEC's (Organisation of Petroleum Exporting Countries) assertive role in breaking foreign control over oil prices. The rise in both price and production, combined with gaining effective control of the oil industry (which resulted from renegotiation of the 1954 agreement with the International Consortium), raised the share of oil in government revenues to 86 per cent

(Siavoshi, 1990, p. 27; Najmabadi, 1987a, p. 215). The state was now able to act independently of social forces by relying on two external sources of support, that is, oil revenue and US military, technological and financial backing. Another aspect of the state's increasing externality was its tight control over society which included state domination of the economy, ideological rule and political repression. In these respects, the state negated civil society by attempting to assume all its functions.

In the 1970s the state followed a policy of ideological transformation of Iranian society. The Shah devised the larger than life ideology of 'Great Civilisation' to accompany the arrival of Iranian society into the ranks of prosperous countries. By 1977 the ideology of 'Great Civilisation' was in full swing and dominated every aspect of Iranian life. The history of Iran had been rewritten and the Iranian calendar itself was changed to convey the sense of a continuous non-Islamic civilisation in Iran. An image of power and military strength was projected through accumulation of the most sophisticated and up-to-date armoury. Like the great ancient kings Cyrus and Daryus, the Shah prided himself on leading a strong and loyal army and on having at his disposal a sophisticated spy network known as the 'Shah's eyes and ears'. The modern equivalent of the latter was the deadly secret police SAVAK. Like the ancient civilisation, modern Iran was politically and ideologically led by a single political party, the Rastakhiz (Resurgence) Party was set up on the ruins of the Iranian Constitution to lead the country into the age of 'The Great Civilisation'.

An image of prosperity and compatibility with Western civilisation was also created: nuclear power generators were built; prestigious festivals of music, art and culture were set up; delegations were sent to major international conferences; and sportsmen and women were sent to compete in the Olympics. The most glamorous holiday resorts, casinos, hotels, palaces, high-rise buildings and stadiums were built; the entertainment business and pop music were promoted; and mass media dominated people's lives. Traditional practice and life-style were systematically demoted. The life-style of the royal family was presented as the example to be aspired to by ordinary people and imitated by the newly rising, luxury-seeking, consumerist, upper and middle classes; it became fashionable for well-to-do Iranians to shop extravagantly in Western department stores and take seasonal holidays in Western ski and beach resorts.

The ideology of 'Great Civilisation' included a gender dimension. The royal family was presented as the ideal model for the family in Iran. The Shah, as the ideal Iranian man was powerful, masculine, single-minded, moralistic, protective and the undisputed head of his family and nation. He believed in the participation of women in society but would not tolerate women 'who tried to imitate men'. He was not 'influenced by any woman in his life' and 'respected women as long as they were beautiful, feminine, and moderately clever' (Fallaci, 1976, pp. 271–2). He believed that 'women's natural endowments required them to be primarily wives and mothers, but if they needed to take up other roles society should provide the opportunity for them to do so' (Pahlavi, 1960, p. 235). He disliked Western feminism and believed that Iranian women had 'neither the need nor the desire' to interest themselves in such nonsense (*ibid.*). The Queen, represented the ideal stereotype of emancipated Iranian woman, and, as such, had everything that the Shah desired in a woman. As a woman she was beautiful, feminine and elegant; as a wife she was loyal, subservient and caring; as a mother she was devoted and conscientious. She believed that her prime responsibility in life was looking after her husband and children but her role as a Queen required her to take an interest in extra-familial affairs. She left the serious business of the state in the hands of her husband and took up 'feminine' pursuits such as social welfare, education, art and culture (Blanch, 1978).

The official ideology embraced the women's movement even more tightly. In 1966 The High Council of Women's Organisations, which consisted of a number of independent women's organisations, was abolished in the interest of further uniformity and tighter control from above. The Women's Organisation of Iran (WOI) was founded under the presidency of Princess Ashraf and the vice-presidency of Mrs Farideh Diba, the Queen's mother (Sanasarian, 1982, pp. 83–93). The supreme board of the organisation consisted of one woman, Mrs Farrokhru Parsa, who was the minister of education, and nine men who held the positions of speaker of the senate, speaker of the parliament, minister of justice, minister of economy, minister of the interior, minister of health, mayor of Tehran, and the chief of police. This was the second women's organisation to come into existence since the constitutional period which had male leadership. The Ladies' Centre set up by Reza Shah and the Women's Organisations of Iran both involved women at grass-roots level and men at decision-making level. The WOI set up various committees in charge of health, literacy, education, law, social welfare, handicrafts, international affairs, provincial affairs, membership and fund raising. The committees were chaired by upper-class women connected with the royal court (*Iran Almanac*, 1967, p. 522). The first general meeting of the organisation held in February 1966 was attended by 7,000 women which passed the constitution of the organisation and pledged itself to open branches all over the country. Members of the WOI were prohibited from taking part in political activities but the WOI developed close cooperation on women's issues with women Majles deputies and senators and the New

Iran Party. With the establishment of the WOI, both the objectives and the activities of women became subject to directives from above, especially since no other independent women's organisation was allowed to exist (Najmabadi, 1991).

The Women's Organisation of Iran became a closed, hierarchical and non-democratic institution and suffered from the decay and corruption inherent in such institutions. But this did not necessarily make it a mere puppet of the Shah. Like other official organisations, the WOI developed its own identity and culture. Many royalist women who were active in it were genuinely interested in the problem of women's subordination and had been campaigning for women's rights since the 1940s. The identity, culture and interests of the WOI did not necessarily coincide with those of the Shah in every single instance (Afkhami, 1984). The WOI played an important role in promoting positive policies on women within the state machinery (Najmabadi, 1991, pp. 62–3). In 1975 the secretary of the WOI, Mahnaz Afkhami, was promoted to the newly created post of Minister of Women's Affairs. The constitution of the WOI was amended to include 'preparing and coordinating women for active participation in Iran's national development within the confines of the Rastakhiz Party' (Sanasarian, 1982, p. 83). Ms Afkhami announced that the branches of the Women's Organisation of Iran around the country encouraged women to participate in Rastakhiz Party activities (*Iran Almanac*, 1976, p. 352). In 1976 out of the 5,100,000 members of the party 1,450,000 were women and 2,885 women had declared their candidacy for the election for 'democratic councils', which were supposed to be the grass-root bases of the Party (*Iran Almanac*, 1977, p. 422). The ideology of 'The Great Civilisation' in Iran was supported and applauded by the majority of Western governments and their mass media. Images of a modernising monarch achieving tremendous progress despite the enormous economic and social odds filled the Western press in the 1970s.

But the artificiality of 'The Great Civilisation' was occasionally perceived by a small minority of Western social scientists, humanitarian organisations and media reporters anxious to carry out balanced studies. Indeed, the golden age of civilisation in Iran was being perceived quite differently by various categories of Iranians. The ruthless drive of the Iranian state in the 1970s to build an image of grandeur and international prestige meant that despite the huge oil revenues, the real experience of many urban Iranians consisted of a daily struggle against high inflation, shortage of basic foodstuffs, a severe housing shortage and high urban and rural unemployment. The government's agricultural policies created a mass of rural migrant workers who found insecure employment on construction sites in urban centres and lived in shanty towns which developed rapidly on the margins of the cities. The collapse of the construction boom in the late 1970s created unemployment amongst the shanty town dwellers and the high rate of inflation reduced their standard of living sometimes to the point of starvation. Shanty towns around the capital were an ugly open sore, wounding the conscience of the socially minded middle class and the intelligentsia. They were also a source of embarrassment to the modernising monarch and a potential base for populist opposition to the Shah.

But despair and frustration in the 1970s was not limited to the underprivileged. The contamination of all aspects of the economy and society by the growing cancer of corruption affected most of the urban strata. The stake the Pahlavi Court held in social and economic development was a major source of corruption throughout society. The immediate family and the relatives of the Shah were all major shareholders in private companies, export and import businesses, construction firms, agribusinesses, factories, private hospitals and schools, and any other profitable venture that was going on. It was a common experience for the capital-holding, upper and middle classes to be overrun by the royal family in their attempt to set up a business or acquire shares.

Moreover, most of the top jobs in the civil service and in government controlled services, such as national radio and television, went to those connected with the Court. Many wage-earning middle-class people were frustrated in their attempts to get promotion. This was true even in the army where many officers from lower-class backgrounds or without high connections, or unwilling to be ingratiating towards the leadership never rose above the rank of colonel before retirement. The same also applied to welfare organisations. Most welfare centres, hospitals, clinics and other projects dealing with social services were chaired or directed by the Pahlavi family and independent organisations were either squeezed out or made ineffective and insignificant. The Shah himself announced with pride that the Queen was the head of more than forty organisations dealing with education, welfare, health, medicine, culture, art and research (Pahlavi, 1975, p. 206). The state bureaucracy which had an extremely tight hierarchical structure was steeped in corruption and bribery. The bureaucracy operated with an ideology of non-accountability towards those whom they served and acted in a disdainful manner towards the poor and the needy. Despite the concrete benefits that some from the lower classes received through social and medical insurance and welfare and education, their overall experience in dealing with state-run organisations was that of frustration and humiliation.

The above policies and practices followed by the state and the Court created a sense of estrangement of state from society. But political repression proved to be the most alienating aspect of Iranian society in the 1970s. It would not be an exaggeration to say that the degree of disparity of power between the monarch and the people in the 1970s was unprecedented hitherto in the modern history of Iran. The Shah enjoyed the backing of a modern army and a sophisticated deadly secret service. The state had a free hand in monopolising economic, social and political institutions to the benefit of the official ideology. The Shah expected his subjects either to follow his political dictates or remain passive and apolitical. Those who refused to be manipulated or blackmailed into silence by the possibility of personal material gain, and followed a third way of open political opposition, suffered the full brunt of the SAVAK repression. In 1975, the Shah announced that political pluralism did not meet the political needs of the era of 'The Great Civilisation'.

The two-party political system was abolished and the Rastakhiz Party was introduced to provide ideological leadership for the nation in the age of 'The Great Civilisation' (Pahlavi, 1975, pp. 199–205). The party opened branches all over the country and demanded mass membership. Rumours of SAVAK surveillance of non-members and official pressure brought to bear on the employees of state and private organisations to become members meant that the party soon acquired a large affiliation. The emphasis of the Shah on the ideological (rather than political) role of the party turned it into something resembling the ideological wing of the SAVAK. The party penetrated educational, welfare and other social institutions and conducted ideological campaigns in them. This completed the state's domination of society and increased its separation from the civil society. It was within this context that the gender policies of the modernising state were constructed.

Modernisation of the family

By the late 1960s the only area affecting women's rights that had not been touched upon by the state was the family. The main demands put forward by the women's movement since the constitutional period, namely education, unveiling, desegregation of the sexes, raising the age of marriage, entry into the professions, political rights and improvement of women's rights within the family, had all been achieved, albeit to a limited extent and in an undemocratic manner, except for the last which had not received any attention.

After the achievement of political rights, the attention of women activists turned to the question of family. In 1964 Tehran University's Institute of Social Studies conducted a study on marriage and found that the average age of marriage was between twenty-five and twenty-nine for men and fifteen and nineteen for women. From a study of 1,094 marriage contracts in Tehran and Kermanshah, it was found that 65 per cent of all contracts made in Tehran and 47 per cent in Kermanshah contained stipulations by women to prevent their husbands from exercising polygamy (*Iran Almanac*, 1964, p. 544). It was also reported in a national daily newspaper that 78,000 families were polygamous in Iran. The number of households in 1966 census was 5,069,320 (Friesen & Moore, 1977, p. 112). The newspaper article argued against polygamy by saying that because the number of men exceeded the number of women, the practice of polygamy meant that many young men had to be without a wife and that is why there were 1.5 million eligible bachelors in the country (*ibid.*, p. 541). In the same year, The Society for the Protection of Family Life called a press conference and complained about the lack of interest on the part of women Majles deputies in improving women's legal position: 'After a year of equal suffrage rights of women, not a single woman or man deputy elected with women's votes, has taken a step to safeguard women's rights in family matters. A husband can still throw out his wife any time he feels like it' (*ibid.*).

In 1967, a bill was presented to the Majles by the New Iran Party which proposed to reform the Iranian family structure. The bill was codrafted by the WOI and became known as the Family Protection Law. The bill, it was claimed, preserved and protected family life by restricting or making illegal these prevalent practices which damaged the stability and health of the family. These practices were defined as arbitrary divorce, polygamy based on pleasure, and the man's right to child custody. The Family Protection Law was not meant to replace the Civil Code of 1931 and the Marriage Act of 1937, but to amend these in a few areas which were considered contrary to the requirements of a modern society. The old laws prevailed in general, except when they came into conflict with the Family Protection Law. On these points, the courts were obliged to act according to the latter.

The Family Protection Law of 1967 consisted of 24 Articles. Articles 1–7 reintroduced secularisation of marriage and divorce registration which had, since it was first legislated in the Civil Code, returned to the control of the clergy. Article 8 specified that divorce could only be initiated through submission of an application to a family protection court. These courts were obliged to attempt to bring about a reconciliation and, if that failed, to issue a certificate of irreconcilability, after which the divorce could be registered in divorce registry offices. Article 9 put the responsibility for reaching agreement on maintenance and custody of children on the couple and obliged the courts to intervene only if that arrangement broke down. This applied if both partners were willing to divorce and there was no conflict over child custody and maintenance. Otherwise, Article 13 left responsibility for determining and fixing child custody and maintenance to the courts which would decide on the basis of what was beneficial to the welfare of the child.

Article 14 specified the wife or husband's imprisonment for over five years and his or her disappearance as legitimate grounds for divorce in addition to those other grounds specified in Articles 1121–1132 of the Civil Code. The woman was also given permission to initiate divorce if her husband took another wife without her consent. Article 15 required the husband to seek permission from the court if he wanted to take a second wife and specified punishment if he failed to do so. When permission was sought, the courts would decide on the basis of evidence given and through enquiries, including the testimony of the first wife. The rest of the Family Protection Law of 1967 endorsed relevant articles of the Civil Code and the Marriage Act (Naqvi, 1967).

In 1971, a six-day women's family planning conference was organised by the WOI and the ministry of health. The legal age of marriage was discussed and recommendations were made on raising it for women and abolishing the provision of Article 1041 of the Civil code which allowed women to marry under the age of fifteen in special circumstances (*Iran Almanac*, 1972, p. 567). In 1972, the committee studying the Family Protection Law of 1967 recommended amendments to do with child custody, joint ownership of family assets, and payment of alimony to divorced women out of the assets held by the family (*ibid.*).

In 1973, the Association of Women Lawyers criticised the Family Protection Law of 1967 for allowing men to take a second wife even if it was with the consent of the first wife and also for depriving a wife from the right to ask for divorce if her husband suffered from a contagious disease (*Iran Almanac*, 1973, p. 434). The Women's Organisation of Iran also announced that a special committee had been set up to look into the Family Protection Law to recommend necessary amendments. In 1975, the Majles passed a bill proposing amendments to it. The 1975 amended Family Protection Law had 28 Articles. It raised the age of marriage to twenty for men and eighteen for women, but asked the family protection courts to consider applications from women over fifteen (Article 23). Article 18 gave equal rights to men and women in applying to the courts to stop the wife or husband from taking employment which was detrimental to the family. But the courts could not stop a man from working unless it was satisfied that this would not interfere with financial and other affairs of the family. Articles 16 and 17 tightened up Article 15 of the 1967 Law by specifying the conditions under which the courts can allow a man to take a second wife. These included permission of the first wife. While in the 1967 Law if a man was financially able there was nothing to stop the courts from allowing him to take a second wife, the 1975 amendment made the court's agreement conditional upon the agreement of the first wife, her lack of consent to sex, mental illness, barrenness or disappearance. Both laws, however, specified that the woman had the right to ask for divorce if she disapproved of the court's decision to allow her husband to take a second wife (Ghorbani, 1989, pp. 144–60).

The final area of state policy on the family was abortion. The background to this was pressure to control population growth. Comparison of the 1956 and 1966 censuses revealed that the rate of growth of the population had increased to 3 per cent and the population was even younger than in 1956. The state initiated an extensive programme of family planning in 1967 (Momeni, 1977, p. vii). A study of abortions carried out in Farah Maternity Hospital in Tehran, conducted in 1969, revealed an increasing rate of abortion from 11 to 15 per cent since the beginning of the family planning programme, and concluded that the programme had not yet been effective in preventing unwanted pregnancies in lower socio-economic groups (Jalali & Payman & Majd, 1977, p. 275).

A further study conducted in 1974 in Tehran's Women's Hospital pointed to a steady increase in the number of abortions (*Iran Almanac*, 1975, p. 418). The report indicated that 60 per cent of the 30,699 miscarriages referred to the hospital in the previous ten years had been self-induced. According to the report, these abortions had been attempted by inexperienced people using drastic methods such as administering citric acid, opium or permanganate and even rupturing the uterus with knitting needles. In 1977 abortion was made legal. Under the new Abortion Law, doctors were permitted to perform an abortion if the couple requesting it submitted reasons acceptable to the physician on humanitarian grounds, if the foetus was not older than twelve weeks, and if the abortion would not endanger the mother's life. Abortion was also allowed in cases where the baby would be born with an incurable disease, and the mother's permission was specified as sufficient to procure an abortion (*Iran Almanac*, 1977, p. 423).

The family laws of the 1960s and 1970s were the flagship of the state's modernisation policy. Despite the state pretence that these laws were aimed at liberating women and revolutionising their position, there were other motives behind them, such as population control, and they had a much more limited aim than was pretended. In reality, far from being part of a coherent gender policy, this legislation responded to immediate and conflicting pressures. On the one hand, the rapid growth of population with its explosive economic and political implications put enormous pressure on the state to devise polices to control it. The result was an extensive family planning programme, and in the same year, a family law which raised the age of marriage and limited polygamy. Later, free abortion was also provided to compensate for the lack of effectiveness of the family planning programme among the lower classes. These population control policies coincided with the aims of the women's lobby since no doubt whatever the motive behind them these policies had a positive consequence for those women who had access to the law. They gave women a longer pre-marriage life and hence increased the possibility of education and employment, they gave women some choice in the type of marriage they entered into or remained in, and they gave women some control over their bodies. Furthermore, the existence and rights of unmarried pregnant women were for the first time acknowledged because of the provision of free abortion.

Other social pressures on the state which coincided with women's demands included those for stable families and child welfare. Curbing the male right to arbitrary divorce decreased the rate of divorce in the decade following the passage of the Family Protection Law of 1967 from 16.5 in 1966 to annual rates of 9.8 to 11 in subsequent years (Vatandoust, 1985, pp. 121–2). The move towards the monogamous family also worked to stabilise the family, although the ratio of polygamous to monogamous households was reported to be insignificant anyway (Momeni, 1977, p. 175). This may be one of the reasons why it was not worthwhile for the state to risk conflict with the clergy by banning polygamy.

Moreover, the prevalent ideas of child psychology and welfare did not agree with some of the practices resulting from the existing child custody laws. Forcible separation of children from mothers after divorce when many mothers were not allowed any access, was one. Many fathers, given custody, tended to place the child with female relatives as it was not culturally approved for them to raise their children on their own. As a result, children of divorced parents were in danger of being deprived of both parents, hence the social pressure towards the improvement of mothers' custody rights. The pressures of modern society affected the Islamic state in the same way (see Part 3). The setting up of the family protection courts was also in line with state policy of continuing along the secularisation route set out by Reza Shah to curb the power of the clergy.

On the other hand, however, the state was subject to other forces which contradicted those policies with emancipatory potential for women. The social conservatism of state officials and the Shah himself, in particular, was an important one. Another was the threat of clerical revolt which was potentially possible because of the autonomy of the institution of Shiism (as described in chapter 1), despite the political quietism of the majority of the clergy during this period. These negative pressures were also reflected in the family laws of this period. Despite consecutive legislation, the family laws of Iran in the late 1970s still considered the man as the head of the household. Divorce was still considered a 'natural' right for a man while a woman had permission to initiate divorce 'on behalf of her husband'. A man still had the right to demand sexual intercourse from his wife and lawfully force her to comply. Polygamy was still considered the right of the husband despite being curbed. A woman still had to obtain her husband's permission to travel and take up a separate place of residence. There was still a lower legal age of marriage for women, and for her first marriage a woman still had to have her father's permission. Women still inherited less than men. There were countless other male privileges, which put together would undisputedly prove the dominance of patriarchal family relations in this period.

Familial changes, then, on the whole only scratched the surface of the problem of male–female inequality and the law still concentrated on curbing the excess of male power in the family rather than fundamentally shifting it. As a result of social conservatism, the male dominated family and the subordinate position of women within it continued to be upheld despite the confirmed need to adjust the structure of the family to changing social conditions.

Modernisation of women's social position

It is often said that under the Pahlavis the legal position of women changed more rapidly than their social position (Pakizegi, 1978, p. 217). The contrary seems to be a better reflection of the situation of urban middle-class women who were targeted as the main beneficiaries of state reforms. The Pahlavi legislation lagged far behind the progress that individual women made in social and economic fields. Indeed, it could be argued justifiably that women's progress occurred despite limited and inadequate legal change and irrespective of a contradictory state ideology and social policy. It has already been shown how the majority of reforms concerning the family did not go deep enough to fundamentally alter the patriarchal basis of the family and women's role in it. In the same way, state policy affecting women's social position was of a limited and contradictory nature.

The state constructed the modern woman in at least three different ways. On the one hand, urban centres were exposed to the conception of women as sex-objects through the mass media. On the other hand, state policy on the family attempted to regulate female sexuality in accordance with the Islamic *shariat*. Thirdly, in responding to the pressures of national development, the state formulated policies which contained emancipatory potentials for women. These different and sometimes conflicting intentions were reflected in gender policies of the 1960s and 1970s. The response to developmental and political pressures resulted in a series of laws which were intended to facilitate women's participation in society. The Family Protection Law of 1967 and its 1975 amendments included a conception of women as income earners by changing the divorce and custody rules in favour of women. These laws also reflected the growing social equality of men and women by making the family protection court rather than the husband the point of reference in family matters.

In 1967, the Constitution of 1906 was amended to make it possible for the Queen to exercise regency in the event of the Shah's death before their son reached the age of twenty. The monarch, however, remained male in the Constitution (Bagley, 1971, p. 54). In 1968 the Majles passed a law on women's social services. Female high school graduates who were unmarried and did not have dependents to care for were required to enter the Women's Literacy and Health Corps and serve in rural or backward urban areas for two years. In the same year, the last of the public positions closed to women, the judiciary, opened its doors to them. In 1970, the Passport Law which required women to have written permission from their husbands for each trip abroad was criticised by Senator Mehrangiz Manuchehrian, a women's rights campaigner since the 1950s. As the head of the Association of Women Lawyers which was now a pro-establishment organisation, she argued that the Passport Law discriminated against women:

> The question is one of the equality of men and women, recognised by the Shah and People Revolution as a major point, and also by the universal Declaration of Human Rights. All citizens should be equal in the eyes of the law. No rights should depend upon the physiological characteristics of a citizen. Article 14 of the Passport Act disregards all this, and I think stands in violation of the Constitution, because the Constitution lays down conditions under which a citizen's right to travel can be restricted. There is no restriction on the basis of sex. Article 14 of the Constitution states that no Iranian may be exiled, or prevented from residing in a place, or forced to reside in a place. (*Iran Almanac*, 1972, p. 568)

Six years later the government announced that a woman would not be required to obtain her husband's permission for each trip abroad and once permission was granted it would be sufficient for multiple trips. This was another example of the government's gender policies in the 1970s which allowed amendments but not fundamental social change. The last legal change introduced in the 1970s was the 1977 bill presented to the Senate which proposed to allow a woman to work part-time until her child(ren) reached the age of three (*Keyhan Havai*, 47). This bill did not become law under the Shah, but it was passed later as an Islamic law in the Islamic Republic (see Part 3).

The legislation of this period affecting women's social roles speaks for itself: it aims to respond to the requirements of a modern economy and society yet is piecemeal, conservative and firmly placed within male dominated social relations. A comparison of the actual legal changes with the demands made by official women's movement can further demonstrate the limitations of state policy on women. Throughout the 1970s, the demands of the Women's Organisation of Iran and other pro-establishment women proved far more radical than the reforms that the state was willing to entertain. In 1975, the Women's Organisation of Iran held a conference to mark the fortieth anniversary of the unveiling of women in Iran and the beginning of the United Nations' International Women's Year. The conference passed an eleven-point resolution which called for the 'complete elimination of discrimination against women [and] equal opportunity and welfare for women from all walks of life'. The points included in the resolution were as follows:

> Equal rights for Iranian men and women, and the improvement of laws, regulations, and methods of implementation which may in some way prove discriminatory and detrimental to women.
>
> Extension of social security coverage to housewives.
>
> Job security for working mothers who are temporarily prevented by work from caring for their children because of working.
>
> Requiring public and private organisations to provide facilities for working mothers.
>
> Elimination of any form of discrimination in the distribution of jobs between men and women.
>
> Utilisation of women in varied tasks, and basic measures to elevate women from low paying positions to productive jobs with higher returns, and their participation in planning and decision-making posts.
>
> Provision of part-time employment for housewives, and the creation of productive activities in rural areas for women during periods of seasonal underemployment.
>
> Application of the Labour and Social Insurance Laws to cottage industries employing girls and women.
>
> A multi-dimensional campaign to increase public awareness of the true status of women in the family and society and combating of unwarranted beliefs and prejudices which prevent the full social and economic participation of women.
>
> Extension of educational programmes in order to inform women of their legal rights and the existing means for utilising these rights. (*Iran Almanac*, 1975, p. 419)

The resolution did not lead to government action or legislation. The more limited women's demands, the more chance there was of positive government response. The limited and conservative legal change was complemented in the 1970s with a state ideology which stereotyped women and men. At the same time that some pro-establishment women were co-ordinating a campaign against sexism in society, the Shah expressed his personal views about women in saying 'You're equal in the eyes of the law but not, excuse my saying so, in ability ... You've never produced a Michelangelo or a Bach. You've never even produced a great chef ... You've produced nothing great, nothing!' (Fallaci, 1976).

This was a further legitimisation of the hard grip of male domination over social relations which made the social experience of many women one of powerlessness and frustration, and affected the pattern of women's participation in education, employment and politics by reinforcing the negative aspects of prevalent gender relations. Despite state propaganda, which was widely believed and repeated in the Western media, women's social position was not being revolutionised for the better as a result of state policies.

The pattern of women's participation in education, employment and politics reflected the fact that modernisation was not a homogenous and coherent process affecting women in a total and consistent way. The ways in which the positions of rural and urban women changed in the 1960s and 1970s is a stark example of this.

Rural women and development

Erika Friedl has documented some of these changes in a village in the Boir Ahmad area of South West Iran (Friedl, 1981, pp. 13–18). The breakdown of tribal structure resulted in the loss of economic and political functions. The land reform of the 1960s initially turned tribal peasants into independent farmers, but subsequent government policy of introducing capitalist farming in reality made profits impossible from small scale farming, and as a result most farmers lost the economic independence they had won in the land reform to urban usurers. By the mid-1970s agricultural work, which was based on the family as the basic productive unit, had been largely replaced by seasonal or permanent wage labour and salaried employment in and outside the village.

These developments had a drastic effect on the economic role and public and domestic status of rural women. On the one hand, it opened up the possibility of employment for a minority of village women as teachers, midwives and office workers, although there was more demand than jobs. But, on the other hand, these developments destroyed women's productive role and turned them into consumers. While, in the past, women used to produce up to 90 per cent of all daily necessities of the household, which they controlled and distributed, they ended up as a result of the process of modernisation being edged out of production. Friedl observed that 'The house is no longer where a woman's productivity is centred, but where the husband's economic success is demonstrated' (*ibid.*, p. 17).

Another example of the way in which rural women were affected by modernisation is provided by Haleh Afshar in her study of the village of Asiaback in central Iran (Afshar, 1985). Here, women's productive role changed from that of agricultural worker to carpet weaving which increased the family's cash income substantially. Contrary to the expectation that socially productive work will lead to emancipation, this development resulted in further subordination of women:

> women receive no payment for either spinning or weaving. The carpets are sold by the men. . . . Women have no access to the sphere of circulation and do not own their produce or their means of production. Neither are they able to sell their labour. Their ability to weave carpets has enslaved them even further in an unpaid relation of production which is kept separate from the money economy of the men. (*Ibid.*, pp.76–7).

The general impact of the land reform on village women was also assessed to be generally negative in other studies (Hegland, 1986 and 1992). As a direct result of the land reform, the need for female and child labour on peasant family plots increased tremendously. This was intensified as a result of male migration to towns in search of construction or industrial jobs (Tabari, 1980, p. 21). During 1956–66, agricultural production as a whole decreased from 48.9 to 28.0. But a 1973 study of agricultural activities in selective rural areas showed that in Nain male productive activity decreased from 74.2 in 1966 to 66.4 per cent in 1973 while female productive activity increased from 30.2 to 37.6 per cent (Dallalfar, 1987, p. 19). The above process increased the exploitation of peasant women especially since technological innovations did not reach women and also because they worked either as family workers or were paid half of the male wage (Najmabadi, 1987b, p. 220). The expansion of the carpet market intensified the exploitation of rural women. More than 90 per cent of all carpet weavers during the period 1965–71 were female and 40 per cent of these were under the age of fifteen (Tabari, 1980, p. 21). It was estimated in 1972 that 70 per cent of all cloth weaving employment was in the rural sector (Halliday, 1979, p. 191). Indeed women's participation in industry increased from 55 per cent in 1966 to 64 per cent in 1972. The majority of these industries and their female workers were based in the rural sector.

These women suffered from intolerable working conditions and low pay. Despite their substantial contribution to the economy, rural women's work was not reflected in the official statistics. The censuses of 1956 (the first in Iran), 1966 and 1976 gave the percentage of economically active women in rural areas as 9.2, 14.2 and 16.5 respectively (Mirani, 1983, p. 79; Statistical Centre of Iran, 1980, p. 34), while most rural women were involved in some form of productive work (Sedghi and Afshar, 1976, p. 205; Dallalfar, 1987). The state targeted rural women for literacy, health and family planning programmes. Yet the benefits gained by these women were minimal as a result of public ignorance and the incompatibility of state policies with rural women's living conditions. Despite the large number of agencies designated for rural areas, few were operating effectively at the local level (Bauer, 1983, p. 144). Some of these measures were not implemented to any extent: only 1 per cent of Iran's 60,000 villages had day nurseries in 1974 (Afshar, 1985, p. 67). The success of other measures such as family planning was marked by incompetence (Mossavar-Rahmani, 1983, p. 254). The literacy rate among rural women stood in 1956, 1966 and 1976 at 1.2, 4.3 and 16.5 per cent respectively (SCI, 1989, p. 11) which means that in a span of twenty years it only increased by about 15 per cent. Modernisation of rural women, then, did not on the whole seem to have integrated them into the modern economy in a meaningful and positive way with emancipatory consequences.

Urban women and development

As to the situation of urban women, again, the process of modernisation worked differently for different categories. Urban women from lower strata included those who had migrated from rural areas to towns. These women represented a growing number since, by 1978, the urban population of Iran increased from one-third to half of the total population. Migrant women either followed their menfolk to towns or moved there independently. The latter group constituted one-third of the total number of women who moved from villages to towns independently. The overwhelming majority of this group moved to towns in search of work and the rest for education or other purposes (Mirani, 1983, p. 73). In the 1970s almost all sectors of the urban population experienced an increase in family income. Although the cash benefits of increasing oil revenue went mostly to the upper and middle classes, the lower strata, too, benefited. Despite enormous unemployment, housing and other social problems faced by seasonal and settled migrants (Kazemi, 1980), urban life improved their cash income and acquisition of consumer goods and prestige foods. It also provided access to better education, health care and social amenities, and particularly improved their social life and access to modern entertainment.

Janet Bauer's study of migrant women in south Tehran has provided some insight into the effects of migration and modernisation on these women, although in general the position of women from lower strata of urban and rural sectors remains under-studied. The study concluded that the process of economic development and demographic change affected these migrant households in a number of ways: it placed the younger generation, especially males, in an advantageous position for participation in non-domestic activity and hence affected the relation of authority, particularly that of the mother, within the family; it did not result in a weakening of patriarchal control over women; it resulted in restriction of women's mobility in the neighbourhood and their enhanced veiling and segregation; the age of first marriage for both men and women rose and most girls received schooling, but young women were expected to marry and become housewives; women who were employed outside the home were mainly divorced or widowed, but they too were subject to male authority within the family (Bauer, 1985). Women in poor migrant neighbourhoods were exposed to two conflicting role models in the 1970s. On the one hand, they were exposed to portrayals of unveiled, modern and sophisticated women of the entertainment world or members of the royal family on their television screens, and in films and magazines, all of which were popular means of entertainment even for poor migrant households. On the other hand, the social activities of these women consisted of attending the religious gatherings of *rowzeh*, *sofreh* or visiting the sacred shrines. In these gatherings a different type of woman was being addressed and constructed by the male or female preacher who was at the centre of these gatherings. The preacher's tales of the sacrifices made for Islam by the devoted daughter of the Prophet Mohammad and Shii *emaman* and the virtues of the chaste women of Islam were often accompanied by criticism of un-Islamic appearance and behaviour of women in the rich districts of north Tehran (Bauer, 1985).

Those women amongst the lower strata who worked tended to be employed as domestic workers, cooks, cleaners, and workshop and factory workers. Urban lower-class women also traditionally worked at home as seamstresses, beauticians and hairdressers. The rate of illiteracy amongst these women was higher than average rate for urban women which stood at 55 per cent in 1976 (SCI, 1989, p. 11), and they had little job security or protection from harassment by employers. The labour laws of the 1970s left a lot to be desired both in terms of the protection of the rights of women workers and their implementation. They worked long hours under unsuitable conditions and were paid less than men.

Young women from the relatively more affluent lower or middle strata who had better access to education and vocational training turned to office work, sales, or professions such as nursing and teaching. Female education expanded rapidly in the 1960s and 1970s. The average annual growth rate of enrolment of female students in different levels of education during 1961–71 was 13 per cent for primary schools, 30 per cent for high schools, 88 per cent for technical and vocational colleges; 76 per cent for teacher training institutions and 65 per cent for higher education (Sedghi and Ashraf, 1976, p. 207). Women attended university in great numbers, but fewer women succeeded in competing with men for scarce university places and they mostly studied traditionally 'feminine' subjects such as literature and the humanities (Mirani, 1983).

Most female high school and college graduates took up employment in the service sector. An estimated 53 per cent of women employed in urban centres worked in the service sector. Teaching was the number one profession among women and nursing was almost exclusively a female profession, at least at its non-managerial levels. Clerical, administrative and secretarial jobs were as popular among women as teaching and nursing. Women still had very little opportunity to enter highly specialised and prestigious professions such as medicine and law.

Female employment in urban centres reached its peak in the mid-1960s and declined until the mid-1970s. This meant that despite their outward image as emancipated working women, Iranian middle-class women were in fact leaving work during the 1970s. The percentage of economically active women in urban areas changed from 9.3 per cent in 1956 to 9.9 in 1966. It then dropped to 7.5 in 1971, after which it rose to 9 per cent in 1976. This pattern was not favourable, compared with a steady and consistent rise in rural women's economic activity from 9.2 in 1956 to 14.2 per cent in 1966, to 15.7 in 1971, and 16.5 in 1976 (SCI, 1980, p. 34). The decline was particularly great in the 10–19 age group and was explained in terms of the increase in urban women's uptake of education during this period (Mirani, 1983, p. 77). However, the economic activity of women in all age groups was downward in this period. This must have been facilitated by a mixture of economic and social factors, including the fact that state ideology encouraged women's role as home makers. Furthermore, the reluctance of men to allow female members of the family to take up paid employment when they themselves were earning enough as a result of the economic boom may have contributed as well. Male prejudice and the practical problems faced by women in getting and keeping a job also must have deterred many middle-class women who could depend on a man's income from entering paid employment. This called into question the state's commitment to the integration of women in national development.

In the 1970s, when the employment rate for women was rising again, the type of employment came under criticism. According to a study conducted by the Women's Organisation of Iran in 1975 regarding the pattern of female employment: 'There has not been a shift away from "women's jobs" to jobs that are technical in nature and the number of women in prestigious professions is too low: in 1974, only 1 in 7 or possibly 10 doctors in the country were women and out of 12,000 engineers surveyed 350 were women' (WOI, 1975, p. 8).

The study also identified the kinds of discrimination women faced in the employment market and at work: they had to be more highly skilled than men to gain employment, were inhibited by stereotyping at work and were given fewer opportunities for promotion because they were regarded as less knowledgeable, serious and hard-working than men. Women who made significant progress at work were considered to be different from 'average' women (*ibid.*, pp. 37–42). This was supported by other studies of women's experience in education and employment which demonstrated the odds against which women struggled in these fields (Vatandoust, 1985, pp. 125–6). Women also commonly faced sexual harassment in university or at work and were expected to earn promotion by flirting and bestowing sexual favours on their male superiors. Another form of harassment was preventing women from wearing Islamic clothing at work or on university campuses since it was considered a political statement against the state-propagated image of womanhood. Another aspect of women's employment which drew criticism was the absence of women from top jobs, and the findings of the above mentioned study were that women's engagement in the top four tiers of jobs in leading industries and professions in both public and private sectors was very insignificant indeed. Of 4,438 'top jobs' surveyed, only 340 or under 8 per cent were held by women, 3 per cent of which was related to the nursing profession (*ibid.*, p. 10). The same pattern of token presence of women was the case in politics, as summed up in the following comment:

> Following [women's enfranchisement in 1963], of the total of 197 members elected to the Majles . . . six were women and, of the total of 60 senators, two were women. In comparison, in the present Majles (terminating in September 1975), of the total of 270 members, 18 were women and of the 60 senators, two were women. In the recent election, of the total of 97 female candidates of the Rastakhiz Party . . . 21 were elected: one female senator and 20 for the Majles. Thus as compared with the 1971 elections, recent electoral politics witnessed a decrease of one female senator and an increase of two female deputies in the Majles . . . Up to now, there has been only one female minister. (Sedghi and Ashraf, 1976, p. 208)

So, as demonstrated in the case of rural women the effect of modernisation on urban women was varied. It did result in the integration of urban women into the economy and opened many hitherto closed fields of activity to middle and upper-class women. But it did not necessarily affect women's employment in a consistent and predictable way. Moreover, women were integrated into the formal economy in a subordinate way, and in many ways, the state ideology and legislation undid the progress made by individual women as a result of economic and social developments, by their reinforcement of negative aspects of the dominant gender relation. The modernisation process not only subjected women to the general onslaught of 'The Great Civilisation', but also made women suffer from extra pressures brought upon them by their families and communities. As the bearers of the honour of the family, women were caught between contradictory expectations. The state on the one hand opened the doors to them to go out to the university and take up paid employment, and on the other hand, constructed them as sex-objects. The family demanded the extra income brought in by the woman, but refused to release her from patriarchal control. Many well-educated women ended up as housewives against their wishes because of pressure from men or the state's inability to provide jobs.

Furthermore, many women who had been raised with the expectation of eternal protection and security in the house of a father and then a husband, in return for nothing more than being allowed to perform their 'natural functions' as wife and mother, found to their disappointment 'the old normative order slipping away from them without any empowering alternatives' being created (Kandiyoti, 1991b, p. 29). The gap between the ideal patriarchal order, in which sex roles were clearly defined, and the contradictory demands of the modern state and family on women could only increase in the age of 'The Great Civilisation'. Women's response was to search for alternative ways of being, and as the following pages show, they found a few. Some women continued to work within the state machinery to further the goals of modernisation from above. Others sought to extend the boundaries of gender relations by demanding sexual liberation for women. Some saw the alternative in a communist political order. Others found their salvation in a new Shiism – one which was not a simple retreat into 'tradition' as has been suggested sometimes.

Response to 'The Great Civilisation'

In the 1960s and 1970s, a number of responses developed against the ideology of 'The Great Civilisation'. The tremendous gap created in the state–citizen relationship as a result of the increasing disparity between the state's propagation of the ideology of 'The Great Civilisation' and the ordinary citizen's experience of life, came to be filled by other socio-political alternatives. Like the process of modernisation, the social responses to it, too, were varied and developed in many secular and religious directions. But they had many common features as well.

Oppositional responses to modernisation had a number of common features. To begin with, their development was rooted in the changing conceptions of the West and its role in Iran. The social and political experiences of the intelligentsia since the Constitutional Revolution resulted in the 1960s and 1970s in a reversal of the turn of the century admiration for Western civilisation. Then, the adoption of Western state, society and family values was seen as desirable for Iran because the West represented strength, modernity and progress. Now, the West was under criticism from within and without for its exploitation of other nations, its diminishing social morality and its collapsing family system. The Westernisation of Iran under the Pahlavis, it was believed, did not bring about the political freedom, national independence and social progress that the constitutionalists of the turn of the century had aspired to. On the contrary, modernisation had reinforced foreign dependence and was now threatening the moral fabric of society. Furthermore, the illusion that state modernisation and women's emancipation were necessary corollaries was shattered because of the contradictory effects and unfulfilled promises of Westernisation.

All this made it imperative for the new generation of the intelligentsia to put aside the West as a viable model for Iranian society and develop alternative models which presented the right solutions for society's ills. The new alternatives, however, were not based on a wholesale rejection of anything that was not Iranian. Contrary to the common dichotomisation of Islamic opposition politics as 'indigenous' and 'authentic', and secular opposition politics as 'Westernised', all socio-political responses against modernisation drew upon both external and internal sources of inspiration and support.

Although both secular and religious opposition movements made a claim to authenticity, nevertheless they could all pick and choose from a variety of socially available conceptions in developing their opposition to 'The Great Civilisation'. The sources of inspiration were history, literature, art, religion and knowledge of world events and international movements. Information about political and social movements in other parts of the world penetrated through distorted news in the state controlled press, which readers learnt to interpret for themselves, and was disseminated through foreign press and media, Iranians travelling abroad, and so on. The student revolt in Europe, protests in the United States against the Vietnam war, the Algerian struggle for independence, the rise of guerrilla movements in Latin America, the Palestinian struggle against Israel and many other world events constituted a source of inspiration for Iranian intellectuals, both secular and religious, in the 1960s and 1970s, and gave rise to new interpretations of history, politics and religion.

Another common feature of opposition alternatives to modernisation was their appeal to the middle and lower sections of society. Contrary to opposition movements in the first half or so of this century which drew their leaders and members primarily, but not exclusively, from the middle and upper classes, the major oppositional movements of the post-1963 era drew their leadership and ranks mainly from the lower and middle classes. Finally, despite their different outlook, all political responses to modernisation included their own particular definition of gender relations and proposed a particular position for women.

Secular opposition to modernisation

Secular opposition response to modernisation as it related to women developed in at least three directions. The first one, which was very much a minority position confined to intellectual women of the middle and upper classes, attempted to go beyond both the conception of woman as a sex-object and the moralist criticism of it. It advocated an open society which allowed sexual liberation for women. It is no surprise that this response has come to be associated with a woman. Forough Farrokhzad, a famous poet who was killed in a car accident in 1967, epitomised the demand for breaking the legitimate boundaries of gender relations, advocated by both the state and its moralist opponents, to reach total liberation for women (Farrokhzad, 1985; Malek, 1984; Milani, 1992). The second secular response to modernisation suggested that Iranian society should shake off the *gharbzadegi* with which it had become polluted. The concept of *gharbzadegi*, literally meaning to be struck by the West, was popularised by Jalal Al-Ahmad, a well respected literary figure (Al-Ahmad, 1981). He criticised 'polluted' popular culture and called upon Iranians to abandon their unreserved embrace of Western materialism and consumerism. This cultural alternative constructed women as 'modern-yet-modest'. It rejected 'the painted dolls of the Pahlavi regime' and advocated preservation of modesty for modern Iranian women. (Najmabadi, 1991, pp.65–6) The concept of *gharbzadegi* in its secular form was a new way of tackling the old dilemma inherited from the constitutionalists of the turn of the century: how to benefit from the West without losing the authenticity of Iranian culture. But the collapse of nationalist politics in the 1960s prevented this response from developing in its secular form. This alternative to modernisation was soon taken over and transformed into a religious radical form by Shii modernists.

The third secular alternative to 'The Great Civilisation' was provided by the Marxist–Leninist left. This takes us to the process of development of radical secular politics in the aftermath of the 1953 *coup d'état* and the 1963 political upheaval. Political repression in the 1960s and 1970s changed the nature of left politics by driving it underground and in to exile. The era of moderate politics and the demand for constitutional monarchy seemed to have ended. The battle between political rivals had been fought and the Shah had won by, first, carrying out the social reforms that nationalists had asked for and, second, going so far in the direction of autocracy as to make the demand for his return to constitutional rule meaningless. The Tudeh Party was banished into exile where it underwent internal debates and splits in the 1960s. It also came under concerted criticism for its policies during the Mosaddeq era. The Tudeh Party was branded among the Iranian left in the 1970s as a 'traitor' for letting down the anti-Shah nationalist movement by allying with Ayatollah Kashani's movement and facilitating the 1953 coup which had resulted in another round of Pahlavi dictatorship.

As a result of the collapse of the moderate opposition, violent political action became the only possibility for opposition in the 1960s and 1970s and university campuses became fertile grounds for the formation of underground cells. In the 1960s a number of underground groups were formed by disillusioned members of the Tudeh Party and the National Front (Jebheye Melli), which advocated a violent response to the Shah's violent political repression. Out of these groups, two main guerrilla organisations were founded, namely, the Organisation of Fadaiyan Guerrillas of Iranian People (Sazeman Cherikhaye Fadai Khalgh) (hereafter Fadaiyan Khalgh) and the Organisation of Mojahedin of Iranian People (Sazeman Mojahedin Khalgh Iran) (hereafter Mojahedin Khalgh). These underground groups concentrated on ideological and guerrilla training in the 1960s and presented their own particular analyses of the Iranian society. The literature produced by these groups gained popularity among university students and made a major contribution to the post-Tudeh Party Marxist–Leninist ideology in Iran. The outbreak of armed struggle against the Shah's regime should be seen in the international context of an ongoing guerrilla movement in Latin America. The success in destabilising some pro-American regimes in the region presented some hope to Iranian Marxist–Leninists. The growth nearer to home of the Palestinian guerrilla movements pitted against Zionism and imperialism was also an important background factor, as were the student revolts in the West which influenced a growing number of Iranian students abroad. Between 1971 and 1975 the guerrilla movement initiated and carried out a number of missions such as armed robberies, attacks on police stations, kidnapping and execution, of the regime's officials, disruption of public celebrations, bombing of sensitive installations and hijacking of Iran Air planes. They also published numerous underground papers, propagating the theory and practice of armed struggle.

The difference among guerrilla organisations, whose numbers were on the increase, was in politics rather than ideology. They differed in their allegiance to communist regimes such as the Soviet Union, China, Cuba, Vietnam or Albania and this affected their political analyses of international relations. Yet they were unified in their ideology of anti-imperialism and anti-capitalism. There was an ideological difference between the Mojahedin Khalgh and other groups as the former resorted to Shiism for legitimacy. During the 1970s, however, the Mojahedin's Islam did not make them any different from other guerrilla groups. Ideological differences between the Mojahedin and secular guerrilla groups became more apparent at later stages in their struggles. The ideological unity of guerrilla organisations resulted from their common criticism of the Shah as 'the puppet of American imperialism' and of his regime as the instrument of Western economic and cultural imperialism in Iran, and also from their common conviction that armed struggle was the only route to the overthrow of the Shah and the salvation of Iran from imperialism. In the midst of a political vacuum which existed on the oppositional political scene and in the absence of continuity in political action, many of the concepts developed within Marxist–Leninist ideology concerning Iran's relationship with the West were deeply internalised by the younger generation of Iranian intelligentsia. These concepts constituted some of the means by which the anti-Shah mass movement was fought during 1977–9.

Marxist–Leninist groups conducted a limited but influential campaign in the 1970s in protest against state policies on women. This campaign covered both historical and current analyses of women. At the historical level, Marxist–Leninists applied Frederick Engels' analysis of women's historical subordination to the position of women in Iran (*On the Question of Women*, 1971). This analysis remained detached from particular historical events and developments in Iran. What was said about the historical development of women's position in Iran could be said about any other society equally. At the current level, the Marxist–Leninist analysis of women was carried out within the framework of dependency theory. 'Imperialism' played the same role in Marxist–Leninist theory that 'Islam' played in modernisation theory in explaining where the blame lay for the oppression of women. Women were defined as victims of Iran's dependence on the West and state policies on women were dismissed as tools of the imperialist exploitation of Iranian women. Within this framework, the objective of modernisation was seen to be the utilisation of women as consumers and cheap labour to further the interests of American imperialism in Iran. Women who were seen to have benefited from modernisation were considered accomplices in this imperialist conspiracy. While lower-class women were portrayed as passive victims of the regime's oppression, affluent women were condemned as sex-objects, accomplices of the Shah and oppressors of lower-class women.

Marxist-Leninist analysis led to some genuine and relevant critical descriptions of the experiences of deprived groups such as working-class women, rural women and urban prostitutes (*On the Oppression of Women in Iran*, 1972). Moreover, the limitations of state legislation in tackling women's problems were discussed and the prevalent backward social attitudes towards women were analysed and criticised (Committee for Women's Liberation in Iran, 1978). Furthermore, Marxist–Leninist analysis led to a set of demands for women's liberation. The Marxist–Leninist movement articulated its aspirations for women in the single and general demand of full equality of rights for men and women in all spheres. It was common to qualify the above demand, however, by a statement to the effect that comprehensive equality of men and women was not possible within a capitalist society. Therefore, this demand was one to be made under capitalism but to be realised only under socialism.

With regard to the guerrilla organisations' treatment of women members, actual practice was often a far cry from the equality of treatment for men and women which they advocated in theory. Women's participation in the guerrilla movement was fairly significant and the movement drew many female members and sympathisers from the lower and middle classes (Abrahamian, 1980a). Many guerilla heroines emerged from the decade of armed struggle against the state, including the legendary Ashraf Dehghani (Azari, 1983, pp. 183–4).

However, the experience of many of the female members and sympathisers was that of discrimination and double standards within the guerilla groups. The Marxist–Leninist remedy for the treatment of women as sex-objects was the 'masculinisation' of women. The Marxist–Leninist woman dressed similarly to her male comrade, wore her hair short, did not use make-up and avoided wearing high-heeled shoes. She was encouraged to be tough and to suppress her emotions. But even compliance with this did not earn her equal treatment within the organisation. Sexual stereotyping operated here, too, and women members and sympathisers were expected to perform their female duties as well as being freedom fighters. A Marxist–Leninist pamphlet complained about some female comrades who were talking about sharing housework with men:

> It has recently become fashionable among educated and progressive women to complain about women's housework and childrearing duties .... Those who are concerned with their own individual liberation are no more than bourgeois and daydreaming intellectuals. ... Anyone demanding women to give up domestic responsibilities, or perform them partially and sharing them with men should know that this will not lead to the mobilisation of the masses. The masses know very well that under present conditions, housework, reproduction and the rearing of children are a necessity to ensure the continuance of the struggle of the masses. (Confederation of Iranian Students Abroad, 1976, p. 6).

Women's 'individual liberation' was seen as contradictory to the 'liberation of the masses' and this was used as a means of patronising the Marxist–Leninist woman into accepting a subordinate position within the organisation. She rarely reached the top decision-making levels and spent most of her time serving male colleagues. With regard to sexuality, here too she faced double standards. Although sex outside marriage was prohibited on ideological grounds for both male and female members, nevertheless if her male colleague was carried away by sexual desires he was easily forgiven. She, on the contrary, faced stigma and disciplinary measures for sexual laxity (Azari, 1984, pp. 80–91).

The Marxist–Leninist guerilla movement presented the most influential secular alternative to modernisation in the 1970s. Despite its isolation from the 'masses', which it aimed to represent, the movement managed to construct a vision of a future society in Iran and the position of women within it which assumed prime importance later in the context of the Iranian Revolution of 1977–9. The movement considered the salvation of Iran to lie in the overthrow of capitalism and the relation of dependency to the West which sustained it. Women were assigned an important role in both maintaining and overthrowing the existing system. Women's participation in the guerilla movement reflected the pattern of women's entry to all spheres of society. But women's 'masculinisation' in appearance and action represented a new willingness by the secular forces to transcend the boundaries of gender relations to an unprecedented degree.

Islamic opposition to modernisation

The 1960s and 1970s also witnessed the rise of the religious response to modernisation. Contrary to some expectations, the process of modernisation in Iran did not uproot religion. What was strongly suppressed by the state was the political power of the clergy. The state allowed Islam to flourish at grass-roots level while controlling the political digression of the institution of Shiism. The religious response to Western-style modernisation was not a return to a pre-modern 'tradition'. On the contrary, it 'consumed the products of development', integrated itself within modern structures and institutions, and reconstructed a modern political ideology (Baykan, 1990).

The development of the practice of Ejtehad

The post-1963 era was a period of major theological debate and spiritual contemplation within the institution of Shiism (Akhavi, 1980, pp. 117–29). The apolitical clergy concentrated on studying and training their students in seminaries. The spread of literacy and the clergy's need to maintain contact with an increasingly urbanised and Westernised population gave rise to a new phenomenon, the publication of *touziholmasael* (book of religious instructions). These books of religious instructions had their roots in the tradition set by Mohammad Bagher Majlesi and Sheykh Morteza Ansari in the eighteenth and nineteenth centuries respectively (see chapter 1). After the death in 1961 of Ayatollah Borujerdi, who was the sole *marjae taghlid* of his time, several similar ranking *mojtahedin* became *marjae taghlid*. This resulted in the development of the institution of *ejtehad* and increased the need for the *mojtahedin* to publish their views on various aspects of Shii concern to help their devotees to choose one to follow.

The *touziholmasael* was intended to regulate the lives of Shii followers and answer their religious enquiries. In the 1960s and 1970s, the libraries of Iranian homes were expected to include a copy of the *Qoran*, a copy of *Nahj ol-Balagheh* [Sayings of *emam* Ali] and a copy of *touziholmasael* from the *marjae taghlid* which was followed by the head of the household. The flourishing of *touziholmasaels* and other books of religious instruction which devoted substantial attention to women and the family was an indication of the clergy's determination to preserve their authority over these issues on the face of modernisation.

The principles of the *shariat* on the family had already been codified under Reza Shah in the form of the Civil Code. But the fact that, despite this, the clergy attempted to describe the same principles in an overtly religious language in their books, indicated that they found it necessary to keep their hold on the family as a religious territory. Political suppression of the clergy resulted in the strengthening of their claim over the family. In the atmosphere of state modernisation, the clergy's renewed claim over women and the family turned this issue into an arena of power struggle between the state and the Shii establishment. Ayatollah Khomeini's *touziholmasael* is a good example of how women and the family were constructed in the books of religious instruction. Khomeini's *touziholmasael* was preoccupied with the protection of the Muslim community from the onslaughts of modernisation. This was attempted by means of instructions which aimed to keep men and women in their respective places in the family and increase to maximum degree the reproductive capacity of the Muslim community (Khomeini, n.d.b).

In summary, incest was defined very narrowly; the age of marriage for men was low and women were encouraged to marry before reaching the age of puberty; men were allowed to practise polygamy and *sigheh* marriage as a matter of right. In all of this, the emphasis was on reproduction. Men were encouraged to conduct their main sexual activity with a view to reproduction and allowed to have sex for pleasure only on an additional basis. But for women sex and reproduction was inseparable at all times. Male sexuality was defined as active and female sexuality as passive. Women were told that it was a religious duty for them to submit to their husbands' sexual wishes (*ibid.*, pp. 259–88). Pregnant women were treated favourably by Ayatollah Khomeini and a whole series of instructions were presented on breastfeeding.

Khomeini considered the man as the head of the household and enjoined women not to leave the house without their husbands' permission. Virgin women were instructed not to marry without the consent of their fathers, and children were not given into the custody of the father in the event of divorce. The divorced mother could look after children on behalf of the father until a female child reached the age of seven and a male child the age of two. Divorce was a natural right for men, but women could insert stipulations in their marriage contracts to specify under what conditions they might have permission to ask for divorce. Women inherited half the amount men did, and the testimony of one man was equal to the testimony of two women. Women were prohibited from entering the judiciary and, in any case, they could not work without their husbands' consent. Ayatollah Khomeini's response to the Family Protection Law of 1967 was a warning to the faithful against compliance with it:

> The law that has recently been passed by the illegal Majles under the name of the Family Protection Law in order to destroy Muslim family life, is against Islam, and both its originators and implementers are guilty before the *shariat*. Women who are divorced in family courts should consider their divorce as null, and if they re-marry they are committing adultery. Whoever marries such women knowingly is also an adulterer, and should be punished according to the *shariat* by whipping. The children of these men and women are illegitimate and are not entitled to inheritance. (Khomeini, n.d.b, p. 314)

Ayatollah Khomeini, however, was at the time a lone political voice in exile. The majority of Shii clerics inside Iran went along with the Family Protection Law, especially since it did not overtly contradict the *shariat*. Even in matters such as abortion and family planning, there was little public opposition from the clergy. There was a general acceptance of family planning among the clergy (Friesen and Moore, 1977, p. 118). On abortion, views were more divided. Some prohibited sterilisation and rejected abortion at any stage of pregnancy (*ibid.*). Others considered abortion up to the 120th day of pregnancy acceptable. The latter view held by non-opposition clergy such as Ayatollah Beheshti came to the top in the 1970s (Mosavvar-Rahmani, 1983).

The modernisation of Shiism

But the main development within the institution of Shiism in this period was the modernisation of Shii ideology. The development of Shii modernity, which began with the setting up of the Liberation Movement of Iran in the early 1960s by Mehdi Bazargan and Ayatollah Taleghani, reached new dimensions in the late 1960s and 1970s. Various circles of clerics and laymen who dedicated themselves to the modernisation of Shiism held seminars, wrote books and initiated debates on almost all aspects of Shii ideology and institutions (Akhavi, 1980). The direction in which some of Shii rethinking was moving, for example in relation to the family, was in accordance with state policies in the broad sense and was therefore tolerated or even encouraged by the state. On other developments within Shiism, particularly in those which had political implications, the state was intolerant and repressive. Political debate, then, had to be carried out clandestinely or in exile.

Shii modernism involved a major rethinking and rationalisation of the family. It propagated a new concept of Shii woman through its publications and sermons. Ayatollah Motahhari was one of the main proponents of Shii modern thinking on the family. Motahhari's major book on the family was *The System of Women's Rights in Islam* (1978) which was originally a collection of articles published in a glossy, pro-establishment women's magazine *Zan Ruz* (Woman of Today). Motahhari's book was a polemic against the defenders of male–female equality as reflected in the United Nation's Declaration of Human Rights. Motahhari rejected the Declaration of Human Rights on two grounds and argued against the Western tendency to measure the status of women in different societies in terms of its observance. First, he saw the Declaration as being based on the philosophy of 'individualism' which was in his view contrary to Islam. The latter gave priority to the rights of society over the rights of the individual and that, he said, is why Muslims were obliged to observe social rules as stated in the *Qoran*. Second, the call for 'equality' of rights irrespective of sex, he argued, was unacceptable in Islam because it confused 'equality' with 'similarity' or sameness of rights. Motahhari developed a systematic and comprehensive explanation of the 'equal but different' rights of men and women in the Islamic family and society. This involved new and liberal interpretations of *Qoranic* verses on women (Arbery, 1955). The core of Motahhari's argument should be sought in his differentiation of the sphere of 'social' from that of the 'family'. 'Civil society', he argued, was a human creation and individuals entered it as equals; they only gradually acquired unequal positions and rights through their different personalities and talents.

The sphere of the 'family', however, was governed by 'natural laws' as opposed to laws made by humankind which governed civil society. Here, individuals were born with different initial rights, abilities and needs. The law of nature put them in dissimilar positions from the start. That is why men and women have different positions within the family, and hence their different rights and responsibilities. Islam, Motahhari argued, recognised this and the *Qoran* instructed the Muslims accordingly. The position of men and women differed with regard to marriage, divorce, child custody and inheritance. Motahhari rationalised these differences with reference to biological and psychological differences between men and women: man is rational, woman is emotional; man is strong, woman is weak; nature has invested in man the need to love and protect woman, and in woman the need to be loved and protected; man is a slave of passion, woman is a prisoner of love and affection; man is zealous, woman is jealous. He therefore created a rigid stereotype of the sexes.

Motahhari believed that the well-being of society depended on preserving the separation of the 'family' from 'civil society'. The former was the site of operation of sexuality and the latter of social activity. Islam's concern was, he argued, to keep these two kinds of activities within their respective spheres. The mixing of the two would only create chaos and a society which was in contradiction to human nature. In his view, the social and individual problems faced by the West were all due to the penetration of sexual relations into civil society and to their merging with social relations. In his view, the merging of these two spheres culminated in the act of adultery (*zena*) and that was why Islam set up such elaborate mechanisms for the regulation of sexuality. Islam, Motahhari argued, fully acknowledged women's sexuality and did not condemn it as a sin. One of these mechanisms was women's sexual and emotional satisfaction within the sphere of the family so that they would not look for satisfaction outside marriage. A woman's task of motherhood, Motahhari argued, made the home the natural place for her activities. Nevertheless, her social and economic activity should not be denied. In fact, women's involvement in particular occupations was considered a social obligation because it helped to preserve the separation of the two spheres by preventing a close interaction of men and women within the wider society. These tasks included nursing, practising medicine, dressmaking, teaching, and so on. Women, he argued, should not be prevented from holding other occupations and activities so far as they kept to modest clothing and avoided close interaction with the male sex.

In Motahhari's view, Islamic *hejab* was an important device created to preserve the separation of the sphere of 'family' from 'civil society' and it was women's responsibility to preserve it (Motahhari, 1974). Other devices for keeping the two spheres separate included polygamy, *sigheh* and rules related to child custody. Motahhari claimed that monogamy was the 'natural' form of marriage and that true Islam had confined polygamy strictly to certain social circumstances. In fact, he argued, it was the practice of polygamy which saved monogamy in the Islamic East. His logic was that if polygamy had not been allowed under certain conditions, such as in times of war and mass migration, chaos would have taken over and adultery would have burned the roots of monogamy.

So, in Motahhari's view, since love and affection could never be satisfied in polygamy as they would in monogamy, the former was not allowed unless certain conditions were met. This was the basis on which modernist clergy such as Motahhari tolerated the restriction of polygamy in the Family Protection Law. Another device, specific to Shiism and prohibited by other Islamic sects, was *sigheh* marriage. The aim here, as Motahhari explained, was purely the satisfaction of sexual needs and this kind of marriage should also take place only under certain circumstances. The requirements of modern life, he argued, prohibited married men from exercising it. He considered its practice justified only for the unmarried, since the requirements of modern life such as the duration of education, and so on, resulted in late marriages. *Sigheh* helped in these cases to prevent adultery. The right of the father to child custody was another device to keep sex away from society, since it left the divorced woman free to remarry and hence prevented women from experiencing sexual and emotional frustration which could lead to adultery.

Motahhari's modernisation of the Shii family involved a transferring of the family from the realm of religion to the realm of nature. To bring the Shii conception of family in line with dominant social relations, he created stereotypes of 'femininity' and 'masculinity' which he saw as being based on men and women's natural endowments. In doing so, he defined monogamy as the natural form of family and advocated a partial release of women from the home to take up social and political responsibilities. Motahhari's modern Shii woman was remarkably close to the Shah's expectation of women since the latter, too, rejected Western feminism on the ground that 'women possess certain unique endowments and with those go unique responsibilities' (H.R.S. Pahlavi, 1960, p. 235).

Radicalisation of Shiism

Another direction in which Shii modernism moved was that of radical politics. The new generation of Muslims began to sidestep traditional Islamic politics by bringing state and religion together in a way that had not been experienced by Muslims since the formative years of Islam. The most influential attempts in this direction were made by two diametrically different Shii thinkers, Ayatollah Khomeini and Ali Shariati, a Western educated layman. Both were dissatisfied with the traditional relationship between the state and the institution of Shiism and believed that state domination over religion would result in the elimination of Islam from Iran.

Away from his home, the religious city of Qom, and from the reforms that were being initiated within the Shii establishment inside Iran, Khomeini delivered a series of lectures in exile in Najaf which were published in 1971 under the title of *Hokumat Eslami* (The Islamic Government) (Khomeini, n.d.c). These lectures reflected a lone crusade to reform the prevalent Shii theory of government. In them, Khomeini argued that the traditional view within Shiism towards the question of temporal government was not relevant any more and needed to be changed. It was no longer sufficient for Shiis, he argued, to be content with giving support to the most just and fair temporal ruler. On the contrary, he believed the time had come for the clergy themselves to assume political power and establish an Islamic government. Ayatollah Khomeini instructed fellow clergy in these lectures how to achieve Islamic government and explained the principles that governed the guardianship of the Islamic Jurist (*Velayat Faqih*). He believed that the clergy should concentrate on the political education of their followers and use every religious service for the benefit of political agitation and propaganda. The main point to be taught to people was that 'religion is not separate from politics'. Khomeini argued that Islamic government was 'the rule of God over people': it was the administration of God's rule in society by the most learned and just Shii *faqih* of the time. Once such a Shii *faqih* is located, it is his duty to assume the guardianship of society in the absence of the Hidden *emam*, and it is the duty of every Shii to obey him (*ibid.*, pp. 19, 46).

Shariati's approach to political Islam differed radically from Ayatollah Khomeini's. Shariati studied sociology at the University of Paris in the 1960s. He became deeply interested in existentialism and involved himself with the Algerian Liberation Movement. He applied his knowledge of Western philosophy and third world liberation movements to a reassessment of Shiism. Shariati's knowledge of the field of Islamic studies and Western orientalism enabled him to arrive at a 'sociology of Islam' which he based on a historical analysis of Shiism (Shariati, 1979). The reform he proposed for Shiism was posed upon a rejection of 'Safavid Shii', which was the Shiism traditionally practised by the Iranian clergy, in favour of 'Alavid Shii' which he defined as the Shiism practised by early Shii *emaman* in the formative years of Islam. In this way, he claimed to have 'purified' Iranian Shiism from local practices and customs that had 'diluted' it throughout the centuries. Shariati's Alavid Shiism was an ideological vehicle for the liberation of the Shii community from a society based on injustice and corruption to the utopia of the 'unitary class-less society' (*Jameeh bi-tabagheh touhidi*). In this ideal Islamic society, politics and religion were inseparable and so were state and society. The *emam* and the 'community' were one and democracy was genuine and inherent in the system as opposed to Western elitist democracy which was corrupt and money-led, and Eastern workers' democracy which was totalitarian (Shariati, 1978).

One of the most important aspects of Shariati's political ideology was in relation to women. Shariati's ideas were radical and hit a chord with the younger generation. He built upon Jalal Al-Ahmad's criticism of Western materialist culture and his call on Iranian intellectuals to abandon *gharbzadegi* to provide relevant new concepts for the young Iranian Muslim. The establishment of a religious centre known as Hoseiniyeh Ershad in 1965 as a centre for Shii study of modern social issues was a result of the new atmosphere of involvement of young people in Islamic politics. The spread of Shii culture took place irrespective of political repression. While any attempt to spread Marxist–Leninist culture met with severe political repression, the spread of Islamic culture proved too illusive and slippery to be suppressed effectively by the state. Even after Hoseiniyeh Ershad was closed down by the government and Shariati was arrested and later exiled to France, tapes of his lectures continued to be distributed.

In addresses to women, expanded in the early 1970s in his *Fatemeh is Fatemeh* and other works on women (Shariati, 1975, 1976, 1980), Shariati typically avoided getting involved in the issue of the family and the position of women within it since these had been established as the traditional subjects of contemplation by the clergy. Instead, he concentrated on the issue of women's oppression in modern Iranian society as a 'sex object'. For Shariati, women's oppression in third world countries was a direct result of 'cultural imperialism' which he defined as the 'greatest conspiracy against humanity'. 'Cultural imperialism', he argued, aimed at depriving third world nations of their character and traditional values, and thus of any kind of resistance, so that the third world could be better exploited economically. Shariati's conception of woman should be fitted into this picture. Woman, the pillar of the family, was considered as a perfect target by Western conspirators. Shariati recalled Fanon's argument that the manipulation of Algerian society became a possibility for French conspirators only when they came up with the idea of winning over the women. He argued that in Iran, too, possession of women had taken place through turning women into 'Western dolls'. This was the main component of a package deal, he argued, the conspirators wanted the raw materials and natural resources of Iranian society, and in turn, exported their culture in the form of 'freedom, ethics, techniques, culture, art and pornography' to this land. They sent these generously, and in doing so had the support of the political establishment, the mass media, propaganda, as well as the use of social, political and educational facilities of the country to justify it.

Shariati believed that the image of woman created by capitalism had two functions: first, as a sex-object she was trained to destroy the concentration and energy of the worker, intellectual and professional, by filling their leisure time in order to prevent them from thinking about class struggle and anti-capitalist activities. Secondly, capitalism in order to encourage consumption, to make people more dependent and thus to increase production, created the woman as a consumer. Woman, who was the main source of inspiration throughout history, he argued, came to be used as a sexual image so that the transformation of the values and ethics of a traditional-spiritual society into an absurd consumer society could take place. Shariati considered women in Islamic countries as an important element in preserving tradition and social and cultural relations, and most important of all, as a key to the consumption pattern of society. He believed that due to her sensitivity, a woman would be the first to accept the 'new Western civilisation', that is, the new consumerism, especially when her own society had nothing to offer her except suffering in the name of religion and tradition.

Shariati argued that woman in the Muslim society has been the last to benefit from human rights, social facilities, and a full development of her potential. Hence, in the name of Islam, the very rights and possibilities given to her by Islam have been taken away from her and she is reduced to the level of a 'washing machine' and her human personality to that of a 'breeding machine'. In his view, women in the corrupt traditional society, which was painted with a phoney cover of religion, lived a degrading life as daughters, wives, mothers. All this contributed to the attraction women felt for consuming and living a life of 'luxurious absurdity'. In Shariati's words, this accounts for the five-hundred-fold increase in the use of make-up in Iran from 1956 to 1966. He recalled Fanon again, saying that we were responsible if our women responded to the 'sweet murmurings' of the colonisers about their 'lost rights'. Women were confused and trapped within these two systems, Shariati argued: if they didn't want to join the consumers a dull and unjust tradition awaited them, and if they ran away from this the consumer life-style awaited them. What should they do, then? What was the way for a woman if she decided to choose to 'think' and to 'make' herself? Who should she 'model' herself on? Here Shariati constructed a 'model' for the Shii Iranian women to follow – the figure of Fatemeh, the Prophet's daughter.

Shariati's book on Fatemeh built up the ideal type of Fatemeh and made her image relevant to the modern world. Shariati did not separate the 'family' from 'society' as the sphere of operation of the laws of nature. Shariati's concern was not with the 'family', but with the 'woman'. Shariati's ideal woman was not to be deterred from taking up her social responsibilities because of the limitations of the family. Shariati, of course, was not anti-family; far from it. His way of releasing women from familial constraint was the politicisation of the whole family. Fatemeh's family was the ideal Shii family and her father and husband lead her to social responsibility and participation in political struggles. But what were Fatemeh's rights as compared to those of her menfolk? Shariati says

> although Islam is strongly against 'prejudice' against women, it does not support 'equality' for them ... Nature has created man and woman as complementary beings in life and society. This is why unlike Western civilisation, Islam offers men and women their 'natural rights' and not 'similar rights'. This is the most profound word to be said on the matter and its depth and value should be clear to those conscious readers who would dare to think and see without seeking Europe's permission. (Shariati, 1976, p. 5)

In Shariati's writings, however, the inequality or dissimilarity of the rights of Fatemeh and her menfolk were not spelled out except on the subject of sexuality. In his attempt to free women from being 'sexual objects' Shariati desexualised women; there was no place for women's 'sexual instinct' in his theory. Shariati's Fatemeh was simple, pure, shy, chaste and virtuous (*ibid.*, p. 6). In order to work side-by-side and participate in the Shii struggle, the new militant Shii youth, both male and female, were called upon to purify their souls from 'Freudian sexual liberation' (Shariati, 1975, p. 27). The thousands of young people who attended Shariati's lectures in Tehran tended to accept this. The new Shii militant woman wore a scarf over her head and desexualised her body by wearing loose-fitting clothes. Her militant Shii brother grew a beard, buried his heart, and modestly averted his gaze. Shariati's popular Shiism offered a new perspective on life within the contemporary indigenous and international context. It also provided communal identity and a sense of solidarity, where hard competition for the satisfaction of material needs had dominated young people's lives (Zubaida, 1989c).

The development of Shii modernism, and the flourishing of Islamic politics in the 1970s, contradicted the expectation that the process of modernisation would uproot religion in Iran. It became obvious that Shiism, too, was moving ahead with the times and was undergoing constant development. Religion was not declining as a result of the imposition of the ideology of 'Great Civilisation', but was evolving and changing. In developing new alternatives, Shiism was not rejecting modernity with its idealistic implications of economic prosperity, social justice, political freedom and national independence. But it was criticising Pahlavi style modernisation which was associated with a kind of Westernisation which emphasised materialistic and vulgar aspects of Western culture. Indeed, like other contending political ideologies, Shiism was claiming to have presented the only viable root, that is the Islamic modernist one, to the attainment of the ideals of modernity. In none of its forms, was a return to a pre-modern past and pre-industrial life advocated by Shii oppositional alternatives. These alternatives called for justice, democracy, a fairer distribution of wealth and moral integrity, and in so doing referred to both indigenous and exogenous sources.

To conclude, the discourse of modernity, which had been the dominant political discourse in Iran since the turn of the century, experienced an unprecedented degree of diversification in the 1970s as a result of the development of secular and religious responses to state modernisation. This process of diversification soon turned into disintegration by a revolutionary process which unfolded during the period 1977–9.

Part 2

The discourse of revolution

The process of diversification of the discourse of modernity reached its peak during the late 1970s, when a revolutionary process brought the modernising state into fatal conflict with the opposition forces. During 1977–9, a transitional discourse of revolution became dominant which facilitated the transformation of the state from a modernising one to an Islamising one. Part 2 will be concerned with this revolutionary process and how it constructed women.

The transitional discourse of revolution was a framework within which a variety of political forces united against the modernising state. Unity was made possible by including those values of modernity with which both secular and Islamic opposition forces could identify. As was the case during the Constitutional Revolution of 1905–11, these rather vague and idealistic values included political freedom, equality, economic development and social justice. The unity around such historically cherished values of modernity and the radicalisation of the political scene helped to transform the discourse of modernity into the transitional discourse of revolution. The transitional discourse revolved around a redefinition of Iran's relationship with the West and had particular characteristics. It was a heterogenous discourse which contained a variety of, sometimes contradictory, secular and Islamic concepts and analyses. It mobilised around the rejection of the Pahlavi regime and its Western supporters and succeeded by unifying under the ideological and organisational hegemony of Shiism.

The specificity of the institution of Shiism, the place it occupied in pre-revolutionary Iran, and its relationship with the state set the background for the role of the Shii movement in the discourse of revolution. The Shii clergy had played an important role in the Constitutional Revolution and supported the move towards modernity, albeit with some reservations. Some clerics had been coopted and silenced by the state, and hence had condoned the establishment of a nation-state and state modernisation, and others had modernised and radicalised the Shii opposition movement. The state's attempt to describe the Shii movement as 'black reaction', then, was not very convincing. Moreover, the institution of Shiism historically had enjoyed a independence from the state and maintained its own links and channels of communication with ordinary people. In the absence of other political forces with stronger links and more established channels of communication, then, the Shii opposition movement was in a strong position to take the lead in in the anti-Pahlavi revolution.

The revolutionary hegemony of Shiism ensured a strong emphasis on rejection of 'cultural imperialism'. This created the contrasting aspects of the two twentieth-century revolutions in Iran. While the Constitutional Revolution aimed to achieve economic and political independence through the emulation of secular European models of modernity, progress and strength, the emphasis in the Revolution of 1977–9 was on achieving cultural independence through the construction of an 'indigenous' and 'authentic' Islamic model of modernity and progress in Iran.

It was within this context that gender was constructed as a revolutionary discourse. The redefinition of Iran's relationship with Western powers entailed a redefinition of gender relations. The emphasis on cultural independence and the hegemony of the Islamic models of independence and modernity determined the content of the revolutionary discourse of gender. The participation of women, the revolutionary demands on gender, the gender symbols of the Revolution, the gender addresses of the revolutionary leadership and the male–female ambience established within the Revolution all helped to construct the 'authentic' Muslim militant Iranian woman.

What accounted for the transformation from modernisation to revolution should be sought in the political developments of 1977–9, which will be discussed in chapter 6. The formation of the discourse of revolution was a result of the transformation of the power relationship between the political ideologies of 'Great Civilisation', Shiism and Marxist–Leninism within the discourse of modernisation. In 1976, when the ideology of 'Great Civilisation' was at its peak, the disparity of institutional power and perceived legitimacy between the three political ideologies was substantial. Most Marxist–Leninist leaders had been killed in guerrilla operations or under SAVAK torture. Opposition Shii leaders such as Ayatollah Khomeini, Ayatollah Taleghani and Ali Shariati were in internal or external exile. The National Front and the Tudeh Party had been relegated to past history. The only tangible political opposition was coming from university students. The student movement launched sporadic political attacks against the regime and university campuses were turned into battlegrounds between the students and the riot police. The Confederation of Iranian Students Abroad was at the height of its political activities against the Shah. The state nevertheless regarded student activism as a nuisance and the Shah believed that the oppositional sentiments of youth were a result of childhood complexes caused by bad parental upbringing.

However, the power relationship between the ideologies of 'Great Civilisation', Shiism and Marxism–Leninism changed rapidly during the course of the next two years. By the beginning of 1979, the contrast with 1976 was enormous. The Shah himself was in exile, Shii political ideology had secured leadership of a popular anti-Shah uprising; and Marxist–Leninist political ideology was being torn apart by, on the one hand, the necessity to unite against the Shah under Shii leadership and, on the other, the desire to assert itself as an independent force within the sweeping revolutionary tide. What accounted for this transformation should be sought in the political developments of 1977–9.

Part 2 will also be concerned with the post-revolutionary transformation from modernisation to Islamisation, which will be analysed in chapter 7. This was a long and difficult process of political power struggle and ideological conflict, and women's issues occupied a prominent place within the contending political ideologies. The process of transition entailed a gradual disintegration of the discourse of revolution and the post-revolutionary transitional period became the scene of intense debate over the new culturally authentic and economically and politically independent society, and the place of women within it. During the Revolution, the main boundary in relation to gender was drawn between the 'Iranian nation' and the 'imperialist culture' and the revolutionary discourse was the affirmation of an 'authentic' cultural identity in relation to gender in contrast to the 'alien' and 'imported' Western one. After the Revolution, the definitions of gender relations multiplied and the battle turned inwards. The battle of gender identity which ensued gave rise to a diverse but vocal feminist movement.

The post-revolutionary transitional period was marked by a difficult struggle for power between the Islamic leadership and other secular and Islamic forces and led to the success of the hardline Shii clergy in gaining exclusive state power. From this process emerged the Constitution of the Islamic Republic which constructed a particular set of patriarchal gender relations. The Constitution responded to the requirements of the modern world by aiming to remove the tension between the family and the nation in relation to women. While, under Pahlavi rule the clergy considered women's absorption into the national process as contradictory to their role within the family, the Constitution of the Islamic Republic granted women rights and obligations both as creators of the Islamic family and nurturers of the Islamic nation.

The analysis of the discourse of revolution which will be presented in following chapters, goes against the conception of the Iranian Revolution of 1977–9 as an explosion against modernity. This idea is often based on an analysis of the pre-revolutionary decade as the period in which a return was made to 'indigenous' culture and religion against the exogenously inspired policies of the state. This is a far too simplistic interpretation of diverse social responses to the Pahlavi state in the two decades which preceded the Revolution.

Indeed, I will argue that the explanation of the Islamic leadership of the Revolution and anti-Western revolutionary slogans should be sought in the revolutionary process itself as it unfolded during 1977–9, and not in the pre-revolutionary opposition to modernisation or a pre-determined judgement about the outcome of the Revolution. The specificity of Shiism, for example, has been identified as one of the root causes of the Revolution (Kramer, 1987). Moreover, the socio-political developments in Iran in the latter part of the Shah's rule have been theorised sometimes as the 'cause' of the Revolution and the Islamic Republic which followed it (Abrahamian, 1980b). Within this framework, the Iranian Revolution has been understood as a reaction to a variety of national grievances which included political protest against autocracy, psychological rejection of rapid modernisation and cultural desire for a return to traditional Islam. The subsequent development of the Islamic Republic has been explained as the natural consequence of an Islamic revolution which has embodied the latter's aspirations against modernity and for traditional Islam (Arjomand, 1988; Sadowski, 1993). However, the causal explanations of the Revolution are susceptible to the fundamental criticism that the aforementioned socio-political developments could have led to a variety of political outcomes other than a revolution. For although many of the social and political factors present in the pre-revolutionary process were activated during the revolutionary process, nevertheless they did not necessarily lead to and constitute the causes of the Revolution (Zubaida, 1989b).

It is my contention that the explanation for the Revolution should be sought in the process of formation and establishment of the discourse of revolution itself. Furthermore, the dominance of Islamic organisational networks, concepts and symbols within the discourse of revolution do not necessarily prove the inevitability of the establishment of the Islamic Republic in its present form, nor do they establish the Islamic Republic as a return to traditional Islam. On the contrary, the analysis of the transitional period demonstrates that, far from being inevitable, the establishment of the Islamic Republic in its particular form was the outcome of a transitional period which exhibited specific features, including a process of power struggle. The new Constitution which emerged from this process proved to be neither a return to tradition nor Islamic in any pre-defined sense. On the contrary, it solicited reference to modern concepts and institutions and made a claim to modernity, independence and progress (Zubaida, 1989a).

6 Gender as a revolutionary discourse

The Revolution of 1977–9 contained a number of features which were particularly pertinent to the construction of gender as revolutionary discourse. The discourse of revolution was established during 1977–9 in several stages including political liberalisation, human rights protests, mass demonstrations, appearance of fractions within the state, mass urban revolt and revolutionary takeover of state power (Milani, 1988; Arjomand, 1988). Let us briefly consider each stage.

Political liberalisation and protest

The formation of the discourse of revolution was triggered by the Shah's introduction of the concept of 'open political space' (*fazaye baz siasi*) (*Keyhan Havai*, 1). The Shah's newly found interest in political liberalisation has been attributed to a number of factors. These included his illness, the failure of his one-party political system and the change of emphasis in American foreign policy from unconditional support of the Pahlavi state to concern over human rights in Iran. By 1976, the Shah had privately acknowledged the failure of the Rastakhiz Party to secure an orderly transfer of power to the crown prince in the likely event of his death from cancer. He therefore turned to the option of securing political stability for his own remaining years and the post-succession era, through a limited and tightly controlled programme of political liberalisation (Ioannides, 1984, pp. 29–30).

While the Shah was entertaining the idea of broader political participation, the Carter administration hinted about a possible link between the Shah's human rights record and the US sale of arms to Iran. Once again, as in the early sixties, a democrat US administration forced the Shah to initiate some loosening of his tight grip over the political system. The Shah found himself intending to liberalise within an international atmosphere of criticism over human rights violations in Iran. He responded by defending the human rights record of his regime, attacking the ideological basis of the human rights' movement, and introducing a gradual and careful programme of political liberalisation. The official press published interviews with the Queen who emphasized the importance of accepting constructive criticism and fighting corruption and dishonesty (*Keyhan Havai*, 2). In March 1977, it was announced that terrorists who had not committed murder would be freed. The Shah granted amnesty to 256 political prisoners. In April he permitted foreign lawyers to attend the trial of eleven dissidents. In May he met the representatives of Amnesty International and the International Commission of Jurists and allowed the Red Cross to visit political prisoners. In June the government amended the rules of procedure in military courts and indicated that civilians would be tried in open civilian courts. The Rastakhiz Party announced that 'free discussion' and 'constructive criticism' were welcome (Abrahamian, 1978, p. 5). The Shah also suggested in an interview that he would not hesitate to loosen his grip over political control. He told a French reporter that he was planning to let go of control once the right degree of strength and preparation was achieved (*Keyhan Havai*, 3). The efforts of the Shah to introduce carefully controlled liberalisation culminated in the dismissal of Prime Minister Hoveyda. His replacement was Jamshid Amuzegar, an economist educated in the US and the general secretary of the Rastakhiz Party who projected an image of modernism and competence.

Human rights protests

Although the change of US foreign policy remained at a mere rhetorical level and the Shah continued to enjoy the military, economic and political support of the Carter administration, American acknowledgement of human rights violations in Iran played an important role in activating internal opposition against the Shah which resurfaced and demanded political and civil rights. The Shah began to lose his chance of initiating controlled political participation as previously banned groups came out into the open independently and new groups emerged. Once in the open, these groups set their own terms for political opposition and made their own demands. The first groups to surface were composed of lawyers, writers and well-known politicians from the Mosaddeq era. Given the degree of publicity the issue of human rights in Iran had received internationally, these well-known intellectuals felt less at risk since their arrest and imprisonment would have further damaged the reputation of the regime. They also protested in groups to decrease the chance of arrest. These groups and individuals wrote open letters to the Shah, accusing the regime of ruining the economy, destroying agriculture, and violating the 1906 Constitution. They demanded abolition of the one-party system, genuine and honest elections, release of political prisoners and freedom of the press and assembly. In Qom, theology students demanded the return of Ayatollah Khomeini from exile. In October, the Association of Writers organised ten poetry reading evenings in the Iran–German Cultural Institute. Between 8,000 and 10,000 people participated in these gatherings and tape recordings of the events were circulated widely.

In November 1977, the Shah's visit to the United States was seen off by an open letter written by a prominent writer, Ali-Asghar Haj-Seyyed-Javadi, which strongly criticised virtually all aspects of his reign. In the United States, the Shah was greeted by thousands of Iranian students protesting against violations of human rights in Iran. The return visit of President Carter to Iran provoked further student demonstrations. The Fadaiyan Khalgh organisation planted a bomb in the Iran–America Society and distributed leaflets that attacked the Shah for 'employing 35,000 American advisors for his army while the country had only 12,500 doctors for 33 million people' (Fadaiyan Khalgh, 1977). By the autumn of 1977, internal opposition had clearly taken the force out of the Shah's intended programme of political liberalisation. The Shah was now cornered into a defensive position.

Mass demonstrations

While the Shah was tackling the problem of how to liberalise without permitting a challenge to his personal authority, a new development created an extraordinary momentum for the opposition. In January 1978, the publication of an insulting article about Ayatollah Khomeini in a mainstream daily newspaper brought the phenomenon of religious riots into the arena of opposition protest. In response to the above article, about 4,000 theology students assembled in a mosque in Qom and voiced the following demands:

> implementation of the Constitution, separation of powers, abolition of the bureau of censorship, freedom of speech, freedom for political prisoners, freedom for citizens to form religious associations, dissolution of the Resurgence Party, the reopening of Tehran University, closed as a result of the poetry-reading sessions, an end to police violence against students, state assistance to farmers, the reopening of Feyzieh, a seminary in Qom closed by the police, and the return of Ayatollah Khomeini ... (Abrahamian, 1978, p. 6)

Theology students and their sympathisers left the mosque to march through the city and in clashes with the police 70 were killed and over 500 were injured (*ibid.*). After the Qom killings Ayatollah Shariatmadari who was a high ranking quietist *mojtahed* emerged as one of the most influential internal leaders of the religious protest movement who demanded proper implementation of the 1906 Constitution. A cycle of religious riots on the fortieth day of previous riots emerged which faced police violence. In May 1978, Ayatollah Shariatmadari called for a day of national mourning which was welcomed by many sections of the population. Once the process of transformation of local religious riots into nation-wide anti-Shah action began to shape up, wider sections of society joined in the protest. The traditional political and oppositional alliance between the clergy, merchants and intelligentsia which dated back to the constitutional period was revived once again. Thousands of students clashed with the police all over the country and Tehran University was occupied by the army. Hundreds of professional and self-employed middle-class people joined with the urban masses and swelled the ranks of the rioters. In June 1978, a general strike was called to commemorate the fifteenth anniversary of the June 1963 religious riots against the Shah's White Revolution which had led to the exile of Ayatollah Khomeini. In the same month the burning down of a cinema was blamed on SAVAK and the deaths of hundreds in that incident led to the spread of riots which resulted in many banks, restaurants, and cinemas being burnt down in revenge. In September 1978, riots culminated in an incident in a Tehran square where a peaceful gathering of people was machine-gunned by the army and thousands of men, women and children were killed. That day, 8 September, became known as 'black Friday'.

While the riots were spreading all over the country, new political groups continued to form and existing ones kept up their pressure (*Iranshahr*, 1, 2). Independent trade unions were formed by university lecturers and lawyers who invited prominent Western lawyers to participate in a four-day conference on human rights. The Association of Lawyers also presented a draft scheme for the trial of offenders, criticised the trial procedure of political prisoners, and demanded the release of Ayatollah Taheri who had recently been detained. The representatives of merchants and traders again and again demanded the abolition of the government controlled Chamber of Commerce and the formation of independent democratic unions (*Keyhan Havai*, 4, 5, 6, 7, 8, 9, 10).

Fractions within the state

By May 1978, opposition spread within the state and the government fell into confusion and disorder. After decades of passivity, the Majles became a platform for heated speeches about the importance of observing the Constitution, and experienced convulsion and disorder after speeches made by the representative from Tabriz, Bani-Ahmad (*Keyhan Havai*, 11). The crisis of the Rastakhiz Party reached its zenith. A government spokesman announced that membership of the Rastakhiz Party was not compulsory. A number of Majles representatives withdrew their membership which was followed by a wave of other withdrawals (*Keyhan Havai*, 12). Various sectors of the state apparatus formed their own pressure groups (*Keyhan Havai*, 13, 14, 15, 16, 17, 18, 19). The Rastakhiz Party was divided into three wings: the right, centre and left, each demanding independence. The government was soon forced to announce that political groups could register for the next election (*Keyhan Havai*, 20).

Amid confusion amongst the parliamentarians and in the Rastakhiz Party, the Shah dismissed General Nasiri as the head of SAVAK, and dissolved the Ministry of Science and Higher Education which controlled the universities, thus granting independence to them. On the anniversary of the Constitutional Revolution, the Shah announced that political freedom in Iran would in the near future match that of European countries (*Keyhan Havai*, 21). He also showed tolerance about the riots by saying that the 'breaking of windows and attacking of banks is the price we have to pay for freedom' (*Keyhan Havai*, 22). In yet another speech he acknowledged that 'many mistakes have been made in the past' and promised that 'Iran is taking steps towards liberalisation' (*Keyhan Havai*, 23). The Shah also granted political amnesty to opposition groups abroad provided 'they respected the Constitution', and promised that members of the Confederation of Iranian Students Abroad would not be persecuted if they returned home (*Keyhan Havai*, 24). The invitation was extended to Ayatollah Khomeini but he rejected it and announced that he would not return to Iran until the Shah was overthrown. The extent and intensity of religious riots and the capacity of the Shii leadership inside Iran to remain at the forefront of the anti-Shah movement persuaded the Shah to pay more attention to religious demands than he had previously done. Prime Minister Amuzegar was soon replaced with Sharif-Emami (in August 1978) who was considered better able to deal with the religious opposition due to his own clerical family background. Sharif-Emami proclaimed his government to be 'the government of national unity' and pledged freedom of the press and political activity as well as the independence of the judiciary. He promised strict observation of Islamic rites, a crackdown on corruption, the closing of casinos, the establishment of a code of conduct for the royal family, removal of the red light district (*shahr now*) from the centre of Tehran, a return to the Islamic calendar, and the abolition of the Ministry for Women's Affairs and the Family Protection Law.

Despite the Shah's optimism, Sharif-Emami was not acceptable to the religious opposition. His previous association with the Court as the head of the Pahlavi Foundation and the head of the Senate for fifteen years, and the fact that the event of 'black Friday' and the imposition of martial law happened just after his appointment as prime minister, went heavily against him. The opposition took advantage of some of Sharif-Emami's reforms to strengthen its position against the Shah and ignored the rest of his concessions. As soon as the freedom of the press and political association was announced, the press gave more space to the opposition. Dozens of new political parties sprang up and the old ones brought their activities into the open. These included some of the old National Front parties such as the Liberation Movement of Iran (Nehzat Azadi Iran), The Toilers Party (Hezb Zahmatkeshan), The Third Force (Niruye Sevvom), The Pan-Iranist Party (Hezb Pan-Iranist), and others (*Keyhan Havai*, 25). The general secretary of the Rastakhiz Party, Javad Said, announced his resignation in October at a press conference and said that various parties that had been formed within the Rastakhiz Party would from then on become independent. Soon after, the premises of the Rastakhiz Party were taken over by the Board of Judiciary for Combatting Corruption, and the party was officially dissolved (*Keyhan Havai*, 26).

Mass urban revolt

The anti-Shah protests of 1977 and early 1978 developed into a political revolution in the autumn of 1978. The Shah appealed for order but new sections of society kept joining in and the waves of protest strikes swept across the country. The strike at Tehran oil refinery was followed by strikes in the Abadan refinery, the largest in the Middle East, and other major industries and factories. Striking workers formed committees, issued regular communiqués, publicised their demands, and opened bank accounts to collect relief funds for workers (*Iranshahr*, 3). The demands of the striking workers were clearly political: the abolition of martial law, dismantling of SAVAK and prosecution of General Nasiri who was the head of SAVAK, release of political prisoners and return of exiled leaders, exclusion of foreign advisors, nullification of exploitative foreign contracts. Many other political demands in solidarity with other striking industries and professions featured prominently in the communiqués of various strike committees. The workers of the National Bank of Iran joined in the strike and the workers of the Central Bank of Iran circulated lists of names of those who had transferred large sums of foreign currency abroad. Soon railways, airlines, newspapers and universities came to a standstill. Even the employees of Court-associated organisations such as the Centre for Intellectual Development (Kanun Parvaresh Fekri) and the Women's Organisation of Iran joined in the strikes. Rumours swept the country that the Shah was planning to abdicate in favour of his son. The Shah, however, denied this and said that 'the transition of power should take its natural course' (*Keyhan Havai*, 27).

By November 1978, it became obvious that the 'government of national reconciliation' had lost control. The army was still very much involved in suppressing demonstrations and many leaders of political parties, of human rights organisations, as well as a number of clerics, were being detained on and off for short periods. In the Majles, the deputies staged walkouts against government proposals and accused the government of arresting and shooting innocent people (*Keyhan Havai*, 28). Finally, in November 1978, Sharif-Emami's government collapsed. The Shah turned to his final option and formed a military government headed by General Azhari, with the aim of bringing the situation under control by military force. Government troops occupied the oil refineries, industrial centres and factories, and radio and television stations. Many of the organisers of demonstrations and strikes were arrested and many demonstrators were shot during street clashes with the army. For a while the streets of Tehran were deserted and workers returned to work. But soon people began to defy the curfew and sporadic demonstrations and clashes continued all over the country. Ayatollah Taleghani called on the people to protest from their rooftops and the sound of chanting, 'God is Great' (*Allah-o-Akbar*), filled the nights. Oil workers refused to produce for purposes other than domestic consumption. Slowdowns continued to cripple the system. Tension built up and culminated in mass demonstrations in defiance of martial law on the religiously significant days of 10 and 11 December. Nearly 1 million people marched in the streets of Tehran and demanded 'freedom, independence and Islamic Republic'. Banners demanded the overthrow of the Shah, the destruction of American power in Iran and arms for the people. By the end of December, once again widespread strikes and stoppages brought all major industries and services to a standstill and General Azhari was forced to resign.

It was during the premiership of Sharif-Emami and Azhari that the main features of a political revolution emerged in Iran. Participation in the anti-Shah movement extended to most social groups and an effective network of organisation and mobilisation was created, revolutionary aspirations and demands were articulated, a common revolutionary language was created, class and gender relations were redefined, and an effective charismatic leadership emerged which adopted a maximalist line.

The revolutionary takeover of the state

After the failure of the military government of General Azhari to bring the demonstrations and strikes under control, the Shah was forced to look for yet another political alternative. Shapour Bakhtiar, a National Front leader, managed to reach an agreement with the Shah to set up what he felt was the only socially viable alternative for Iran. The National Front immediately expelled Bakhtiar and dissociated itself from his negotiations with the Shah. Bakhtiar was not at all happy with the way the anti-Shah movement was going. The domination of the clergy, the extremism of its demands and slogans, and the portrayal of the future political system as Islamic went against his deep-seated nationalist ideal of a democratic constitutional monarchy in Iran. In December 1978 Bakhtiar became prime minister and presented his programme: the Shah's departure from Iran, appointment of a Regency Council, lifting of martial law, freeing of political prisoners, dismantling of SAVAK, an end to the sale of oil to Israel and South Africa, and Ayatollah Khomeini's return to Iran (*Keyhan Havai*, 29). The United States declared its support for Bakhtiar and the army promised to back the legal government and gave its assurance that there would be no military coup after the Shah's departure. The US Embassy and General Huyser, who was a White House special envoy, played important parts in these arrangements (Rubin, 1980, p.246). Finally, the Shah left the country and waves of celebration swept across Iran.

However, the extent of the opposition to Bakhtiar's government became apparent when the press, which had just begun to republish after a two-month old strike, wrote: 'The Shah is gone; now it's America's turn.' Ayatollah Khomeini rejected President Carter's appeal to give Bakhtiar's government a chance and called for the overthrow of American power in Iran. On 19 January, millions of people took to the streets throughout the country to protest against Bakhtiar and a small pro-Bakhtiar demonstration had to be abandoned because of clashes and injuries. In subsequent protests many banks and government buildings were attacked by demonstrators. The red light district of Tehran was burnt down and many prostitutes lost their homes and possessions in the fire (*Keyhan Havai*, 30). The offices of the Women's Organisation of Iran were also set on fire. Various human rights groups and political parties issued declarations against Bakhtiar's government.

As Bakhtiar's government was becoming increasingly isolated and unsupported, the Regency Council collapsed after the resignation of its president. The US government arranged for a secret meeting between

Ramsey Clark and Ayatollah Khomeini in Paris. On 17 January, Khomeini announced the formation of a Council of Islamic Revolution with the secret assistance of the Liberation Movement. The National Front, the Mojahedin organisation and the Tudeh Party announced their allegiance to the new council. The Fadaiyan demanded that a 'Council of Iranian Revolution' should be formed to include striking workers, and warned against the consequences of 'monopolising the Revolution'. On 1 February, Khomeini returned to Iran and was welcomed by massive demonstrations and celebrations in his support. A new political structure began to emerge. Khomeini formed a provisional government and named Mehdi Bazargan as the 'real' prime minister (*Keyhan Havai*, 31, 32, 33, 34). The army was still backing Bakhtiar, but in doing so it faced loss of authority, defections and internal confrontations on a wide scale. Bazargan negotiated with the American government, the army and SAVAK to withdraw support from Bakhtiar's government (Rubin, 1980, pp. 239–40, 251).

On 9 February, the Imperial Guard suppressed a rebellion by Homafaran air force trainees. The next day the Homafaran rebellion was backed by thousands of members of local revolutionary committees (*komiteh Enghelab*), the Mojahedin, the Fadaiyan and members of the public. Armed crowds marched to police stations, military bases, army and SAVAK buildings and prisons, invaded and looted the armoury and released prisoners (*Keyhan Havai*, 35). Army units joined the crowds on a massive scale. The army withdrew its support from Bakhtiar and allowed a non-violent transition of power to the Provisional Government of Mehdi Bazargan. Bakhtiar's government fell and on 14 February the Council of Islamic Revolution took over (*ibid.*).

The development of revolutionary leadership

The leadership of the anti-Shah movement was fluid and somewhat unpredictable. As the movement grew and took its course, its leadership developed and took shape. It began under the leadership of a small group of secular intellectuals, developed into a multiple secular and religious leadership, and finally narrowed down to the leadership of Ayatollah Khomeini as the highest authority in the oppositional movement.

During 1977 secular intellectuals such as lawyers, writers, university teachers, and an older generation of politicians from the National Front and the Liberation Movement initiated a new assault against the Shah's regime on the issue of human rights. This initiative took place when the regime was seen as omnipotent and invulnerable, and therefore put such prominent intellectuals into the leadership position. The long-established Marxist–Leninist and Shii movements continued their activities, but for the moment assumed a background leadership role. The appearance of religious riots changed the situation rapidly. The new situation brought about the involvement of the crowds and changed the nature and character of the leadership as a result. Secular intellectuals continued their protests on human rights and their number increased day by day. But the emergence of street protests created another category of leadership alongside theirs, a Shii leadership which could mobilise and lead the crowds of protestors because, historically and structurally, it was the only group in opposition which was in a position to do so. The economic independence of the institution of Shiism from the state, the relative dependence of the state on its legitimisation by the Shii establishment, and the traditional links between clergy and people all assumed particular importance in the revolutionary context. This was because no other oppositional group could bring crowds of protestors into the street as a result of the state's total suppression and isolation of secular forces. Therefore, the clergy had its own particular independent oppositional lever and established its leadership in the area of mass protest. In the first half of 1978, as anti-Shah struggles developed and more and more freedom of speech and assembly came into being, it became possible for the Marxist–Leninist movement to come out into the open and form a wider ideological constituency. They soon created their own independent space within the oppositional movement. The leadership of the left was firmly in the hands of the Fadaiyan and the Mojahedin organisation and other left-wing groups and tendencies were pushed to the periphery.

By the summer of 1978, then, a situation of multiple constituencies and multiple leadership existed within the anti-Shah movement. Each leadership group – the human rights pioneers, the Shii clergy, and the Fadaiyan organisation – controlled heterogeneous constituencies. The Shii clergy dominated a constituency which included various Shii political tendencies. The clerical leadership was itself heterogeneous, including both moderate and hardline opponents of the Shah. However, the situation of multiple leadership began to change with the ever-growing success of the mass protests. The ability of the Shii establishment to coordinate mass protests gave political credibility to the clergy within the opposition, but it was actually the success of the mass protests in destabilising the Shah's regime that won them the leadership of the anti-Shah movement. The regime proved more vulnerable to mass demonstrations and strikes than to any other form of oppositional activity. The Iranian Revolution was, of course, won through a combination of protest and negotiation, but at the end of the day the bargaining power of the opponents depended on the number of people they could bring into the streets. In circumstances in which a mass following was the ultimate indicator of power, the ability of the clergy to pull out the crowds proved fatal not only to the regime of the Shah but also to other oppositional groupings. Moreover, Ayatollah Khomeini's rise to the position of spiritual leader of the anti-Shah movement occurred through a political process in which a new leadership image was constructed for him, and secular leaders were brought into line one by one.

Shii leadership

Prior to October 1978, the leadership of the crowds of protestors was firmly in the hands of internal Shii leadership. At this time Ayatollah Khomeini was not in a position to coordinate the activities of the opposition against the Shah. Organising and formulating the immediate demands of public protests was, then, left in the hands of the internal Shii leadership. Prior to October 1978, Shii leadership supported the demands made by most sections of the opposition, that is, the proper implementation of the 1906 Constitution. Apart from the isolated pledge of the guerrilla movement to overthrow the Shah and US imperialism in Iran, and Ayatollah Khomeini's assertion that the Shah's regime was illegal and should be overthrown, no other oppositional group challenged the very existence of the regime. The extreme positions adopted by the Marxist–Leninist movement and Ayatollah Khomeini were not mainstream ones at this stage.

The situation, however, changed after October. During the last few months of the Revolution, the external Shii leadership rose to a position of prominence and overshadowed not only the internal Shii leadership but also the leadership claims of all other sections of the opposition. This process started when in October 1978 Ayatollah Khomeini was deported by the Iraqi government and took up residence in a Parisian suburb. He was immediately surrounded by Western-educated aides and established a headquarters for the supporters of the anti-Shah movement. His image was enhanced by the presence and contribution of his aides who were much better informed about the characteristics of anti-Shah movement and were in touch with the aspirations and demands of various sections of the population and opposition political groups. Ayatollah Khomeini's frequent interviews with the foreign press and regular communiqués issued by his headquarters helped to publicise the cause of the anti-Shah movement abroad, and created a new image for him as a popular, charismatic and progressive Shii leader. Khomeini's 1960s image amongst the urban upper and middle classes as a dogmatic, reactionary and backward looking cleric faded away rapidly. Easier communication links with the opposition inside Iran by means of telephone, air, cassette recordings, press, radio and television turned Khomeini's residence into a centre of communication and negotiation over the events in Iran, and enabled him to assert his views and his new image more effectively both at home and abroad. This helped him win widespread public support inside Iran and thus outweigh the leadership claims of other groups.

Moreover, Khomeini was the only political leader who managed to save himself from tail-ending the spontaneous protests. Instead, he succeeded in situating himself ahead of every section of the anti-Shah movement. He managed to persuade most sections of the population to consider him as the spiritual leader of their movement, a leader above party political affiliations. His responsibility was seen as providing general guidance for the anti-Shah movement and the anti-imperialist, anti-Pahlavi direction of Iranian society in general. Khomeini ruled out the possibility of direct rule by the clergy after the Shah's overthrow. The public was persuaded that the mundane aspects of running a country would be beyond the role of a spiritual leader such as Khomeini. It was common to hear among people with various Shii and secular political positions the view that after the overthrow of the Shah, Khomeini would assume a role similar to that of the Pope and the religious city of Qom would become the Vatican of Iran. It was expected that the future state, even if Islamic, would operate independently from the institution of Shiism.

As a result, Khomeini's personal politics seemed irrelevant. His book of religious instruction (*touziholmasael*) which contained attitudes degrading to women, for example, and his conception of an 'Islamic government', which emphasized the necessity of rule of the *faqih* over society, were seen to be outdated. It was believed that these views had been written long before the revolutionary situation in the context of Pahlavi rule. Once the Shah's rule was overthrown, it was believed, Khomeini would never be in a position to implement such policies and would not need to do so anyway. It was argued that what Khomeini really wanted now was to bring Iran out of dependency and establish the rule of social justice, democratic participation and economic fairness. Ayatollah Khomeini's personal interviews reiterated these views over and over again (Nobari, 1978). Within an atmosphere in which the Shii institution was coordinating a mass movement against the Shah, when there were daily massacres of innocent unarmed protestors, and where anger and distrust of the Shah's regime was prevalent, a blind trust towards the revolutionary leadership and solidarity and altruism towards the anti-Shah opposition dominated the public mood. In such circumstances Ayatollah Khomeini's political reassurances could not but work with the general public.

Marxist–Leninist leadership

While oppositional activities by secular constitutionalists and proponents of human rights were weakening the foundations of the political ideology of 'The Great Civilisation', the political ideology of Marxism–Leninism was growing and multiplying.

One of the main pre-revolutionary developments which affected the direction of the movement during the Revolution was the violent shake-up of the Mojahedin organisation. In 1976, the Mojahedin split into two opposing sections. A group of Mojahedin denounced the path of armed struggle and the reference to Islam, and split to set up a secular guerilla organisation by the name of Peykar Khalgh. This split served to strengthen the Islamic identity of the original Mojahedin Khalgh Organisation, who made extensive reference to the teachings of Ali Shariati and advocated Islamic *hejab* for female members. The Mojahedin adopted Shariati's concept of the 'Islamic Unitary Society' and proposed to struggle towards the attainment of a classless Islamic state (see chapter 5). The Mojahedin, however, retained many aspects of their Marxist–Leninist ideology. They aimed to expand into a Leninist-type party and play a vanguard role in leading Iranian society into 'Islamic socialism'.

The secular Fadaiyan and the Islamic Mojahedin became the main Marxist–Leninist groups in Iran in the 1970s. The atmosphere of opposition inside Iran made it possible for the Mojahedin and the Fadaiyan to import the literature which they published abroad. These were distributed clandestinely inside Iran and contributed to the growth of the new secular and religious opposition to the Shah. In 1977, the Mojahedin and the Fadaiyan adopted a dual approach towards the anti-Shah protests of the intelligentsia who demanded human rights and democratic institutions in Iran. They, on the one hand, encouraged their followers to support any form of opposition to the Shah. But their official pronouncements, on the other hand, considered anti-imperialist struggles as the most important in Iran and opposed the demand for human rights and democratic struggle as deviationist (Mojahedin Khalgh, 1978; Fadaiyan Khalgh, 1978a).

Both Islamic and secular Marxist–Leninists proposed alternative social and political systems for Iran. They opposed gradual reform and piecemeal change and prescribed a complete transformation of all aspects of society, beginning with the overthrow of the existing social system which they believed was intricately interwoven with the interests of American imperialism. They therefore objected to the National Front's emphasis on the primacy of the struggle against the Pahlavi dictatorship as opposed to the struggle for the overthrow of American imperialism in

Iran, and warned the people that 'the liberal bourgeois opposition is by nature conciliatory and unable to support working-class struggles to the end. The reformist-constitutionalist opposition is bound to sell out the radical demands of the movement to the regime' (Peykar Organisation, 1978). The Marxist–Leninist movement also accused the Association of Writers of 'nesting in the house of foreigners', because the latter organised poetry readings in the Iran–German Cultural Institute, of having received orders from foreigners, and of reducing the anti-imperialist struggles of the Iranian masses to a 'Hyde Park Corner show' (Moazen, 1978, p. 692). The main contribution of the Marxist–Leninist groups to the protest movement was armed struggle. The Fadaiyan staged armed attacks against police stations involved in suppressing demonstrations and also assassinated army officers who had ordered the troops to shoot at demonstrators. After every bloody event, the Fadaiyan issued declarations condemning the regime and informing the public of their armed actions. They also continuously warned 'the masses' against the 'conspiracies' of the reformists and constitutionalists and argued that the only valid leadership of the anti-Shah movement belonged to organisations which defended the rights of the toilers (Fadaiyan Khalgh, 1978a).

The Mojahedin and the Fadaiyan welcomed the appearance of religious riots in the political scene. Throughout the 1960s and 1970s they had struggled clandestinely and as a result had not had the opportunity to establish links with the very classes they aimed to represent. The appearance of the protesting crowds in the streets gave them their first chance of contact with the masses. The most recent time a Marxist–Leninist organisation had been able to pull crowds of its own into the streets independently of the clergy and the bazaar, was the Tudeh Party during the Mosaddeq era. It was not surprising, then, to find that the Marxist–Leninist opposition regarded the 'masses' as sacred and a mass following was seen to be the biggest political prize of all. The Mojahedin and the Fadaiyan organisations turned out to be too eager to support any kind of mass protest and were readily and promptly absorbed into religious riots organised by the anti-communist clergy and the bazaar.

The Marxist–Leninist movement also welcomed Ayatollah Khomeini's uncompromising stance towards the Americans and the Shah and his disapproval of those secular and Shii leaders who believed in a dialogue with the Shah's regime. Therefore, despite the fact that Khomeini forbade his supporters to form an alliance with communists while promising freedom of political activity in a future Islamic society (Nobari, 1978, p. 13), he was the only leader trusted by Marxist–Leninists. As far as most Marxist–Leninists were concerned, the important thing was that the masses were in the street opposing the Shah and it was considered as irrelevant who led them at this stage (CISA, 1978, p. 23). The attraction of being 'with the masses' and the disparity of power which existed between the state and the crowds, the former being armed with the most sophisticated weapons and instruments of repression and torture and the latter being equipped only with anti-Shah slogans and flowers for the soldiers, brought home the necessity of unity. The question of unity, then, assumed great importance. Unity was defined by the Shii leadership as uniting under the banner of Islam. Many eyewitness accounts existed of non-Shii groups being prevented from marching or demonstrating under their own separate banners. The Shii leadership kept a jealously guarded monopoly on placards and slogans used in anti-Shah demonstrations.

For the secular opposition, unity meant covering up old ideological differences and obeying the rules laid down by the Shii leadership. The veil, for example, was easily accepted by the secular opposition as a 'symbol' of resistance to the Shah. Many Marxist–Leninist men and women shouted 'freedom, independence, Islamic Republic' when facing armed riot police. Some of the excesses of the religious leaders and followers were criticised. A Fadaiyan leaflet, which did not have their name on it, criticised the clergy for creating rifts in the ranks of the opposition by adopting an anti-left attitude (Fadaiyan Khalgh, 1978b). Independent socialists, too, reflected their anxiety about concepts such as the 'Islamic Republic' and 'Islamic government' in the pages of independent newspapers such as *Iranshahr* published abroad. Many left-wing women had mixed feelings about various aspects of the participation of women in the Revolution. The dominance of veiled women, intolerance towards the left, the occasional compulsory separation of the demonstrators into male and female sections, and the total domination of the Revolution by the clergy, all worried these women. But worries and mixed feelings of such nature were bound to remain a private concern for these women. Within the sweeping tide of anti-Shah feelings, worries like these had no power to mobilise public attention and concern. It was only a few days before the overthrow of the state that the left came out against these practices publicly and dared to declare their independent existence. In January 1979, the first Marxist demonstration took place in the streets of Tehran when about 10,000–30,000 men and women sympathisers of various Marxist–Leninist groups carried the banners of the Fadaiyan and demonstrated against the intolerance of religious leaders towards the left while at the same time pledging allegiance to Ayatollah Khomeini. The marchers complained that, 'Religious officials forbid us from expressing ourselves. They tear down our posters. They expel us with brute force from their parades' (*Middle East Report*, 1979, p. 32).

Throughout the Revolution, therefore, the Marxist–Leninist movement felt anxious about the Shii leadership of the Revolution but on the whole supported its anti-Shah stance. There was a fairly strong sense of solidarity within the Marxist–Leninist movement. The only Marxist–Leninist organisation alienated from left solidarity was the Tudeh Party. The newly revived Tudeh Party, however, adopted a totally appeasing approach towards the Shii leadership (Tudeh Party, 1978a; Middle East Report, 1979, p. 30). Its unreserved support for the Shii leadership further alienated it from other Marxist–Leninist groups (Fadaiyan Khalgh, 1978a). Tudeh support for the clergy was based on the theory that the anti-Shah movement was a 'nationalist-bourgeois revolution' led by the 'national bourgeoisie' represented by the clergy. The Tudeh Party believed that it was necessary to support the national bourgeoisie to create a democratic atmosphere which would be a prerequisite for any 'socialist-workers' revolution (ibid.). Very soon, the Tudeh Party went so far as to reorganise its own leadership in order to be able to come out in full support of the clergy. The general secretary of the party, Iraj Eskandari, was replaced by Nureddin Kianuri, who promptly announced that the programme of the party was compatible with that of the Shii leadership.

By January 1979, the Marxist–Leninist leadership had been outmanoeuvred by the religious leadership. The leadership of the Fadaiyan could not possibly compete with that of Khomeini. The approach adopted by Ayatollah Khomeini towards the Mojahedin was somewhat different from that which he took towards other Marxist–Leninist groups. He largely ignored the Mojahedin and neither attacked nor supported their actions. For him and for the majority of other religious leaders, the Mojahedin's pledge to establish an Islamic socialism was a deviation from Islam and a bridge that could lead Muslim youth to Marxism. The Mojahedin, however, supported the religious leadership wholeheartedly throughout the Revolution and established a close relationship with Ayatollah Taleghani, the co-founder of the Liberation Movement of Iran, due to contacts and friendships developed in the Shah's prisons.

Nationalist leadership

As the anti-Shah movement developed, those who continued to give priority to values such as individual freedom, human rights and democracy increasingly became less popular. The National Front which traditionally adhered to such values often came under attack for being 'liberal', 'soft' and 'pro-American', and was soon washed away by the tide of hardline anti-imperialist attitudes of the dominant Shii leadership.

The moderate wing of the Shii leadership itself did not remain influential for long. Ayatollah Shariatmadari was soon criticised for being pro-American and soft on the Shah. The Liberation Movement, led by Mehdi Bazargan, was also swept aside by the tide of anti-imperialist sentiments. Moderate nationalist leaders such as Sanjabi, Shariatmadari and Bazargan wanted a peaceful and controlled transition to constitutional government. They wanted to end the bloodshed, restore order and prevent a military takeover, and were willing to negotiate with the Shah and the US to achieve their aims. Bazargan and Sanjabi communicated with the American Embassy regarding their oppositional demands and the intentions of the US government (Ioannides, 1984, pp. 30–1). After Sharif-Emami was appointed as premier, both Sanjabi and Bazargan hoped that the Constitution would be properly implemented. Sanjabi emphasised that he was ready to negotiate with the new government. The National Front, he said, did not plan to govern in the short term and would aim to establish democracy and reinstate the Constitution (*Keyhan Havai*, 36). Bazargan expressed his worry that the wave of spontaneous protests had reduced the political parties to followers instead of leaders. He blamed lack of effective leadership by secular political parties (*ibid.*). He believed that every time Iranians rebelled spontaneously and violently they failed and ended up with another dictatorship (Rubin, 1980, p. 222). But, at the same time, the nationalists were also aware that any effort made to block the momentum of the Revolution might turn out to be worse than taking their chances with it.

Moderate leaders, therefore, frequently appeared indecisive and, while privately expressing anxiety about Khomeini's maximalist line, did not publicly oppose him (Chehabi, 1990, pp. 223–52; Siavoshi, 1990, pp. 129–72). It was common to hear from religious and secular people alike statements such as 'Sanjabi and Bazargan really want to make a deal with the Shah. They are bourgeois. We only have confidence in Khomeini for he is the only one who really wants the Shah to leave' (Middle East Report, 1979, p. 19). Within the revolutionary culture of the day, anyone exhibiting any interest in coming to terms with the American presence in Iran and compromising with the Shah was deemed unfit for leadership. During the last few months of the Revolution, Ayatollah Khomeini's residence became the focal point for negotiations regarding the political future of Iran. Sanjabi and Bazargan and representatives of the bazaar visited Khomeini during October and November 1978 (*Keyhan Havai*, 37). Khomeini and Sanjabi issued a joint declaration about Islam and democracy, and Sanjabi rejected the Shah's invitation to form a National Front government over and over again. In December, the National Front issued a declaration which condemned the regime of the Shah as illegal and called for its overthrow (*Keyhan Havai*, 38). For the first time, Ayatollah Shariatmadari threatened the regime with violent demonstrations if the demands of the opposition were not met (*Keyhan Havai*, 39). By December, the total loyalty and subservience of the nationalist leadership to Khomeini was complete and another stage in the process of his rise to absolute leadership was completed.

Organisation, mobilisation and participation

The organisation, mobilisation and participation features of the Revolution had an important impact on the construction of the Islamic national model of modernity and the notion of womanhood that it entailed. The organisation of the Revolution through grass-roots networks provided an alternative to the state's model of managing the society from above. The mass urban model of mobilisation challenged the existing mode of government by exclusion. Women's mass participation was a challenge to the state ideology of Westernisation and its accompanying notion of womanhood. The alternative model of national independence, strength and progress was an Islamic populism based on grass-roots action and participation. The assertion of the rights of popular classes was considered as the new modernism and a sign of progress within the oppositional movement.

The politicisation and mobilisation of the networks of mosques, Islamic associations, centres of pilgrimage, *rowzeh* and *sofreh* networks played an important role in the success of the Revolution. The Revolution progressed through undetermined chains of events, confrontations, and sets of actions and reactions. But under the surface of spontaneous action and reaction, the movement was being organised by a network of grass-roots organisations. These organisations were flexible and fluid, and moved rapidly to embrace and organise the latest developments of the day. The grass-roots organisations constantly changed and adapted themselves to the changing situation. Riots were organised in association with major religious centres in towns and villages. This was because of the historical autonomy of the institution of Shiism, as described before, and the policies of the Pahlavi state which prevented political parties from forming organic links with the masses. During the 1970s, as one writer put it 'No other opposition group could master a network of 180,000 members with 90,000 cadres (*molla*) ... some 50 leaders (Ayatollah), 5,000 'officers' (*hojat ol-eslams*) ... 11,000 theological students (*tollab*), and a whole mass of ordinary members, such as Islamic teachers, preachers, prayer guides and procession organisers' (Ramy, 1983, p. 77).

The rapid growth of the grass-roots network meant that, by the autumn of 1978, most localities in urban centres and some in rural centres were organising their own daily events and activities through the local mosques and revolutionary committees (*komiteh enghelab*), which received support and funds from the main religious centres and local population. During the last two months of 1978 most young people became involved in street protests which often resulted in clashes with the army. In many localities, the mosque and the revolutionary committee were one and the same and constituted the sole power centre of that area. In other localities, dual power centres were created by the mosque and the secular-oriented revolutionary committee, either cooperating or competing with each other for power depending on the situation. Some revolutionary committees were controlled by the clergy, others were controlled by the Mojahedin or the Fadaiyan. In ethnic provinces such as Kurdistan, Baluchestan and Khusestan, local liberation movements were in control of revolutionary committees. Many factories, industries and other places of work, too, formed their own revolutionary committees which coordinated strikes and other activities of their constituency. The revolutionary committees of the oil, textile and manufacturing industries were some examples (Middle East Report, 1979, p. 33). The cadres at the forefront of neighbourhood and workplace revolutionary committees were mainly men, with women playing a supporting role, except for the revolutionary committees controlled by the Mojahedin and the Fadaiyan where women directly participated in the operations of revolutionary committees.

The role of grass-roots organisations was not confined to organising demonstrations and policing the locality. Through the network of local revolutionary committees, revolutionary literature and tapes were produced and distributed and anti-establishment rhetoric and slogans were devised and spread. In this area, too, the mosques and revolutionary committees were flexible, fluid and responsive to the oppositional mood. The slogans and placards carried in large demonstrations were under the control of the mosques and revolutionary committees (Fischer and Abedi, 1989). The same slogan would suddenly be on everyone's lips. But a popular slogan would change as soon as a new chain of events came about. Immediately after a speech by the Shah, his prime minister, or the military governor, new oppositional slogans, rhymes, couplets and songs were composed and widely circulated. They often reflected the spirit of Ayatollah Khomeini's declarations.

The political network of mosques and revolutionary committees created revolutionary symbols and popularised changes of emphasis in Shii ideology. The content of symbols and the revolutionisation of Shii ideology will be examined later. But the role played by the revolutionary network to popularise these was instrumental in the development of the discourse of revolution. As the army killed and injured thousands of demonstrators, the powerlessness of the demonstrators in a military sense was compensated for in a psychological sense by revolutionary symbols and ideology. The writings which appeared on the walls told the demonstrators that fields of tulips were growing from the blood of martyrs to cover the whole country. The images of Shii heroism and martyrdom and the revolutionary concept of Muslim womanhood spread rapidly within the revolutionary network. But it would be wrong to conclude from the Islamic nature of revolutionary networks that their prime concern was the spread of Islam or that revolutionary networks were limited to Islamic ones. The civil disobedience which broke the backbone of the Pahlavi regime included strikes and walkouts as well as street demonstrations. Professional guild associations and workers' committees in public and private institutions and government agencies and ministries were very much part of the revolutionary network and their oppositional actions were instrumental in the paralysis of the state.

With regard to the class component of the Revolution, the organisational features of the Revolution facilitated representation of most economic and political interests. But contrary to assumptions made by most class analyses of the anti-Shah movement, the economic class interests and political demands of the participants did not necessarily correspond (Zubaida, 1989b). This was mainly because other social and historical loyalties and interests cut across those of economic classes, and similar political demands were formed by economically heterogeneous social groups. More often than not within the revolutionary context, the political demands of the participants depended on multiple factors such as membership of social networks like the bazaar, Shii institutions, or the university; historical association or animosity against the royal family or the state; and other religious, ethnic and familial loyalties. Social categories such as the intelligentsia, the clergy and bazaar merchants who played important roles in the Revolution did not constitute a single economic class. These were politically heterogeneous groups which assumed distinct political identities within the revolutionary context. The political interests of these groups were determined by the revolutionary process. Moreover, collective political demands were developed during the course of the anti-Shah movement and popular revolutionary slogans contained contradictory class interest components.

The nature of women's participation in the above oppositional activities reflected both the pattern of their integration into society in the preceding few decades, and featured the revolutionary construction of the new 'authentic' woman. Women were represented in most secular political groups but in smaller numbers. The associations formed by lawyers, writers, university lecturers, civil servants, and teachers were all mixed but had a low female membership. Here, women mainly participated within the rank and file, and token numbers of female leaders emerged. The associations of writers and university lecturers had few women leaders between them and the Association of Lawyers elected only one woman to its board of management. The leadership of the political parties, whether royalist, constitutionalist, nationalist, religious, secular, or Marxist–Leninist was in men's hands. Women's representation was even smaller in technical professions and the associations which represented them. The associations of engineers and doctors, and the committees formed by employees and labourers at industrial and technical complexes did not include any women. Women were best represented within the associations formed by teachers, nurses, government employees and students.

The human rights movement did not represent women's specific interests. In the 1970s many of the victims of human rights violations were women. The human rights organisations circulated documents regarding the treatment of women in prisons and the use of physical, psychological and sexual torture against women. But the particularly severe nature of the violations of the rights of women prisoners did not result in the formation of women-specific human rights groups as neither the defenders of human rights nor the victims of human rights violations regarded gender-specific issues relevant. Moreover, women's participation in moderate political parties was particularly weak. Contrary to the enthusiastic support given by women to the constitutional movement at the turn of the century, Iranian women in the late 1970s did not have much taste for constitutional monarchy. Women's membership within the rank and file of the moderate nationalist and reformist parties was not significant. None of the middle of the road political parties formed or revived during the premiership of Sharif-Emami made a specific appeal to women. The pro-establishment parties did not do so in order not to offend and agitate the religious opposition, and anti-state parties were wary of taking up the question of women's rights because of its association with the policies of the Shah's regime. In short, the moderate political opposition failed to present an alternative conception of women to that of the Pahlavi state.

Contrary to the moderate political parties, radical political ideologies took up the question of women's oppression under the Shah and mobilised large numbers of women around it. While moderate political parties bypassed the new mood of interest in the question of women and continued to subscribe to existing gender relations, the radical political ideologies pointed to women as the source of change within society and promised radical reorganisation of gender relations in a future egalitarian society. The new oppositional context which was created after the appearance of religious riots and the political concessions made by Sharif-Emami's government opened up new areas for women's oppositional activities. Women became massively involved in anti-Shah demonstrations and strikes, and the established trend of women's absorption into the political ideologies of Shiism and Marxist–Leninism was intensified. Women joined the crowds of protestors as early as spring 1978 and throughout the Revolution participated in almost all kinds of oppositional activities.

As will be examined in more detail later, during the anti-Shah movement gender divisions of role and space diminished substantially (Betteridge, 1983, p. 121). The movement was not governed by a sexual division of labour except with regard to leadership. The leadership of the mass movement was exclusively male, and female leaders did not emerge. As long as women participated as rank and file, they were left free to choose for themselves which aspects of the struggle they wished to take up. Women participated in peaceful and violent mass demonstrations; they dug trenches and fought in street battles; they joined strikes, boycotts and stoppages at work; they participated in the activities of local militia groups, and took part in guerilla attacks against government installations. In August 1978, six women were put on trial by the state for 'creating disorder in Tehran bazaar' (*Keyhan Havai*, 40). Women sometimes constituted more than one third of the demonstrators (MERIP Reports, 1979, p. 15). Many women were killed during street clashes with the riot police. Women went to demonstrations expecting violence and shoot-outs and many of them dressed appropriately to avoid being exposed if shot (*Ketab Jomeh*, 1, p. 90). Many women were killed in the 'Cinema Rex' and 'black Friday' events and some were killed in guerrilla activities. Women sometimes led the processions and offered flowers to the soldiers to prevent them from shooting. This tactic usually had a traumatic effect on young soldiers. Women's participation in strikes was widespread in all major public and private organisations and industries. In the last few months of the Revolution even the employees of the state's Women's Organisation of Iran joined the strikes (Sanasarian, 1982, p. 117).

But in addition to personal participation in revolutionary events, the main role played by women was that of sustaining and nourishing the revolutionary movement. Women supported and organised the oppositional activities of their families, relatives, friends and neighbours. They faced the deaths or injuries of their loved ones with courage and strength. Women felt it to be a revolutionary duty to give blood and keep the hospitals going by offering clean bedding. Female doctors and nurses worked round the clock to provide medical assistance to the wounded in hospitals and those in hiding in homes. Women often offered the protection of their homes to the demonstrators being chased by the riot police. They fed and offered beds to friends of their husbands, brothers, sisters, sons and daughters who stayed with them during the curfew hours to plan the next day's actions. Women supported neighbourhood oppositional activities. They offered food to the local mosque and protected the local militia. Women played an important role in the circulation of oppositional literature and tapes and spread the latest BBC news and revolutionary slogans in a short span of time through women-specific networks of *rowzeh* and *sofreh*. The enthusiasm shown by women in their effort to transform their ideals and expectations of society, radically, and practically overnight, was an important contribution to the transformation of gender relations into a revolutionary discourse.

Women's participation in the anti-Shah movement cannot be fully and satisfactorily explained by reference to class patterns. Women participated as political subjects and their political demands were constructed within the general oppositional context. As one writer put it 'Most women, poor or not, became involved in the marching and protests, discussions and organising only to the extent that personal situations provided the role models, information, and support which made it efficacious for them to take part' (Hegland, 1983a, p.181).

Many generalisations about the pattern of participation of lower and middle-class women, which equate economic class with political views and rely heavily on the presumed political unity of women from the same economic classes, remain at the level of mere assumption. Doubt has been raised by informed studies of the participation of various strata of women such as the poor and the ideologically motivated Shii women. It has been demonstrated that poor women, too, had differing political opinions despite their common economic position, and being poor did not universally drive them to support the Revolution (Bauer, 1983).

Revolutionary demands and symbols

Revolutionary demands and symbols had a role as important as organisation, mobilisation and participation in the construction of cultural populism and the culturally authentic conception of women. Once mass mobilisation was achieved, the Revolution became a space for voicing historical and structural frustrations. The grievances of the peasants against the landlords and those of the workers against the capitalists featured prominently amongst revolutionary demands. But these grievances were not voiced by a class of workers or peasants as a 'class for itself'. They were voiced by mixed social strata referred to as 'the poor' or the *mostazaf*, the majority of whom were rural migrants and shanty-town dwellers. The demands of the poor were taken up by the anti-Shah movement as a matter of priority. These and the economic demands of the more privileged classes were constructed collectively and there was no question of contradictory class demands within the revolutionary movement. The opposition regarded the state as guilty of defending the rich against the poor, protecting big business against small business, and giving priority to finance capital as opposed to productive capital. The revolutionary movement demanded proper housing and social security for the poor as well as the abolition of the state's Chamber of Commerce and the dis-involvement of the royal family in commercial deals. All of these demands were seen as complementary. Economically motivated political demands were complemented by political and cultural demands. Again and again demonstrators shouted slogans against state corruption, dictatorship, political centralisation, suppression of freedoms, destruction of the indigenous culture, and tradition and religion. The same policies of the Shah that had been tolerated or even supported for decades were now defined as oppressive.

The manner in which the Revolution defined the *ancien régime* attempted to account for all oppression. This included the oppression of women. The new oppositional context created new terms for debating the question of women. The discourse of revolution divided the issue of women's emancipation into two components: 'women's formal rights ' and 'women's social value'. The former were considered to be mere cosmetic changes in the legal status of women brought about by the Shah's regime and were therefore rejected. The latter was defined as the indicator of women's real emancipation within society and was therefore subscribed to. In rejecting the attempts of the regime and its women's organisation to champion the cause of women's liberation in Iran, revolutionary women refused to mobilise around the question of women's rights. It became a contradiction in terms to oppose the Shah on the basis of a demand for the improvement of women's formal rights. Revolutionary leaders talked about 'special worth and respect' for women and this message was able to mobilise thousands of women into revolutionary action. After all, the end result of the Pahlavi state's female emancipation was seen to be the *gharbzadeh* woman of the seventies. This was a woman who lived under the influence of Western culture and therefore 'came to embody at once all social ills: she was a super-consumer of imperialist/dependent/capitalist/foreign goods; she was a propagator of the corrupt culture of the West; she was undermining the moral fabric of society; she was a parasite beyond any redemption' (Najmabadi, 1991, p. 65). Ayatollah Khomeini conveyed his pride in the way women rejected the *gharbzadeh* woman by their participation in the Revolution: 'Any nation that has women like the Iranian women will surely be victorious' (Haines, 1980, p. 99). He promised them real freedom, equality and dignity. Khomeini's statements were couched in general terms and allowed women to interpret them in their own ways. He emphasised over and over again that:

> As for women, Islam has never been against their freedom. It is, to the contrary, opposed to the idea of woman-as-object and it gives her back her dignity. A woman is man's equal; she and he are both free to choose their lives and their occupations. But the Shah's regime is trying to prevent women from becoming free by plunging them into immorality. It is against this that Islam rears up. This regime has destroyed the freedom of women as well as men. Women as well as men swell the population of Iranian prisons, and this is where freedom is threatened. We want to free them from the corruption menacing them. (Nobari, 1978, p. 13)

Khomeini's messages of support and encouragement gave women a feeling of security and importance. Terms such as 'freedom', 'dignity', 'immorality' and 'corruption' remained undefined by the Shii leader and, affected by the atmosphere of opposition to the Shah, women tended to read into them their own positive meanings. Khomeini, however, was quite specific about some of the issues of concern to women. He emphasised in an interview that women would be free to choose their own clothing within the framework of decency (*The Guardian*, 1), and revolutionary women believed him. The prospect of veiling being imposed forcibly on women in the future seemed inconceivable within the context of an anti-autocratic revolution. The conditions were ripe for the Shii leadership to persuade most sections of the nation to fight the Shah under the united banner of cultural nationalism, even if an Islamicised one.

Revolutionary symbols and role models further defined the authentic cultural construction of women. An important symbol of resistance to the imported 'culture' which appeared in the revolutionary movement was women's *hejab*. To wear the *hejab* became a woman's way of enacting the revolutionary demand of respect and social value for women. The *hejab* became the symbol of rejection of Pahlavi values. Reza Shah's programme of modernisation of women's position in the 1930s began by forcibly unveiling women on a massive scale (see chapter 3). Women were then forced to adopt Western clothes and change their values overnight in accordance with their dress. The popularity of *hejab* during the Revolution was a sign of their rejection of forcibly imposed values.

On the issue of *hejab*, too, the majority public opinion changed from seeing the *hejab* as a sign of backwardness to considering it the sign of social value for women. For decades, *hejab* in the form of the *chador* had only been worn on a regular basis by religious or poor women. Other women only wore it for funerals, pilgrimages to Shii shrines and on other religious occasions. When feelings towards the adoption of Western values changed during the 1970s and more and more women turned to Islamic values, the *chador* was still considered traditional and the new Islamic women turned to a more modern form of *hejab*, that is, headscarves and loose dresses and trousers. The name *hejab*, meaning modest clothes for women, became popular then.

But with the Revolution, the desire to raise the status of the poor and the traditionalist and the necessity to create overt symbols of resistance to Pahlavi values brought all forms of *hejab* including the *chador* back into popularity. But contrary to some suggestions, the adoption of *hejab* by some women during the Revolution was not necessarily related to their class background. Women from different classes wore *hejab* for different reasons (Betteridge, 1983). While some did so because it symbolised their protest against the treatment of women as sex-objects, other women wore it as a religious duty.

Some women wore the *chador* when participating in demonstrations which took place on religiously significant days, but did not wear it in other demonstrations. Many secular women felt confusion about the question of *hejab*. The old meaning of *hejab* was changing (Milani, 1992; Abu Odeh, 1993). While in the past it used to signify lack of access and inhibition for women, it was now being conceived of as enabling and empowering. It was felt as enabling because it allowed access to public spheres where access by women had always been accompanied by sexual harassment and humiliation, such as walking on the street, using public transport or participating in mixed demonstrations; and it was felt as empowering because it portrayed women as free, non-sexual, politically aware, and in solidarity with the Revolution. A minority of secular women rejected wearing *hejab* under any circumstances, but many others chose to wear it in the revolutionary context because of its new meanings.

The Iranian revolutionary discourse was about new forms and representations of the anti-Shah protest. Images of thousands of marching veiled women and portraits of Ayatollah Khomeini being led by heavily clad little girls were bound to make strong impressions on the enemy. Symbolic language was adopted to help internalise often complex economic, social and political criticisms of the regime. Collective demands were often expressed by labelling the enemy in symbolic language. The demand for social justice, equality and independence was expressed by labelling the American government as the 'Great Satan' and the regime of the Shah as demonic, or *taghuti*. The revolutionaries did not have to be religious and strictly pro-Khomeini to identify with this language. It was a language of opposition more than the language of Shiism. A language, in other words, specially made for the Revolution. Symbolism was accompanied by a revolutionary change of emphasis in Shii ideology. The active Shiism articulated by Ali Shariati assumed popularity and dominance amongst the educated, as well as the illiterate. The struggles of the Shii *emaman* against Sunni Caliphs, which culminated in the battle of *Karbala* and resulted in the death of Hosein the third *emam*, became positive points of reference: 'it became practical to stress that the *Karbala* paradigm is not a passive weeping for Hosein but rather an active fighting for Hosein's ideals, and it is not merely a personal and individual commitment but a social one' (Fischer, 1980, p. 213).

The image of Hosein changed from that of 'Hosein as intercessor' to 'Hosein as exemplar'. The quietist Shii ideology of adaptation to existing relations of power gave way to the revolutionary ideology of struggle against tyranny (Hegland, 1983b, p. 235). Likewise, the cultural emphasis of quietist times regarding female role models changed and gave way to a new revolutionary emphasis. The role model of Fatemeh, the Prophet's daughter and mother of the second and third *emaman*, changed from that of a wife and mother to that of a revolutionary Shii woman. The role played by Zeynab, Fatemeh's daughter and the sister of *emam* Hosein, in Shii struggles against the Sunni Caliphs came to the fore. Zeynab's political speech against Yazid and her supporting role in the *Karbala* battle were cited by the new Shii woman with pride. The traditional mourning processions of the religious month of *moharram* were suspended for the first time since they came into practice in Iran more than a century ago in the Qajar period. Instead of commemorating the historical battle of *Karbala* by religious processions and passion plays as they would normally do, the actual battle of *Karbala* against the tyranny of the Shah was enacted in the streets of Tehran. Thousands of demonstrators poured into the streets in the religious month of *moharram* to protest against the Shah, the Yazid of modern times.

Traditionally, women were excluded from religious processions but now thousands of veiled women took part. For many of them this was an opportunity to feel as close as men did to the *Karbala* battle, the recitations of which they had listened to all their lives. The anti-Shah demonstrations which took place on religiously significant days were treated by many women as religious occasions and a rare opportunity to play an equal part in religious activities. The content of most religious ceremonies such as *rowzeh* and *sofreh*, too, changed. No longer were they weeping sessions at sermons describing the sufferings of the *emaman* and their offspring. Instead, political speeches were presented and women wept for the martyrs of the anti-Shah movement. The audience gained strength and courage from collective prayers and mourning to make even more spectacular sacrifices. The male or female *akhund* who gave the sermons, provided direction and encouragement for renewed action. It was almost as if a new Shiism had been born. Most old-fashioned concepts advocated by the *mollas* were pushed into the background and the foreground was occupied by refreshingly modern Shii concepts. These had nothing to do with the kind of Shiism the Shah was trying to label as 'black reaction'. His reaction, therefore, remained irrelevant.

The all-embracing slogan of 'freedom, independence, Islamic Republic' which became the trademark of the Iranian Revolution was a condensation of a wide range of economic, political and cultural grievances against the Pahlavi regime and a manifestation of the alternatives sought. The issue of women's liberation was made central to the revolutionary demand for the overthrow of the Shah and was voiced by a nation of men and women on behalf of women. Mass demonstrations shouted slogans against the conception of women as 'sex-objects' and demanded 'respect' and 'social value' for women. The Pahlavi dynasty was labelled as the 'spreader of prostitution' and the 'corrupter of women and family'. It was demanded that the 'alien Western culture' adopted by the regime of the Shah be uprooted. Like class demands, gender demands too were situated at the heart of the slogan of 'freedom, independence, Islamic Republic'.

Male–female interaction in the Revolution

An important aspect of the revolutionisation of gender relations was the enactment of new gender relations within the Revolution. The alternative 'culturally appropriate' mode of male–female interaction being demanded necessitated a reorganisation of gender relations within the revolutionary movement. If the regime was accused of treating women as sex objects, then, women could not be treated as such within the revolutionary movement. The same applied to other oppressed groups. If the Shah's regime treated the poor with disdain, the revolutionary movement had to offer them respect.

Throughout the mass demonstrations of 1978, participants experienced new conceptions of status hierarchy. The poor and the traditionalist enjoyed a higher status than the rich and the modernist. The way of life of the poor and the traditionalist was adopted as the revolutionary way of life. Simple life styles and traditional cultural values became fashionable, replacing the extravagant habits of the upper and middle classes. The poor were not required to aspire towards the extravagant life styles of the rich any more. They were now respected and had status and power of their own as the 'real' victims of the Shah's regime.

Women, too, had been victims of the Shah's regime and were to be respected and valued as a result. Ayatollah Khomeini said in countless interviews that women were valued above men in Islam, and demonstrators enacted his words. Women, who in the past could not walk in the streets on their own without being accosted or physically molested, were now able to move about freely. They now participated in huge mixed demonstrations when before they had dreaded using mixed public transport. To a lot of women, the most liberating experience of the Revolution was the sense of freedom to mix with men without being harassed. Women were now addressed as 'sisters' and treated as such. Verbal and physical abuse of women diminished overnight. The same male fellow student or colleague who had made sexual insinuations in the past now lowered his gaze and spoke in a non-sexual language. Eye witness accounts of mixed demonstrations reported an enormous sense of mutual respect and solidarity amongst male and female participants.

The question of the sexual division of responsibility did not come in the way of male–female solidarity against the Shah. Women, on the whole, were left free to decide which aspect of the struggle they wanted to take up. It was possible to make choices. If women wanted to dig trenches or expose themselves to the soldiers' bullets in the front line of the demonstrations, no one stopped them and they were not forced to conform to a fixed division of labour within the revolutionary movement. Many women had the blessing of their families when they took part in street demonstrations, but those who didn't found it easier to disobey. The religious leadership encouraged women to disobey their husbands and fathers on political grounds and found precedents for such conduct in the life of Shii female role models. Defending their newly found political independence, women cited the example of Zeynab, who reputedly divorced her husband so as to be able to support the Shii struggle against Sunni tyranny (Betteridge, 1983, p. 120). Women felt independent and free, and the more they were respected and the more they were valued, the more they joined in. Women had found a new secure place within the revolutionary culture and were determined to fill it. Within the revolutionary culture, the status of men and women was raised by making sacrifices and providing martyrs to the Revolution. Many wives and mothers intensified their struggles after losing a loved one.

In short, participation in the Revolution as a woman guaranteed an exceptionally rich and liberating experience and many women could not resist going along with it. As far as the immediate revolutionary experience of many women went, revolutionary Shiism was not a male dominated culture. Women had freely participated in the Revolution, they had experienced respect and a sense of value, and they had freely constructed and followed their chosen models of female heroism. The political role of Zeynab and her response to the *Karbala* battle was cited with pride as an example for the new Shii woman. This Shiism, many women believed, was far from being a backward ideology. If anything, it was forward looking and revolutionary. The immense sense of male–female solidarity within the revolutionary rank and file was coupled with a sense of communalism and pride in making the state and its Western supporters feel helpless.

This constituted the substance of the revolutionary identity in which many divergent groups of participants lost themselves. The question of what would happen after the Revolution could not arise under these circumstances. Indeed it was a characteristic of this Revolution to be an end in itself. Female and male participants were both in search of a new national and gender identity and the Revolution gave them exactly that.

Summary

The discourse of revolution contained a number of features which were particularly pertinent to the construction of gender as a revolutionary discourse. Some important features were characteristic of the revolutionary build-up: the creation of a new oppositional space due to the state's attempt to introduce controlled liberalisation and the accompanying change of emphasis in US foreign policy; the way in which the oppositional activities of prominent intellectuals were complemented by a movement of civil disobedience; the extraordinary oppositional momentum created by the phenomenon of mass demonstrations and cyclical riots; the state's response to the anti-Shah movement being divided, chaotic and contradictory; and the power relationship between different factions of the coalition leadership. If one or a combination of these features had happened differently, in substance or pace, instead of a revolution we might now be talking about a suppressed oppositional movement by the secular intelligentsia, an urban revolt which led to the liberalisation of the Pahlavi regime, or a number of other scenarios. The structural deficiencies of, and cultural developments in, Iran during the Shah's rule would not have led necessarily to an anti-Pahlavi revolution if it were not for the particular way in which the revolutionary process built up.

Moreover, the ways in which the revolutionary leadership developed, the organisation and mobilisation aspects of the Revolution, the pattern of women's participation, and the revolutionary demands and symbols, all contributed to the particular outcome of the Revolution and its construction of women. The Revolution was above all an affirmation of the imagined community of nation (Anderson, 1983). It was a search for national identity and provided its participants with communion and solidarity.

The new national identity was being constructed in relation to a redefinition of Iran's relationship with the 'imperialist' powers. Cultural nationalism was the framework within which national identity and other features of the Revolution was situated. This of course does not mean that the discourse of revolution contained a single conception of national identity. On the contrary, the shifting boundaries of Islam, nationalism and socialism provided varied references to national identity. The breakdown of the state's claim to a unified national identity achieved through modernisation was creating a diversity of identities. What was singular about the revolutionary process was the search for national identity itself and the success of Islamic cultural nationalism in asserting itself over other identities. The new identity, then, had to be defined *vis-à-vis* that propagated by the state and its Western supporters: it had to have a strong nationalist substance and its content had to be dominated by Islamic language and symbolism. Moreover, the new national identity had to have a claim to modernity, progress and strength. The rejection of 'Westernisation' entailed the construction of 'Islamic modernity'. Islamic concepts and institutions were reconstructed in relation to current definitions of modernity and progress to provide the basis for a viable rejection of the West. In other words, the term of the debate was still modernisation and the solution to Iran's problems was being sought in Islamic modernity.

It was within this framework that gender was constructed as a revolutionary discourse. The search for an authentic Islamic national model of modernity, progress and strength entailed revolutionising gender relations. This was manifested within the revolutionary process in a variety of ways. The participation of women; revolutionary demands on gender; the organisation, mobilisation and gender symbols; gender addresses of the revolutionary leadership and male–female interaction were some of the features of the revolutionary movement which revolutionised hitherto dominant gender relations.

7 Women and the political transition from modernisation to Islamisation

The post-Pahlavi political order which came into being in February 1979, went through more than two years of revolutionary transition (Bakhash, 1984; Milani, 1988). It finally settled into an Islamic theocracy in 1981 after the annihilation of internal political opposition was complete. The salient feature of the transitional period, which developed in several stages, was the struggle for political control and state power. Each transitional stage was dominated by an intense power struggle amongst a changing set of political contestants.

Transitional leadership and political culture

The grounds on which the constantly evolving process of political and ideological contest took place in the transitional period had already been laid by the anti-imperialist and populist ideology of the Revolution and the balance of political forces within it.

With regard to the structure of the transitional state, the collapse of the Pahlavi regime resulted in an immediate take-over of state power by the revolutionary coalition of Islamic and nationalist forces. The Council of the Islamic Revolution which had been set up in the final month of the Revolution by Ayatollah Khomeini presided over the immediate transitional tasks. The revolutionary leadership kept some parts of the pre-revolutionary state machinery intact and replaced others with the institutions which were conceived during the Revolution. The old Constitution was retained temporarily, except for the part which related to the role of the monarch. The Majles and the Senate were dissolved and their members were persecuted. The Council of Revolution took over the legislative function temporarily until it could be handed over to an elected Majles. A Provisional Government was set up as the executive arm of the Council of Revolution and replaced Bakhtiar's government. It was given the mandate to plan and oversee the transformation of the old political system into a new one, and hand over the executive power to an elected body when this was achieved. A new revolutionary court accountable to the Council of Revolution was also set up to administer swift punishment to the Shah's officials.

Transitional leadership

As to the participants in state power, the Shii leadership, composed of influential clerics and lay ideologues, dominated the Council of Revolution. This membership, though united in their following of Ayatollah Khomeini, was heterogenous and represented a range of ideological and political views within the revolutionary and modernist trends of Shiism. Members included, on one side of the spectrum, Ayatollah Beheshti, Hojatoleslam Hashemi Rafsanjani and Hojatoleslam Javad Bahonar who constituted the hardline faction. They kept close to Ayatollah Khomeini's views and founded the Islamic Republican Party (hereafter IRP) which soon became the power base of the Council of Revolution and coordinated the activities of the hardline followers of Khomeini. On the other side of the spectrum there were members, such as Ayatollah Taleghani and Abolhasan Banisadr, who were independent minded and more in line with the nationalist, pro-democracy and modernist trend of Shiism than with Ayatollah Khomeini's authoritative legalism.

During the transitional period, these Islamic nationalists differentiated their identity from the hardline clergy by, first, insisting that 'true Islam' was compatible with modern life, and that many aspects of Western progress should be emulated in Iran, and second, that the Islamisation of Iranian society was a gradual process and should be based on long-term education of the people as opposed to force (Banisadr, 1982a). Contrary to the Council of Revolution, the Provisional Government was run totally by non-clerics and its membership consisted of the Islamic and secular nationalist leaders. Mehdi Bazargan became prime minister. Members of his party and a number of secular leaders of the National Front such as Karim Sanjabi, Daryoush Foruhar and Sadr Haj-seyyed-Javadi filled the cabinet posts. The Provisional Government was given the task of planning and overseeing the transition from constitutional monarchy to a new political order. Ayatollah Khomeini occupied the role of spiritual leader. His special position within the transitional state placed him at the centre of the decision-making process yet beyond the mundane affairs of state and unaccountable for political mistakes. He was the initiator of the policies of the transitional state and final arbiter of all political conflicts. Khomeini had overall control over the state. The Council of Revolution and the Provisional Government were dependent on his approval and support.

With regard to those political forces which were excluded from state power, a wide spectrum of Islamic, nationalist, secularist, reformist and socialist political parties and groups were established. These groups which had gained a degree of popular mandate as a result of their role in the success of the Revolution, included the Mojahedin Organisation and the secular Marxist–Leninist movement headed by the Fadaiyan Organisation. The Tudeh Party too resumed political activity. Within the nationalist range, the National Front parties resumed some independent activity despite their leaders' participation in the Provisional Government. The National Front became a purely secular force and returned to its liberal nationalist ideology. The Liberation Movement and other Islamic trends which were once part of the Second and the Third National Front were now in a strong leadership position in their own right and did not wish to go under the same banner with secular forces. A new arrival was the National Democratic Front, a social democratic party which was founded by Mosaddeq's grandson Hedayatollah Matindaftari. Moreover, the multitude of human rights associations and professional and civil groups which had mushroomed during the Revolution consolidated their position in the transitional stage.

As to the dynamic of the transitional state, the main determinant of the direction of the state was the question of the future of the Islamic leadership. This question had already arisen during the Revolution and Ayatollah Khomeini had addressed it with typical ambiguity. On the one hand, he had called for an Islamic Republic and, on the other, he had reassured his secular allies that the clergy did not intend to exercise direct political rule. The transitional state initially reiterated this ambiguity. The Provisional Government was filled with non-cleric members, but the central position of power was occupied by Ayatollah Khomeini and the clergy controlled the Council of Revolution. However, the concept of an Islamic Republic as featured in revolutionary slogans was not clear to anyone. Ayatollah Khomeini's views in his book *The Islamic Government* did not include the concept of an Islamic Republic, neither did it clarify the nature of the Islamic state.

The political leadership of Islam in the transitional phase was considered by most secular forces as temporary and was expected to wither away once the permanent machinery of political rule was in place. They had been promised an independent and free society and did not expect a huge following for Islamic forces in the context of freely contested elections. It was hoped that once the revolutionary fever subsided, the crowd-pulling power of the clergy would diminish and the concept of separation of religion from politics, which had been the dominant political mode of thought in Iran since the Constitutional Revolution, would prevail again. The secular forces expected Ayatollah Khomeini to take a back seat in politics and to devote his time to the spiritual guidance of the nation. To support this view, they relied on substantial participation in the Revolution by those sectors of the urban population, such as intellectuals, professionals and others who were not normally associated with Islamic sentiments. Moreover, secular forces had experienced the Revolution as an expression of their cultural nationalism and defined the role of Islam in terms of national unification. They tended to emphasise the liberating aspects of the Revolution over the religious ones.

The transitional Islamic leadership which now had control of the state, also had to consider the permanency of its position, and in doing so shared and feared the anticipation of the secular forces that there would be a gradual slipping of political power from their hands into the hands of secularists. The clergy were wary of the existence of quite a considerable secularist sentiment amongst the urban population and knew that if Islamic leadership was dispersed there was little hope for an Islamic Iran. The nature and extent of the clergy's involvement in the state was indeed an open matter and would be determined through political negotiation and power struggle. Therefore, the Islamic leadership had to either capitalise there and then on the tremendous popular support and political power they enjoyed or lose everything. This awareness determined the direction of state policy. To consolidate its position on a permanent basis, the Islamic leadership monopolised the seats of power and adopted a multiple strategy for political survival. These included manipulation of the radical political culture, rapid Islamisation, political suppression and the establishment of a theocratic state. These strategies gave rise to a fierce power struggle within the state and determined the nature of state policy, the state's relationship with dependent and independent political organisations, and the activities of these organisations and their relationship with each other.

Clerical manipulation of political radicalism

The transitional political culture was a radical one. Anti-imperialism was the name of the game. The Revolution had created an anti-imperialist revolutionary ideology and a mass of radicalised youth who had acquired arms, established grass-roots organisations and were poised to take radical initiatives. Most secular and Islamic political views subscribed to political radicalism and competed in extending its boundaries. The transitional leadership could choose either to suppress grass-roots politics or to bring it under political control and channel it into the desired route. Initial state policy on this was not unified. While the Provisional Government was trying to deradicalise the political atmosphere, the

Council of Revolution followed the policy of political manipulation of radical youth. Ayatollah Khomeini provided the lead by encouraging diffusion of power and advising his officials to keep the crowds mobilised.

Following Khomeini's lead, his hardline clerical supporters in the Council of Revolution extended their efforts to consolidate their political base by bringing the radicalised youth and grass-roots organisations under their control. Contrary to the wishes of the Provisional Government, the clergy facilitated the establishment of pockets of independent political power and brought them under their own leadership. The IRP, itself a loosely organised body, coordinated the activities of the grass-roots organisations and mobilised them when it needed the presence of a crowd in the streets to legitimise its politics. The revolutionary committees were gradually purged of their Mojahedin and Fadaiyan membership and turned into the eyes and ears of the clergy. They were used as an alternative security force to preserve order, prevent 'counter-revolutionary' activities in the locality, guard important public buildings and watch out for 'un-Islamic' behaviour. The committees set up road blocks and checkpoints in the streets, searched houses, arrested and imprisoned suspects and confiscated property. The 'Islamic societies' (Anjoman Eslami) which had flourished in offices, factories and educational institutions were purged of their secular membership and then put in charge of 'purification' of the work place. These Islamic societies intervened in labour disputes, purged 'counter-revolutionary' employees and in some places even took over management responsibilities.

In May 1979, Khomeini formally established a grass-roots army, The Revolutionary Guards Corp, in order to mobilise revolutionary youth in a pro-clergy army. This became an important centre of power and ran prisons and made arrests. A number of welfare organisations were also founded such as the Foundation of Disinherited (Bonyad Mostazafin) which replaced the Pahlavi Foundation. Moreover, Ayatollah Khomeini and his hardline supporters put themselves in the forefront of the war against the 'alien culture' of the West and East and their internal sources of support, that is, the Westernised middle class and the left. The hardline clergy initiated periodic explosions of anti-imperialist fervour such as the occupation of the US Embassy by the 'Students of *emam*'s Line' (students devoted to Khomini's beliefs), which went down well with the hard left and kept up the radical political atmosphere. In doing so, the clergy manipulated its control over the grass-roots organisations to create an atmosphere of spontaneous popular action against imperialism. The 'people' became a bargaining chip in the hands of the clergy, and were used to increase the power of the clergy and to alienate and disarm political opponents. The clergy's support and manipulation of the grass-roots revolutionary network turned into a serious point of contention between different factions of the transitional state. The Provisional Government found that its authority was eroded by independent pockets of power and the creation of a dual system of law and order.

The added pressure of foreign policy crises created by the clergy's anti-Western policies eroded the Provisional Government's policy of normalisation of the domestic economy and foreign relations. This eventually made the position of the Provisional Government untenable.

The establishment of the Islamic Republic

Ayatollah Khomeini and his hardline supporters saw their political future in the establishment of an Islamic Republic, although they only had a vague notion of the kind of state it would be. The Islamic Republic and its fundamental tenets were constructed step by step through the mechanism of political debate and power struggle, and the end result was a constitution which reflected a mixture of Islamic, Western and Eastern (meaning communist) concepts and models.

The Islamic leadership put everything it had into the establishment of an Islamic Republic which included political manipulation of its supporters and suppression of its opponents. When the Provisional Government was preparing for a plebiscite on a future political system, the political parties called for an open referendum to give the widest possible options to the public, and presented their own choices. The Islamic parties proposed a 'Democratic Islamic Republic', secular nationalists called for a 'Republic of Iran', and the left campaigned for a 'Democratic Republic of Iran'. Ayatollah Khomeini, however, refused to hold an open referendum and dismissed out of hand the proposals put forward by various political parties. He insisted that people had already chosen the 'Islamic Republic' as their future political system when they demonstrated against the Shah and demanded an Islamic Republic. The referendum, which took place on 31 March 1979, asked the nation to vote yes or no to an Islamic Republic. In response to Khomeini's intransigence and the denial of their right to put their opinion to the public, some political parties of the left such as the National Democratic Front and the Fadaiyan Khalgh boycotted the referendum. The Mojahedin Khalgh, the Tudeh Party, The Liberation Movement, the National Front, and the Islamic People's Republican Party, too, objected to the imposition of Khomeini's choice, but asked their supporters to vote yes to the Islamic Republic. The IRP and its allies waged a religious campaign for the yes vote, and Ayatollah Khomeini lowered the voting age to 16. The Islamic Republic was supported by 98 per cent of the voting population and the boycotting parties were branded as the enemies of the Islamic Republic.

The next step for the clergy was the consolidation of their position through an Islamic constitution. The process of production and formal adoption of a constitution involved several months of debate and power struggle (Bakhash, 1984). In this process, too, Ayatollah Khomeini finally came out as the winner. After an initial acceptance of the draft constitution presented by the Provisional Government, he asserted his authority over the manner of its ratification. The opposition's demand for an elected Constituent Assembly, composed of representatives of major sectors of society to revise and ratify the constitution, was rejected by Khomeini who wanted an Assembly of Experts with a limited number of appointed members.

Elections for the Assembly of Experts took place in August 1979 under the hardline clergy's tight control over the mass media. Doubts over the fairness of the election and the inability of the political parties to campaign freely due to a counter-campaign of intimidation by Khomeini's supporters, led to boycott of the election by a variety of opposition groups. The Mojahedin, the Fadaiyan and the Tudeh Party put up candidates but did not stand a chance in the face of the massive mobilisation of votes by the Islamic alliance. The total manipulation of the voting process by the hardline clergy resulted in the election of at least fifty candidates associated with the IRP, one of whom was the only woman representative in the Assembly of Experts. The rest of the members were candidates of minorities and representatives from other Islamic and nationalist leadership factions. The Constitution that emerged from the Assembly of Experts and was approved in December 1979 by the public was totally different from the draft one. It incorporated Ayatollah Khomeini's political doctrine and established the 'divine authority' of the *faqih* over state and society. The role of the *faqih* was taken over by Ayatollah Khomeini as the highest ranking Shii jurist. The Constitution of the Islamic Republic emphasised the primacy of Islamic law and legitimised the dominance of the clergy within the state. The main features of the Islamic state included the institution of *faqih* who held extensive powers and responsibilities; the independence of the legislative, executive and judiciary arms of the state from each other; an elected Majles with responsibility for primary legislation; a Council of Guardians with responsibility for checking the Islamic credentials of the laws passed by the Majles; a president who was a ceremonial figure; and a cabinet led by the prime minister who was appointed by the president and confirmed by the Majles.

The Constitution, in its establishment of clerical rule, brought about a profound change in the relationship between the state and the institution of Shiism as it existed under Pahlavi rule. Indeed, the Islamic Republic proved to be a turning point for Iranian Shiism. The predominant trend in Shii theory since the Safavid dynasty had been acceptance of temporal rule, and the Shii clergy had traditionally supported the monarchy. Although the Constitution of 1906 included a provision for clerical scrutiny of parliamentary legislation, this was ignored in practice and the Constitution was regarded as secular. Nevertheless, the Constitution had been supported by the clergy and since the Constitutional Revolution the clergy had many times rallied behind the demand for the Pahlavi Shahs to return to constitutional rule. Even in the 1960s and 1970s, Ayatollah Khomeini's extremist position that the *Qoran* and the rule of Ali should be the basis of government in a Muslim society, was a minority view among the Shii clergy (Bonine & Keddie,1981, p. 3). Furthermore, the history of Shiism reflected the heterogeneity of the position of Shii *mojtahedin*. The Shii *marjae taghlid* traditionally exercised religious and political autonomy and had authority over his followers. But the dominant Shii tradition was overturned by the establishment of the practice of guardianship of *faqih*. Shiism became highly radical, hierarchical and centralist (Arjomand, 1988). This was combined with totalitarianism and destroyed the autonomy of the *mojtahedin*. The Shii clergy were brought in line, politically and religiously, one after the other by the hardliners in power. Indeed, the challenge presented to the state by a Shii *mojtahed*, such as in the case of Ayatollahs Shariatmadari and Zanjani, was taken much more seriously and dealt with more swiftly by Ayatollah Khomeini than was the case with other opposition. The Shii state found it necessary to suppress the heterogeneity of Shii theory and practice. The state's success in this further contributed to the rise of the hardline clergy within the transitional phase.

Elimination of Islamic diversity and secular opposition

With the ratification of the Constitution of the Islamic Republic in December 1979, political events in the transitional period began to focus on the question of who should occupy new seats of power. The hardline clergy, having secured the principles of clerical rule, now had to have a strategy for stopping everyone else from occupying the new power bases.

By this time, the hardline clergy and their fanatical street mobs had already severely limited the freedom of expression of the secular forces. In August 1979 the first opportunity presented itself to the IRP and its grass-roots supporters to attack the oppositional left when the prosecutor general banned *Ayandegan*, an independent left-wing newspaper, for a dubious reason. The offices and printing equipment of *Ayandegan* were confiscated and taken over by the IRP for publication of the Islamic newspaper (*Sobh Azadegan*). The closure of *Ayandegan*, which presented an independent left-wing point of view, was protested against by the National Democratic Front which organised a major demonstration in support of freedom of the press. The demonstration was attacked by Islamic mobs who called themselves *hezbollahi*, and a number of demonstrators were injured. The National Democratic Front was banned the next day and a warrant was issued for the arrest of its leader. The headquarters of the Fadaiyan Khalgh, too, was attacked, and their offices were confiscated by the revolutionary guards. Increasing curtailment of democratic rights followed. The Mojahedin and the Fadaiyan were driven underground and their newspapers were banned.

After the left, it became the Provisional Government's turn to be uprooted. The Provisional Government faced enormous odds. Its position was constantly weakened by a combination of factors: an assertion of independent power by grass-roots organisations and their disregard of law and order, the authoritative leadership and Islamisation policies of Ayatollah Khomeini, ruthless rivalry by the Council of Revolution, strong criticism by the left, and the dwindling confidence of the democratic forces in its effectiveness, all contributed to the demise of the Provisional Government. The image of Bazargan's government as technocratic, moderate, gradualist and compromising towards the West had made the position of the Provisional Government unsustainable within the dominant radical uncompromising anti-imperialist political culture. The last straw that broke its back was the occupation of the US Embassy and the taking of American hostages by a group of young Islamic radicals led by the hardline clergy and supported by Ayatollah Khomeini. Amid huge anti-imperialist demonstrations organised by both the Islamic forces and the Marxist–Leninist left, and the release of documents seized in the US Embassy proving communication between the Provisional Government and the US government, Mehdi Bazargan resigned. Ayatollah Khomeini promptly dissolved the Provisional Government and instructed the Council of Revolution to take over its functions. The documents obtained during the occupation of the US Embassy were further used to eliminate the only formidable clerical opposition, that is, Ayatollah Shariatmadari and his Islamic Republican People's Party. With the fall of the Provisional Government, the silencing of Ayatollah Shariatmadari and death of Ayatollah Taleghani, Islamic resistance to the excesses of the hardline clergy and their political tool, the IRP, was almost eliminated.

By the end of 1979, that is, less than a year after the victory of the Revolution, the only remaining alternative voice within the state belonged to Abolhasan Banisadr and a few other less influential political figures. These became the next political rivals of the hardline clergy. In

January 1980, a presidential election took place and as a result of the last minute withdrawal of the IRP candidate for a constitutional reason, the independent candidate Abolhasan Banisadr was elected. The IRP considered Banisadr as a 'liberal' and regarded his policies as a continuation of those of the Provisional Government. The hardline clergy warned that they could only support Banisadr if he pursued a militant Islamic policy in domestic and international affairs. The stage was set for a long battle over political supremacy. The IRP forced Banisadr to accept their choice of prime minister, Mohammed Ali Rajai, and filled the newly elected Majles seats with IRP candidates. This was easily achieved, as the credentials of independent candidates were scrutinised and elected representatives from the nationalist camp such as Sanjabi, Khosrow Qashqai and Madani were refused seats. The Majles that met in August 1980 had a 60 per cent majority of IRP candidates. In the ensuing power struggle with Banisadr, the IRP used its Majles majority and the constitutional position of the prime minister to make the president a symbolic head of state and prevent him from exercising real power. In all of the many clashes that developed between Banisadr and the IRP over the choice of prime minister, membership of the cabinet, appointment of the commander of the Revolutionary Guards Corps and control of mass media, Banisadr ended up as the loser and the IRP managed to assert its own policies. Where Banisadr succeeded in seriously threatening his rival's confidence was in his support from the public and the opposition.

Banisadr soon became a rallying point for the Islamic and secular opposition. His regular verbal attacks on the IRP at public meetings attracted large crowds. He presented a much more threatening resistance to the IRP than Bazargan and his cabinet ever managed to do. The IRP retaliated by implicating the National Front in a conspiracy to overthrow the Islamic Republic and in July 1980 the headquarters of the National Front was attacked and its newspaper was closed down. The headquarters of the Tudeh Party was also attacked but they were later allowed to resume activity and continue to publish their newspaper. A few months later, Bazargan's newspaper, *Mizan*, was closed down. IRP club-wielders broke up many demonstrations and protests against these attacks and in favour of President Banisadr. These demonstrations and protests were organised by various sectors including the bazaar, writers, academics, lawyers and political organisations such as the Mojahedin.

By the spring of 1981, animosity between the two camps had reached an unprecedented degree. Banisadr's position as the commander-in-chief of the army, which was fighting a war with Iraq, and his presence in the war zone and absence from Tehran was used by the IRP to spread rumours that he was plotting a military coup. Eventually, in June 1981, the IRP used parliamentary procedure to dismiss Banisadr. This led to a bloody battle in the streets of Tehran which was started by revolutionary guards attacking a peaceful pro-Banisadr demonstration organised by the Mojahedin and other supporters.

The last avenue of political freedom was closed after the June 1981 event and, with all opposition driven underground or into exile and thousands of young radicals shot or imprisoned, the Islamic Republic settled into an Islamic theocracy. Unable to compete with the rigour and logic of its secular and Islamic opponents, and fearful of the covert secularist and materialist sentiments of the urban population supported by centuries of a temporal state in Iran, Ayatollah Khomeini and those who identified with him gained permanent state power by political suppression and violations of democratic rights.

Rapid Islamisation

Rapid Islamisation was another strategy adopted by the hardline clergy to consolidate their political position. Early Islamisation was intended to strengthen the Islamic features of society whilst the clergy was in leadership position and popular, and to delegitimise pre-revolutionary secular concepts. On this, too, disagreement occurred between various factions of the state. On the one hand, Ayatollah Khomeini and his hardline supporters pursued rapid Islamisation and, on the other, the Provisional Government and later President Banisadr and their Islamic and secular supporters considered early Islamisation a rash and out of place policy.

The Provisional Government's argument against Islamisation emphasised that the transitional state had a temporary caretaker status whose primary task was to prepare the ground for transfer of power to a legitimate and popularly mandated state. Mehdi Bazargan, the prime minister, repeatedly argued that the existing economic, social and legal structures should be preserved during the transitional period because the Provisional Government did not have a mandate to change the law, which could only be done by an elected government. President Banisadr and his faction within the state, too, argued against forceful Islamisation on the ground that it would have a negative long-term effect on the popularity of the Islamic state and the willingness of the nation to adopt Islam wholeheartedly. Nevertheless, the arguments against forceful Islamisation fell on deaf ears and the Provisional Government found itself in the forefront of Ayatollah Khomeini's Islamisation drive.

Ayatollah Khomeini's Islamisation policy got off the ground with gender relations as one of its first and foremost targets. On 26 February

1979, only two weeks after the victory of the Revolution, Ayatollah Khomeini's office announced that the Family Protection Law was to be abrogated. On 3 March, it was announced that women would be barred from becoming judges. On 6 March, Khomeini said in a speech that women should wear *hejab* in their place of work. On 29 March, it was announced that beaches would be segregated, and a few days later the public was informed of the segregation of sport. This was followed a few weeks later by the announcement of the abolition of coeducational schools. On 30 March, came the first news of the flogging of a man and a woman for adultery by a revolutionary committee in the northern town of Roodsar. This was followed a couple of months later by the first stoning of a woman for adultery in Behshahr.

Within a few months of the victory of the Revolution, most aspects of women's position had been the subject of Ayatollah Khomeini's comment and intervention. Resistance to his Islamisation measures was forthcoming from certain categories of women and their political allies which will be explained in more detail shortly. Indeed, Khomeini and his hardline supporters had to retreat many times from outright Islamisation and resign themselves to partial reforms. But, on the whole, they were able to push through different degrees of Islamisation of women's position in relation to family, education, employment, segregation, *hejab*, sexual relations and penal law. Two years after the Revolution, *hejab* was in full force; women had lost the right to initiate divorce and have child custody; they had been barred from becoming a judge or a president; they could not attend school if they were married; they could not study and work in a range of subjects and jobs; and they had been totally subjugated to male power. Some of these changes were not implemented effectively and coherently for some time to come (such as aspects of the new family laws). But they clarified the state's official position on women. Indeed, no other pre-revolutionary feature of Iranian society was touched upon so rapidly and so thoroughly during the transitional period.

The rapid Islamisation of women's position pointed once again to the centrality of gender relations in the political ideology of Islam. The fact that Islamisation of the family and sexual relations was prioritised, demonstrated that the new political order had to be constructed around a transformed gender relations. Ayatollah Khomeini was adamant that without the Islamic family and women's *hejab* there could be no Islamic society. Women were the markers of the boundaries of the Islamic community and the makers of Islamic identity. Even those factions of the transitional state which opposed forcible Islamisation acknowledged this. Ayatollah Mahmud Taleghani, the nationalist and pro-democracy cleric, said in response to protests against Khomeini's pronouncement on Women's *hejab*, that although *hejab* should not be forced on women, nevertheless it should be voluntarily taken up because 'we want to show that there has been a revolution, a profound change' (Taleghani, 1979 p.107). This profound change was to be marked by the appearance and behaviour of women. Indeed agreement on this extended beyond Islamic forces and became universal amongst political ideologies in the transitional period; whether secular or Islamic, they all propagated their own particular formula for women's appearance, behaviour and legal status.

However, all post-revolutionary political ideologies faced two important questions during the transitional period: which model of womanhood should be adopted for the new society, and how long could revolutionary unity continue? Ayatollah Khomeini's hasty Islamisation was an attempt to mark the revolutionary change that had occurred with Islamic legislation and symbols before other political ideologies got the chance to put down their markers. But, by so doing, he created a battlefield on gender: did the forcefully Islamised woman represent the revolutionary model of womanhood that had been sought? For secular women and their political allies, Ayatollah Khomeini's Islamisation measures constituted a betrayal of the revolutionary construction of women. Women were praised as revolutionaries when they participated in the Revolution, afterwards they were asked to go back to their homes. For the Islamic moderate, the state's hasty Islamisation measures were unnecessarily forceful and could tarnish the image of the Islamic leadership. For the diehard Islamic supporter, these measures put the Westernised woman of the Pahlavi era in her proper Islamic place.

The battle of gender resulted in further diversification of the opposition forces. A variety of women's groups with secular and Islamic stances were set up to defend their favoured model of womanhood. Secular political groups set up their separate women's sections to safeguard women's rights. Islamic nationalists and reformers wrote articles and made speeches in defence of a progressive interpretation of Islamic gender relations. The hardliners mobilised women to defend their true Islamic identity.

By bringing the question of women's position onto the political agenda, the Islamisation policy forced the break-up of the revolutionary construction of gender. The boundary of gender identity which had been drawn during the Revolution by opposing Iranian national identity to that of a Western imported identity, lost its unifying significance. Political ideologies were forced by Ayatollah Khomeini's Islamisation policy to enter into a battle over gender identity whilst revolutionary anti-imperialist feelings were still running high. The issue of women's rights became the point on which the internal and external political boundaries of gender intersected.

Women's spontaneous response to Islamisation

The first and strongest reaction to Ayatollah Khomeini's Islamisation attempt came from secular women on the eve of International Women's Day celebrations on 8 March. A celebration had been planned by a consortium of Marxist–Leninist women's groups as the first such celebration since the early 1950s when it used to be organised by the Tudeh Party. The celebration, however, was turned into a protest as a result of Ayatollah Khomeini's pronouncements about the suspension of the Family Protection Law and women's *hejab* at work, and the dismissal of women judges by the Ministry of Justice, all of which had taken place in the span of a week, before the International Women's Day. These policies changed the scale and status of International Women's Day from a fringe event organised by a fringe movement, into a massive spontaneous protest movement composed of various strata of women. The protestors included young and old, rich and poor, veiled and unveiled. But the majority were secular women including students, professionals, the unemployed or housewives, from the middle and upper classes.

On 8 March, thousands of women poured into the streets to protest. Spontaneous meetings were held and marches got under way in different directions towards Tehran University, the Prime Minister's Office and the Ministry of Justice. The protestors carried banners defending equality of rights and democratic freedoms. Incidents of fanatical mobs attacking the demonstrators were reported. Nonetheless, women continued to hold protest meetings throughout the day. Two days later, further demonstrations against the imposition of *hejab* took place, again quite spontaneously. A mass meeting was held at the Ministry of Justice to demand 'freedom of choice in clothes', 'equal civil rights with men', 'abolishment of all discrimination in law against women, particularly in relation to the family', and guarantees regarding 'freedom of speech and association'. Women then asked the prime minister, Mehdi Bazargan, to declare his views on their demands (*Ettelaat*, 1).

Another demonstration took place on the same day in front of the National Television, to protest against the news blackout of 8 March demonstrations. Small pockets of veiled women staged counter-demonstrations demanding compulsory veiling for all women. Their zealous male supporters, armed with knives, broken bottles, clubs, stones and snowballs, attacked women protestors and caused many injuries. Revolutionary guards who had previously watched the incidents passively or shot into the air to disperse women made some attempt this time to protect women demonstrators (*ibid.*).

In response to the crisis, the prime minister reassured the protestors that the message of Ayatollah Khomeini had been misunderstood and that there were no plans to make *hejab* compulsory. Ayatollah Khomeini and his representatives retreated by ordering their army of religious zealots to refrain from attacking women demonstrators (*Keyhan*, 1). The next day, the government's spokesman, Mr Amir-Entezam, announced that the Family Protection Law would remain in force until a new law was drafted to replace it. He added that 'despite the fact that the prime minister and his family are proponents of reasonable *hejab*, nevertheless he and his cabinet do not believe in compulsory veiling' (*ibid.*).

The National Television, too, responded to women's demands for the lifting of the news blackout by showing footage of the women's demonstrations. This was done, however, in an intimidating manner and was aimed at discrediting the women's protest movement by associating it with the Shah's regime, the SAVAK, and the Westernised rich (*Ayandegan*, 2). The solidarity expressed by Western women through the participation of Kate Millet, the American radical feminist, in these demonstrations was made an issue by the authorities, and she and her companion were promptly deported from Iran (*Keyhan*, 2). The head of National Radio and Television, Sadegh Ghotbzadeh, was later attacked by a group of angry women who objected to his treatment of women's demonstrations in the media (*Keyhan Havai*, 41).

The announcement by the government, and no doubt the campaign of intimidation by the mass media, prompted some of the Marxist–Leninist organisations to withdraw support from the demonstrations planned for 11 March, and many ordinary women who had been spontaneously drawn to protest marches also stayed away. Nevertheless, that day's rally in the University of Tehran drew some 20,000 women. After hearing several speeches women marched towards the Azadi (Freedom) Square. As the march proceeded, women from offices, hospitals and schools abandoned their work and joined in or waved to the demonstrators enthusiastically. The march, however, drew other types of enthusiasts too. Fanatical mobs began to attack the demonstrators and showered them with verbal abuse. Revolutionary guards watched passively and did nothing to defend the demonstrators. The circle of aggressive mobs armed with weapons became tighter and tighter and the women were finally forced to abandon their destination and disperse in order to avoid further clashes and injury (Millet, 1982).

Women's demonstrations presented an opportunity for the hardline clergy to draw the boundaries of legitimate protests by the secular forces. It became obvious that mass demonstration was not going to be an accepted means of oppositional protest in a post-revolutionary society. Women's spontaneous protests, therefore, lost momentum and their diverse mass participation ended. Women's rights activism became much more confined and politically divided thereafter. Women organised themselves within professional associations and around professional issues, or they set up women's sections within their preferred political organisations. The most vocal women's protest was that of women lawyers who had been barred from becoming judges. During the period March to June 1979, that is from the date it was announced that women's appointment as judges would stop until the date of the swearing-in ceremony of new judges which excluded women nominees, women lawyers and trainees organised numerous sit-ins and protest meetings. Protests by women lawyers were very well supported and most secular and Islamic nationalist and reformist political organisations backed them. The protests did not, of course, change Ayatollah Khomeini's mind and women judges and trainees were forced to switch to administrative posts in the judiciary. Women civil servants were also quite active and organised protest actions around their professional concerns.

In June 1979, women employees of the Communication Corporation protested against the closure of the day-care centre at their work place. Their protest was halted by a threat of mass lay-offs (*Ettelaat*, 2). After Ayatollah Khomeini's June 1980 decree on 'administrative revolution' which required women to wear *hejab* in all government offices, protest action was taken by women civil servants in the government departments and agencies. A couple of thousand women demonstrated in front of the office of President Banisadr demanding the reversal of compulsory *hejab*. Some women refused to comply with the order and were promptly dismissed from their jobs.

The success of the hardline clergy in breaking up women's spontaneous protests and the failure of women's organisations and their political allies to safeguard women's rights remained a subject of debate and recrimination amongst the secular opposition for sometime in the future. Many protesting women at the time felt unsupported and even betrayed by their natural political allies who paid lip service to women's rights but refused to put up active resistance to the clergy's Islamisation advances.

Here again the question of political priorities was raised. Should revolutionary unity have been preserved at any price in the post-revolutionary transitional period? Should anti-imperialism have been made the main concern of political groups whilst the infringements of democratic and women's rights were taking place? Should the opposition have gone along with the Islamisation policy in order to remain united in the face of the 'imperialist threat'? These questions preoccupied the secular opposition for the rest of the decade.

The Islamic nationalist response

Women's spontaneous protest against Islamisation created a crisis of identity for the Provisional Government and its Islamic nationalist and modernist supporters. On the one hand, they retained the conception of women's emancipation and its relevance to national progress. Furthermore, being gradualist, non-authoritarian, and adhering to individual rights, they disliked rapid and forceful Islamisation by Ayatollah Khomeini. But, on the other hand, the Provisional Government and its allies subscribed, to different degrees, to cultural nationalism which entailed social conservatism and a belief in female modesty. This made it possible for them to forge a political alliance with the clergy and tolerate the latter's anti-emancipatory views on women for the good of higher national aims. An historical example of this was when in the 1960s the Shah's electoral reform to enfranchise women came under attack by Ayatollah Khomeini and other clerics. The position adopted by the Liberation Movement of Iran then was a denial that the clergy held backward views on women. Despite supporting the Shah's electoral reform, the nationalist movement found itself allied with the clerics who opposed it. This was because the clergy's protest gave the nationalists an opportunity to register their own protest against what they regarded as a higher national issue, that is, the Shah's infringement of the Constitution and the parliamentary system (see chapter 4).

Now the stakes were even higher for the nationalists in the Provisional Government. Their Islamic ally, Ayatollah Khomeini, was hailed as a revolutionary hero under whose leadership their previous enemy, the Shah, had been overthrown. The revolutionary political culture had turned the moderates into the vulnerable party in this alliance. Moreover, there was still a danger of a pro-Pahlavi military coup or some kind of external threat by the West as a show of support for the Shah. The Provisional Government, then, had to keep a delicate balance between opposing Ayatollah Khomeini and being true to their beliefs on women's emancipation in order to 'preserve the national interest', that is, to avoid rocking the boat for the transitional state (*Keyhan*, 3). The Provisional Government, then, adopted a dual strategy to deal with this crisis; on the one hand, reassuring women and denying that Khomeini intended to impose *hejab* on women or abolish the Family Protection Law (*ibid.*) and, on the other hand, appeasing Khomeini by emphasising that women should adopt Islamic clothing and modest behaviour by their own free will. This policy was also defended in the official newspaper of the Liberation Movement, which wrote 'Forcing *hejab* on women is the wrong policy and would have an adverse effect on women. Since the Revolution, a lot of women have turned to *hejab* of their own free will and this trend is continuing. Women should be encouraged to adopt modest clothing but we should not make *hejab* an issue to feed the propaganda machinery of the enemies' (*Mizan*, 1).

However, what this double strategy amounted to was political subordination to the hardline clergy and loss of support amongst secular forces. The Provisional Government was seen to be going along with the clergy's violations of women's rights. Being rejected by secular forces as 'weak', 'indecisive', and 'compromising', it became easier for the hardline clergy to squeeze the Provisional Government out of the power struggle (Chehabi, 1990, pp. 253–77).

The same pattern of power struggle was repeated over and over again: Ayatollah Khomeini called for the Islamisation of one or the other aspect of women's position; the hardline clergy pushed the measure through in a forceful manner; the Provisional Government resisted at first, sometimes causing a temporary retreat on Islamisation, but later conceded in order to avoid confrontation with Ayatollah Khomeini. The more the hardline clerics advanced in their control of power, the less vocal the Provisional Government became against the infringements of women's rights. Once again in the contemporary political history of Iran, a nationalist government chose to compromise women's rights in the interest of power politics and national unity (see chapter 4).

During the life-time of the Provisional Government, the Liberation Movement remained conspicuously silent on women's issues, particularly so in relation to the Islamisation of the family. Perhaps this was an area in which the Liberation Movement and the clergy were more in agreement. The minister of justice, Sadr Haj-Seyyed Javadi, who was from the Liberation Movement, defended some of the changes in the Family Protection Law and the prohibition of women from becoming judges (*Keyhan*, 4). But the Liberation Movement and its women's section became more vocal after the collapse of the Provisional Government. On the question of women's family rights, the women's section of the Liberation Movement objected to polygamy but did not present a detailed view on it (*Mizan*, 2). The Liberation Movement was critical of the Constitution because, contrary to the earlier draft prepared by the Provisional Government which was later rejected by the Assembly of Experts, it did not satisfy 'individual rights and social freedoms' (*Mizan*, 3). The Islamic penal law put forward by the hardline clergy, which had serious implications for women, was one of the issues which the Liberation Movement took seriously and organised a series of public meetings to protest against (*Mizan*, 4).

On the whole, the views expressed by the women's section of the Liberation Movement were similar to those expressed by the Islamic women's movement. The similarities included celebration of the state's official women's day which was the birthday of Fatemeh, the prophet's daughter, reference to her as the role-model for Iranian women, emphasis on the primacy of women's motherhood role, and encouragement of women to 'belong both to the family and the society', all of which were typical of the progressive wing of the Islamic women's movement (*Mizan*, 5). Indeed, the Liberation Movement's women's section established a close relationship with the Women's Society of the Islamic Revolution through its leader, Ms Azam Taleghani, who was the daughter of Ayatollah Taleghani. But the Liberation Movement insisted on the preservation of individual rights as specified in the Declaration of Human Rights and hence supported the concept of equality of rights between men and women (*ibid.*), which the pro-establishment Islamic women activists rejected following the teachings of Ayatollah Motahhari (see chapter 5).

The same dilemmas were also faced by other prominent Islamic nationalists such as Abolhasan Banisadr. As a member of the Council of Revolution in 1979 and as the first president of the Islamic Republic, Banisadr contributed to the debate on the question of *hejab*. During the 'administrative revolution' in the summer of 1980 which involved attempts to impose *hejab* and caused women's angry response, Banisadr defended the concept of *hejab* for women but rejected its forcible imposition (*Ettelaat*, 3). In defending *hejab* for women, he became well known for his indirect confirmation in a televised debate that women should wear the *hejab* because of 'scientific proof' that women's hair discharged special rays which attracted men (Banisadr, 1980). Banisadr's later denials that he did not believe in such a theory did not impress the secular middle class and he remained associated with the pseudo-scientific justification of *hejab* (Banisadr, 1982b). But although he did not oppose Khomeini directly on the issue of *hejab*, Banisadr made an unsuccessful attempt in his capacity as president to mediate between the hardline clergy and women protestors on *hejab*. On 5 July 1980, thousands of women gathered in front of the president's office to protest against compulsory *hejab*. Banisadr's response was to ask women to accept *hejab* at work as a means of 'fighting the consumer culture [and creating] a non-confrontational atmosphere in the work place'. He advised women that they should create harmony in society by 'wearing the same clothes as millions of their sisters' and that '*emam* [Khomeini], whom you call father, had not unjustly invited women to wear *hejab*' (*Enghelab Eslami*, 1). Banisadr promised women to take responsibility on this matter and asked them to trust him to 'try and resolve this problem' (IWIMA, 1980). He held meetings with Khomeini's son and his other associates on this issue and discussed the prospect of a long-term social strategy towards *hejab* (*Enghelab Eslami*, 2). But the imposition of *hejab* remained the Islamic Republic's official policy.

Another Islamic reformist response to Ayatollah Khomeini's Islamisation of women came from the Islamic women's movement which gathered force and created a vocal Islamic feminist movement during and after the transitional period. The Women's Society of Islamic Revolution (WSIR) was founded soon after the Revolution by a group of women to preserve and build upon the revolutionary demand for a culturally authentic gender identity. The popular pro-Pahlavi women's magazine, *Zan Ruz*, was also taken over by an editorial board of Islamic feminists and transformed into a popular Muslim women's magazine. Most of these women activists had been educated in the West. Fereshteh Hashemi, Shahin Tabatabai and Zahra Rahnavard, all held doctorates from American universities. Others were connected to respected religious leaders and/or had made a name for themselves as a result of their political activities against the Pahlavi regime. Azam Taleghani was a cofounder of the society. The WSIR set up branches in provincial towns and started a programme of awareness raising for women. The Islamic reformist women set out to create a vision of the 'ideal Islamic society' and the role of women in it. The idealisation of the future Islamic society entailed a criticism of the past and present. The Islamic feminist theory of women's oppression and liberation began to take shape. This was constructed in opposition to 'traditional Islam'. The 'true Islam', according to Islamic feminists, transcended the 'traditional, deviatory and colonised Islam' in relation to women (Hashemi, 1981a). The failures of traditional Islam were considered to be rooted in the male dominated culture and the distorted interpretations of Islamic laws:

> in the current Islamic system women in our society are second-class citizens. From the moment of birth, sorrow is expressed: 'What a pity she is not a boy!'; in adolescence she is constantly reminded of the differences between her situation and that of young boys; when she gets married she is told 'go to your husband's home in a white wedding gown and come out in white shroud', that is, in all quarrels and disputes it is she who must keep silent. Finally as she becomes middle-aged and reaches old age, instead of one master every son becomes a new master, especially if her husband dies . . . Are these all the rights that Islam gives to women? . . . How can these Islamic laws and practices be said to support women? (*Zan Ruz*, 1)

The 'true Islam' was, on the contrary also superior to the 'West' and the 'East' in its treatment of women. The West, it was argued, considered women as objects of sex and consumerism, and the communist East failed to liberate women because of its emphasis on women's productive role. Both, it was emphasised, failed women. While these systems benefited from exploiting women, women themselves were left unprotected, unrealised and unhappy (Rahnavard, 1979, pp. 32–7). Contrary to the above systems, Islam was considered to be capable of enabling a woman to become 'a perfect, multi-dimensional being' (*ibid.*). True Islam, it was argued, combined equality of opportunity for men and women to develop their talents and capacities and to participate in all aspects of social life, because it acknowledged women's maternal instinct and their essential role within the family (Yeganeh & Keddie, 1986). However, the expectation of Islamic reformist women to receive support from the state and play a role in the formation of state policies was not realised. Far from supporting the WSIR, the hardline faction of the state attempted to manipulate and control it. As far as the clerical leadership was concerned, there was no need for free debate on the position of women and no place for an independent women's organisation to promote it. Women complained that the state refused to fund the WSIR (*Mizan*, 6). Later, when some Islamic feminists criticised the policy of imposed Islamisation the meetings of WSIR were attacked by IRP supporters and its premises in some cities were looted and stoned (*Ettelaat*, 4). The IRP attempted to drive out reformist women from the WSIR and put its own supporters in control to make it possible to mobilise women for state-initiated demonstrations and gatherings.

Ayatollah Khomeini's Islamisation measures did not receive the whole-hearted support of Islamic feminists. While the IRP was busily organising women's demonstrations in support of Khomeini's edicts on *hejab* and the family, women ideologues were putting forward Islamic alternatives in relation to women. Azam Taleghani and Zahra Rahnavard warned the authorities about the negative effects of forcing the *hejab* on women. They emphasised that the issue of *hejab* should not be blown out of proportion in relation to other necessary changes, that *hejab* should not be made specific to women and both men and women should be required to wear Islamic clothing, and that *hejab* should not be defined as anything more than simple and decent clothing which covers the body in a non-arousing way (*Keyhan*, 5). The WSIR convened a seminar on *hejab* and its resolution called for 'compulsory public decency instead of *hejab*' (*Ettelaat*, 5). The seminar was followed by open letters and proposals from other ideologues of the Islamic women's movement to the authorities. On the question of barring women from becoming judges, Islamic feminists argued that 'Women's emotionality is not an acceptable ground for their exemption from judgement' and proposed that 'Muslim women should be able to take their legal problems to female judges as much as possible, just as they take their medical problems to female doctors' (Hashemi, 1981b).

But the attempts of the Islamic feminists to gain a role in determining policy on *hejab* was not successful. Policy continued to be determined by Ayatollah Khomeini and his hardline followers in the Council of Islamic Revolution. Islamic reformists and feminists faced the same political dilemma as others: whether or not to insist on their interpretation of Islam and risk the breakdown of revolutionary unity against imperialism. Despite putting forward alternative points of view, they did not oppose the Islamisation measures of the hardline clergy openly and unequivocally. The criticisms made by Islamic nationalists and feminists were often heavily qualified and contained affirmation of loyalty to Ayatollah Khomeini and rejection of the secular opposition. Islamic feminists drew a rigid line between their defence of women's rights and that of the secular feminists. Despite their sympathy with secular women's protests against compulsory *hejab* and erosion of women's rights within the family, the Islamic feminists refused to associate themselves with the secular women's movement. Women's issues did not constitute a ground for unity amongst women who held different ideologies.

The secular nationalist response

In comparison with the Liberation Movement, the other major partner in the Provisional Government,the National Front, was able to adopt a more critical stand towards the early Islamisation of women's rights. This was the case for a number of reasons. The National Front had become fully secular since those Islamic parties which affiliated to it in the past, such as the Liberation Movement, were now independent. The National Front had less at stake since its leaders occupied the cabinet posts which did not involve them in women's issues. Moreover, the National Front soon broke with the Provisional Government when its leader Karim Sanjabi resigned his post as foreign minister in protest against the intervention of the clergy in foreign policy. This allowed the National Front to express criticism. Its women's section, too, seemed to be more assertive than that of the Liberation Movement. Nevertheless, the National Front leaders did collude with the clergy's infringements of women's rights to some extent as a result of their role in the Provisional Government. They, too, when in government subjected women's interest to that of the nation, as they saw it. In the transitional period, the National Front tried to revive its membership and publicise its vision of post-revolutionary society by launching a campaign (Siavoshi, 1990, pp. 151–65). As part of this campaign, Karim Sanjabi emphasised the National Front's view of women in the new post-revolutionary society: 'In the future political system no efforts will be spared so the women can participate in all aspects of the society while preserving their eminent human character. Society must provide all necessary conditions for the flourishing of women's talents and mobilise them to participate in the reconstruction of the society shoulder to shoulder with men, enjoying equal rights and responsibilities with them' (*Payam Jebheye Melli*, 1).

The National Front presented its point of view on women's issues regularly, adopting cautious liberal language in its criticism of the Islamisation measures. It objected to the imposition of *hejab* and demanded equality of rights for men and women 'so that women who are the basis of the family can build a healthy family and raise the free men and women of tomorrow' (*Keyhan*, 6). The women's section of the National Front supported women's right to practice as judges and organised protest meetings. They argued that the infringement of women's right to choose their profession contravened the Declaration of Human Rights:

> Throughout the Revolution, one principle has been demanded by all social classes and sections more than any other, and that is 'freedom' and 'equality'. Now, in the dawn of victory, freedom and equality, irrespective of class and sex is being threatened. The concept of the Declaration of Human Rights has been again and again supported by all freedom-lovers of this country. Now it seems that the intentions of the Declaration are being violated and are losing their credibility. One instance of the Declaration is the freedom of choice of occupation. The meaning of this is that everybody has the right to choose his or her occupation, irrespective of sex. We consider this the right of a woman to reach the position she deserves. One of the important instances of the violation of human rights by the present government is the question of the practice of law by women. The Women's Organisation of National Front supports the rights of women to practise law and considers the indifference shown by the government as an insult to all heroic and militant women of Iran. The Women's Organisation of National Front, in support of women's rights, will participate in the protest gathering in Tehran University on 2 May 1979, and invites all supporters of just demands of women lawyers also to do so. (Women's Section of the National Front, 1979, p. 228)

The National Front women also objected to Prime Minister Bazargan's traditional manner of addressing the meetings as 'Sirs', and wrote in protest 'Mr Prime Minister, women of this country are capable of participation in all spheres of society. If you fail to see them in the gathering of top managers, governors and ministers, it is because the government has failed to provide the opportunity for them to participate ... You and other state officials have ignored women and filled the decision-making posts with men' (*Payam Jebheye Melli*, 1).

The National Front criticised women's position in the Constitution as 'inadequate and full of shortcomings' and objected to the male-dominated nature of the Assembly of Experts which drafted and ratified the Constitution. In relation to family law, it criticised the new family courts for 'making the position of women within the family insecure'. It also took up the issue of women's employment rights and protested against the fact that the 'purification' of the public sector had adversely affected women. The new Islamic penal law, too, was subjected to criticism on the ground that 'it was an insult to the dignity of women' (*Payam Jebheye Melli*, 2). These criticisms, however, were being made after the Islamic and secular nationalists had lost state power to the hardline clergy. It was now argued that 'national interest' demanded opposition to the clergy's discriminatory laws on women. But when the nationalist Provisional Government was in power, it based its approach to women's rights on the objective of preserving revolutionary unity, and hence colluded with Ayatollah Khomeini's infringements of women's rights in order to preserve the 'national interest' *vis-à-vis* the West.

The Islamic left response

The Mojahedin Khalgh Organisation entered the transitional period projecting the image of a forward looking, radical and progressive Islamic force. They had played an important role in the construction of the 'revolutionary Muslim woman' during the Revolution. The Mojahed woman was portrayed as the living example of the new ideal of womanhood. The Mojahedin's identity resided in the proclaimed militancy and equality of its male and female supporters. However, during the lifetime of the Provisional Government, the Mojahedin adopted extreme caution in condemning the infringements of women's rights. Their response to women's protests against state Islamisation was a statement which conveyed three messages to women. The first message was a warning to women against deviating from the main struggle:

> The struggle is intricate and the enemy is lying in ambush. The fundamental bases of imperialism have not been uprooted from our society and consequently the future of the Revolution is still in danger. In these conditions it is only by recognition of major problems and their distinction from minor ones, avoiding minor details, concentrating all our popular forces, and the elimination of the internal bases of imperialism, that we can turn the poisonous atmosphere into a permanent and desirable breath of freedom. (Mojahedin Khalgh, 1979a)

By choosing to issue a warning to women rather than to the government, the Mojahedin made it clear where their allegiance lay. They showed little sympathy for the type of 'middle-class' educated and secular woman who had reacted angrily to the infringement of her 'Pahlavi granted' rights. To the Mojahedin, these women were reminiscent of the 'contemptuous and cynical imposition of the Shah's sister, this embodiment of Western corruption and arrogance, as the symbol of the free women of Iran' (Mojahedin Khalgh, 1979b). The Mojahedin did not respect the 'formal rights' granted to women under the Shah and therefore rejected women's prioritisation of these rights over the political unity of the country. The Mojahedin's second message to women was that they should shelve their women-specific demands and channel their efforts into anti-imperialist struggles to achieve the 'classless' society which would then automatically bring about their full equality, because 'As has been the case from its first day, our Revolution cannot but be the expression of freedom and liberation of all classes and popular forces, disregarding any differences and sexual, racial, class and ideological distinctions. Therefore, our Revolution cannot accept any denial of the total political and social freedom of our women' (Mojahedin Khalgh, 1979a, pp. 126–7).

This was quite a popular conviction amongst the hard left at that time and many women activists subscribed to it. But the Mojahedin immediately contradicted their promise of equality for women in their ideal society by their third message to women. The Mojahedin's third message was that the forceful imposition of *hejab* was an 'unacceptable and irrational act', not because of the importance of freedom of choice but because 'the heavy burden of the imperialist culture cannot be eliminated all at once and other than through a long term and gradual process' (Mojahedin Khalgh, 1979b). The Mojahedin emphasised that

> *hejab*, as a revolutionary foundation of Islam is in fact nothing but a social effort for the sake of the observance and protection of morality in society. It is without doubt one of the necessities of an all-embracing social, material and spiritual development; and we are sure that our revolutionary sisters and mothers, as they have so far proved in practice, also have observed this necessity and will continue to do so. (*Ibid.*)

In other words, the message was that although they did not believe in forceful imposition of *hejab*, the Mojahedin saw it as a 'necessity' for the development of post-revolutionary society in the favoured direction, and that they believed in its universalisation 'through a long term and gradual process' (*ibid.*).

The Mojahedin's concept of *hejab* was of course different from that which was traditionally associated with women's submissiveness and isolation. They argued that the type of *hejab* which is 'aimed at the denial of any social activity to women' is neither Islamic nor desirable (*ibid.*). The roots of traditional forms of *hejab* were attributed to the customs of the upper classes in ancient Iran and hence rejected. But the rejection of traditional *hejab* aside, the Mojahedin offered little reasoning on the 'necessity' of *hejab* for today's woman. The Mojahed women's *hejab* seemed to have more to do with revolutionary symbolism and identity than religious precepts. It entailed identification with the masses and distancing from the stereotype that became known as the 'middle class Westernised woman'; it symbolised resistance to 'cultural imperialism'; and it was the only apparent and obvious proof of the Mojahedin's subscription to the Islam of the masses. This was particularly an issue for the Mojahedin Organisation, because the majority of its members were middle-class college-student types (Abrahamian, 1989). The Mojahedin could not, therefore, take their links with the masses for granted. They had to work on establishing a mass basis hard and fast. The Mojahedin leader, Masud Rajavi, emphasised later in exile that 'in times of revolution, clothing acquires particular significance: remember that in the Chinese revolution women's clothes changed too' (Rajavi, 1982). The importance of 'not alienating the masses' by rejecting *hejab* was emphasised over and over again by the Mojahedin (Vardasbi, 1981). The Mojahedin's message on *hejab* to the demonstrating women did not suggest a return to traditional *hejab* and all that went with it. But it smacked of a conspiracy by the 'working-class vanguard party' to lead women to uniformity and mass identity, where there was no place for individual choice and personal taste. The secular women demonstrators did not find this prospect comforting.

The Mojahedin also kept conspicuously silent on other infringements of women's rights (Mojahedin Khalgh, 1980a). There was hardly a word of justification or opposition from the Mojahedin about the prohibition on women becoming judges, when most of the secular opposition objected to it. The policy of segregation in education, sport and leisure, too, did not draw any protest from the Mojahedin. Neither did the Mojahedin support secular political and pressure groups who were being pushed out of the political scene by IRP organised mobs. They remained largely silent while non-Islamic newspapers and groups were being systematically terrorised, feeling confident that they would not be the next target of the anti-democratic trend within the ruling clergy (Abrahamian, 1989). On the issue of family law, the Mojahedin did not respond to the Islamisation of women's position within the family. In an educational pamphlet written for the Mojahed rank and file, the Mojahedin rejected 'the superficial understanding of the inequality between men and women' on the grounds that 'the restoration of the lost historical rights of women could not be achieved simply by passing a few laws giving women the right to divorce, the right to vote, etc. This was a mere legalistic approach which did not reflect the historical oppression which had made women second class human beings' (Mojahedin Khalgh, 1979b). Instead, the pamphlet suggested that 'women's liberation requires constant struggle for the transformation of economic, social, political and cultural relations' (*ibid.*). What this meant with regard to the position of women in the family included the salvation of the family from 'capitalist consumption', preventing motherhood from 'overshadowing all their [women's] other roles' and 'preventing the holy process of marriage, which in a healthy society is primarily based on ideological merits of the participants', from being reduced in the capitalist society 'to the level of a trade and exchange' (*ibid.*).

Here again, the issue of the family was used to create a particular identity for the Mojahed member. Guidance and encouragement on marriage amongst comrades was provided, and it was ensured that the married Mojahed woman would not be taken out of action by the demands of husband and child. All this was based on a historical analysis of women's oppression which concluded that the Mojahed woman should put all her efforts into the struggle towards the ideal society in which her rights would be realised. There was no space for her involvement in 'legalistic' struggles on women's rights here and now. Unlike most other political organisations, the Mojahedin did not organise a separate women's section and remained faithful to their policy on women throughout the transitional period. They avoided confrontation with the state on women's rights but consistently presented their own ideology on women, and by doing so drew a line between their views on women and those of the Ayatollah Khomeini and the hardline clergy. The Mojahedin stipulated equality of rights for men and women in all their programmes. Their programme under the title of 'Conjunctural Expectations from the Islamic Republic' which was published in March 1979, included 'total fulfilment of women's political and social rights' and demanded 'elimination of class exploitation of women by providing equal wages for equal work' (Mojahedin Khalgh, 1979c).

The Mojahedin Organisation refused to support the draft constitution presented by the Provisional Government on the ground that 'it had a Western capitalist spirit' (*Ayandegan*, 3). They put up candidates for election to the Assembly of Experts with a democratic programme which included 'women's political and economic equality with men' (*Keyhan*, 7). This of course left the issue of male–female equality in culturally sensitive areas such as the family outside the arena of political debate in order to avoid antagonising Ayatollah Khomeini who was busy reforming the position of men and women in the family (Mojahedin Khalgh, 1980b). The Mojahedin's candidates did not, however, get into the Assembly of

Experts. They criticised the reactionary comments made by some deputies in the Assembly in relation to the clauses on women in the Constitution by saying that 'The closed minds of some members of the Assembly of Experts represent a feudal view of woman as a wife who stays at home and bears children with no productive role or social duty. As if they are not aware of the toiling women of the north and their responsibility for heavy productive duties in the rice fields' (Mojahedin Khalgh, 1979b). Since there was no sign of the Mojahedin's approved policies being reflected in the new Constitution, they boycotted the referendum on it. The Mojahedin later participated in the presidential election putting up their leader Masud Rajavi as a candidate. One of the promises of Rajavi was to amend the Constitution of the Islamic Republic to overcome its shortcomings including those on the question of women (*Ettelaat*, 6). But Ayatollah Khomeini refused to accept Rajavi's candidacy on the ground that the Mojahedin had not endorsed the Constitution in the referendum, and the Mojahedin candidate was left out of the presidential race. The Mojahedin's other attempt to gain access to political power was their participation in the Majles election in January 1980. Again, the Mojahedin included equality of rights for women in their election campaign. In an interview, the Mojahedin's second-in-command Musa Khiabani explained their emphasis on the importance of 'women's economic and political equality':

> To talk about male–female equality without emphasis on their economic and political equality is meaningless. In our *touhidi* [unitary] point of view, the criteria for the individual's value is in his or her productive and revolutionary credentials ... It is a polytheistic viewpoint, based on class interests, to consider men and women's inequality in politics and economy as natural ... According to this viewpoint, women are primarily a means of reproduction which should be solely occupied with household chores. This viewpoint has nothing to do with Islam ... Obviously, the kind of emancipation we have in mind for women is clearly different from the bourgeois freedoms and licences which are in fact another type of oppression for women. (*Bamdad*, 1)

Once again the Mojahedin made their priorities on women clear: that women's release from domestic duties into production and party political activities had to come first and women's liberation would follow. In this scheme there was no toleration for demand for 'bourgeois' freedoms.

Despite targeting women for recruitment, the Mojahedin organisation did not make their record on female participation public. It was a common sight during and after the Revolution to see Mojahed men and women in the streets in more or less equal numbers. But when it came to counting the members who had been killed during clashes with the revolutionary guards or under torture or by execution, male members constituted 85 per cent of the rank and file (Abrahamian, 1989, p. 227). Out of 799 women martyrs, 556 were aged between 19 and 25; 125 were aged under 18; and 10 over 38; 147 were students, 65 teachers, 21 housewives. The largest number came from Tehran; 507 of them were executed and 35 died under torture (Rezvani, 1985, p. 18). It is not clear whether this reflected the percentage of women in the rank and file or whether it was an indication of the type of activities that male and female members engaged in. It may well have been the case that this was the result of an organisational or personal division of labour in which women took less dangerous tasks.

Moreover, the Mojahedin did not seem to have a particular policy of promoting women members to the leadership role. Only a handful of Mojahed women gained prominence during this period for their candidacy for elections or martyrdom. The Mojahed woman was shy and restrained contrary to her counterparts in the secular left groups. On the whole, however, the Mojahedin's record of female participation, although not particularly different from those of secular Marxist–Leninist groups, was a substantial improvement on that of the other Islamic and secular political organisations.

The secular left response

Spontaneous protests by secular women put the issue of women's formal rights, which had failed to become a mobilising force during the Revolution, firmly back on the political agenda. Women's mass protests against Islamisation demonstrated that women's rights was now a slogan around which women could be mobilised. This was a factor which secular Marxist–Leninist forces, who were desperate for public support, had to take into account in formulating their response to Ayatollah Khomeini's Islamisation policy.

But in doing so, they too faced the same predicament: whether or not to oppose Ayatollah Khomeini's Islamisation policy and risk the break-up of national unity against imperialism. The response to this dilemma divided the left into two broad camps: those who emphasised the primacy of anti-imperialist struggles and others who prioritised the preservation of democratic freedoms and individual rights.

One of the main exponents of the former view was the Tudeh Party, which adopted a policy of supporting the hardline faction of the state. The Tudeh Party, funded and supported by the Soviet Union, followed the Soviet foreign policy of wooing the post-revolutionary Iranian state into the Eastern camp. The Tudeh thesis of the 'non-capitalist road to socialism' proposed a leap to socialism through an anti-imperialist revolution (Tudeh Party, 1979). In this theory, leadership of the revolutionary leap was in the hands of the 'national bourgeoisie' represented by the hardline anti-imperialist faction of the state.

The moderate reformist faction of the revolutionary leadership, represented by the Provisional Government and later by President Banisadr, was portrayed in this theory as the defender of the interests of the 'dependent bourgeoisie' and the stooge of American imperialism. The opposition put forward by the moderate faction in the state to the hardline clergy's excesses in foreign policy and infringements of democratic rights was interpreted by the Tudeh Party as an American conspiracy to weaken the anti-imperialist struggles of the post-revolutionary state. This did not stop the Tudeh Party from putting forward its own Marxist–Leninist programme on women. The Tudeh Party reorganised its women's section, the Democratic Organisation of Iranian Women (hereafter DOIW), and resumed publication of its magazine *Bidari Ma* [Our Awakening]. It also organised educational and health projects for women in poor districts of Tehran (DOIW, 1982a). But the Tudeh Party's prioritisation of national unity prevented it from criticising the hardline faction of the state directly and openly. Even with regard to those state policies which were in opposition to the Tudeh Party's own policies, its approach was submissive and appeasing. Unwilling to criticise the state on 'deviatory issues' such as women's rights and individual freedoms, the Tudeh Party aimed to redirect women's protests against Islamisation into anti-imperialist activities. The Tudeh Party's message to the secular protestors against their infringements of women's rights was that:

> Your destiny is closely intertwined with that of the Revolution. The day the Revolution succeeds in dealing the final blow to imperialism and enforcing the *emam*'s anti-despotic anti-imperialist and popular line, you will also find your rightful place in the young Republic. Dogmatic elements sowing division and causing discontent among our people and drawing a distasteful picture of the Islamic Republic of Iran will then be isolated. However, this lofty aim cannot be achieved without your active participation in the general struggle of our people and without your persistent and indefatigable fight for your rights. (DOIW, 1982b)

The position of the largest and most popular post-revolutionary Marxist–Leninist organisation, the Fadaiyan Khalgh, was more complex than that of the Tudeh Party. The Fadaiyan Organisation, on the one hand, insisted on the primacy of anti-imperialist struggles over all other forms of political activities, and on the other hand, openly objected to the despotic tendencies and Islamisation policies of the hardline faction of the transitional state. This resulted in the Fadaiyan's conditional support for the women's protest movement. The Fadaiyan condemned the state's Islamisation of women's position and praised women for fighting for their rights. But women were also warned against the hijacking of their movement by the 'liberals and other representatives of dependent capitalism who are pretending to be the defenders of women's rights' (*Kar*, 1).

The Fadaiyan Organisation set up the National Union of Women (Ettehad Melli Zanan) to ensure women's mobilisation into their rank and file as well as securing leadership roles for pro-Fadaiyan women within the women's movement. The Fadaiyan attempted to contain and control the direction of the secular women's movement. They succeeded in toning it down by refusing to support and participate in women's further demonstrations on the grounds that 'despite the fact that the state has retreated on women's issues, bourgeois women are persisting in their protests and are thereby trying to deviate women's protests by prolonging the life of the regime' (*Kar*, 2). The dual tendency in Fadaiyan policy towards the transitional state came to a head and resulted in an organisational split into the 'Minority' and the 'Majority' factions in June 1980 (*Kar*, 3). The latter adopted a similar policy to that of the Tudeh Party and the two collaborated closely with each other. The Minority Fadaiyan faction stepped up its criticism of the Islamic state and remained firm in its anti-imperialist convictions. The first Minority Fadaiyan congress considered imperialist domination and dependent capitalism as the main obstacles to the development of productive forces and the attainment of a socialist society. But it also emphasised that leadership of the anti-imperialist revolution cannot be assumed by 'reactionary Islamic ideologues' because 'their class interests were tied to the anti-socialist interests of Western imperialism' (*Kar*, 4). The congress instructed its followers to resist the despotic policies of the state and side with the democratic struggles of the working class 'to create the right conditions for a socialist leadership of the anti-imperialist revolution' (*ibid.*). The Minority Fadaiyan adopted a more straightforward policy towards secular women's protests against state infringement of their rights. In their analysis of women's struggles in the transitional period, the Minority Fadaiyan concluded that 'the existence of an independent and democratic women's movement is a necessity in this conjuncture of our nation's struggle against the anti-democratic ruling class' (*Kar*, 5).

At the other end of the spectrum on the left, there were those Marxist–Leninist and social democratic groups which took a longer term view of the development of Iranian society into socialism. The Organisation of Communist Unity (Sazeman Vahdat Komonisti), The Worker's Path (Rah Kargar), the Left Unity (Ettehad Chap) and the National Democratic Front (Jebheye Democratic Melli) represented the second trend within the left which, despite their differing analyses, prioritised democratic rights and individual freedoms over the revolutionary overthrow of foreign domination in Iran. These organisations were supportive of women's protests against Islamisation and actively participated in them. The National Democratic Front was among the first to object to Ayatollah Khomeini's Islamisation edicts openly and loudly. It provided concrete support to women protestors and campaigned for the formation of an independent women's movement (Matindaftari, 1982). Many of its women supporters were active in the women's protest movement. The response of the National Democratic Front to the state's infringements of freedom of the press was equally strong. It organised the largest protest march against the closure of the *Ayandegan* newspaper and led the way on rejecting the Islamic Republic as a viable political system for post-revolutionary Iran. The National Democratic Front's unequivocal opposition to Ayatollah Khomeini's Islamisation measures made it the earliest target of denunciation and harassment by the hardline clergy and their street mobs.

The two different positions on anti-imperialism and democratic struggle within the left were also reflected within the socialist women's movement. In attempting to absorb women into their ranks, most Marxist–Leninist organisations found it necessary to set up an adjacent women's organisation. These groups formed a relatively large and vocal socialist women's movement. The socialist women's organisations worked strictly within the theoretical and political framework provided by their parent organisations. They had to define their response to state policy in relation to their leaders' position on anti-imperialism and Islam. The policy of the parent organisation determined whether a socialist women's group confronted the Islamisation policy of the state or kept silent about it, and whether or not it cooperated with other women's groups.

During the transitional period, then, the main features of the socialist women's movement were political dependency and the theoretical dominance of Marxism–Leninism. This being the case, the socialist women's movement was dominated by the question of the compatibility of the women's movement with anti-imperialist struggles. The Tudeh Party's DOIW led the way for those socialist women's groups which subordinated the women's movement to the anti-imperialist movement. The belief was that due to 'various plots and subversive activities of counter-revolutionaries and imperialist agents inside and outside the country', the anti-imperialist revolution was in danger and therefore all efforts should be directed to its defence (DOIW, 1982b).

In accordance with this view, the programme of the DOIW for women was low-key and non-confrontational. It included the standard Marxist–Leninist demand for 'equality of rights for men and women in all spheres of life', as well as 'participation of women in government at all levels ranging from the village council to the presidency', and 'appointment by parliament of a commission to draw up equal and just family law' (DOIW, 1982b). The DOIW criticised the imposition of *hejab* indirectly as 'deviating from the main objective of combating imperialism' but this was complemented with praise for Ayatollah Khomeini's firm stand against the West (*Jahan Zanan*, 1). The Islamisation policy on women was blamed on 'certain bigoted elements and pseudo-religious individuals who have infiltrated the revolutionary institutions' and the Provisional Government and Islamic reformists such as President Banisadr were named as representatives of this misguided position (DOIW, 1982b). Ayatollah Khomeini's edicts on the family were 'constructively criticised' and justified at the same time. The return to the Civil Code of 1931 was considered as 'unwise' due to the fact that 'the Civil Code was a Pahlavi law, established by Reza Khan inspired by imperialist domination of Iran' (Tudeh Party, 1980). The banning of abortion was justified on the ground that 'the basic problems facing the vast majority of women in Iran are quite different from the problems of the elite' and that 'having a large family was in fact one of the necessities of peasant life in Iran' (DOIW, 1982b).

Those women's groups who were following the opposite political line were able to campaign more openly on women's issues and play a role in women's protests against Islamisation. The pro-Fadaiyan National Union of Women, the Organisation of Women's Emancipation (Sazeman Rahai Zan) which was attached to the Organisation of Communist Unity, and the women's section of the National Democratic Front, all demanded a greater space for the women's movement insisting that 'women's struggle for their rights was inseparable from the struggle against imperialism' (WSC, 1979). Contrary to the DOIW, these women's groups were prepared to confront the hardline faction of the state on its Islamisation policies, but like the DOIW they too refused to support the moderate and reformist factions of the state.

Within the socialist women's movement, the dominant analysis of the Provisional Government and President Banisadr's camp was that their pro-Western political outlook was a reflection of their class interest which was that of the dependent bourgeoisie. There was therefore no question of alliance between Islamic reformists and the socialist women's movement. The DOIW often found it convenient to support the Islamic feminists' criticisms of state policies instead of making its own direct criticism of the state (DOIW, 1982b). But this did not result in cooperation between the DOIW and Islamic feminists due to the latter's distrust of socialists. Contrary to the DOIW, the anti-state socialist women's groups made an issue of the state's Islamic ideology. They condemned Islamic ideology as backward and reactionary and rejected the anti-capitalist and anti-imperialist claims of the Islamic state on the basis that this was a particularly reactionary form of capitalist state which was incapable of leading the country out of dependency and backwardness. The socialist women's movement, then, defined its main task as the struggle against the Islamic Republic. The anti-state socialist women's groups believed that the state's Islamisation measures were aimed at confining women to the home:

> Compulsory veiling, preventing women from holding judicial posts, sexual segregation of swimming areas, execution and flogging of women on charges of prostitution and adultery, re-establishing polygamy and temporary marriage, practically annulling the Family Protection Law, and the recent segregation of schools – these are but some of the measures of the ruling class against half the population of the society, women. These measures aim, step by step, to eliminate women from social and productive life, to push them back from positions that have been gained through long struggles, and to limit them to the four walls of the patriarchal household. These reflect the reactionary outlook of the people in power today. Today our problem is not simply that the people in power and powerful clergy prevent the development of half the productive forces of society, but that they are trying to throw women back fourteen centuries, a rather strange and incredible state of affairs that is taking place in front of our shocked eyes and those of the rest of the world. (OWE, 1979a)

In opposition to Islamisation policy, the anti-state women's groups demanded the liberation of the working class and equality for women. They wrote 'The regressive legislation of the Assembly of Experts does not represent the anti-imperialist demands of the people and must therefore be condemned. Rather, in a framework of democracy and liberation, we should put forward laws to protect the rights of national sovereignty for all toilers of this country and determine full equal rights for men and women in Iran' (WSC, 1979). The restoration of women's full rights within the family was another main demand of the anti-state socialist women's groups:

> The abolition of the Family Protection Law and the revival of the Civil Code [has meant] that men's unrestrained desires to marry more than one woman will now become legal and a man will enjoy the full and unconditional right to divorce. Even the stipulation of women's right to divorce in the marriage certificate would not diminish man's complete right to divorce. The woman has to have permission from her husband to enter a profession and even as a mother she would be deprived of the right to custody of her children if she is divorced . . . We condemn the reversal of women's rights in the family and demand equal familial rights for men and women. (NUW, 1979b, p. 154)

The socialist women's programmes and demands for women were uniform and quite limited in scope. Theoretical work did not have priority because Marxism–Leninism had equipped women's groups with ready-made formulas about women's oppression and liberation. To the majority of socialist women's groups, there was one 'woman question' and one 'Marxist position on women'. The theoretical consensus on women produced uniform political demands on the part of the socialist women's organisations. The primary objective of the movement was defined as women's participation in production. The most revolutionary demands were considered to be related to the condition of women toilers. Equality before the law in every aspect was the gist of the demands put forward by socialist feminists.

These demands were raised in a reactive manner in response to the state's Islamisation policies and not as part of a systematic feminist strategy formulated specifically in relation to the situation. Equality of rights for men and women was taken as a vehicle for reaching socialism, defined as the only society capable of creating real equality. The demand for equality was so general and abstract that it was untranslatable into concrete policies for here and now. It could have been made in any society and on behalf of any category of women. Moreover, to propose concrete policies presumes pragmatism and willingness to negotiate and compromise. This was not possible because of the dependence of the socialist women's group on Marxist–Leninist organisations. While cries were reaching the sky over what was being done to women by the Islamic state, opportunities for effective alliance against Islamisation were being missed by the socialist women's movement. Being wary of supporting the reformist faction of the transitional state in its efforts against the impositions of the hardline faction, the socialist women's movement effectively isolated itself from the political scene in which concrete policies on women were being formulated. Women's groups ended up proposing revolutionary demands in isolation.

In relating to each other, socialist women's groups were equally rigid and uncompromising. Since their parent organisations were competing for mass support and needed to create a distinctive identity for themselves, women's groups were often prevented from joint action. It was common practice amongst women's organisations to specify in their constitutions which other groups they would refuse to cooperate with. For example, the National Union of Women announced that it would not cooperate with any women's organisations 'who have not stated their political positions clearly, or those who situate women in opposition to revolutionary forces or with reactionary groups who attempt to mobilise women along deviatory and secondary issues at this sensitive time . . . [or] any group or party dependent on the United States of America, the Soviet Union, China or any other foreign power' (NUW, 1979b).

The sectarianism which prevailed within the left also operated within the socialist women's movement. It was a common practice for women's groups to call for unity between the few women's groups which were prepared to work together. But unity was defined as the acceptance of the terms and conditions of one side by others. Every one of these women's organisations wanted unity under its own banner. The formation of the Women's Solidarity Committee in the Autumn of 1979 reflected the problem. This coalition was formed by a number of women's groups to set up a joint conference on women. The NUW was one of the founding groups, but it later withdrew from participation because of its failure to impose its own terms and conditions upon the others. It only managed to send a message of support to the conference (OWE, 1979b).

The failure of Marxist–Leninist organisations to support women's protests and the theoretical and political dependence of socialist women's groups came under increasing criticism. As the success of the hardline clergy in Islamising women's rights and suppressing political opposition increased, the political and theoretical influence of Marxism–Leninism amongst the left decreased. This was particularly the case amongst the socialist women's movement. Political sectarianism, isolation from mainstream politics and dependency on organisations which did not prioritise women's issues were considered to be some of the reasons for the failure of the left in general, and the secular women's movement in particular. By 1981, when state repression succeeded in the eradication of all open political dissent inside the country, there was a substantial call within the socialist women's movement for an independent secular feminist movement which was free from Marxist–Leninist dogma and nationalist compromise.

Women, family and nation in the Constitution of the Islamic Republic

The Constitution of the Islamic Republic was the formalised expression of the revolutionary transformation from modernisation to Islamisation. It was a product of the aforementioned process of power struggle and political repression, and reflected the clash of ideas and balance of forces within the transitional period.

A number of observations can be made about the Constitution and its construction of women. First, the Islamic alternative on women proposed in the Constitution in opposition to 'alien Western concepts' was far from a 'pure Islamic construct', if such a thing ever existed. On the contrary, the Constitution borrowed from a variety of indigenous and exogenous models of womanhood and reflected a compromise between conflicting sets of ideas. Indeed, it was the context of revolutionary populism and anti-imperialism which determined which concepts and ideas on women found their way into the Constitution as 'Islamic' and which were excluded as 'un-Islamic'. Second, the prominent place given to women in the Constitution reflected the depth of interest expressed by all competing ideologies in the transitional period about the relationship between gender and nation. The Constitution demonstrated that the creation of an Islamic nation was dependent on the Islamisation of gender relations. It constructed the new 'Islamic' link between nation and gender and specified a corresponding position for women.

Finally, the Constitution aimed to solve the problem of tension between women's roles in the family and society which had remained unresolved. To recap, under both Pahlavi Shahs the state's modernisation policies aimed, on the one hand, to integrate women into the process of national development and, on the other hand, to preserve male domination and female subordination within the family. Moreover, the position adopted by the autonomous institution of Shiism *vis-à-vis* state policy on women deepened this tension by separating the sphere of 'social' from 'family' and defining the former as the preserve of the state and the latter as the preserve of the clergy. Now that in the Islamic Republic the state and Shiism were one, there was no need for this tension to continue. For the first time, the clergy was in control of both women's social and familial roles. The result was a total reversal of the history of clerical opposition to women's participation in the economy, politics and society. The same clerics, such as Ayatollah Khomeini, who objected so strongly to women's enfranchisement before the Revolution in the name of Islam, were now prepared to grant women the right to vote in the Constitution of the Islamic Republic. With these points in mind, let us consider the way in which the Constitution of the Islamic Republic constructed women.

The opening chapter of the Constitution described the principles on which the Islamic Republic was based. These included: 'the complete expulsion of imperialism and the prevention of foreign influence'; 'the elimination of all forms of tyranny and autocracy and all attempts to monopolise power'; 'the securing of political freedoms within the limits of the law'; 'ensuring the participation of entire people in the determination of their political, economic, social and cultural destiny'; 'the abolition of all forms of impermissible discrimination and the provision of just opportunities for all in both material and non-material matters'; 'securing the comprehensive rights of all citizens, both women and men, and the establishment of judicial security for all, as well as the equality of all before the law' (Constitution of the Islamic Republic, 1980, Article 3: e, f, g, h, i, n). The Constitution drew upon the above conceptions to construct an 'Islamic nation' which was defined as a collective unity:

> In accordance with the verse 'This your nation is a single nation, and I am your Lord, so worship Me', all Muslims form a single nation, and the government of the Islamic Republic of Iran has the duty of formulating its general policies with a view to the merging and union of all Muslim peoples, and it must constantly strive to bring about the political, economic and cultural unity of the Islamic world. (*Ibid.*, Article 10)

Two main characteristics of the 'Islamic nation' were specified in the Constitution. First, the 'Islamic nation' was founded on 'the family'. The Constitution emphasised that 'Since the family is the fundamental unit of the Islamic society, all pertinent laws, regulations, and programmes must tend to facilitate the foundation of a family and to protect the sanctity and stability of family relations on the basis of the law and the ethics of Islam' (*ibid.*, Article 11).

Second, the 'Islamic nation' privileged women as a particular section of 'Muslims' with special rights and responsibilities. This was because of their 'greater oppression under the despotic regime' and their 'weighty responsibilities' in Islamic society: 'In the creation of Islamic social institutions ... women should benefit from a particularly large augmentation of their rights, because of the greater oppression that they suffered under the despotic regime. ... Given the weighty responsibilities that woman thus assumes, she is accorded in Islam great value and nobility' (*ibid.*, pp. 21–2).

The Constitution considered women and the family as the main element in the identity of the 'Islamic nation' as opposed to other nations. Women, as the link between family and Islamic society featured prominently in the Constitution's twelve chapters and 174 articles, which set out to explain 'the political, social, cultural and economic institutions and relations there are to exist in our society [and] to establish an ideal and model society on the basis of Islamic criteria' (*ibid.*, p. 19). Women were constructed in the Constitution as 'fellow strugglers' and an indispensable element in the process of social and political change: 'The Islamic Revolution of Iran was nurtured by the blood of hundreds of young believers, women and men, who met the firing squads at dawn with cries of *Allah-o-Akbar*, or who were gunned down by the enemy in streets and market-places' (*ibid.*, 1980, p. 15). Women were seen in partnership with men and acknowledged as a diverse force: 'The widespread solidarity between men and women of all segments of society, belonging to both religious and political wings of the movement, played a clearly influential role in the struggle. Women were active and massively present in a most obvious manner in all stages of this great struggle' (*ibid.*, p. 17). The *Qoran* was also quoted as saying that 'The men and women believers are the protectors of each other; they enjoin the good and forbid the evil' (*ibid.*, Article 8). Women were also treated as full citizens with the right to education, employment and equality before the law. The rights of people (men and women) were described in chapter 3 of the Constitution. These rights which have specific implications for women's positions were described as follows:

Article 3: The government of the Islamic Republic has the duty of directing all its resources to the following goals:

...

c. free education and physical training for everyone at all levels.

...

h. ensuring the participation of the entire people in the determination of their political, economic, social and cultural destiny. ...
i. the abolition of all forms of impermissible discrimination and the provision of just opportunities for all, in both material and non-material matters ...

...

n. securing the comprehensive rights of all citizens, both men and women, and the establishment of judicial security for all, as well as the equality of all before the law.

Article 20: All citizens of the nation, both women and men, equally enjoy the protection of the law and enjoy all human, political, economic, social, and cultural rights, in conformity with Islamic criteria.
Article 28: Everyone has the right to choose any employment s/he wishes, if it is not opposed to Islam, the public interest, or to the right of others. The government has the duty ... to provide every citizen with the opportunity to work, and to create equal conditions for obtaining it.
Article 30: The government must provide all citizens with free education to the end of middle school, and must expand higher education to the level required by the country for self-sufficiency.
Article 43: ... the economy of the Islamic Republic is to be based on, among others, the following criteria:
a. the provision of basic necessities to all citizens. ...
b. assuring conditions and possibilities of employment for everyone. ...
d. respect for the right to choose freely one's job. ...

Article 151: Military training for citizens in accordance with Islamic law.

But being citizen and revolutionary were not the only dimensions of womanhood. Women were also defined on the basis of the family and their role as mothers. The 'Islamic family' allowed the woman to 'recover her momentous and precious function of motherhood' and thereby become a 'true woman' (*ibid.*, p.22). But how did these different dimensions of womanhood relate to each other? In the Constitution, women as citizens and political beings were subjugated to women as mothers. Since the woman's role within the family was a special one, motherhood was not considered equal in status with other dimensions of womanhood. Motherhood was the essence of a woman's being and as a result all other dimensions of womanhood were conditional upon it. Examples of how women's citizenship and political roles were dependent on her motherhood role were plentiful in the Constitution. The image of women's participation in the Revolution as presented in the Constitution is one example: 'The common sight of mothers with infants in their arms running towards the scene of battle and the barrels of machine guns demonstrated the essential and decisive role played by this major segment of society in the struggle' (*ibid.*, p. 17).

The greater exploitation of women in pre-revolutionary society was believed to be due to distracting women from their familial and motherhood responsibilities by treating them as 'sex-objects'. The social responsibilities of the new Muslim woman was based on her regaining her motherhood role and putting it in the service of the Islamic Revolution:

> The family is the fundamental unit of society and the major centre for the growth and advancement of man [human-being]. Compatibility with respect to belief and ideal is the main consideration in the establishment of a family, for the family provides the primary basis of man's [human-being's] development and growth. It is the duty of Islamic government to facilitate this goal. . . . This view of the family unit delivers women from being regarded as an object or as an instrument in the service of consumerism and consumption. Not only does woman recover thereby her momentous and precious function of motherhood, rearing alert and active human beings, she also becomes the fellow struggler of men in all the different areas of life. (*Ibid.*, p. 22)

Women were conceptualised as mothers or potential mothers when their specific rights were spelled out in Article 21. The government was instructed to 'assure the rights of women in all respects in conformity with Islamic criteria' and accomplish the following goals:

a. create a favourable environment for the growth of woman's personality and the restoration of her rights, tangible and intangible;
b. the protection of mothers, particularly during pregnancy and child-rearing, and the protection of children without guardians;
c. the creation of a competent court to protect and preserve the family;
d. the provision of special insurance for widows and aged and destitute women;
e. the granting of guardianship of children to their mothers whenever suitable in order to protect the interests of the children, in the absence of a legal guardian.

In short, women were granted social and political rights because they were mothers or potential mothers. The importance of women's familial role to the identity of the 'Islamic nation' was also indicated by the way in which her rights were subjected to the extra-constitutional criteria of 'conformity with Islamic law'. The state, which 'must work towards the creation of an Islamic society' was given the responsibility of ensuring the conformity of women's position with Islamic law (*ibid.*, p. 23). The Constitution referred to 'Islamic law' as an extra-constitutional criteria in many of its articles. This was particularly the case in relation to women, especially in Articles 20, 21, 151 and 163. This resulted in the subjection of the Constitution to a divine law outside and above it. It also created a great deal of confusion and contradiction in the text of the Constitution.

This was the case because despite the references to it, 'Islamic law' was not defined. As a result, the final form of women's constitutional rights was left to be determined by the state outside the boundaries of the Constitution. To take one example, Article 20 stated that men and women should enjoy equal rights 'in conformity with Islamic criteria'. The precise nature of the equality of women with men in Islamic society was left vague and put in the hands of the state to determine. Article 21, which was about protection of mothers and the family, also, put the obligation of assuring the 'rights of women in all respects in conformity with Islamic criteria' on the shoulders of the state. It avoided clarification on what the rights of women in conformity with the Islamic criteria were.

Article 151 qualified the requirement that the government should provide military training 'for all of its citizens' by stating that it should be done 'in conformity with Islamic criteria'. It therefore left it unclear whether or not women had the right to participate in the military defence of the country. Article 163 specified that 'the attributes and qualifications of judges will be determined by law, in accordance with the criteria of *faqih*' (*ibid.*, Article 163). Here again, whether or not a person's gender was a qualification for becoming a judge was left to the unspecified opinion of the *faqih* of the time.

Moreover, the qualifying criteria of 'conformity with Islam' was used selectively and caused contradictions. While women's rights and equality of rights between men and women were required to conform with Islamic criteria, others were not. Articles 3, 28, 30 and 43 dealt with subjects such as citizens' rights to education and employment; yet these articles were not subject to conform with Islamic law. Article 3 (n) and Article 20 addressed similar rights. The former made an unequivocal statement about equality of rights while the latter subjected equality of rights to Islamic criteria. Article 21 (e), contradicted Article 3 (n) because the equality of rights promised in the latter was not observed in the former, where men were treated as legal guardians of children and women as substitutes in the absence of the real guardian. Indeed, this article contradicted all previous emphases on the importance of motherhood by prioritising the patriarchal rights of the father.

The Constitution of the Islamic Republic constructed a particular set of patriarchal gender relations which aimed to remove the historical tension between the family and the nation in relation to women. Women's loyalty could now be shared between the family and the nation. The woman was constructed as a mother; the mother as creator of the Islamic family; and the family as the foundation of the Islamic nation. Women were granted rights and obligations as the creators and nurturers of the Islamic family and nation. The state was given the task of creating 'Muslim mothers' and of putting them in the service of the Islamic nation. The rights and responsibilities of 'Muslim mothers', however, were left to be determined by the Islamic state in conformity with an unspecified Islamic law.

Part 3

The discourse of Islamisation

Part 3 will focus on the discourse of Islamisation and examine the development and implementation of the Islamic Republic's policies on women.

The transitional discourse of revolution facilitated the transformation of the discourse of modernity into the discourse of Islamisation. The discourse of Islamisation shared with the discourse of modernity the need to acquire economic development, technological progress and political strength to achieve national independence. This required reliance on modern institutions and practices which included women's national participation. But it differed from the discourse of modernity in advocating an 'Islamic' route to national independence. While the latter emphasised secularism and Westernisation, the discourse of Islamisation aimed to achieve national independence by creating a modern Muslim nation, a model which it claimed could be emulated by other Muslim societies.

The establishment of the discourse of Islamisation was the result of a process of power struggle and political repression. The Islamic Republic that emerged from the transitional period set out to implement constitutional gender relations and actualise the proposed ideal Islamic family. The Constitution had advocated a set of patriarchal gender relations which preserved male control over women while granting women the right to be active mothers and citizens. The ideal 'Islamic' family was defined in opposition to 'Western' definitions of family and sexuality and hailed as the culturally authentic and appropriate form of family for a modern Muslim society. The post-transitional Islamic state promised its male and female citizens fulfilment of their 'natural' rights. It made a bargain with women to be obedient wives and active citizens in return for protection by men and the Islamic state (Kandiyoti, 1991b). Women mobilised into an Islamic women's movement to protect their bargain with the state and defend their gains from it.

The actualisation of the Islamic family and nation involved extensive Islamisation of women. The state introduced a range of legislation and codes of behaviour within the framework of the Constitution to establish and reinforce various aspects of Islamic gender relation. The first aspect related to the definition of 'Islamic family'. Policies were developed on marriage, family planning, familial relations, divorce and custody to Islamise and standardise the Iranian household. The Islamic Republic's policies on the family will be discussed in chapter 8.

The second aspect related to women's participation in national processes. Policies were formulated on women's education, employment and political participation to ensure that the Islamic nation continued to benefit from the creative and nurturing qualities of its female citizens. The Islamic Republic's policies on women's national participation will be discussed in chapter 9.

The third aspect of Islamic gender relations concerned formation of strategies to enable the family and the nation to remain in harmony in relation to women. Policies were developed on gender segregation and the punishment of adultery to desexualise male–female social contact and hence protect the sanctity of the Islamic family. The Islamic Republic's policies on gender segregation will be discussed in chapter 10, and a summary of the main points raised in Part 3 will also be presented.

1 A Tehrani woman skiing in Aliabad ski resort in the outskirts of Tehran wearing appropriate Islamic clothes
Photo: N. Kasraian, 1992

2 Retired prostitute playing 'Taar' in her home in Sirus Avenue in Tehran
Photo: H. Zolfaghari, 1993

3 Women listening to a sermon in Ayatollah Khomeini's shrine in Tehran on the anniversary of his death
Photo: H. Zolfaghari, 1993

4 Tehrani women shopping in Mosalla Friday market in Abasabad in Tehran
Photo: H. Zolfaghari, 1993

5 Women leading the procession to mark the opening of 'women's olympic' competitions in Tehran
Photo: H. Zolfaghari, 1993

6 A lower-class family in their house in Sirus Avenue in the south of Tehran
Photo: H. Zolfaghari, 1993

7 Women using a Caspian Sea beach in Mazandaran wearing appropriate Islamic clothes
Photo: N. Kasraian, 1992

8 The Islamic construction of family

The Islamic state's actualisation of the patriarchal ideal was set against a context of Islamic diversity, power struggle, political repression, ideological control, economic stagnation, war, destruction, international isolation and an uneasy coexistence of state populism and decreasing popularity.

Let us pause briefly before discussing the Islamic Republic's policy on family to consider this socio-political context.

The socio-political context in the first decade of the Islamic Republic

One of the most distinct aspects of the Islamic Republic in its first decade was the reign of terror. In respect of political suppression and control, the Islamic Republic gained a formidable reputation for employing ruthless means to root out internal dissent. Widespread political arrests, disproportionate punishment of 'political offenders', indefinite detainments without trial, inhumane prison conditions, horrific tortures of political prisoners and inhumane treatment of their families, all became the hallmarks of Islamic justice.

Political suppression in the Islamic Republic was directed towards both the secular and Islamic forces. After the annihilation of the secular and Islamic left opposition, it was the turn of the silenced and subjugated Islamic and secular nationalist opposition inside the country to be given the full Islamic treatment. Many former aides and allies of the Islamic leadership were implicated in 'conspiracies against Islam' and imprisoned or executed. The National Front was silenced and its leaders were forced into hiding. The Liberation Movement, too, went underground but its infrequent clandestine oppositional voice was tolerated. Tribal and ethnic rebellions were suppressed brutally, and military offensives against the Kurds succeeded in bringing Kurdish nationalism under control. Even Shii tribes, such as Qashqais, who had supported the Revolution did not escape suppression (Beck, 1992).

Despite its successes in suppressing political opposition, however, the regime was still afraid of its politically heterogeneous citizens. The Majles was not allowed to become representative and democratic: elections were manipulated and tampered with, candidates were prevented from standing, elected representatives were vetoed and some were refused their seats or expelled later. Political representation became the exclusive right of a hard core of Islamic supporters, and political debate became the exclusive privilege of a close circle of the regime's officials. But the Islamic Republic was incapable of allowing even its own officials to exercise freedom of expression. The ongoing political debate within the state was conducted within rigidly set boundaries and at times resulted in political casualties. The 'Maktabi' and 'Hojatiyeh' rivalries and 'pragmatist' and 'extremist' power struggles replaced earlier struggles between the Shii hardliners, the left and the nationalists. The political system had an inbuilt tendency towards extremism and the position of those who advocated moderation and compromise was always vulnerable. The moderates only prospered when Khomeini chose to protect them out of necessity and pragmatic considerations.

The central concern of the Islamic state was relations with the West. Political realities affected the 'Islamisation' of foreign policy and resulted in conflicting priorities. The war with Iraq, which resulted in economic devastation of the country and a staggering loss of life as well as the Islamic Republic's isolation, was a clear demonstration of this. The damage inflicted on Iran's economy by the war and its political consequences were recognised by the pragmatists within the state who made many unsuccessful attempts to change the direction of Iran's foreign policy in favour of compromise and peace. Yet other priorities of the Islamic leadership resulted in the continuation of the conflict until it was practically impossible to sustain this policy.

The war accelerated the growth of revolutionary organisations who used it as an opportunity to consolidate their hold over the population. It gave legitimacy to radical populist trends since the war was used for mobilisation of the masses. It put a lid on economic demands and legitimised the ideology of sacrifice and austerity. It also prevented the revolutionary fever from subsiding and reaffirmed the Shii ideology and Ayatollah Khomeini's leadership through the popular embrace of martyrdom for the cause of Islam and *emam*. The question of post-war reconstruction, too, galvanised old conflicts and diversity of policy within the Islamic state and resulted in political casualties.

The importance of a radical foreign policy for the regime arose from its mobilising value. The failure of the hardline leadership to deliver tangible economic prosperity and social justice to its people led the regime to rely on mass mobilisation through political and ideological propaganda. The condemnation of the West for conspiracy against Islam and *mostazafin* continuously proved to be a mobilising issue. Alongside this, the regime relied heavily on ideological propaganda and social conformity to keep the population ready for mobilisation and prevent social and political diversity from gaining ground. The press and mass media, Friday prayers and mosques were all put at the service of revolutionary Islamic propaganda, denunciation of the West and internal enemies, and enforcement of Islamic education for citizens. Both propaganda and Islamic education penetrated schools, universities, prisons, offices and streets. Those seeking education or employment were required to pass ideological tests (Habibi, 1989). Secular ways of life were destroyed and Muslim and non-Muslim alike were forced to conform to what was defined as the proper Islamic way of life. Women were particularly pressurised to fit into their Islamic role. In short, the state expanded its sphere of influence over every aspect of civil and personal life in a way that the Pahlavi states had not been willing or able to do.

Economic development, too, was a reflection of both the diversity of responses to economic realities and the power struggle within the Islamic state. Despite an explicit statement in the Constitution that the economic system was to be based on long-term planning, a clear economic development policy did not emerge. The economy was managed on the basis of *ad hoc* decisions and conflicting policies. Broadly speaking, two opposing tendencies emerged within the state on the question of economy. During the first decade of the Islamic Republic, on the one hand, radical populist factions within the government and the Majles pushed for more state intervention and the imposition of limits on private property. On the other hand, the orthodox clergy, jurists in the Council of Guardians and some moderate Majles deputies argued for the protection of private property and limited nationalisation of capital and industry. The power struggle over economic policy resulted in a number of outcomes in different contexts, ranging from temporary compromises to total stalemate on issues such as the nationalisation of urban land, redistribution of agricultural land and nationalisation of foreign trade.

The Council of Guardians refused on many occasions to approve those Majles bills which extended state control over the economy. The government attempted to by-pass the Council of Guardians by implementing policies which had no legal foundation (Bakhash, 1984). The economic programme failed to bring about Islamic justice, or to increase agricultural and industrial output and free the nation from dependence on foreign food and technological supplies. If anything, the Islamic Republic's economic mismanagement and the devastation caused by the war against Iraq increased the country's dependence on the West (Parvin & Taghavi, 1988).

The state had to rely increasingly on oil revenue to finance the war and to import substantial proportion of the nation's food and other basic goods from abroad. The ever expanding black market, racketeering and soaring inflation affected the delivery of economic benefits to the lower and middle income sectors (Amirahmadi, 1990). Increasingly, the state had to maintain the loyalty of its supporters by charitable handouts. The war resulted in the mobilisation on a massive scale of volunteers who had to be maintained by the state in addition to the regular security and armed forces. The network of state-funded charities had to expand substantially to reward the war wounded, the families of the martyrs, war widows and the like. The war and war-related patronage could hardly be financed by the decreasing oil revenues. Therefore, the state often turned to illegal means of financing its welfare programmes. Illegal taxes and confiscations of private property and wealth became a regular source of income for state supported organisations.

By the time of Ayatollah Khomeini's death, despite a decade of anti-imperialism, Islamisation, political control, ideological propaganda and populist policies, the objectives of the Islamic Republic were far from being achieved. Despite the fact that the regime was still capable of generating political excitement and continued to operate on the basis of mass mobilisation, it had lost the support of many sectors of the population. The process of decreasing genuine support and increasing social and ideological conformity caused by fear and helplessness, started early in the aftermath of the Revolution and continued throughout the 1980s. Political repression, Islamic imposition, and economic stagnation deeply affected all urban and rural sectors and lost support for the regime, albeit in different degrees, amongst all social groups.

Economic mismanagement was a major confidence loser. The 1986 census showed that only 39 per cent of the population over the age of ten were economically active, out of which only 33.47 per cent were officially considered employed (SCI, 1988b, pp. 8–9). The reign of terror and the exercise of harsh Islamic justice was another issue which outraged many remaining secular and Islamic supporters of the regime. By the end of the first decade, the tremendous popular support that the revolutionary leadership had enjoyed amongst men and women in the immediate aftermath of the Revolution had shrunk to a hard core of political devotees.

The Islamic Republic's gender policies were developed and implemented within the above social context. The Constitution provided the general framework for the Islamisation of gender relations. But within this framework, the formulation and implementation of gender policies were closely tied with the Islamic Republic's political and economic development and reflected the heterogeneity of state policy, the diversity of Islamic thought, political debate and power struggle. Contrary to ahistorical conceptions of Islam, gender policies of the Islamic state were not a straight replica of the *Qoran* or the *shariat*. The dominant conceptions of gender in the Islamic Republic were, rather, constructed with reference to Islamic modernisation, or Islamisation, in the context of immediate social and political relations and processes in the post-revolutionary society.

Development of legal institutions

The establishment of clerical rule brought about a profound change in the clergy's influence in the legislature as well as the judiciary. In particular, the reversal of the Pahlavi secularisation resulted in the clergy having an unprecedented degree of influence over the legal position of women. Nevertheless, in the first decade of the Islamic Republic, the legal institutions established to tackle the Islamisation of the family were heterogenous and the sources of family law were multiple. The Islamic Republic did not inherit a ready-made and coherent family law, but constructed one in response to issues arising in post-revolutionary society and with reference to a variety of Islamic and secular legal sources.

The process of construction of the 'Islamic family' began with Ayatollah Khomeini's suspension of the Family Protection laws of 1967 and 1975 a few days after the victory of the Revolution (*Keyhan*, 8). The Family Protection Law had signified the abandonment of the Shii *shariat* in favour of the Westernisation of the Iranian family (see chapter 5). This suspension effectively returned the legal status of the family to the Civil Code of 1931, which had been drafted under Reza Shah on the basis of a relatively liberal interpretation of the Shii *shariat* (see chapter 3). This, however, was not immediately implemented due to strong protests from the secular opposition and nationalist allies (see chapter 7). In April 1979, Ayatollah Mahdavi Kani, a member of the Council of Revolution, reiterated Khomeini's earlier call for the suspension of the Family Protection Law by announcing that since Islam had granted the right of divorce to men, they should not be required to go to courts for divorce. This was an invitation to men to by-pass the family protection courts which dealt with divorce, custody and other family matters. Under the Family Protection Law, divorce was issued by the family protection courts and then registered at notary public offices. Ayatollah Kani suggested that men could simply register their divorce in the notary public offices without producing a court permission.

Protest was raised again that the abrogation of the Family Protection

Law should not take place before it could be replaced by a new law which was drafted through proper legal channels. Two months later a leaked document was published by the Council for Coordination of Women's Rights, a socialist women's group, which pointed to a secret memorandum issued by Ayatollah Mahdavi Kani to the family protection courts. The memorandum instructed the courts to issue divorce to men on demand without taking them through court procedure, so that despite a pretence of following the lawful route men could exercise their Islamic right (*Ayandegan*, 4). The Provisional Government's denial of the secret instruction did not convince the opposition (National Union of Women, 1979c).

Despite its earlier announcement that the Family Protection Law would remain effective (*Keyhan*, 9) the Provisional Government finally conceded. In August 1979, Ayatollah Khomeini's hardline supporters finally won the battle. The minister of justice in the Provisional Government, Sadr Haj-Seyyed-Javadi, officially announced that the Family Protection Law was abrogated and although the family protection courts would continue to exist, they would not issue verdicts which were considered to be against the Shii *shariat*. This compelled the family protection courts to base their verdicts on the old Civil Code which preceded it (*Keyhan*, 10). In October 1979, a proposal for the replacement of the family protection courts with special civil courts was presented by the minister of justice to the Council of Revolution, which was approved (*Keyhan*, 11).

The new courts, however, were mandated to deal with divorce only if there was a dispute involved. In cases where there was mutual consent and both husband and wife had agreed to the divorce, the man could register it, in the presence of two male witnesses, in notary offices without permission from the court (*Keyhan*, 12). This was a compromise solution and the concept of a family court, albeit a watered down one, was retained despite the Family Protection Law being theoretically removed from the statute books. The jurisdiction of the special civil courts also included disputes related to marriage, annulment, *mehrieh*, *nafagheh*, child custody, wills and inheritance (*Zan Ruz*, 2). The government soon announced that many branches of the special civil courts would be set up around the country. It started with five branches in Tehran and by 1981 there were eighty branches throughout the country (*Keyhan*, 13). The courts were headed by a cleric who was assisted by a lay lawyer and a secretary (*Ettelaat*, 7). The family was one of the few areas of civil life which was subjected to legislation in the life time of the Provisional Government. The legal basis for this was, strictly speaking, questionable since the Islamic Republic's Constitution had not yet been drafted and neither the Council of Revolution nor the Provisional Government were elected bodies and their mandates excluded passing civil laws.

The Civil Code, however, stopped being the main family law in March 1981 when the hardline prime minister in President Banisadr's government, Mohammad Ali Rajai, presented a bill which amended the Special Civil Courts Act of 1979 passed by the Council of Revolution. The amendment specified that, 'In cases where there is no guidance on family matters either from the Council of Revolution or the Majles, the special civil courts will base their judgements in relation to family disputes on Ayatollah Khomeini's *fatavi*' (*Mizan*, 7). This bill diversified the legitimate sources of legal guidance on the family and gave the clergy in charge of the special civil courts a choice of family laws to interpret and select from. A further complication was added in August 1982, when Ayatollah Khomeini intervened. Angry about the persistence of what he called '*taghuti* laws', meaning the laws passed under Pahlavi shahs, he ordered the 'purification' of the judiciary and asked for the conformity of all laws with the *shariat*.

This meant that those parts of the Civil Code which gave a different interpretation of the *shariat* had to be subordinated to the instructions in Ayatollah Khomeini's *touziholmasael*. An instance of such difference of interpretation was explained by Hojatoleslam Mahdavi Kermani, the head of the special civil courts. According to him, the courts had been deciding the age of consent on the basis of the Civil Code which suggested fifteen for girls and eighteen for boys. But after Khomeini's decree to rid the laws of Pahlavi influence, the courts had to rely exclusively on Khomeini's book, which was more strict than the Civil Code, by prescribing a minimum age of marriage of nine for girls and fifteen for boys (*Keyhan*, 12). Asked whether Islamisation of the law applied to religious minorities, he emphasised that minority religious authorities had been granted jurisdiction over their members in family matters. But should a non-Muslim married couple choose to take their family disputes to special civil courts, then they would be subjected to *shariat* rules (*ibid.*).

In November 1984, Hojatoleslam Kermani gave another example of the multiplicity of sources of legal guidance on the family when he talked about the existence of two legal opinions on polygamy. According to him, 'the Council of Guardians consider polygamy as man's unconditional right' but 'those who administer the law [the special civil courts] believe that the first wife's permission needs to be obtained'. He complained that this duality in the law had resulted in the inability of the courts to enforce sanctions against those who take second wives without the court's permission, which 'has resulted in many illegal marriages' (*Keyhan (London)*, 1). This meant that despite its abrogation, parts of the Family

Protection Law were still in force. Another clash of legal opinion between the special civil courts and the Council of Guardians happened over the establishment and remit of the newly set up special civil appeal court. In January 1985, the High Council of Judiciary (Shoraye Aliye Ghazai) announced that a special civil appeal court had been set up to look into those family disputes which had not been satisfactorily resolved by the special civil courts (*Ettelaat*, 8).

This was a compromise decision between the Council of Guardian's rejection of an appeal court on *shariat* grounds and the proposal by the special civil courts for the establishment of an appeal court with an extensive remit. The jurisdiction of the special civil appeal court was confined to appeals on three specific counts. First, if one or both parties to the dispute claimed that the judge in the special civil court was incompetent. Second, if the decision of the special civil court was against the *shariat*. Third, if the special civil court judge had neglected major evidence. The appeal court could not review disputes and sustain or overturn the decision of the special civil court if one or both sides of the dispute were not satisfied with the original court verdict (*Zan Ruz*, 2).

The complications arising from the multiplicity of family laws were exacerbated by the multiplicity of centres of administration. Disagreement amongst different factions of the state on the Family Protection Law and its final dismantlement, affected the regular functioning of the courts and a large backlog of cases was created. This resulted in a decrease in the rate of divorce in the aftermath of Revolution (Aghajanian, 1988, p.159). The High Council of the Judiciary announced that since the newly founded special civil courts were unable to deal with 80,000 cases outstanding from the family protection courts as well as new applications, a network of smaller and quicker '*shariat* courts' would be set up. These 'informal' courts were set up inside the revolutionary committees and were given a remit to resolve family disputes within a week (*Keyhan*, 14). Furthermore, since there were not enough branches of special civil courts to cover the whole country, the High Council of the Judiciary instructed the public courts to take on family disputes in the absence of a special civil court in the area (Ghorbani, 1989, p. 215).

The result of family disputes being dealt with in three different courts was uncoordinated and contradictory verdicts which resulted in public complaints. Azam Taleghani, a woman Majles deputy, complained in the Majles on behalf of her constituency that 'the verdicts of the family courts are not coordinated'. She demanded action on this and asked for a 'female consultant to be stationed in every court' (*Keyhan*, 15). But it took more than two years for the authorities to attempt to rationalise the legal system in relation to the handling of family disputes. The first stage of this rationalisation was the cancellation of informal '*shariat* courts' and a halt on referral of family disputes to the public courts. The second stage was the coordination of the special civil courts.

In April 1983, a seminar was set up by Ayatollah Sanei, the Public Prosecutor, to bring the special civil court judges together to discuss the coordination of their work. Another seminar was set up by the Women's Society of Islamic Revolution to discuss women's complaints against the treatment of family disputes by the courts. Hojatoleslam Mahdavi Kermani, the head of the special civil courts, participated in this seminar to learn about women's problems (*Keyhan*, 16). Referring to these discussions, Ayatollah Sanei said in an interview that the Civil Code was in essence in accordance with the *shariat* and therefore satisfactory as the basic law. But he promised to introduce new laws where necessary, to complement it (*ibid.*). In February 1984, a Committee on the Family was set up in the Majles by the efforts of women deputies. Maryam Behruzi, one of the founders, explained that the Committee held regular meetings with the special civil court judges to discuss family rights and propose solutions for women's problems in the family. The Committee had been preparing proposals for submission to the High Council of the Judiciary (*Keyhan*, 17).

A year later, Firuzeh Golmohammadi, a member of the editorial board of an Islamic women's magazine, protested on Islamic Women's Day that 'the law and its implementors often fail to give women their due rights in family disputes'. She described the problem as a 'lack of existence of truly Islamic family law'. The family law that is being implemented, she argued, was the old Civil Code which was being used as the 'mother law'. The Civil Code, she believed, was too restrictive on women's Islamic rights. She protested that complementary laws promised by the public prosecutor had not yet materialised. She also raised the problem of the lack of general awareness about women's true Islamic rights (*ibid.*).

The problems of unclear law, uncoordinated court verdicts and unsatisfactory treatment of women by the courts were discussed openly in the pages of *Zan Ruz* which was becoming increasingly assertive on women's rights. These problems were described vividly in an interview with Mohammad Ali Ebrahimkhani, the head of a unit responsible for the administration of decisions taken in the special civil courts (hereafter the Unit). According to him, the Special Civil Courts Act of 1979 anticipated the introduction of further legislation to create this Unit to safeguard the implementation of the courts' decisions on the family.

But since this promised legislation did not materialise, the Unit was temporarily set up to alleviate some of the urgent administrative problems. He summarised the difficulties faced by the Unit as inconsistent decisions by judges, lack of clarity in the law, and absence of legislation to enforce the courts' decisions. Since the Unit did not have any legal backing, most of these decisions were unenforceable. Moreover, the Unit's work suffered from severe lack of funding and lack of cooperation by the disciplinary forces (*Zan Ruz*, 3). The problem of lack of clarity of family laws arose, according to him, because, since the abrogation of the Family Protection Law, not enough laws had been introduced to cover all areas previously covered by the former. As a result, when the Unit faced certain problems such as the kidnapping of a child under the custody of one parent by the other parent, there was no other choice than to use the Family Protection Law as the only body of law which provided guidance on this matter. Mr Ebrahimkhani also pointed to the difference of approach between the courts and the administrators of the courts' decisions: 'While the courts are more *shariat* oriented in their approach to family disputes, we are more law oriented.' He complained that the judges preferred to rely on personal interpretations of the *shariat*. Some courts did not allow secular lawyers to represent their clients at all and others behaved badly towards them (*ibid.*).

In 1989, an authoritative collection of the Islamic Republic's family laws brought together a number of legally valid sources of guidance on the family. These included the Civil Code of 1931, the Family Protection Law (1967 and 1975), the Special Civil Courts Act 1979, other related legislation passed by the Majles and the Council of Guardians, regulations and opinions aimed at coordinating the decisions of the special civil courts issued by the High Council of the Judiciary and General Board of Supreme Court (Heyat Omumi Divan Aliye Keshvar), and the various *fatavi* by Ayatollah Khomeini and Ayatollah Montazeri (Ghorbani, 1989).

The way in which different authorities in family law related to each other was administratively hierarchical but the *mojtahed* who presided over the special civil court had the autonomy to decide which source of law to base his judgement on. The Majles introduced new legislation and amended the old, which included amendments to various articles of the Civil Code (Mohaqeq-Damad, 1986). But Majles interventions in family law, as described before, were very limited indeed. Furthermore, some of the laws passed by the Majles did not find their way to the statute books because they were deemed to be against the *shariat* by the Council of Guardians. The main bulk of legal reform in the Islamic Republic took place through rules and opinions rather than laws (*ibid.*). The High Council of the Judiciary and the General Board of the Supreme Court introduced regulations and issued judgements in response to conflicting decisions by the special civil courts and the appeal courts. These were often based on a combination of legal sources and referred to both pre-revolutionary secular laws and *shariat* laws as exemplified by Ayatollahs Khomeini and Montazeri. These interventions were, however, considered 'consultative' and the courts were not obliged to accept them (*ibid.*, pp. 215–25, 226–7).

Having examined the general characteristics of the legal system and the sources of family law, I will now turn to the state's policy of Islamisation which affected various aspects of the family including marriage, family planning, family relations, divorce, child custody, widowhood and inheritance.

Marriage

The state policy on marriage focused on the construction of marriage as the only legitimate site of sexual pleasure and reproduction, and its universalisation. To achieve this, the state adopted a number of strategies: the minimum age of marriage was lowered, restriction on polygamy was removed; financial assistance was offered to newly wed couples, and a campaign was waged on the virtues of marriage and Islamic matrimonial rights.

Lowering the age of marriage

With regard to marriage age, the foregoing description demonstrates that due to the multiplicity of legal sources the legitimate age of marriage remained a source of contention. Although the Civil Code specified the minimum age of thirteen for women, in practice it was left to the judge to decide whether a woman was mature enough to marry. The determining criteria was proof of physical maturity for sexual intercourse. The courts granted 'certificate of exemption' to women as young as ten or eleven if they had started to menstruate (*Keyhan*, 18). In addition to the age condition, women had to obtain paternal consent for the first marriage (as a virgin) (*Ettelaat*, 9). Another condition which had to be met in relation to marriage was prohibition of matrimony between close relatives by blood or marriage (Mohaqeq-Damad, 1986, p. 379). But other than these, there were no restrictions or conditions attached to the marriage of a Muslim man to a Muslim woman.

Removing restrictions on polygamy

Another strategy for the universalisation of marriage was polygamy. The abolition of the Family Protection Law removed previously existing restrictions on polygamy which required a man to obtain permission from his first wife or from the court before embarking on his second marriage. The removal of this restriction meant that a man could marry up to four permanent wives without any legal problems. The law relating to *sigheh* marriage did not change and remained as it was in the Civil Code, since the Family Protection Law had not introduced any changes. However, contrary to the Pahlavi era where *sigheh* had been reduced to a practice limited to religious circles around the Shii shrines and where it was looked upon, officially and socially, with disdain, *sigheh* in the Islamic Republic was officially promoted as a legitimate and desirable means of containing the harmful and disruptive male (and to a limited extent female) sexual drives (Haeri, 1989).

The Islamic Republic encouraged a proliferation of the practice of *sigheh* in many different forms including sexual *sigheh*, procreational *sigheh* and non-sexual *sigheh* (Haeri, 1989). Sexual and procreational *sigheh* were encouraged for men who were not married or were away from their wives, but in reality many married men indulged in them. These types of *sigheh* flourished around sacred shrines, and the circle of people involved in them, either as intermediaries or partners, widened considerably. A cleric explained that of 500 female theology students in Qom in 1981–2 'more than two hundred were in *sigheh* to either one of their teachers or a fellow religious student'. Another *molla* described the network of *sigheh* as an 'underground Mafia organisation [that] everyone knows about . . . but nobody talks about'. Sexual *sigheh* was also applied as a means of both repentance and punishment (*ibid.*, pp. 165, 192, 99–100). Prostitutes detained in rehabilitation centres were encouraged to become *sigheh* to revolutionary guards and many did so willingly or unwillingly. In prisons too, virgin women prisoners were forced into *sigheh* with their jailors before being executed, since according to religious beliefs they would otherwise go to heaven (Amnesty International, 1987).

Another type of *sigheh* encouraged and practised was the non-sexual one. This form of *sigheh* functioned as a way of overcoming segregation rules as it made association of men and women who engaged in it lawful. Non-sexual *sigheh* was practised for various reasons by men and women who wanted or needed to mix with someone from the opposite sex for a social reason. Young men and women who went to rural areas, as part of state mobilisation and reconstruction programmes, were encouraged to enter into non-sexual *sigheh* to be able to cooperate closely with each other without breaking the segregation code (Haeri, 1989, p. 95). Non-sexual *sigheh* was also advocated for prospective married couples to use the opportunity of lawful association to get to know each other without endangering the honour of the woman. An Islamic magazine for young people advocated this type of association as 'religiously sanctioned social intercourse' (*Javanan*, 1). Even the secular upper and middle classes carried fake *sigheh* documents when in mixed company to protect themselves against the consequences of breaking the segregation rules (*ibid.*, pp. 161–3).

The state campaign on marriage

The extension of the legal boundaries of marriage was accompanied by a campaign by Islamic leaders to encourage the nation to engage in the many forms of marriage available to them. Hojatoleslam Rafsanjani told Muslims that the individual, the family and the state all had a duty to encourage and facilitate marriage. The individual had a duty to find a partner and choose one who was pious, the family had a duty to encourage marriage by its offspring, and the Islamic state was responsible for facilitating marriage through financial and legal means. Ayatollah Montazeri warned parents against ignoring the sexual urges of their children: 'If you do not facilitate marriage of your offspring to ensure the satisfaction of their sexual needs, you will be facilitating corruption and prostitution' (*Keyhan*, 19). He therefore asked parents not to be too selective in their choice of future son or daughter-in-law (*ibid.*).

The campaign to boost the rate of marriage also included financial and other-worldly rewards for Muslim men and women. Various charities were set up to provide economic incentives for marriage, and banks offered special marriage loans. The *Emam*'s Aid Committee (Komiteh Emdad Emam) announced that 3 per cent of all household goods produced in the country will be allocated to this committee by the Ministry of Trade exclusively for sale as dowries to couples who were to be married (*Keyhan*, 20). The Islamic Republic Services Foundation (Bonyad Khadamat Jomhuri Eslami) announced that a grant loan of 100,000 to 500,000 rials would be offered to the newly married (*Keyhan*, 21). The Bank of Mellat, too, offered a special marriage loan to professionals such as teachers (*Ettelaat*, 10). Women were told that the war returners had a special place in heaven and women who married them would share it with them. Ayatollah Khomeini personally presided over the marriage ceremony of a revolutionary guard who had returned disabled from the war with Iraq (*Keyhan*, 22). The Martyrs' Foundation (Bonyad Shahid) set up a match-making office to arrange marriage for war widows and revolutionary guards. It was believed that the number of war widows reached 200,000 (*Keyhan London*, 1). The Marriage Foundation was another match-making organisation which was funded to bring men and women together for the purpose of marriage.

Another aspect of the campaign for the universalisation of the family was awareness raising amongst the Islamic populace about the principles of Islamic marriage and the rights and duties of married partners. This was considered so important that Ayatollah Mahdavi Kani suggested that prospective brides and grooms 'should receive training on marriage and matrimonial responsibilities just as people are trained for employment' (*Zan Ruz*, 4). A series of speeches, sermons, newspaper articles and radio and television programmes were launched by the Islamic leaders to raise public awareness about the Islamic family. The philosophical basis of Islamic marriage was explained by Hojatoleslam Rafsanjani at a Friday prayer sermon: 'The Creator of life, created men and women differently and based his plan for their rights and responsibilities on their natural biological and psychological capacities' (*Ettelaat*, 11). He spelt out these differences in a standard biological determinist fashion which was examined earlier in the work of Ayatollah Motahhari in the 1970s (see chapter 5).

Another Islamic leader in a series of newspaper articles explained the principles of Islamic marriage and the system of rights and responsibilities which emanated from 'natural' differences between men and women (*Ettelaat*, 12). In these articles, marriage was constructed as a 'legal institution' based on a contract between a man and a woman. The universalisation of Islamic marriage was considered to be essential for counteracting the 'decadent' influence exerted by sexual freedom in the West. The calamities that would fall upon the Islamic nation if Islamic marriage were rejected in favour of Western style free association of men and women, were listed by Hojatoleslam Rafsanjani as 'sexual communism', 'prostitution', 'illegitimate children' and 'AIDS' (*Ettelaat*, 13).

Women's Islamic rights in marriage

Now what were the principles of the Islamic marriage and what did it entail for men and women? Islamic marriage, the Islamic leaders explained, was a divine system for ensuring the reproduction and thereby survival of the Muslim community. It was based on an agreement between the man, who possessed economic means, and the woman, who possessed sexual and reproductive apparatus, to exchange these commodities for the sake of well being and regeneration of the human race. Islamic marriage was then a commercial transaction based on an exchange of commodities between partners (Haeri, 1989, pp. 28–32). In the archetypal bargain, the man's share was to be the head of the family, to have exclusive rights and control over sexual intercourse with his wife; to be obeyed at all times; to be fed and looked after; and to be provided with offspring to whom he would give his name and extend his guardianship. He would also receive in inheritance one half of his wife's wealth, if no children were involved, and one quarter if there were any children.

The woman's share was to receive *mehrieh* (in money or goods), which she could claim at any moment and if not received she could legitimately refrain from sexual intercourse with her husband. She was entitled to sexual intercourse as frequently as once every four months. The wife was also entitled to receive maintenance within her husband's means. She had control over her personal wealth and could dispose of it as she wished. To secure the husband's side of the bargain, the wife faced a number of sanctions if she did not comply with her responsibilities. Her maintenance could be cut legitimately if she refused sexual intercourse with her husband. She did not have the right to use contraception without the knowledge and agreement of her husband. She could not take up employment without her husband's permission. Neither could she dissolve the marriage on her own initiative. If the man decided to end the marriage, she would not receive maintenance or be entitled to the guardianship of her children if they were above a certain age.

If woman was the object of sale in permanent marriage, she was the object of lease (*mostajereh*) in temporary marriage (Haeri, 1989, p. 31). *Sigheh*, like permanent marriage, was a contract of exchange. Here, a sum of money was exchanged for sexual or other services rendered by the woman for a specified period of time. If any aspects of *sigheh* such as the bride price, the duration of the marriage or the agreement on the service to be rendered by the woman is missed from the contract, *sigheh* would be null and void and hence unlawful. The difference between permanent and temporary marriages was explained by a cleric as analogous to the difference between 'buying a house . . . and . . . renting a car' (*ibid.*). *Sigheh contract* may be presided over by a clergyman and be registered and documented as well. But none of these requirements were legally enforced. The contract was often set and sealed by the partners without the presence of witnesses and with no legal documentation. The *sigheh* wife was not entitled to maintenance unless specified in the contract. The *Sigheh* partners could not inherit from each other, but their offspring were considered as their legitimate heirs. The *Sigheh* woman was granted greater freedom of movement than a permanent wife. But she too, did not have the right to refuse intercourse.

Islamic diversity on marriage

But the state policy on marriage was neither unified nor a complete success. There existed a difference of opinion regarding polygamy, and many of the above-mentioned policies were subjected to criticism on Islamic grounds. Moreover, the intervention of various cultural, economic and political factors affected the successful realisation of the Islamic Republic's policy of universalisation of marriage and led to a 'crisis of marriage'. The initial attempt to extend the legal boundaries of marriage to the maximum possible level under Islam was criticised by factions of the Islamic leadership who advocated a more cautious approach towards polygamy. As noted earlier, those special civil court judges who favoured retaining the previous restrictions on polygamy, as set in Family Protection Law, failed to obtain *shariat* sanction for it from the Council of Guardians. They therefore resorted to other legal and administrative tactics to restrict polygamy.

One of the legal loopholes used was the right and freedom of a woman to accept or refuse marriage. This was used in two ways to restrict male polygamy. First, women were encouraged to stipulate conditions in their marriage contract under which they would have the right to initiate divorce. Women could choose to stipulate polygamy as one of those conditions (*Iran Times*, 1). Second, a woman's right to accept or refuse marriage was supported by putting an obligation on the man to tell the truth about himself to the woman he was seeking to marry. This was legally ensured by making it an offence for the man to lie about his health, education, job, income or marital status (Ghorbani, 1989, p. 221). So, a woman could either find out about her prospective husband's other wife prior to marrying him and decide whether or not to marry him; or if she was tricked into marrying a married man, she could obtain a divorce without his agreement. In theory, then, women were given a choice in entering into polygamous marriage.

But the most vocal opposition to the above mentioned policies on marriage and polygamy was presented by sections of the Islamic women's movement. The *Zan Ruz* magazine turned into a platform for the expression of Islamic feminist opposition on the family. Women Majles deputies and other Islamic women leaders, too, voiced women's concerns over the prevalent policies and practices on the family. Islamic women, having accepted the philosophy and principles of the Islamic conception of marriage as a contract, set out to defend and improve the woman's side of the marriage bargain. The state policy on polygamy was criticised for being lax on men and unjust to women (*Zan Ruz*, 5). Contrary to the official encouragement of polygamy, Islamic women argued for its strict control and demanded that 'permission for polygamy should be granted by a qualified court only in the case of necessities of either social or individual kinds' (*Zan Ruz*, 6). The necessities proposed differed very little from those specified in the 1975 Family Protection Law.

It was pointed out that the man's power to remarry was arbitrary and the woman's power to prevent it was too restricted. The new restrictions introduced on polygamy were criticised for being insufficient. They only offered, it was argued, limited protection to women as these restrictions only applied to new marriages, and amongst these, only to those in which a woman had exercised her right to stipulate divorce conditions in the marriage contract. In practice, it was argued, women's economic, social and psychological vulnerability acted as strong incentives to prevent them from initiating divorce especially if children were involved.

The same type of pressures, it was argued, encouraged women to marry without setting too many conditions in advance (*Ettelaat*, 14). Cultural factors were also blamed for prohibiting women from exercising their right to stipulate divorce conditions in their marriage contract: marriages had been cancelled because the bride's insistence to talk about divorce conditions had offended the groom and his family; some families considered it bad luck to talk about divorce at the outset of a young couple's union; other families were too interested in giving their daughters away to insist on divorce conditions (*Ettelaat*, 15). The marriage registration system, too, proved to be a problem. There were reports that some notary public offices refused to conduct marriage ceremonies when the bride insisted on stipulating divorce conditions in the marriage contract (*ibid.*).

The rights and responsibilities of men and women towards each other within marriage were judged by the Islamic women leaders to be biased in men's favour. Attempts were made to redefine male–female responsibilities within the family to strengthen the women's side of the marriage bargain. Islamic feminists emphasised the 'partnership' aspect of marriage as opposed to the interpretation based on male supremacy (*Zan Ruz*, 7). A woman leader argued that 'the same Islam which says men are women's guardians also says that it is a woman's right to be paid by the husband for breast feeding. Women are under no religious obligation to do housework. They should be paid for their management of household' (*Ettelaat*, 16).

The pages of women's magazines were filled with heartrending stories of hardship and suffering of women in the hands of despotic husbands. Most of the reported cases reflected the extreme economic and legal vulnerability of *mostazaf* women who had maintained mass support for the Islamic regime. A three-year study of suicide amongst women, which was conducted in a Mashad hospital, concluded that 67 per cent of women's suicides were caused by marriage problems (*Zan Ruz*, 8). In another survey, 75 per cent of women who were divorcing said that their husbands regularly beat them (*Keyhan*, 23). Muslim women, as the individual women's stories illustrated, were being failed by the Islamic state's policies and courts of law (*Zan Ruz*, 9).

This opposition was no doubt instrumental in the introduction of further legal remedies for women. Some of the initial family rights granted to men in such a total and complete way, were gradually watered down. The husband's right to prevent his wife from taking up employment was limited. The High Council of the Judiciary ruled that if a woman worked before marriage or took a job with her husband's agreement after marriage, he could not lawfully prevent her from continuing to work. Even if a woman had started work without her husband's permission, the ruling stated, he could only prevent her from working if he could prove that her job was contrary to the interest and reputation of the family (Ghorbani, 1989, p.223).

A new marriage contract was devised to help women have some control over the kind of marriage they entered into. The marriage contract spelled out those infringements of women's rights which could give them the right to initiate divorce. These included the husband's refusal to pay *nafagheh* or serious misbehaviour on his part; the husband's long-term illness or insanity or his employment in jobs demeaning to her and her family; the husband's imprisonment for over five years or his addiction or unreasonable absence from home for over six months; the husband's infertility or impotence and his marriage to another woman without her consent (*Iran Times*, 1). Most of these stipulations had already existed within the Family Protection Law.

On the social and cultural fronts, too, the policies of the fanatical factions of the Islamic leadership ran into problems. By 1985, the newspapers were already talking about 'the crisis of marriage'. Hojatoleslam Rafsanjani complained that despite the Islamic Republic's ideological receptivity to marriage, the age of marriage had in fact risen (*Ettelaat*, 17). Statistical evidence supported this. The trend of increase in the age of marriage in the 1970s had not substantially reversed as a result of the Islamic Republic's policies (*Keyhan*, 24). The mean age of marriage increased within a similar range from 18.4 in 1966 to 19.7 in 1986. Moreover, statistics demonstrated that the number of registered marriages had not substantially and consistently increased after the initial upsurge in 1979 (SCI, 1988c, p. 62; 1990, p. 12). The large increase in the number of marriages in the first post-revolutionary year was considered to be an initial reaction to the lowering of the age of marriage and partly due to revolutionary optimism about life (Aghajanian, 1988, pp. 156–8). This data does not take into account the possibility of increase in unregistered monogamous and polygamous permanent marriages and *sigheh* marriages.

The crisis of marriage

The factors commonly listed as having contributed to the crisis of marriage included the housing shortage, decreasing incomes, unemployment and other economic problems. It was suggested that these problems had prohibited marriage and had contributed to the 'increase in venereal diseases, especially so since prostitution had gone underground' (*Ettelaat*, 18). A study of marriage recommended that 'before encouraging marriage, the right conditions should be created for it' (*ibid.*). The policy of financial rewards for marriage, too, were abandoned as a result of economic constraints. Although state aid for marriage and pregnancy continued to increase by a small percentage every year, nevertheless it represented a real decline in comparison with the increasing number of war widows and young supporters whom the state aimed to help (SCI, 1990, p.38). Many state funded schemes to assist married couples ran out of funds. The *emam*'s Aid Committee announced the cancellation of its marriage loans and grants due to war time financial pressures (*Keyhan (London)*, 2). According to some estimates, the high cost of the marriage ceremony and of setting up a conjugal household, prevented 1.5 million marriages from taking place every year (*Keyhan (London)*, 3).

Another blow was struck at the state policy of universal marriage by the problem of population control. As will be demonstrated shortly in the discussion of the state's population control and family planning policies, the official attitude towards polygamy shifted substantially in favour of restriction, once the economic and political consequences of the population explosion became apparent to policy makers. Hojatoleslam Rafsanjani took the lead in reversing the policy on polygamy by arguing for its restriction on the grounds that 'in Iran the male population is about 5 per cent greater than the female population and therefore there was no social justification for taking more than one wife'. He emphasised that 'monogamy should be the norm for at least 95 per cent of marriages' and polygamy should be practised only if absolutely necessary (*Ettelaat*, 19). The censuses of 1956, 1966, 1976 and 1986 confirmed that the sex ratio in Iran had been, respectively, 104, 107, 106 and 105 men for every 100 women (SCI, 1990, p.7).

Rafsanjani's position on temporary marriage was, as he explained in a Friday prayer sermon, that '*sigheh* is considered in Islam as a safety valve to prevent explosion . . . It is not there for men to satisfy their voluptuousness and ruin their families' (*Keyhan*, 25). The cultural acceptability of *sigheh*, too, remained in question. Despite the official propagation of the philosophy of *sigheh* and its proliferation in practice, it remained socially stigmatised. A well-documented study of *sigheh* demonstrated that the pre-revolutionary attitude of disdain towards *sigheh* resulting from its conceptual association with prostitution persisted in the Islamic Republic. Those who practised it tended to keep their activities secret and this also applied to the clerics who fervently defended its philosophy (Haeri, 1989, p. 165). Cultural disapproval of *sigheh* prevented its legitimisation and institutionalisation during the first decade of the Islamic Republic despite state propaganda in its favour.

Family planning

The development of family planning policy in the Islamic Republic followed the typical pattern. The family planning programme of the previous regime was scrapped immediately after the Revolution and the position of Islam on family planning was constructed in opposition to that of the Pahlavi state. However, the new Islamic policy created enormous problems and resulted in an uncontrollable rate of population growth. The issue of population control was soon an issue in the power struggle between hardliners and moderates, and after a period of intense debate Islamic policy was reversed to the pre-revolutionary one. But the effectiveness of the policy change was hampered by lack of cooperation by the hardliners, lack of sufficient funds due to economic stagnation, and weak management of the problem.

Population growth as anti-imperialist policy

In the late 1970s, Iran had a population growth rate of 2.7 which was gradually decreasing as a result of the Pahlavi state's population control policy. This policy included legalisation of abortion, under certain conditions, and sterilisation, distribution of free contraceptives, campaigns for smaller families, and the setting up of family planning clinics in urban and rural areas (see chapter 5). After the Revolution, there was a period of uncertainty about population control and family planning. The Provisional Government was aware of the problems associated with the high birth rate but as an anti-Shah measure it dismantled the family planning clinics and brought family planning under the control of the Ministry of Public Health. In March 1979, the minister of public health, Dr Sami, sought guidance from Ayatollah Shariatmadari about the compatibility of family planning with the *shariat* in order to calm the rumours that the sale of contraceptives had been banned. The reply was that contraception was allowed in Islam providing it did not result in the impairment or destruction of the fetus (*Iranshahr*, 4). A few months later, the Minister of Public Health sent a report to Ayatollah Khomeini about the rate of population increase and its social and economic consequences. Ayatollah Khomeini's view was that, while abortion and sterilisation were not allowed in Islam, the use of contraceptive was permitted providing that they were not harmful to the woman and the husband agreed to their use (*Ettelaat*, 20).

Contraception was not, of course, a new issue, nor was it the invention of the Pahlavi state. It had been normal practice for centuries and medical texts as far back as the early tenth century had discussed it (Mossavar-Rahamani, 1983, p. 255). Moreover, there was a history of diversity of thought on this issue amongst the Shii *mojtahedin*. A contemporary example of this was Ayatollah Shariatmadari's and Ayatollah Beheshti's approval of the state's family planning policy under the Shah (*ibid.*). During the post-revolutionary transitional period, the historical conceptions of family planning were drawn into the context of immediate political relations and new positions were adopted on this issue. The political necessity of opposing the Pahlavi regime gave rise to a new consensus on family planning as expressed by Ayatollah Khomeini.

After the collapse of the Provisional Government and the takeover of state power by the hardline clergy, the issue of population growth and its control through family planning gained a new dimension. What was at stake was the link between a woman's motherhood role and reproduction of the Islamic nation. Population control and family planning were condemned as an imperialist conspiracy to violate the rights of the Islamic nation and impair its growth and prosperity. This policy was put forward by the Islamic Republic's delegation at the international conference on population and development which took place in China in 1981. Mrs Monireh Gorji, a Majles deputy, opposed the conference resolution in favour of population control on the ground that it was an imperialist conspiracy to control the population of Muslim nations and argued that, 'Population control goes against the anti-imperialist objectives of the Islamic nations' (*Keyhan*, 26). Her second objection was that 'Islam puts more emphasis on the quality of human life and the role of the mother than on population growth' (*ibid.*).

A third dimension of population control and family planning was emphasised by Hojatoleslam Rafsanjani in a Friday prayer sermon. He argued that birth control was against women's Islamic duty to bear children and that in Islam 'women do not have the right to avoid pregnancy and feeding of their infants' (*Ettelaat*, 21). Rafsanjani added that there may, however, be situations where society can support birth control (*ibid.*). This was an assertion of the state's control over the Islamic nation. Women were being prevented from exercising free choice on birth control and thereby of taking control over the Islamic population.

Ayatollah Khomeini had emphasised that women's control of their fertility without their husband's permission was against Islam. Rafsanjani added another means of control over female fertility by asserting the state's right over the nation and its reproducers, women.

Population control as pragmatic policy

The rejection of birth control as a means of curtailing population increase remained official policy until the middle of the 1980s. But economic realities and their political consequences began to erode the determination of the Islamic Republic to increase the size of its anti-imperialist nation. The chronically ill economy, the devastation of national resources as a result of the war against Iraq, high unemployment and the housing crisis, all contributed to the Islamic state's awakening to the political consequences of rapid population growth under the existing circumstances.

The process of reversal of policy began in 1988 through the state's initiation of public debate on the issue of population control. A letter from Hojatoleslam Mohammad Yazdi drew attention to the dangers of uncontrolled population increase. A reply was published which argued that population control was against 'Mohammad's [the Prophet] aim to spread Islam', and asked, 'now that the oppressed Muslims are struggling against imperialist oppressors, why do we want to control the increase in the numbers of *mostazafin*?' (*Keyhan Havai*, 42).

The political dangers of rapid population growth in an atmosphere of economic stagnation and political uncertainty was, however, too pressing at this time to allow the efforts of the hardliners to be effective against population control. By 1989 the policy on population control had been fully reversed. Newspapers provided regular factual information about the rate of population increase. In 1989, the population of Iran reached 55 million with an annual rate of increase of 3.2. Of this, 29 million lived in urban areas and 26 million in rural areas, which made emigration from rural to urban areas a political issue (*Keyhan (London)*, 4). In July 1989, Dr Malekafzali, Deputy Minister of Health, announced the government's policy on population control. He explained that the policy would be based on distribution of free contraceptives through the newly set up health centres in rural and urban areas which would cover 90 per cent of the population. The contraceptives, including IUD, pills and condoms, had been imported from Western countries, he announced. Asked about the forms of birth control, he emphasised that government policy was in line with Ayatollah Khomeini's instructions that abortion, regardless of the stage of pregnancy, and sterilisation were prohibited in Islam. He also reaffirmed the state's support of the husband's control over his wife's fertility by emphasising that women should not use birth control without their husbands' agreement (*ibid.*).

The policy of birth control received a positive response from the Islamic women's movement. The proceedings of the conference on family planning which took place on the occasion of International Health Day, was reported extensively in Muslim women's magazines. The conference recommended that pregnancies outside the age of 18–35 should be avoided, that there should be at least three years gap between pregnancies and the number of pregnancies should be limited to a maximum of four for each woman (*Zan Ruz*, 10). Women's magazines discussed methods of birth control extensively and recommended a wide variety of contraception including withdrawal, child spacing, breast feeding, condoms, pills, IUD and injections. These discussions contributed to the momentum of the Islamic Republic's campaign on population control and family planning.

By the end of 1989 the Islamic Republic's policy on birth control had developed to such a degree that it was now considered to be the Islamic duty of Muslims not to sacrifice the quality of the Islamic nation for the sake of having large families (*Zan Ruz*, 11). Ayatollah Sanei, speaking at a conference on population control and family planning, supported the official policy on smaller families and strongly condemned 'Muslim men who consider it Islamic to marry three or four women and have seven or eight children from each' (*ibid.*). He talked about the disastrous consequences of ill-treated and badly brought up youngsters for the future prosperity of the Islamic nation. He encouraged Muslim men and women to have fewer children and instead to concentrate on providing a quality Islamic training for them (*ibid.*). Ayatollah Sanei expressed strong 'Islamic opposition' against polygamy and raised the question of the acceptability of abortion as a method of birth control. He revived the Islamic argument in favour of abortion in the early stages of pregnancy and linked it to the interest of the Islamic state by saying that, 'Should the birth of a child cause a problem for the Islamic state or the family, the Islamic state can decide whether to allow abortion before the fetus reaches ten, twenty or forty days' (*ibid.*).

The problem of the high rate of population growth and its political consequences, then, opened the debate on polygamy and abortion in the Islamic Republic. Once again economic and political imperatives defined which practices in relation to the family were or were not acceptable as 'Islamic'.

Divorce

The battle of Islamic opinions on divorce revolved around the question of how to reconcile the man's absolute right and control over divorce with the realities of family life in the Islamic Republic.

Ayatollah Khomeini insisted that divorce belonged to men by right. A woman could only initiate divorce under certain conditions and even then by being granted power of attorney to divorce herself on behalf of her husband. But in marriage, the Ayatollah Khomeini's ruling was that the right to choose or refuse to enter into a marriage belonged to the woman and her family, and the man's role was limited to that of a seeker (*khastegar*). This, Ayatollah Khomeini instructed, gave women the scope to bargain before signing the marriage contract (*Ayandegan*, 5). But this did not take into account the legal developments of the previous two decades in the field of family law. Legal history had in the past registered the catastrophic results of men's absolute right to divorce. A campaign was therefore waged by sections of the Islamic leadership and the Islamic women's movement to improve women's divorce rights within the limits of the *shariat* by transferring the right to divorce from the individual man to the court of law.

Women's divorce rights

The development of divorce law was briefly described earlier in this chapter. It was noted that the establishment of the special civil courts limited the man's right to register divorce in notary public offices in circumstances where both partners agreed to the divorce. The justification given for this was that when there was a dispute about divorce, there needed to be arbitration and those who ran notary public offices did not have the Islamic training to act as just arbiters between the warring partners. Family disputes had to be solved therefore by an Islamic judge who was knowledgeable about the Islamic rights and responsibilities of husband and wife.

This was achieved, but the campaign to limit male control over divorce ended here. The next move was to gradually extend the grounds on which a woman could initiate divorce, or to put it in other words, have the power of attorney to divorce herself on behalf of her husband. Ayatollah Khomeini's instructions were that a woman could ask for a divorce if her man was insane, impotent or infertile, absent from home without reason, imprisoned, or unable to support the woman (Khomeini, n.d.b). These were also the reasons stated in the Civil Code (Mohaqeq-Damad, 1986, pp. 379–415). But the Civil Code had also considered hardship and adversity borne by the wife as a valid ground for divorce (Article 1130). This was reinterpreted by the campaigners, to improve women's divorce rights, to include irreconcilability and violence of a husband towards his wife.

Ayatollah Mahdavi Kani announced in 1983 that women were granted the right to ask for divorce on these grounds. He justified and defended the new rules on the ground that 'in Islam woman is not considered a slave to be forced to live with a man irrespective of her wishes. Far from limiting the man's holy right, this law in fact takes away the wrongful power of the man' (*Ettelaat*, 22). Two years later, a standard marriage contract was introduced, to be signed by both man and woman, which included twelve conditions under which a woman could initiate divorce irrespective of the wishes of her husband. Amongst the conditions inserted in it, two new grounds were added to those stated above (Najmabadi, 1989). One was: 'If the court issues an order certifying that the husband's engagement in certain employment is contrary to the interests of the family and to the reputation of the wife but the husband does not abide by this order'. Another one was: 'If the husband takes another wife without the consent of the first wife, or if according to determination of the court he is not treating them justly' (*Iran Times*, 1).

While divorce through notary public offices was easier than ever before for couples in cases of mutual consent, the special civil courts prided themselves on reconciling about 65 per cent of the couples who filed for divorce (*Keyhan*, 27). The procedure adopted by the special civil courts was that once a divorce was filed, both sides were asked to appoint someone they trusted as their arbiter. The two arbiters were asked to help the couple to reconcile within four weeks. If reconciliation succeeded the file was closed, otherwise the arbiters would negotiate with the couple to determine the terms and conditions of the divorce. The court normally accepted the outcome, but did impose its own decision on the couple if arbitration failed. The use of arbiters was based on the *Qoran* (chapter 'Women', verse 35) which instructed the faithful to arbitrate between the warring partners (*Ettelaat*, 23). In cases where the man had filed the divorce and the woman was against it, if arbitration failed the court would grant the man the right to divorce. If it was the other way round and arbitration failed, the woman could only get permission to divorce, irrespective of her husband's wish, if her reasons were in accordance with the *shariat* (*Keyhan*, 28) (*Ettelaat*, 23).

The plight of women who initiated or faced unwanted divorce were published to demonstrate how women suffered from the courts' lack of awareness about women's true Islamic rights. Regular interviews and reports were provided by the authorities on the work of the special civil courts and the difficulties of implementing the law. Some of the problems associated with the operation of the special civil courts, especially with lack of coordinated and enforceable court verdicts, were discussed earlier in this chapter. Islamic feminists also complained about male bias and discriminatory verdicts by the courts. They said illiteracy and ignorance about the law created major problems for women who approached the courts. A survey of women using the special civil courts concluded that 72 per cent of divorced women in 1987 were illiterate (*Keyhan (London)*, 5). Mrs Marziyeh Dabbagh, a Majles deputy, complained in the Majles about the treatment of women by the courts. She argued that 'In divorce disputes, the special civil courts should pay special attention to the preservation of women's dignity and Islamic rights. Some women are ignorant of their legal rights and this should not result in them losing their entitlements' (*Keyhan Havai*, 43).

Another problem was that court cases took longer on average if divorce was initiated by women (*Ettelaat*, 24). The courts expected women to back up their complaints with stronger evidence than they expected from men (*Keyhan*, 29). The high burden of proof for women who were often more naive and inarticulate than their husbands, resulted in court cases which took years to complete (*Ettelaat*, 24). Mrs Behruzi, another Majles deputy complained that, 'Some special civil courts expect woman to bear all the problems and submit to their husbands' whims under all circumstances. The same courts are willing to grant the man his divorce on the basis of the clumsiest evidence without paying attention to the fate of the wife and children' (*Ettelaat*, 25). These problems were all the more serious because the majority of divorce cases in special civil courts were filed by women (*Zan Ruz*, 12). Divorces through special civil courts, however, constituted only a fraction of all divorces. Mohammad Asghari, a Majles deputy, reported that in 1988 about 15 per cent of all divorces went through the courts, and the remaining 85 per cent in which there was no dispute between the couples were registered by notary public offices without court permission. There was, however, ample evidence that in many such divorces, the wife's agreement had been secured by intimidation and the threat of violence. Women were sometimes divorced without their knowledge and in their absence. Complaints were raised that contrary to the Prophet Mohammad's characterisation of divorce as the most reprehensible practice, the Islamic Republic had increased the ease by which Islamic marriage could be dissolved. This view was substantiated by the rising divorce rate.

Islasmic opposition to rising divorce

The rate of divorce which had a downward trend in the 1970s was reversed in the 1980s (Mirani, 1983). According to official statistics, the proportion of divorce to marriage in the country rose from 8.8 in 1982 to 10.4 in 1986 (Statistical Centre of Iran, 1987, p. 70 and 1988a, p.126). Moreover, official data about divorce and other marriage disputes handled by the special civil courts, showed an increasing trend (SCI, 1988c, p. 205). A Majles deputy exaggeratedly claimed in 1989 that the number of divorces had increased 200 per cent since the Revolution (*Zan Ruz*, 13). A survey indicated that the main causes of divorce in 1987 included financial hardship, lack of compatibility (including ideological differences), addiction of the partner (mostly men), and financial hardship (*Keyhan (London)*, 5).

These complaints prompted initiation of a campaign in the first decade of the Islamic Republic for curtailment of male divorce rights. A bill was introduced in the Majles in July 1989 to transfer the power of divorce from the husband to the special civil court. The man's divorce rights remained as they were, but the rules of divorce registration changed so that, as was the case under the Family Protection Law, all divorces had to have court permission before being registered in notary public offices (*Zan Ruz*, 13). The first and second readings of the Divorce Reform Bill (Layeheh Eslah Talagh) received majority support in the Majles and the bill was submitted to the Council of Guardians for final approval.

The Majles debate on the Divorce Reform Bill articulated a power struggle between men and the state over the control of the family. Those opposing the bill argued for the man's Islamic right to dissolve marriage as and when he wished. Hojatoleslam Ali Abbasi argued that, 'The Islamic *shariat* has explicitly stated that if a man wished to divorce his wife, he can do so without being obliged to give any reason. Despite Islam's disapproval of divorce, it chose to give this authority to the man and no court of law can take away his right' (*Zan Ruz*, 13).

Those who supported the bill, such as Hojatoleslam Asadollah Bayat, gave priority to the state's right over the family, arguing that, 'Those who object to this bill, are disregarding the state's responsibility in relation to the family. They think we are living in a non-Islamic society. But our system is, thank God, a divine Islamic one. The Islamic regime cannot ignore the family and its problems; divorce and unprotected women and children' (*ibid.*).

State control over the Islamic family, then, resulted in the curtailment of men's divorce rights quite in line, at least in theory, with those specified in Pahlavi laws. It took two weeks for the Islamic state to demolish the Family Protection Law in a blast and then ten years to rebuild it again bit by bit. The same family laws which historically had been presented by Pahlavi states as part of a process of secularisation, and were hence opposed by the clergy as against Islam, were now being reconstructed as part of a process of Islamisation by the Islamic state. The difference was not in the Islamic or secular nature of the law, but in the political problems of the era.

Child custody

The concept of 'custody' has a double meaning in Shii *shariat*. The first meaning refers to legal guardianship (*velayat*). This is a right which naturally and automatically belongs to the father and paternal grandfather in his absence. The second meaning refers to fostering (*hezanat*), that is caring for offspring for a fixed period of time without possessing legal guardianship. The former meaning refers to the right of the man, while the latter is considered as a natural, but not automatic, right of the mother and extends in the case of a female child until the age of seven and in the case of male child up to the age of two. The right to foster can be withdrawn from the mother if her moral suitability is in doubt. During the fostering period, the father is financially responsible for the upkeep of the children under the mother's care.

The dominance of the *shariat* definition of custody within Iranian law came to an end in the late 1960s when the Family Protection Law replaced the Civil Code in relation to child custody. The Family Protection Law introduced a different concept of custody which overcame the differentiation in the Civil Code between the concepts of guardianship and fostering. Custody was defined in the new law as a single concept incorporating both fostering and guardianship. The family protection courts took extra-*shariat* factors into account in determining custody and introduced the idea of granting custody on the basis of competencies and capabilities of the parents and welfare of the children (see chapter 5).

The new concept of custody was ruled out after the abolition of the Family Protection Law in the post-revolutionary transitional period. But the return of the *shariat* definition of custody in the Islamic Republic was neither consistent nor without opposition. On the contrary, the development of the custody law in the Islamic Republic was a reflection of the struggle to extend the boundaries of the *shariat* concept of custody to incorporate the ideas of 'child welfare' and 'parental suitability'.

In the battle over child custody, the Islamic women's movement waged a vocal campaign for equality of custody rights between men and women.

This was one issue on which most sections of the women's movement agreed.

Islamic women's campaign for custody

The first attempt to extend the boundaries of the *shariat* concept of custody was made by the judiciary. The head of the special civil courts, Hojatoleslam Mahadvi Kermani announced that the *shariat* law would apply to the custody of children under twelve, but above that age, if they demonstrated maturity, the court would allow them to choose which parent to live with. Financial responsibility, he emphasised, remained with the father if the child was placed with the mother (*Keyhan*, 30). Moreover, the concept that the paternal family of a child had the right of custody over and above that of the natural mother came under attack in the Majles. Mrs Goharolsharieh Dastgheib illustrated her point by drawing the attention of the Majles to the fate of the offspring of 'martyrs' of the Iran–Iraq war:

> Many of the children of our martyrs not only lose their father but also become victims of a custody law which separates them from their mothers. These children despite having suitable, trustworthy and competent mothers, are forcibly separated to live with paternal relatives who claim custody because of some old family grudge against the mother of the child in order to ruin her. This is a misuse of the Islamic law of custody. The Islamic law of custody cannot be implemented in spirit until this un-Islamic behaviour is eliminated. We should protect children from forced guardianship by passing the necessary laws so that the Martyrs Foundation can deal with custody disputes concerning martyrs' families in the right way. We should make sure that the children of martyrs do not end up losing both their father and mother. (*Ettelaat*, 26)

Another female Majles deputy, Mrs Behruzi, reported that one of the most urgent issues raised by her constituents was the prevalent discrimination against women in relation to child custody (*Keyhan*, 31). On the initiative of a few female deputies, the Majles Committee on Legal Matters prepared a proposal about the right of mothers to custody (*Keyhan*, 32). The final reading of this bill took place in December 1981 and was then referred to the Council of Guardians for approval. In March 1982, the Council discussed and rejected the bill on the ground of incompatibility with the *shariat*. The content of the bill was not made public (*Ettehad Mardom*, 1). It took another three years for the custody bill to be revived. In February 1985, the Majles Committee on Revolutionary Institutions discussed the bill and made a number of proposals to amend it to the satisfaction of the Council of Guardians (*Ettelaat*, 28).

The bill on Mothers' Right to Foster Minor and Forlorn Children

(Layeheh Hagh Hezanat Farzandan Saghir va Mahjur Beh Madaran) gave the special civil courts the power to punish the father or paternal family by imprisonment, flogging or fine, if they did not abide by the decision of the court to place the child with the mother. But it evaded the issue of whom the right of custody belonged to in order to overcome the objection by the Council of Guardians. This bill was not supported by women Majles deputies.

The Majles deputies speaking in favour of the bill defended the *shariat* for granting the right of custody to men on two main grounds. First, they pointed to the dangers for Islam of children being raised by unsuitable mothers; second, they emphasised the importance of increasing the chance of widows to remarry by not burdening them with the custody of child(ren) (*Ettehad Mardom*, 2; *Ettelaat*, 27). But women deputies spoke against the bill on the ground that 'it does not address the problems faced by mothers deeply enough'. Mrs Dastgheib argued that the judgements of the special civil courts on custody are often governed by 'legal inconsistencies and procedural difficulties which should be investigated and resolved'. She emphasised that the courts 'do not take into account the child's emotional needs and shift the child like a stone'. She added that 'fathers often take the child away from the mother to have him brought up by an unqualified relative'. In her view 'many children turn to delinquency as a result of wrongful upbringing' (*ibid.*). The same concepts of child psychology and welfare which the pro-establishment women's movement under the previous regime used in arguing for custody for the mother were also referred to by the Islamic women's movement (see chapter 5).

But since the Council of Guardians had already refused to change the *shariat* concept of custody, the only way open to satisfy both sides was to avoid passing a new law or emphasising strict interpretation of the *shariat*. Under the circumstances, where neither side had the power to outdo the other, the Majles and the Council of Guardians reached a compromise to leave it to the special civil courts to solve social problems arising from custody disputes on the basis of the judge's personal interpretation of the *shariat*. Mrs Dastgheib, concluding her speech in opposition to the bill, urged the special civil courts to 'give priority to the emotional needs of the children and not to apply the law rigidly' (*Ettelaat*, 29).

Liberalisation of women's custody rights

The campaign to improve women's custody rights and protect children from forcible separation from mother continued. Islamic women leaders based their campaign on the contradictions of state policy. The state, on the one hand, defined women as mothers and considered their motherhood role as the basis of their dignity and value in Islamic society. On the other hand, it refused to grant women the right to keep and raise their children in the absence of the father. This implied that the Islamic nation's children could not be entrusted to women. Political sensitivity to the fate of the children of war martyrs was seized upon by Islamic women leaders to make inroads into the issue of women's custody rights. The Council of Guardians eventually agreed to grant the war widows, as well as other widows, the right of fostering without extending this right to legal guardianship. The bill which was passed by the Majles specified that:

> The fostering of children whose fathers have reached the high status of martyrdom or have died [from other causes] is with their mother and their customary living expenses should be paid by the legal guardian. If these are paid out of the government budget or by the Martyrs Foundation, the money should go to the mother unless the unsuitability of the mother is established by the court. (Ghorbani, 1989)

Further liberalisation of the custody law was openly demanded by some lay members of the judiciary and the legitimacy of clause 1169 of the Civil Code which limited the 'fostering' of the child by the mother up to the age of seven for girls and two for boys was challenged as 'one opinion within the *shariat* amongst others, which can be challenged by modern minded judges [who could] apply the most relevant interpretation [of the *shariat*] to today's world and set the right direction for the future generation' (*Zan Ruz*, 14). In the closing years of the first decade of the Islamic Republic, political pressure was still directed towards a redefinition of custody.

Women without men

Single women, widows, divorcees, or as they were referred to in the Islamic Republic 'unprotected' or 'deprived' women, were perhaps the most problematic category of people for the Islamic state. They were a symbol of the breakdown of the Islamic vision in which the universality of marriage was supposed to have protected all women. Their existence was considered as a source of evil in society since they were legally devoid of male guardians: neither father, brother nor husband had a right over them. They were therefore open to temptation. Hojatoleslam Rafsanjani expressed the state's anxiety about 'unprotected women' (*zanan bisarparast*) in following words:

> In 1982 in Iran, the population of women between the age of 20 and 50 were numbered 7 million and 45 thousands. From these, about one million were

without a husband ... What should be done with these women? Those who manage society should think about this ... We should not create temptations for our youth and then confront them with punishment. ... We should find a solution for one million deprived human beings. (*Ettelaat*, 30)

Indeed, the 1986 population census showed an even greater group of unmarried people due to the widening gap between population growth and the rate of marriage. Amongst the population aged ten and over, those who had not married at all constituted 41.5 per cent of men and 30.9 per cent of women in urban areas and even higher rates of 41.8 per cent for men and 33.4 per cent for women in rural areas (SCI, 1988b, p. 4). This showed a rise compared with 1976 data (Aghajanian, 1988, p. 156). Hojatoleslam Rafsanjani's solution for the 'deprived women' was marriage. Yet the crisis of marriage, easy divorce, the war and population growth were all contributing to the rising number of unmarried women. Moreover, the Constitution had specifically obliged the Islamic state to look after the 'unprotected' women. The Islamic state, therefore, had to step in on behalf of the man to protect the unmarried woman until the time she could be found a husband.

State policy on protection of unmarried women had two main features. One was a strategy to assist women to acquire their rightful gains from their husbands upon divorce or death. The second feature was state funded welfare programmes for widows and divorcees. Women's Islamic rights included control over their own property and wealth, that is, at least in theory. But the sources of financial support for the majority of women who did not have personal wealth and regular income remained very limited indeed. It was confined in the case of divorcees to *mehrieh* and sometimes *nafagheh*. For widows, there was a limited chance of a state pension, and so inheritance was their other main financial resource.

Islamic policy on women's inheritance

The conventional Islamic rules on women's inheritance were extremely complicated. Whether or not and how much a woman inherited from her husband depended on whether sexual intercourse had taken place during the marriage, whether there were any offspring from the marriage, and many other detailed factors (Mehrpour, 1989). On the whole, as a daughter or as a wife, women inherited half of what men did. They also did not inherit everything that men did. Women could not inherit land and were only entitled to a share from the sale of property and not the property itself (Articles 946 and 947 of the Civil Code).

This was criticised in the late 1980s by some Islamic clerics as 'the conventional but not necessarily the right Islamic interpretation of women's inheritance rights' (*Zan Ruz*, 15). Ayatollah Mohammad Musavi Bojnurdi called upon Shii scholars to amend the Civil Code in the light of a non-conventional interpretation of the Islamic rules of inheritance which advocated more equal inheritance rights for men and women (*ibid.*). However, as far as existing Islamic inheritance rules were concerned, women's right to inherit from her husband in principle did not necessarily mean that she would do so in practice taking into account all detailed factors in her particular circumstances.

Islamic policy on bride price

The question of woman's *mehrieh*, too, was fraught with problems. All women were entitled to their *mehrieh* but most did not benefit from it. *Mehrieh*, as bride price, was normally specified in the marriage contract, and was payable to the woman by the man after consummation of marriage. But traditionally, woman's *mehrieh* was paid by the man upon divorce. One of the common problems, therefore, was its depreciating value. Another problem was that since the value of *mehrieh* had to be within the means of the husband and in accordance with the previous living standards of the wife (Article 1091 of the Civil Code), many poor women who married poor men could only ask for a modest sum.

Moreover, despite their right to it, women did not necessarily receive *mehrieh* as it was subject to withdrawal and abuse. The wife's *mehrieh* could be lawfully withdrawn from women for a variety of reasons. One was if the woman willingly gave it up in return for her husband's agreement to divorce. This was a very common occurrence as expressed in a folk saying meaning 'my *mehrieh* for my freedom' (*mehram halal junam azad*). Another reason for withdrawal of *mehrieh* was a woman's stipulation of conditions in her marriage contract to enable her to initiate divorce later. In return for easy divorce, women had to give up their *mehrieh*. The official marriage contract which specified twelve conditions under which a woman could sue for divorce also specified that if these conditions were invoked by a woman she would have to give up her *mehrieh* (*Iran Times*, 1).

Other contexts for lawful withdrawal of *mehrieh* related to the consummation of marriage. Article 1086 of the Civil Code stated that *mehrieh* would not be paid to a woman if she refused to submit herself sexually to her husband. Article 1088 stated that if the husband died before consummation of marriage, the wife would not be entitled to *mehrieh*. Articles 1098 and 1101 withdrew *mehrieh* if marriage was annulled before its consummation, unless the absence of sexual intercourse was due to the man's impotence. Article 1092 granted the woman half of her *mehrieh* if she was divorced by her husband before consummation (Ghorbani, 1989, p. 91–5). Women were not, therefore, entitled to their *mehrieh* if they did not render the services that they were being paid for, that is, sexual intercourse. Moreover, *mehrieh* was also open to other legitimate and illegitimate abuse by husbands, many of whom failed to comply with Islamic law. Divorce statistics demonstrated that a large number of divorces was due to social problems such as poverty, crime and addiction. In these circumstances, even if a woman had a worthy *mehrieh*, its extraction from the husband at the time of divorce was an unreasonable expectation.

Moreover, even if the marriage was dissolved by the husband or with his agreement and he could afford to pay there was still no guarantee that he would pay, since the law enforcement apparatus did not operate satisfactorily in relation to family disputes (*Zan Ruz*, 16). State assistance to women in securing payment of *mehrieh* remained rhetorical when it came to enforcement. Some effort was made by the state to intervene on behalf of women. Hojatoleslam Erfani, a special civil court judge, suggested that in situations where there was little or no *mehrieh* payable to the wife by the husband, the courts could ask the husband to pay compensation (*hagholzahmeh*) to the wife. The amount, he said, 'depended on the woman's age and years of marriage' (*Keyhan*, 29). But the idea of marriage compensation was not officially endorsed.

Islamic policy on alimony

Similar problems operated in relation to woman's *nafagheh* which, according to the Shii *shariat*, was payable under two circumstances. First, during *eddeh*, or the waiting period. This meant that a divorced woman had to abstain from remarrying or having sexual intercourse with her ex-husband for three menstrual cycles after the divorce. The waiting period varied in different circumstances, but during the specified period woman could continue to reside in her ex-husband's residence whether she was or was not maintained by him (Mohaqeq-Damad, 1986, pp. 314–15). Second, *nafagheh* was also payable to the wife if she was in lawful custody of child(ren) from the marriage. In both cases, again, *nafagheh* could be withdrawn if divorce was due to the woman's immorality or refusal to have sex with her husband (*ibid.*). Women who were over childbearing age and did not have to observe the waiting period did not receive anything.

Like other family related issues, the question of *nafagheh* for divorced women became the subject of intense lobbying by the Islamic women's movement (*Zan Ruz*, 17). Islamic women leaders demanded that divorced women should have the right to half of the family possessions which had been accumulated in the course of the marriage and which were the result of joint effort by husband and wife (*Ettelaat*, 31).

This campaign culminated in a number of Majles proposals. Maryam Behruzi, a woman Majles deputy, explained that the Majles Committee on the Family had put forward two proposals for consideration. One was related to dowry and the other to marriage compensation for divorced woman: 'The latest proposal is that if the judge feels that the divorce request by the man is unjustified and without valid reason, then he should be made to compensate the woman for her work at home during the marriage. This will prevent the man from divorcing his wife when his fancy is taken to another woman' (*Keyhan*, 17).

Another policy proposal was described by Hojatoleslam Moghtadai, the spokesman for the High Council of the Judiciary. He emphasised women's right to stipulate conditions in their marriage contract and said that providing this was done, and 'if divorce was not due to a woman's moral corruption, bad behaviour or refusal to carry out her marital duties, then the man should be obliged by the courts to transfer to her half of the wealth he has gathered during their marriage' (*Keyhan*, 89). But despite its frequent revival, the idea of marriage compensation did not become law in the first decade of the Islamic Republic.

State protection of 'unprotected women'

In addition to inconsequential attempts to improve women's access to *nafagheh*, the Majles introduced a number of laws on the welfare of 'unprotected' women. One of these was the Security of Unprotected Women and Children Law (Ghanun Tamin Zanan va Kudakan Bisarparast). Some welfare programmes had already been launched under the auspices of the Welfare Organisation and various other state funded charities and foundations. These included special programmes set up for 200,000 war widows (*Keyhan (London)*, 1). But there was little coordination and planning involved and each establishment received separate funding and devised separate programmes. In an attempt to influence the priorities of these organisations in favour of women, a number of women Majles deputies demanded that these activities be brought under one cover and made accountable to the Majles. Azam Taleghani demanded that 'the budgets for Martyrs' Foundation, *Emam's* Aid Committee and Welfare Organisation should be amalgamated to cover the welfare of all unprotected women' (*Keyhan*, 33). But this suggestion did not result in a change of policy.

Two years later, a bill was drafted by the Majles Committee on Health and Welfare on the 'Welfare of Unprotected Women'. It received its first reading in the Majles in August 1983. The spokesman for the Committee explained that 'the bill puts an obligation on the government to have a welfare scheme for unmarried women in accordance with clause 21, sub-clause 4 of the Constitution'. In supporting the bill, Mrs Behruzi said, 'unprotected women should be supported by the state and provided with shelter and jobs to become self-sufficient' (*Keyhan*, 34). The second round of the Majles discussion of the bill took place in November 1983 and the bill was ratified. It was in a single clause and stated that 'the government is obliged in accordance with Article 21 of the Constitution, to draft a bill on the welfare of unprotected women and children and present it to Majles for approval within 3 months. The bill should pay special attention to the self-sufficiency of those under consideration' (*Keyhan*, 35).

The required government bill did not, however, materialise during the first decade of the Islamic Republic. The only group of single women who came under state protection, incidentally, through laws made during the Pahlavi regime, were the dependants of deceased state employees. These widows and their under-age children were entitled, as part of the social security law of 1975, to receive a pension (Ghorbani, 1989, pp. 445–57). In 1987, the government improved the pension allowance of the widows of state employees whose husbands had been killed in the war with Iraq, to the equivalent of the husband's last salary (*Keyhan*, 36). The final attempt in the 1980s to revive the idea of marriage compensation, concerned expansion of the Social Security Law to include transfer of one third of the man's social security benefit to the wife upon divorce (*Zan Ruz*, 18). This proposal covered dependants of those men who were insured for unemployment benefit, that is the employees of the state and some in private sector. In 1987, about 2,200,000 men were covered by the Social Security Law (*Keyhan*, 37).

By the end of the first post-revolutionary decade, then, the debate on 'unprotected women' amounted to very little improvement in the situation of women without men. Indeed, the myth of universal male protection for women came under more strain than ever before by the state's pursuit of war and repression. The state's attempt to protect Muslim women or find them husbands did not quite work. According to the 1986 population census, 7.1 per cent of heads of two-parent families were women, meaning they were the main income earners in the family, and 61.7 per cent of those living on their own were women. The 'ideal Islamic family' of husband, wife and children constituted 67.1 per cent of the Iranian households (SCI, 1988b).

9 Women and national participation in the Islamic republic

Once the Islamic family was legally constructed, its links with the Islamic nation had to be strengthened. Women, the creators of the Islamic family, had to nurture the Islamic nation as well as secure its survival and make it prosper.

Despite pressures by conventional clerics who were in favour of the separation of family from society and women's confinement to housekeeping and child rearing tasks, Ayatollah Khomeini adopted a policy of women's participation in national processes (*Zan Ruz*, 19). He, too, believed strongly in the separation of home from society and his pre-revolutionary position was very close to that of the conservatives. But the political imperatives of revolutionary Iran convinced him that the very survival of the Islamic Republic in its formative years depended on the active participation of both men and women in society. This was why, contrary to many expectations, the establishment of a theocratic state did not result in outright prohibition of women from social activities.

Women's participation in national processes was subjected to a wide range of state policies and acquired many forms. Three specific areas of politics, education and employment are selected for discussion here. Together, these areas of women's activities drew a fairly complex picture of the process of construction of policy on women's social participation during the first decade of the Islamic Republic.

Political participation

The participation of women in politics legitimised the state's Islamic policies and created an image of popular support and stability internally and internationally. Ayatollah Khomeini considered women's participation in the anti-Shah Revolution crucial and on many occasions praised the 'lion-heart women whose great effort saved Islam from the captivity of the foreigners [and] who alongside men secured the victory of Islam' (*Keyhan*, 38). Women's power, for Khomeini, emanated from their motherhood role and in his view, 'If nations are deprived of brave and human-making women, they will be defeated and ruined' (*ibid.*). He saw the future of his Islamic movement dependent on the harnessing of women's motherhood power in the right political direction:

> Endless greetings to the committed women who have taken part in the upbringing of children, the teaching of literacy classes and the teaching of our rich *Qoranic* culture. The blessings of God upon the women who have attained the high status of martyrdom in this Revolution and in defending their country. Blessings upon those who are serving the sick and the maimed in hospitals and clinics. Salutations to those mothers who have lost their young ones in the most honourable of ways. (*Mahjubeh*, 1)

Women and crowd politics

After the Revolution, various factions of the state and revolutionary grass-roots organisations attempted to harness women's tremendous mobilisation potential. The IRP took control of the mass mobilisation of *mostazaf* women. It set up the Committee for the Celebration of Women's Day which organised mass rallies every year to mark the birthday of the Prophet's daughter, Fatemeh, which had been named as official Women's Day by Ayatollah Khomeini (*Jomhuri Eslami*, 1). The IRP directed the slogans, demands and the resolutions of these rallies in support of the policies of the hardline clergy. In the early post-revolutionary period women were mobilised against the secular, and later, the Islamic opposition. Oppositional demonstrations and rallies often faced women's counter-demonstrations in support of the hardline factions of the state. A number of these women gained a special reputation for their skills in disrupting anti-government rallies. Zahra Khanum, for example, became famous in Tehran for leading a band of hooligans against the secular women's anti-*hejab* demonstrations in March 1979. State officials often praised these *hezbollahi* women. The IRP also made sure that the women's contingent of the Friday Prayers was fully attended.

In later years, *hezbollahi* women's demonstrations continued to be used to prepare the ground for new policies or rejuvenate old ones. Pro-*hejab* demonstrations, for example, were used by the government as a pretext to tighten up the *hejab* rules in response to 'popular demand'. After the total annihilation of the opposition, Islamic Women's Day rallies grew smaller. Their slogans and resolutions continued to be supportive of mainstream policies, but they also included genuine women's demands.

Women's mass support was manipulated also by the Islamic state and its supporting grass-roots organisations in relation to two other areas important to the survival of the state, that is, elections and war. Women's participation in the elections was of prime importance for the Islamic

Republic's populist image. This was especially so in the context of the number of times people were asked to cast votes in the first decade of the Islamic Republic: two referendums, two elections for the Assembly of Experts, three Majles elections, few Majles by-elections and four presidential elections. In all, people were asked to vote on more than eleven occasions, that is, more than once a year. Prior to each election, an extensive campaign was launched to encourage people to vote. Women's magazines published articles and editorials which described the women's vote as a 'national, political and Islamic duty' (*Zan Ruz*, 20). Ayatollah Khomeini held audiences with women supporters and made speeches, appealing to women around the country to vote (*Keyhan*, 39). A survey of women voters showed that the majority of them were illiterate and many were accompanied by their menfolk when voting (*Zan Ruz*, 21). Another study of voting patterns demonstrated that the number of voters had gone down substantially in later years compared with early elections (*Soroush*, 1).

Women's participation in the war

Women's participation in the Iran–Iraq war was, too, encouraged by the state. Ayatollah Khomeini made several rousing speeches during the war to promote women's supporting role in the War (*Keyhan*, 40). Women's participation took a variety of forms. A survey conducted by a women's magazine about women's support for the war concluded that:

> Women have played an important role in the war through their activities, attitude and encouragement at home, work place and behind the front lines. Victory is only possible if morale is high and women are the main morale boosters. Women have encouraged their husbands and sons to go to war. They have preserved unity and refrained from creating harmful rumours [against the war]. They economise and reject unnecessary consumption. They send money and clothes for the soldiers and war refugees. They raise the awareness of school children about the war. They nurse the wounded and play their role in relief operations behind the front line. Leaving aside some women who ignore the war and carry on with their decadent way of life as if nothing had happened, the majority of Muslim women are helping with the War in one way or another. (*Zan Ruz*, 22)

The type of support expected from women changed emphasis in different stages of the war. Initially, what was expected of women was not more than, as President Banisadr put it, 'helping the country towards self-sufficiency by refraining from over-consumption and boycotting luxury goods'. He also told women that 'I am certain that all of you sisters will shut the door to men who turn their back on the War' (*Keyhan*, 41). But as the war progressed and it became evident that despite the initial victories gained by the Iranian forces there was little hope of an early settlement of the conflict with Iraq, a much more pragmatic and systematic approach was taken towards women's participation in the war. Women were recruited as revolutionary guards and mobilised into the Mobilisation of the Disinherited (Basij Mostazafin), the Construction Struggle (Jahad Sazandegi), the Literacy Campaign (Nehzat Savadamuzi), and Medical Aid (Emdad Pezeshki), and played a fuller role in relief operations in the war zones (*Soroush*, 2).

Women's mobilisation into the revolutionary guards and its rural operation wing, Mobilisation of the Disinherited, was limited mainly to administrative, nursing and educational activities at this stage of the war (*Zan Ruz*, 23). Women revolutionary guards were taught how to use arms but were not expected to use them. As a military trainer explained, 'The sisters do not participate in military activities like the brothers. The sisters are mainly engaged behind the front lines, but they receive training in the use of arms in case they may need it in future' (*Rah Zeinab*, 1). The policy on women's participation in military activities so far was in line with Ayatollah Khomeini's confirmation of the traditional Shii view that women are prohibited from taking part in *Jahad*. Ayatollah Sanei, the chief prosecutor, explained why:

> The reason why women should not participate in the *jahad* is because of the question of honour and chastity. In a war situation women's honour and chastity may be lost which would result in a great psychological blow to Moslems. But although Islam does not allow women to participate in *jahad*, it allows women to take part in defensive *jahad*. The present war is an imposed one. Our youth make sacrifices and women too should defend the country. But women's defence takes the form of nursing, cooking and washing for the wounded and encouragement of husband and sons to go to the front. A young woman whose husband has become a war martyr, has played an equally important role in defence. (*Zan Ruz*, 24)

But a change of fortune for the Iranian forces changed this policy in the latter years of the war (Hooglund, 1989). As the war spread to civilian zones and civilian areas became the target of air raids, the Iranian army, which lacked arms and expertise, was gradually pushed back and defeated by Iraqi forces. The war became more and more unpopular with urban and later rural citizens. The number of volunteers dwindled, war refugees rioted and those whose homes had been destroyed by Iraqi air raids openly demonstrated their discontent. Under these circumstances, the Islamic state, seeing its own survival at stake, attempted a military mobilisation of women (Reeves, 1989; Hendessi, 1990). The change of policy was justified by Ayatollah Khomeini. In a speech to a group of women revolutionary guards in April 1985, he asked women to be prepared to take up arms in defence of Islam, arguing that:

What is not accepted in the *shariat*, is women's participation in primary *jahad*. But when it comes to the question of defence, there is consensus in Islam that women are obliged to take part in every possible way including military defence. Women should receive military training. Of course the environment in which this is done should be Islamic and protective of chastity. Let me make it clear why women's participation in defence is doubly important. With their presence at the war front, women not only bring extra human power, but they also create a special sensitivity in men to fight even harder. Men are sensitive towards women and react more strongly against seeing one woman hurt than a hundred men killed. So, if you [women] participate in the defence of Islam in military and non-military ways, you will create great strength in our soldiers. (*Ettelaat*, 32)

Ayatollah Khomeini's extension of the concept of 'defence' to include the military participation of women in the war and his call for women's military training required mass legitimisation. The Society of Al-Zahra, a women's organisation in Qom, called for a mass demonstration 'in support of the *emam*'s call for women's active participation in the armed defence of the Islamic country' (*Ettelaat*, 33). A women's demonstration took place in Tehran which issued a resolution announcing women's eagerness for armed struggle against the infidel Saddam Hussain and called for women's military training (*Ettelaat*, 34). In April 1986, the Revolutionary Guards Corps announced its programme of military training for women which started by training 500 women (*Ettelaat*, 35). Later in 1986, a number of training camps were set up specifically for the purpose of women's military training (*Keyhan (London)*, 6). But, as it turned out, women did not need to take up arms in defence of Islam. The advances made by the Iraqi army backed by unabated bombardment of civilian targets had gone too far to be stopped by military mobilisation of civilian men and women. One year later, Ayatollah Khomeini presented the only solution left to the Islamic Republic and agreed to end the war.

Islamic women leaders

While women from the lower classes provided the mass support that the Islamic regime needed, the Islamic women leaders struggled to find a role for themselves in the higher echelons of the Islamic society. Women leaders in the Islamic Republic were mobilised into a number of overlapping areas of interest and activity.

The first area of activity and influence for women leaders was the religious one. The training of female religious leaders was regarded as important in the Islamic Republic, and ample opportunities were provided for women to be trained as religious leaders. With the Islamisation of the mainstream education system and the admission of women to theological schools, increasing numbers of women preachers and *mojtahedin* emerged. In no other field were women so encouraged and helped to become active. However, there was a limit to the status women could attain as a Shii scholar. Islam did not allow a *mojtahed* woman to issue religious decrees and if she did they could not be binding.

The second area of activity for Islamic women leaders was social welfare. Islamic women were fairly active in philanthropic organisations and welfare institutions set up by the state to look after its *mostasafin* supporters. Indeed many of the state-funded welfare agencies, charities and foundations which performed a variety of welfare, health and educational roles were run by women. Women who managed such organisations often came from clerical families and were well-connected within the circle of Islamic leadership. To cite an example, the *emam* Khomeini Sanatorium, which assisted the war wounded, was run by Mrs Karrubi, the first wife of Hojatoleslam Karrubi who was an influential Majles deputy. She had an interrupted secondary education (due to her early marriage) but was well versed in the *Qoran*. She managed three branches of the Sanatorium, two for men and one for women (*Zan Ruz*, 25).

Another example was an educational and health charity (Moaseseh Davazdahe Farvardin) run by a collective of several women including Ayatollah Khomeini's daughter, Mrs Farideh Mostafavi. They ran literacy and sewing classes for deprived women in Qom and built public baths and health clinics for women (*Zan Ruz*, 26). Women running these organisations had either been educated in Islamic girls' schools before the revolution or had received Islamic education at home. Some had political credentials in their own right with records of arrest, imprisonment or harassment by SAVAK. But the main credential seemed to be their connection with an approved political leader.

The third area of participation for Islamic women leaders was formal politics. Women's participation in political decision making, however, was much more limited. Women's main involvement in the process of political decision making was in the Majles. But this was of a very limited nature and even more tokenistic than women's participation in parliamentary politics under the Pahlavi regime. Over eleven elections and by-elections during the first decade of the Islamic Republic produced in all six women representatives. In the first election of the Assembly of Experts in charge of drafting the Constitution, over forty women candidates were put forward by a variety of secular and Islamic political parties and organisations. The political manoeuvring and manipulations by the IRP (Islamic Republican Party), ensured that only pro-Islamic Republic candidates were elected and that included the election of the IRP's woman candidate. The IRP's candidate Mrs Monireh Gorji was the only woman representative of the seventy-member Assembly of Experts.

In the 1980 Majles elections twenty-five women candidates ranging from 24 to 60 years of age were put forward by a variety of pro-Islamic Republic and oppositional political parties (*Bamdad*, 2). The dominance of Islamic parties and organisations ensured the success of their candidates. Out of 270 elected Majles deputies, 3 were women, Monireh Gorji, Azam Taleghani and Goharolsharieh Dastgheib. After the annihilation of all opposition in 1981, Majles elections produced fewer women candidates. In a 1981 by-election caused by the assassination of President Rajai, Prime Minister Bahonar and a number of other Majles representatives, two more women were elected to the Majles, Mrs Ategheh Rajai (the assassinated president's widow) and Maryam Behruzi. In the subsequent two elections of 1984 and 1988, three of the existing women Majles deputies were re-elected. In 1984, out of six women candidates only one new woman, Marziyeh Dabbagh, was elected (*Keyhan*, 42). Women candidates were only elected if they were put forward or supported by the dominant political faction. No independent woman candidate was ever elected (*Zan Ruz*, 27).

Women who made inroads into politics came from strict Islamic backgrounds. The profile of the six women who occupied Majles seats in the 1980s demonstrated similar patterns of social background to those who were active in religious and welfare fields. Azam Taleghani was the daughter of Ayatollah Taleghani, a well respected high ranking cleric and co-founder of the Liberation Movement of Iran. She resigned from her Majles seat after the dismissal of President Banisadr in 1981 and kept a low profile. Monireh Gorji, the first woman deputy in the Islamic Republic, was fifty years old with three married daughters. She taught the *Qoran* and Arabic before the Revolution. Mrs Goharolsharieh Dastgheib, Mrs Dabbagh and Mrs Ategheh Rajai were all cofounders of the Islamic Organisation of Committed Iranian Women (Sazeman Eslami Zanan Motahed Iran). All three of them were also teachers and members of the Central Council of the Islamic Society of Teachers (*Keyhan*, 42). Mrs Dabbagh had seven children and was associated with hardline clerics such as Ayatollah Saidi and Mohammad Montazeri. Her anti-Shah activities had led to her imprisonment and exile in Lebanon and Syria. She had also worked closely with the co-founder of the IRP, Dr Javad Bahonar (*ibid.*). Mrs Maryam Behruzi, born in 1945, was married at the age of 15 and had four children. She had given religious talks and *Qoran* lessons to women before the Revolution and had been arrested and imprisoned under the Shah.

Some women Majles deputies used their unique position to voice women's legal and social problems. Despite their tokenistic presence, they played an important role in initiating legislation on women. Their overall achievement, however, was very limited. They lacked power and influence and seemed lost in the male-dominated and authoritative atmosphere of the Majles (*Zan Ruz*, 27). The Majles found little time to reflect on women's issues and when it did, the points of view of women deputies were often marginalised (*ibid.*). As a result of the Majles's preoccupation with the war, economic problems and political faction fighting, many of the Constitutional articles on women were neither legislated nor implemented.

The presence of women in the executive branch of the state was even more limited. Women were barred from becoming president, and post-revolutionary cabinets did not produce any woman ministers. The only role envisaged for women in the government was a consultative one. Women were allocated seats in consultative committees set up by various ministries. Women were also included in the Islamic Republic's delegations to international conferences and events (*Zan Ruz*, 28). In October 1987, the Women's Social and Cultural Council was set up by the High Council of Cultural Revolution to 'make policy recommendations on women'. Thirteen members of the Council were representatives of the High Council of the Judiciary, five ministries, the Qom Seminary, the Islamic Propaganda Agency, two specialists in Islamic science and culture and two women Majles deputies. The objectives of the Council included 'preparing the ground for the growth of women's talents and personality and preserving their rights', 'planning for the fortification of the sacred institution of the family', 'attending to the problems faced by unprotected women and protecting their rights', 'removing obstacles in the way of women's participation in economic, social and political activities' and 'studying and presenting annual reports on women's cultural and social position (*Zan Ruz*, 29). It set up sub-committees on family, education and literacy, employment and others (*Zan Ruz*, 30). During the first two years of their activities, these sub-committees conducted surveys of women's needs and problems in their area of interest and put forward a number of policy proposals (*Zan Ruz*, 27).

Women who were involved with the executive branch of the state were more inclined to be specialists in one field or another and less likely to be hardliners. Although Islamic credentials had to be present, most women representatives in international conferences in later years also tended to be highly educated specialists. Professional women were also called upon for expert reports on various topics. These women drew their support from a small but vocal oppositional faction within the Islamic women's movement.

The fourth area of involvement for Islamic women leaders was the women's movement. As explained before, Ayatollah Khomeini's call for women's *hejab* soon after the Revolution met with a reluctant response from educated Islamic women who did not believe in the forceful imposition of Islam and had their own ideas about the 'true' Islamic position for women. By setting up the Women's Society of the Islamic Revolution and other women's organisations, these women began an unprecedented Islamic feminist movement. However, the expectation of the Islamic reformist women to receive support from the state and play a role in the formation of state policy was not realised. Far from supporting the WSIR, the hardline faction of the state manipulated it by driving out the moderate faction and making it a stronghold for *hezbollahi* women. Women like Azam Taleghani and Fereshteh Hashemi who had been associated with the deposed President Banisadr were forced into silence. Zahra Rahnavard who introduced herself as 'a follower of the party of God, but not belonging to any earthly party' (*Zan Ruz*, 31) was also intimidated into silence. Her magazine, *Rah Zeinab* [Zeinab's Path] was closed down (*Zan Ruz*, 32) and her husband, Mir Hosein Musavi, faced opposition to his Islamic credentials by Majles deputies when he was proposed for the post of prime minister because of his wife's oppositional views on women.

The moderate faction of the women's movement, however, made a come back in the late 1980s. Throughout the early 1980s, being unable to openly criticise state policies on women, this faction filled their magazines, such as *Zan Ruz* and later *Zanan*, with individual tales of hardship, humiliation and suffering of women under male dominated legal and social contracts. Sympathetic voices amongst state officials and influential clerics received coverage in this magazine and the efforts of women Majles deputies on behalf of women were publicised. But, gradually, the oppositional faction of the women's movement consolidated its base amongst both women and the Islamic leadership. The rising circulation of *Zan Ruz* indicated readership amongst women with both pro and anti-Islamic Republic views (Sayyah, 1990). There were also reports of newsagents refusing to sell these magazines because of their oppositional stance on women's question. The *Zan Ruz* policy of voicing women's complaints about inflation, food shortages, the housing crisis, discrimination at work, children's health and schooling, violent husbands and other familial hardships, created a rare public space for women to voice their problems. The oppositional faction of the Islamic women's movement also made alliances with an increasing number of state officials, administrators and clerics who were prepared to criticise the lack of a true Islamic policy on women. Its involvement with international forums such as the United Nations in relation to women-specific programmes demonstrated the ability of the Islamic women's movement to operate within different Islamic and secular alliances in the interest of its aims and objectives (*Zan Ruz*, 33).

Education

Education was considered by the Islamic state as an important strategy for women's integration into national processes. At home, the mother was the transmitter of Islamic values and political culture to the child. In society, this role was played by the school. The woman, as the link between family and nation, had to participate in both processes: as a mother for the child and as a teacher for the pupil. Ayatollah Montazeri reflected official thinking when he told a group of women that:

> The first and foremost school of life is the mother's lap. If we want to achieve a healthy and uncorrupted society which is committed to Islam, we must spare no effort in educating women ... If you [women] want to be blessed by God's compassion, and if you want our future generations to be pious and uncontaminated by worldly diversions, you must create a movement of mass education amongst women. (*Keyhan*, 43)

The role played by women in linking the home and the school was expressed in the following way by an activist in the Islamic women's movement: 'You [women teachers] who are the guardians of millions of future mothers of the Islamic society of Iran, have a great responsibility towards the Continuation and for delivering the Islamic Revolution to the future generation' (*Ettelaat*, 36).

Furthermore, women's presence in educational institutions was a political urgency. The Islamic state had to fill the schools, colleges and universities with its female supporters to counteract the influence of the non-Islamic middle classes. In a country with a young and politically active population, the education system was an important site of ideological struggle, and the Islamic state was determined to take it over and control it by replacing *taghuti* students with Islamic ones. This was emphasised in a statement by the 'Office for Consolidation of Relationship Between *Emam* and People': 'The only guarantee against the victory of liberalism and return to *taghut* is to close the doors of universities to the so-called "expert" and open it to *hezbollahi* brothers and sisters' (*Ettelaat*, 37).

Ayatollah Khomeini himself was unequivocal about the need to educate women. In this respect there was little sign of Khomeini's customary contradictory expressions, and throughout, he gave consistent support to women's education by telling women 'You [women] should endeavour for knowledge and piety. Knowledge is not the monopoly of a particular group but belongs to all and it is the duty of all men and women to acquire knowledge. I hope the authorities will assist you in this and provide the educational and cultural facilities that you need to enable you to succeed' (*Ettelaat*, 38).

The same level of support came from most factions of the Islamic state. The IRP, which was the most powerful and determined hardliner of the ruling factions, stated in its official newspaper that women's education should be considered from the nursery to university level. Many influential Islamic leaders such as Ayatollah Montazeri and Rafsanjani made speeches about the desirability of women's education.

Women's education was particularly important because the Islamic education system trained women as ideologically suitable participants in social, economic and political activities: 'Today the reasons for women's participation in society and the economy are different from those of the previous regime. In the past women were exploited for colonial aims. Now women work in response to specific needs of the Islamic society. Women experts and politicians are needed to cater for women's needs in an Islamic society' (*Zan Ruz*, 34).

The establishment of an Islamic education system

A pre-condition for the education of women (and men) was, however, the creation of an Islamic education system. The early post-revolutionary years witnessed a crusade against the Pahlavi separation of religious and secular education. The secularisation programme of Reza Shah in the 1930s had ended the monopoly of the *mollas* over education. The Islamic Republic devised a 'cultural revolution' to overcome the differentiation between secular and religious education by bringing the mainstream education system under Islamic control. The other purpose served by the cultural revolution was to bring the universities, which had become major centres of left-wing political activity during and after the Revolution, under state control. The cultural revolution started in April 1980 when Ayatollah Khomeini criticised the universities for their Westernised professors, students and text-books. He expressed a fear of the Islamic Republic being undermined by 'Westernised universities and the training of our youth in the interest of the West or East' (*Keyhan*, 45). The Council of the Revolution decided to close down the universities in order to eradicate un-Islamic influences. This resulted in bloody clashes on university campuses between *hezbollahis* and other students. Three days of fighting over the control of the universities led to the death and injury of hundreds of students and the evacuation of anti-government secular and

Islamic political groups from the universities. President Banisadr proclaimed the start of a cultural revolution to Islamise the higher education system. Universities remained closed for over two years while the High Council of Cultural Revolution, consisting of seven members mostly from the IRP, Islamised the education system. The work of the Council of Cultural Revolution was complemented by another body set up in 1986, The Commission for Planning and Administration of Fundamental Change in the Education System (Setad Ejrai va Barnamehrizi Taghyir Bonyadi Nezam Amuzesh va Parvaresh).

The Islamisation of the education system consisted of a number of measures applied to various levels of education. To begin with, the education establishment was coerced into total submission to Islamic ideology. Teachers, lecturers and administrators either agreed to carry the banner of Islamisation or faced dismissal. Islamic student associations played an important role in keeping the pressure on the staff and students of educational institutes.

After the reopening of the universities in 1982, the criteria for admission of students included ideological commitment to the Islamic Republic, and its confirmation by the local mosque was required. Secondly, curricula changes were introduced which included more religious instruction, mandatory teaching of Arabic in secondary schools, dropping of English at primary school level and the teaching of a heavily biased history of Islam and the Islamic Revolution. In short, a large dose of Islamic ideology was injected into school and university curricula (Mehran, 1989). Thirdly, in addition to the ideological content of education, the Islamic structure of the education system was of great interest to the Islamic state. This was where the cultural revolution made its specific impact on women's education.

For the education system to become Islamic, it had to observe and reinforce Islamic gender relations. This was achieved through sexual segregation in the education system, imposition of *hejab* on women, reinforcement of gender division of subjects and adaptation of women's education to the requirements of the Islamic family and the preservation of male dominance in education. Women's education, although highly encouraged in official pronouncements, suffered badly in reality due to a combination of intentional measures and the unintended consequences of those measures. Moreover, despite consistency at the political level, the Islamic Republic's actual policies on education suffered from the usual problems of lack of coordination between multiple centres of decision-making and lack of financial resources due to economic stagnation.

The process of segregation in the education system started in March

1979 when the Ministry of Education announced its intention to abolish coeducational schools (*Ayandegan*, 5). This was followed by the banning of mixed classes in private educational institutions and, later, by attempts to segregate classes in universities and polytechnics. By 1982 all levels of education had been affected by sexual segregation. The shortage of teachers and school premises meant that more often than not segregation led to the dismissal of girl pupils from mixed schools in the absence of allocation of additional resources to girls' schools. The result was a variety of practical and psychological problems for female pupils and their parents and severe overcrowding of existing girls' schools (*Keyhan Havai*, 44). In rural areas, where a larger proportion of children were educated in mixed schools, the problem was more serious due to the shortage of girls' schools in the vicinity. No doubt many young girls dropped out of education in rural areas as a result of the policy of segregation.

Another effect of segregation was felt in private tertiary educational institutions which ran post-secondary school courses including courses which prepared students for university entrance examinations. Many such institutions complained that since the number of female students alone did not make it viable for them to run separate courses for both sexes, they had to refuse to register female students or ask them to change their subjects to those that had sufficient numbers of female applicants to justify running segregated classes for them (*Ettelaat*, 39).

The policy of segregation went hand in hand with that of women's *hejab*. Educational institutions were threatened with prosecution and closure if they did not enforce *hejab* on their female students (*Keyhan*, 45). Islamic uniform became compulsory for school girls over 9 years of age. Women teachers and school administrators were threatened by the Ministry of Education with dismissal if they did not wear *hejab* (*Keyhan*, 46). The pressure on *hejab* was kept up through official encouragement of *hezbollahi* women. President Khamenei told a women's magazine that 'It is up to *hezbollahi* women and pious girls to stop lack of respect for *hejab* by some misguided women in schools, universities and offices' (*Zan Ruz*, 35). Many female students were constantly in trouble at school over their appearance and many were dismissed since their lack of interest in *hejab* was interpreted as a political action against the regime. The extra-educational pressures on female pupils and students sometimes acted as an incentive for them to give up education in favour of marriage. There was even a report of suicide by schoolgirls as a result of psychological pressures and humiliation at school over 'un-Islamic behaviour' (*Zan Ruz*, 36).

Women's education

But the most important aspect of the regulation of women's education was in relation to the reinforcement of the gender division of labour in society. The education system was restructured in such a way as to train men and women in accordance with their 'different natures and capabilities' and the distinct roles which they were supposed to play in society. A conference on the education of the 6–12 year old concluded that, 'The Islamic Republic has inherited an education system which is a Western imitation and should therefore change fundamentally. ... One of the contrasts between the Islamic and Western schooling systems is that the latter trains boys and girls in the same way, but the Islamic system is conscious of male–female differences while considering them equal in creation' (*Zan Ruz*, 37).

The conference recommended, amongst other things, production of separate curricula and text-books for boys and girls. The emphasis in girls' education programmes was not so much on their motherhood function as on their complementary roles at home and society. This was reflected in a number of educational projects set up for girls on a national scale. In 1983, the Ministry of Education announced the setting up of technical schools for girls in rural areas where secondary schools were not available. The curriculum included both theoretical and practical training in a number of rural subjects. In explaining the scheme, the spokesman for the ministry in Fars province encouraged rural girls to take up carpet weaving and bee-keeping which would bring good income to their villages (*Keyhan*, 47). In many rural areas carpet weaving was traditionally done by women in their homes as part of their house-keeping duties for the family's use as well as for earning extra income (see Chapter 5). Girls' technical schools were also set up in provincial towns. The headmistress of one of these schools described the main subjects being taught in her school as childcare, health, hygiene and dress-making (*Zan Ruz*, 38). School girls were not necessarily solely trained for motherhood but were also encouraged to prepare for future employment. The 'feminine subjects' taught at schools were often employment oriented. Schools organised 'employment fairs' to encourage girls to think about future careers (*ibid.*) and work-related educational projects were run in both boys' and girls' schools. One project (Tarh KAD) aimed to bring education and work together by allocating one day a week of school time to practical training in the workshops specially set up for this purpose (*Keyhan*, 48). The areas of training for boys included technology, industry, crafts and trade, but training for girls was service oriented (*Ettelaat*, 40). It is interesting to note that secretarial training, a traditional female occupation, was not included in any of these educational projects since it was considered a confirmation of women as sex-objects (*Zan Ruz*, 39).

In short, the schools did not have many qualms about training the girls for a career. But there was a lot of sensitivity about what career girls should be trained for. Those professions deemed contradictory to the role of women at home were rejected. Indeed many girls who were studying technical subjects in pre-revolutionary technical colleges were forced to change their subjects after the Revolution to those officially approved for women (*Ettelaat*, 41). With regard to female literacy and schooling, the census of 1986 indicated that the rate of literacy amongst urban women had risen from 55.1 in 1976 to 65.2 per cent in 1986. Literacy amongst rural and nomad women was standing at 36 per cent as compared to 16.5 in 1976. Moreover, the trend of female attendance in nursery, primary and secondary schools was upwards when comparing the academic years of 1980–81 and 1983–84 (SCI, 1985, pp. 12, 25). It is not clear, however, whether the upward trend represented a real rise in comparison with the rate of growth of the female population.

The schools, however, were not the only providers of education for girls. A system of non-formal education was maintained for those who were excluded from mainstream schooling either by law or by other impediments. One user group excluded from mainstream schooling by law was the child brides whose numbers were increasing because of the reduction in minimum age of marriage for women. The Islamic education system aimed to protect the 'innocence' of other female pupils by excluding them from schools. These women and many others turned to the non-formal sector for literacy and skills training. Non-formal education was run by charities set up through government or private funding and was mainly managed by women. The Reconstruction Corps, the Institute of Davazdahe Farvardin and many other such charities organised classes for women in many subjects such as literacy, religious studies, training in sewing, typing, design, crafts, cooking, English language, health, child psychology, family relations, nursery training, repairing household instruments and so on (*Ettelaat*, 42). Women were also able to enrol in the Open College and study at home for qualifications through correspondence and tutorials.

This, however, presented a very limited opportunity since the admission of women was restricted by a quota system (*Zan Ruz*, 40). In non-formal education, too, there was no particular reservation about training women for 'suitable' feminine work skills. The official statistics reflected the emphasis in state policy on women's tertiary and adult education. While the trend in women's take-up of teacher training was upwards, the trend for women's training in technical, agricultural training for women was zero by 1982. This data excludes higher education at university level. Women's non-formal education, however, experienced a decline after picking up in the initial post-revolutionary years (Statistical Centre of Iran, 1985, p. 25).

Women's higher education

The same policies operated with regard to women's higher education. Training for professions which were favoured by women was encouraged. Educational institutions which trained teachers, nurses and midwives expanded but shortages in these areas continued. The manager of a teacher training centre explained that the function of these centres was 'to help to propagate the Revolution and Islam by training committed Islamic teachers and dispatching them across the country' (*Zan Ruz*, 41). The limitation here was that since these centres were residential, married women were excluded.

Moreover, the resources allocated to women's training did not meet the demand. Out of twenty-one residential teacher training centres in Tehran, only five were for women (*ibid.*). Nursing colleges which expanded rapidly in provincial towns during the war faced similar constraints. The residential ones excluded married women and the training allowance paid to trainees by non-residential centres was not sufficient to pay their rents. This resulted in a high rate of drop-out (*Ettelaat*, 44). In 1981, a bill was submitted to the Majles for the training of midwives. The bill aimed to train 20,000 midwives by setting up midwifery colleges. The bill did not, however, make it through the busy schedule of the Majles and was shelved (*Keyhan*, 49).

Despite the extended use of women's dormitories and residential colleges, there was a severe shortage of accommodation for women students. University dormitories were often the site of conflict between female students and the authorities as a result of accommodation shortages. There were many protests and rebellions caused by this problem (*Ettelaat*, 43). The housing problem of women students was a major deterrent to their mobility for the purpose of education. Another important problem for women was lack of sufficient creche facilities in educational institutions. In a survey conducted by an Islamic women's magazine, the main reason cited by educationalists for lack of sufficient nursery facilities was lack of funding (*Zan Ruz*, 42). The University of Tehran had demands for 300 nursery places but could only afford places for 85 children. Many women had to leave their children with parents who often lived in far away towns (*ibid.*) Women students protested that despite the government's policy of encouraging marriage, which had resulted in an increase in marriage amongst students, insufficient support was being provided to enable married women students to complete their studies.

But the most rapidly expanding area of women's education was theology. Women's admission to Islamic seminaries had begun in 1975 but it offered only limited opportunities (*Zan Ruz*, 43). Ayatollah Montazeri expressed regret that 'until recently, the Islamic seminaries and other opportunities for studying Islamic theology belonged to men', and talked about the 'necessity of developing and setting up new seminaries in different cities for women' (*Ettelaat*, 45). In 1983, the highly regarded Qom seminary admitted over 400 women with secondary school education between the ages of 16 to 20 after setting an entrance examination (*Keyhan*, 50). In 1985, the Religious Science Complex for women was opened in Qom. This complex known as The Society of Zahra (Jameat ol-Zahra), accepted over 500 female students. It was an initiative of Ayatollah Khomeini himself and was founded by his personal representatives. One of the founders, Ayatollah Jannati, explained that women students were expected to be 'familiar with the alphabet of politics which could not be separated from Islamic government and Islam' (*Ettelaat*, 46). He also warned the students against becoming involved in factionalism (*ibid.*). The curriculum of the Islamic seminaries divided into three stages of introductory, intermediate and advanced. The completion of the first two stages required seven to eight years of study and the advanced stage depended on individual endeavour. In 1984, that is, after nine years of admitting women, no women had yet graduated (*Zan Ruz*, 43).

With regard to women's higher education, the policy adopted by the Islamic Republic proved contradictory and controversial, and as a result had to be amended a number of times. Before the Revolution, women were admitted to all fields of study except mining. During the transitional period, women's entry to higher education remained as before. The Islamisation of the higher education system during the politically extremist period of 1980–4, resulted in a most restrictive policy towards women's entry to 'non-feminine' fields. Women's entry to a whole range of technical, engineering and experimental sciences was prohibited (Ghahreman, 1988). Moreover, restrictions were imposed on women's admission to most medical, environmental and human sciences by specifying a maximum number of places for women, which ranged from 20 to 50 per cent. Women who were attending the prohibited courses were asked either to drop out or change subject. On the whole, 54 per cent of subjects offered by higher education institutes were closed to women (Mojab, 1991). Higher education abroad too, presented problems for women. A Majles bill on education abroad which was ratified in 1985, barred married women students from taking up education abroad unless they were accompanied by their husbands (*Keyhan Havai*, 45). This limitation did not apply to married men. But the gender division of subjects also affected men who were prohibited from entering subjects such as midwifery, family hygiene and sewing. Men were admitted for nursing but were allocated a maximum admission quota of 50 per cent (*ibid.*).

The effect of the state policy on women's higher education was clearly reflected in the official statistics. The number of women in higher education remained steady from the mid-1970s. Women constituted 28.5 per cent of the university students in 1974–5 academic year, 30.8 per cent in 1978–9, and 29.9 per cent in the 1985–6 academic year (Statistical Centre of Iran, 1989, p. 15). However, the pattern of female distribution in various subjects changed. The statistical trend in the first decade of the Islamic Republic indicated a small rise from 37 per cent in 1979 to around 38.5 per cent in 1987, in the number of female students in social sciences and humanities combined; another small rise from 40 to 41 per cent in the same years in educational sciences; and a more substantial rise from 33 to 38 per cent in natural and mathematical sciences. Again in the same years, a substantial drop occurred from 21 to 10 per cent in agricultural subjects; from 9 to 4 per cent in engineering; and from 54 to 45 per cent in medicine and para-medical subjects (Mojab, 1991, pp. 54–8). With regard to education abroad, available statistics indicated that, in 1983, only about 13.5 per cent of students abroad were women (Statistical Centre of Iran, 1985, p. 35).

Change of policy on women's education

In the late 1980s, however, the policy on women's entry to higher education became less restrictive. In May 1989 it was announced that restrictions on women's entry to geology and agriculture were lifted (*Zan Ruz*, 44). Soon after it was announced that women's entry quotas were abolished altogether in medical, para-medical and some engineering fields, and were substantially increased in some technical and industrial subjects (*Zan Ruz*, 45). This was the result of lobbying by the Women's Social and Cultural Council and reflected the unpredictable nature of the Islamic Republic's policies on women.

As in many other areas, the decision-making process was a source of incoherence in education policy. Educational institutions did not have independent status, nor did they have any say in education policy. The High Council of Cultural Revolution was the central body responsible for policy making on education. The Council was composed of seven committees, one of which, the Planning Committee, took final policy decisions on higher education. The Planning Committee was chaired by the minister of education and included representatives from the Council as well as the chairmen of subject committees such as the Committee on Mathematical and Technical Sciences and the Committee on Humanities. These subject committees were in charge of proposing policy in their particular areas which would then be discussed and finalised in the Planning Committee. The minister of education had an equal vote with other members of the Planning Committee and his chairmanship did not accord him any greater power over the Committee. The Ministry of Education, then, could potentially hold views totally different from the policy made by the Council through majority vote. Moreover, high-ranking leaders such as Ayatollah Khomeini and President Khamenei could intervene in education policy independently.

The changes introduced in 1989 on women's higher education reflected the existing contradictions and the *ad hoc* manner in which education policy was made. These changes were initiated through the Women's Social and Cultural Council, one of the seven committees of the High Council of Cultural Revolution. The head of the Women's Social and Cultural Council, Zahra Rahnavard, failed to convince various subject committees to lift or at least raise the female quotas in their subject areas. The minister of education was in agreement with the Women's Council and did not support the High Council's policy on women's higher education. He did not, however, have the necessary power to change the policy or influence the Planning Committee to agree to a change. The Women's Council appealed to President Ali Khamenei to use his influence in support of their campaign. The appeal proved successful and after personal intervention by President Khamenei, the reluctant Planning Committee agreed to some concessions on women's entry to technical and experimental subjects (*Zan Ruz*, 45). The decision-making process reflected the lack of coherence and planning in education policy. These changes were unplanned and their introduction depended on the personal 'good will' of political leaders and the contextual receptivity of the demands of the Islamic women's movement. This change of policy also demonstrated that, far from being rooted in Islam, the Islamic Republic's policies were conjunctural.

Moreover, there was nothing 'Islamic' about many of the arguments originally put forward by members of the High Council of Cultural Revolution's Planning Committee against women's entry to technical and experimental subjects. One of the members had argued that 'when the resources are limited and there is a great urgency for national development, why should the country invest in women, whose personal and familial situation may prevent them from taking up employment in their field of study' (*ibid.*). Another member argued that 'if women are not restricted, they will fill up the courses and there will not be any places left for men' (*ibid.*). Yet another member asked, 'what about women's motherhood and familial duties?' (*Ibid.*). No doubt these arguments were not specific to the Islamic Republic and had been put forward by many male dominated policy-making bodies all over the world. The representatives of the Islamic women's movement rejected these arguments against women's education as 'illegal and discriminatory' and continued to lobby for 'participation of women in all fields of study at higher education level' (*ibid.*).

Employment

No other aspect of women's social involvement presented so much difficulty for the Islamic Republic's policy makers as women's employment. The challenge of women's employment arose from a variety of different and often conflicting ideological, political and economic pressures on the Islamic state. The pressures for and against women's employment were tremendous.

Negative pressures on women's employment

To begin with the negative pressures, the Islamic regime adopted a highly critical approach towards the Pahlavi policy of women's employment and aimed to formulate an 'Islamic' alternative. The commonly held Islamic criticism was that

> Women's employment under the *taghut* was not due to the regime's respect for women, but was an imitation of the West with devious intent. Women were absorbed into the corrupt administration system and performed phoney tasks whilst the intention was to use them as a means to deceive and dupe the youths of this country in order to destroy our culture and rob our economic resources. (*Zan Ruz*, 46)

The post-revolutionary state, then, had to present a policy on women's employment which would be seen as 'different' and 'Islamic'. Moreover, women's employment was a specially sensitive matter for the Islamic regime since it was potentially a serious threat to the role of men as family breadwinners and could undermine the very structure of the Islamic family which was based on the power and authority of the breadwinner. This type of family was being re-instituted legally and ideologically by the Islamic state. A Majles deputy articulated this threat when he argued that 'In Islamic society woman's upkeep is the responsibility of her husband and she should not have to work. . . . If this changes, everything will change; there will be no submission by women' (*Jomhuri Eslami*, 2). Another source of anxiety in relation to women's employment was about motherhood losing its primacy for women. Ayatollah Khomeini was very sensitive to this threat:

> The foreign lackeys tried to divert this respectable section of the society [women] who are instrumental in shaping society by turning them into toys in corrupt hands. There was a conspiracy to make women to turn away their children from their laps and place them in nurseries where they would be deprived of their motherly love and Islamic rearing. . . . If it was not for the transformation we see today in women, they would have succeeded . . . A mother's primary service to society is something else, and that is what the Prophet has talked about and instructed: that women should rear lions and lionesses to offer to Islamic society. (*Keyhan*, 51)

Women were constantly reminded by Islamic leaders of their duty to society and the Revolution and warned against taking their motherhood role lightly:

> Women's main duty is home keeping and child rearing and this is in itself a full-time job. We should not expect women to add generation of income to their tasks. Of course women can engage in side activities such as knitting, sewing and even research and writing. But it should not be forgotten that neither husband nor the wife can dismiss their main responsibilities. (*Ettelaat*, 47)

There were also religious principles to contend with which prohibited women from taking up certain responsibilities such as judgeship. Fear of endangering the moral integrity of the family by women's involvement in certain occupations was another ideological pressure against female employment. Certain professions were considered as 'damaging to the moral integrity of the family' (*Keyhan*, 52). Others such as those which involved travelling or night shifts were considered to 'interfere with the husband's matrimonial rights' since it was seen as woman's responsibility to be sexually available to her husband whenever he wished (*ibid.*).

As to economic pressures against women's employment, the prioritisation of women's role in the family removed some of the economic and developmental incentives in training and employing women as professionals. Women's professional training was considered by some as a 'waste of investment' since 'they either can't find suitable employment or give up work to look after their children' (*Zan Ruz*, 45). There was also a fear of male unemployment in a society where the family was supposed to be based on the concept of a male breadwinner. One official articulated this fear when he complained that 'If women are absorbed into the workforce to the same extent, men have to be excluded from it. This means women will have jobs while men would become unemployed' (*Zan Ruz*, 47).

Positive pressures on women's employment

There were tremendous pressures, on the other hand, for supporting and encouraging women's employment. To begin with, substantial sections of women had traditionally been economically active in Iran. Although official statistics reflected the economically active women as only 12.9 per cent of all women over the age of 10 in 1979 and 8.1 in 1986, in reality a much larger percentage of women contributed to the income of the family (Statistical Centre of Iran, 1988c, p. 65). The Islamic regime had to accept the fact that women had already been integrated into the workforce and any dis-integration policy on a major scale would adversely affect the lower income women, the very section of society which the Revolution needed on its side. Moreover, the Islamic Republic desperately needed women's skills to sustain the war-torn economy. It also needed to maintain a progressive image, especially in the post-revolutionary transitional period, to fend off increasingly vocal internal and international criticisms of its treatment of women.

But, perhaps more important for the Islamic regime, was the political necessity of having women supporters in offices and factories to replace or silence those at the workplace who would not concede to the Islamic regime. Ayatollah Khomeini was very much aware of the need to keep women supporters active in all religious, cultural, political, social and economic spheres. While on the one hand denouncing state nurseries for separating children from their mothers, he was on the other hand encouraging women to participate in the workforce to 'purify' and 'reconstruct' the country which 'they [Pahlavi regime] have ruined' (*Keyhan*, 53). Other Islamic ideologues, men and women, emphasised the political aspect of women's employment by pointing out that 'Women's employment proves their political presence. The Muslim women's presence in work places, which happen to be less penetrated by Islam, is a sign of their political support for the Revolution'; and that 'Women's absence at the workplace is a danger to Islamic society . . . Those who are calling for women to stay at home are contributing to a conspiracy to defeat the Islamic Revolution by driving women out of the political scene' (*Zan Ruz*, 46, 48).

Another pressure which acted in favour of women's employment was the ideological importance of segregation. The Islamic regime needed to create the conditions for preserving sex-segregation by training women to serve other women. If segregation was to be taken seriously, then there was a dire need for more women teachers, doctors, nurses, midwives, social workers and so on. This was a major determinant in the Islamic Republic's policy towards women's employment. Hojatoleslam Rafsanjani, then the speaker of the Majles, encouraged women to participate 'in professions such as teaching and medicine which would result in them helping other women'. Azam Taleghani, a woman Majles deputy, also demanded training of 'more female doctors to treat women' (*Keyhan*, 54, 55). The head of the Teachers Training Centre, Mrs Kheyrshipour, argued that 'women should be served by women professionals in relation to all areas of their needs. That is why families should be prepared to sacrifice a little and bear hardship while women receive training and go out to serve their Islamic society' (*Zan Ruz*, 46).

In short, the conflicting pressures for and against women's employment presented a serious challenge to the Islamic Republic. In response, the Islamic state at first introduced a series of rash and sometimes contradictory measures. After the transitional period, however, it attempted to arrive at a more balanced policy on women's employment by resolving some of the conflicting pressures.

State measures on women's employment

The early post-revolutionary years witnessed a number of attacks on women's employment. Women were prohibited from becoming judges soon after the Revolution (see chapter 7). In March 1979, female judges were told they should apply for administrative posts in the judiciary and trainees were deprived of their appointment decrees (*Ayandegan*, 6). The scale and intensity of protest from all quarters against the dismissal of women judges did not have any effect and finally in June 1979, the swearing-in ceremony of new judges took place without the participation of women nominees. Three months later, the existing female judges were officially transferred to other government departments (*Ayandegan*, 7).

The next step was to cleanse the workplace. The first and foremost target was the public sector, where the intelligentsia of the Pahlavi era had spread roots. Ayatollah Khomeini's call in the summer of 1980 for 'Administrative Revolution' (*enghelab edari*) set the ball rolling. The cleansing operation included the imposition of *hejab* on women employees, segregation of male and female workers, silencing or sacking of non-Islamic employees, replacing secular employees in key posts with Islamic sympathizers, and installing Islamic societies in all state organisations as instruments of control and Islamisation. Women employees were in particular vulnerable in this process. Large numbers of women employees were sacked for protesting against the forceful imposition of *hejab*. The army and the police alone sacked 131 women employees. Some women were sacked for 'colluding with the corruption of Pahlavi state' (*Ettelaat*, 48). The pressures of *hejab*, segregation and the humiliating behaviour of the 'Islamic Societies' towards secular women forced many of them to leave voluntarily. Women were also particularly vulnerable to the 'masculinization' of the workplace. After Ayatollah Khomeini's condemnation of the Pahlavi regime for depriving children of motherly love and Islamic rearing by putting them in nurseries, the government decided to close all workplace nurseries. Working days were also increased from 5 to 6 days a week with detrimental effect for women employees who had children (*Zan Ruz*, 49).

But once the transitional period was over and the Islamic regime felt politically secure after the elimination of all internal opposition, the emphasis began to change from an *ad hoc* replacement of Pahlavi practices to formulation of a more systematic policy on women's employment. The main elements of this policy included emphasis on the ideological importance of training women for certain professions such as education, welfare, health and medicine and adaptation of women's employment to the needs of the 'Islamic family'. The first legislation in this respect was the draft proposal on midwifery training which was presented to the Majles in 1981. The proposal included building more maternity hospitals and midwifery training centres and training of 20,000 midwives (*Keyhan*, 56). Another bill in support of women's employment in favoured professions related to maternity leave for teachers. The bill proposed to extend maternity leave for teachers from 90 days, which applied to women employees of all sectors, to one year which aimed to reward women teachers and encourage more recruitment. The bill was discussed in the Majles but was rejected on the grounds that 'it would discriminate against women employees in other sectors', 'it would create chaos and disorder in the education system' and 'its cost would be a burden for the government'. Mrs Behruzi, one of the three women Majles deputies, argued for the suspension of the bill to provide time to improve its content, but the bill was overwhelmingly rejected (*Keyhan*, 57).

In 1982 a draft labour law was presented to the Majles by the minister of labour and social affairs, Ahmad Tavakoli. The draft law discussed women's work under the heading of 'women and children's labour' which included the following two articles on women's work:

Article 54 – Married women can be employed for jobs which do not interfere with their family responsibilities. In cases where a married woman's work results in infringement of her husbands' matrimonial rights, employment should be conditional to obtaining her husband's permission.

Article 55 – A married woman's work contract should contain terms and conditions related to pregnancy, maternity and childcare. (complementary note: under circumstances where the above is not specified, the prevalent norm will apply). (*Keyhan*, 58)

Hojatoleslam Mahdavi Kani, the head of the special civil courts claimed that family disputes were arising from confusion over women's right to work which was a result of the above proposed laws. He clarified the matter by announcing that:

A woman does not have the right to work without the knowledge and permission of her husband especially so if her work interferes with her matrimonial responsibilities. But on the other hand, the husband cannot withdraw permission unreasonably. If the woman was in employment before marriage and had made it clear to her prospective husband that she intends to continue to work after marriage, then the husband does not have a valid excuse to prevent her from working. (*Keyhan*, 59)

The Labour Law was amended in 1987 to include clauses related to women's health and safety. Article 75 of the new law prohibited the carrying of heavy weights and undertaking dangerous work for women workers. Article 76 prohibited night shifts for women except in relation to educational, health and medical work. Maternity leave was specified as ninety days, half of which should be taken after the child's birth (Article 77). Breast feeding mothers were granted half an hour leave every three hours to feed their baby (Article 79) and companies were obliged to provide the type of nursery suitable to the age and requirements of the workers' pre-school children (*Ettelaat*, 49).

Another new law discussed in 1982 was the Civil Service Recruitment Law (Ghanun Estekhdam Keshvari). The chief executive of the Administration and Recruitment Agency and deputy prime minister, Dr Abbaspour, announced that, 'the new law will propose financial assistance to families where both husband and wife are public sector employees with the aim of enabling the wife to give up work to look after the family'. He added that 'another proposal contained in the new Recruitment Law concerns women's part-time employment in the public sector' (*Keyhan*, 60). A few months later the government presented a draft bill on women's part-time work to the Majles as part of the Civil Service Recruitment Law. In introducing the bill, Mohandes Razavi the deputy prime minister claimed that the bill had been drafted as a result of great demand from women through letters, petitions and questionnaires filled in by women employees of various ministries. He stated that the aim of the bill was to give due value to the Islamic family by enabling working women to perform their motherhood duties (*Keyhan*, 61). This was similar to the bill introduced under the Shah which did not become law (see chapter 5).

The bill consisted of a single article which entitled women employees in the public sector to apply to work part time on the ground of childcare responsibilities. The bill emphasised that the law could only be applied if a request was made by the female employee and was agreed by the highest authority in the ministry or the organisation concerned (*ibid.*). The Majles proposed a further consultation period for this bill, and during this period newspapers printed a questionnaire for public consultation which put great emphasis on the voluntary and Islamic nature of women's part-time work. The questionnaire stated that 'the proposal presented by the government to the Islamic Consultative Majles on women's part-time work has a voluntary nature' and is intended to address the problem of women's economic exploitation 'within the wrongful atmosphere of the primacy of material needs over the spiritual needs of the family'. It contained questions on the comparative importance of family and work and prevalent childcare arrangements (*Keyhan*, 62).

In March 1983, the bill was returned to the Majles for its second discussion. Some Majles deputies who spoke against the bill preferred to see married women banned from employment in order to 'establish the primacy of the family in the Islamic Republic'. Others agreed that women should be employed in certain professions but were worried that the government would end up supporting scores of part-time women who 'would have nothing to do in the office but knitting' (*Jomhuri Eslami*, 3). The bill was finally ratified by the Majles in May 1983 after the third discussion. The specific terms and conditions of the employee's transfer from full to part-time work was referred to the government (*Keyhan*, 63).

These, however, were referred back to the Majles for ratification by the Council of Guardians. The Majles discussed the terms and conditions of women's part-time work in April 1985. The minimum period of one year and maximum of five years employment was specified for part-time work after which women should revert to full-time duties. The working hours were halved and so was the pay. But annual and maternity leave and pension were preserved in full (*Ettelaat*, 50). Women's part-time work finally became law after almost two and a half years of deliberation. In 1987, the government amended the Civil Service Recruitment Law to add three sub-articles to Article 79 which related to conditions of leaving government employment or redeeming. The amendment was an encouragment to women who worked part-time to leave work (*Zan Ruz*, 50). The second article of relevance to women in the Civil Service Recruitment law concerned financial assistance to families. The Majles ratified the granting of a 'family income supplement' to a male employee whose wife was not in employment, unless her employment was in education, health or medical fields (*ibid.*).

Other measures approved by the government during this period included the reversal of the early post-revolutionary decision to close state nurseries. In 1988, the office of the Prime Minister, Mir Hosein Musavi, issued an instruction to all ministries and government organisations to cooperate with the Health and Environment Office in setting up workplace nurseries (*Zan Ruz*, 51). This was the result of a long campaign by the Islamic women's movement and was only achieved when the right type of nursery teachers, i.e., those with Islamic training, were available to run them. The last two pieces of legislation which passed in relation to women's employment concerned maternity leave and retirement. A law ratified in June 1988 specified women's maternity leave as three months for the first three children and an unspecified length of time as sick leave for additional children (Ghorbani, 1989, p. 432–4). The above Majles legislation and government policies related to women's employment in the formal economic sector, to which I will return later.

Women's non-formal economic activities

Women's employment in the non-formal economic sector was on the increase and it was economically and politically important for the government to present a positive response to this. This aspect of women's productive work was a hidden one since as usual it was not reflected in the official statistics. As was the case in Pahlavi era, the Islamic Republic's official statistics only reflected a fraction of women's income generating activities which took place in the formal economic sector which was a traditionally male preserve.

But the kind of productive activities undertaken by women which were largely left out of official statistics increased after the Revolution for a number of reasons. The war-torn economy gave rise to high inflation, high unemployment and low wages. The participation of economically active men in the war and the displacement of population caused by the war, all created a greater need for women to engage in income generating activities. As industry, agriculture and services were not expanding and in fact production was in decline, most lower-class women had to turn to non-formal economic activities. There is anecdotal evidence that increasing numbers of middle-class women, too, took up different types of domestic production and self-employment. It also became usual for men to have second or even third jobs. Some women employees who found their income declining due to wage decreases, inflation or heavier taxes, took up other economic activities in the evenings or earned extra income by working at home for neighbours and friends (*Zan Ruz*, 49). The census of 1986 considered economically active housewives as almost 34 per cent of the economically active population (Statistical Centre of Iran, 1988b, p. 9).

Another expanding non-formal economic sector was the small production units set up by the state and privately funded charities to create income for lower-class women. Many of these workshops were created to make clothes, linen and other goods for the war front. Others were skill training centres which also generated income for women (*Zan Ruz*, 52). Generation of income from traditional female pursuits such as sewing, knitting, cooking and so on in small production units was encouraged for all ages and especially for married women and widows. None of the reservations expressed about women's employment were applied to non-formal income generating activities. Women's workshops were often visited by dignitaries and foreign guests as a sign of encouragement (*Ettelaat*, 51).

Moreover, women had always generated income by working as domestic servants in urban centres and as carpet weavers and labourers in agriculture and animal husbandry in rural areas (see chapter 5). Anecdotal evidence also suggested that there was an increase in the number of domestic servants in the 1980s, and that as agriculture decreased and migration to towns increased women's income generating activities were encouraged in rural areas (*Keyhan*, 64). The official statistics put the proportion of domestic industry (*sanat khanegi*) at 5.6 per cent of all sedentary households in the country. Carpet and rug weaving accounts for over 77.8 per cent, and as noted in chapter 5, these were overwhelmingly run by women (SCI, 1988b, p. 16). So, although non-formal economic activities were not fully reflected in the official statistics, there was sufficient evidence to suggest that this was an expanding sector of the economy, and that in fact an unknown percentage of women who were deemed inactive by the official statistics were involved in income generating activities of this kind.

The economic imperatives and the political importance of providing for the 'unprotected women' prompted government support for the expansion of women's non-formal productive activity. Government policy was explained by the Minister of Labour and Social Affairs, Mr Sarhadizadeh, when opening an exhibition on women's domestic production: 'A lot of women for a variety of reasons such as divorce and losing their breadwinners in the war and so on needed to earn their living, and since we were having problems in creating work in industry and agriculture to absorb these women into the workforce, the only other way of creating an income for these women was to encourage domestic production and self-employment amongst them' (*Zan Ruz*, 53).

Women's formal economic activities

In relation to the Islamic Republic's policy on women's employment in the formal economic sector, the foregoing description of the employment laws passed by the Majles and the policies of the government demonstrated that to meet the challenge of women's employment, the Islamic state on the whole adopted a middle of the road approach. At policy level, the Islamic Republic acknowledged the value of women's work outside the home, yet it adapted women's employment to meet the needs of the family. Women's employment was directed to those professions which were seen to be compatible with 'woman's nature' and her family responsibilities. This was in line with its policy on women's education.

I will now examine how state policy on employment filtered down to the job market and how it affected women's formal economic activity. In this respect, two crucial aspects of women's employment to consider are recruitment policies and working conditions. To get a taste of obstacles faced by women in seeking employment and in their working conditions, it is useful to refer to surveys published in *Zan Ruz* magazine. A study conducted by the Population and Manpower Department of the Planning and Budget Organisation in April 1984 was of job adverts in two newspapers over a period. Over 50 per cent of the adverts asked for male applicants only. The other half did not specify gender. The study concluded that a woman's chance of getting one of the jobs which were open to both sexes, was one-eighth that of men (*Zan Ruz*, 47). Another study by the same organisation concentrated on results produced by the government recruitment agencies in 1985. This survey concluded that throughout the country only 6 per cent of public sector jobs were open to women and the remaining 94 per cent were open only to men (*ibid.*).

In an interview with the Professional Graduates Recruitment Agency for the Public Sector, the official in charge explained that 'Unfortunately we face enormous difficulties in finding jobs for women. Most organisations with job vacancies do not employ women. In technical subjects there are more jobs available but most of them require male candidates. In the human sciences, the difficulty is that although jobs are open to both men and women, there are a lot of qualified women competing for small number of vacancies' (*ibid.*).

Interviews with a number of women graduates in technical professions who had been unable to find jobs demonstrated the range and depth of obstacles to women's recruitment. The main obstacle was their sex. Most of the women had been rejected without an interview. Of those who had been interviewed, one was chosen for a job but later informed that 'the minister has not agreed with employing a woman' (*ibid.*). Another woman, an architect, was accepted on condition that she wore the *chador* while working at the drawing board, which she had to refuse. A woman engineer was told that although she had the relevant qualifications, she could not be given the job because the job required travelling. Another woman architect was told that her qualifications were relevant but the job must go to a man to reduce male unemployment. Interviews were also conducted with women who had been forced by unemployment to work in areas which were unrelated to their training and expertise. A mechanical engineer had to become a school teacher, a graduate architect trained in Italy had to teach Italian to earn a living, a sociologist with post-graduate specialisation in urban planning had to work in an office nursery (*Zan Ruz*, 50).

Another survey of the recruitment policies of various ministries and government organisations demonstrated how government policy was being implemented. The survey found recruitment policy overtly discriminatory to women in a number of agencies including the Ministry of Roads, Ministry of Housing and Urban Planning, the Housing Bank, the Bank of Industry and Mining, the Ministry of Defence and associated agencies, the Ministry of National Industries and associated agencies, the Treasury, and a number of industrial centres and factories (*Zan Ruz*, 47). Some ministries such as the Ministry of Roads adopted a policy of only recruiting men unless in exceptional circumstances, for which written agreement of the relevant minister was a requirement. The Ministry of Defence and associated agencies, such as the Defence Industry Agency, had stopped recruiting women since 1984. The head of the Political and Ideological Department of the Agency, Hojatoleslam Motebahheri, explained that this policy had been adopted on his recommendation. He believed that 'women's main responsibility is motherhood. There are certain other jobs that women can do such as teaching and nursing. But other than that, I am totally against women's employment' (*ibid.*).

As to industrial centres and factories, the findings of the survey demonstrated totally arbitrary recruitment policies. While one factory had stopped recruiting women since 1985, another recruited women for the same type of job. The official in charge of recruitment policy at the National Industry Agency explained that all recruitment in public sector industries was subject to permission from his department. The policy adopted was that women could be recruited, but priority had to be given to men. Pressed to explain the legal basis of this policy, the official confessed that the policy was not based on law but on 'consensus about what was required by the *shariat*' (*ibid.*). The Treasury had banned women's recruitment since 1979. The justification provided by an official was that it was undesirable for women to be sent on work missions, and that it was against the *shariat* for women to sit with men in meetings (*ibid.*). The above policies on women's recruitment emanating from the highest policy-making authorities were strongly criticised. One sympathetic member of the Majles Commission on Administration and Recruitment argued that 'disagreement with women's employment is disagreement with the Constitution which has granted freedom of employment to both men and women' (*Zan Ruz*, 50).

Another member emphasised that 'the only legal prohibition on women's employment is in judgeship. There is no other job that a woman cannot legally do' (*ibid.*). The deputy head of the Administration and Recruitment Agency, Mohandes Ekram Jafari, insisted that government criteria for recruitment was selection of the best candidate and that gender should not be a factor. He put existing differences in implementation down to 'management styles' and agreed to look into the matter further (*ibid.*). Although the above examples of women's recruitment problems are too limited in quantity and extent to allow a reliable assessment of women's employment chances on the whole, nevertheless they were important indicators of the depth of prejudice against employing women.

As to working conditions for women in the public sector, a *Zan Ruz* survey in 1981 indicated that the most 'frequently stated reasons given by women for working were financial need, insecurity of marriage and the need to feel socially useful'. The most frequently mentioned problems included lack of workplace nurseries, long and unsuitable working hours and lack of promotion opportunities for women (*Zan Ruz*, 54). Another survey conducted in 1984 concluded that lack of nursery provision was still the main source of problems for women employees, but housing problems and low pay had become more of a problem compared with 1981 (*Zan Ruz*, 49). Women often protested about discriminatory attitudes at work. In education, where the largest number of women in the public sector worked, men were still occupying most of the decision-making jobs. Women teachers were concentrated at the levels of primary and intermediate schools while male teachers occupied the majority of high school teaching posts (*Ettelaat*, 52). Despite women's substantial role and input into the teaching profession, out of seventy teachers chosen across the country as 'Outstanding Teachers' in 1981 only seven were women (*Zan Ruz*, 55). In a survey on attitudes conducted by a woman's magazine, male employees were found to consider secretarial work 'degrading because it was still considered as a woman's job' (*Rah Zeinab*, 2). Women lawyers faced even worse prejudices. Law courts often refused to admit women lawyers, and female students on law courses were prevented from receiving the same practical training in the courts as their male colleagues. Most women lawyers ended up in administrative jobs with no promotion prospects (*Zan Ruz*, 56).

The official statistics reflected the pattern of women's activities in the formal economic sector. Like modernisation, Islamisation, too, was not a homogeneous process affecting women in a total and consistent way (see chapter 5). Official statistics showed a decline in women's economic activity from 12.9 per cent in 1976 to 8.1 in 1986 for the whole country (SCI, 1988c, p. 65). But within this overall decline, the pattern of women's activity and their representation in various occupational categories varied considerably. The worst decline occurred in the rural sector, where the rate of women's economic activity in the formal sector decreased from 16.5 per cent in 1976 to 7.9 in 1986.

It has been argued that the shifting pattern of rural women's economic activity was only partly due to the policies of the Islamic Republic as: 'Rural Iran was well prepared for this shift before 1979, after two decades of so-called modernisation, economic development and Western-type education had shifted the boundaries of the traditional spheres in the village to such an extent that women could be pushed to the fringes of their world without much resistance' (Friedl, 1992). But urban women experienced a much smaller decline by moving from 9 per cent in 1976 to 8.3 per cent in 1986. Moreover, lower-class women seemed to be more affected than middle-class women. In industry, there was a sharp decline in the proportion of women factory workers, from 20 per cent in 1976 to 7 in 1983 (Moghadam, 1988, p. 16). But since this was accompanied by a high increase in the size of the public sector, it is possible that the overall decline in the economic activity of urban women was not as high as these figures suggested.

Due to the much expanded public sector in the Islamic Republic (SCI, 1988d, p. 19) and increase in the population of urban centres as a result of increased birth and migration rates, the percentage of women employed by the state increased from 16 per cent in 1976 to 28 per cent in 1983 (*ibid.*). Since this increase mainly benefited women with secondary school and tertiary education, it may have reflected the state policy of replacing highly educated secular women by those with lower levels of education, who were regarded as more sympathetic to Islam (*ibid.*). But alongside this upward trend, unemployment amongst both men and women increased substantially in the eighties (SCI, 1988c, p. 65). Another accompanying trend was the steady proportion of women categorised as economically inactive housewives, whose numbers did not seem to change from 68.7 per cent of the total female population over 10 years in 1976 to 68.6 in 1986 (SCI, 1980 and 1988b).

As to women's employment in government departments and specialised occupations, as explained before, state policy came under severe criticism from the opposition faction of the Islamic women's movement. Despite the increasing rate of women's employment in the public sector, a comparison with men was not favourable. While between 1976 to 1986 the annual rate of employment in government departments was 2.5 per cent for both sexes combined, it was minus 1.7 for women (*Zan Ruz*, 47). Moreover, as a whole, men were more evenly distributed across the occupations in the urban sector than women, and only a tiny proportion of women worked in occupations of an educational, scientific, technical or specialist nature; the second largest female concentration was 13.4 per cent in production and transport, and the third and fourth were 8.6 per cent in administration and clerical, and 5.3 per cent in services (SCI, 1988b, p. 9). Women's representation in the largest category was highly skewed towards 'female occupations' such as teaching and nursing (*ibid.*). Men had the highest representation in production and transport, agriculture, sales and trades, and scientific, technical and specialised occupations, and on the whole, were spread more evenly amongst all categories. Men were also better represented in high ranking jobs. Only 0.26 per cent of women were involved in these types of jobs (*ibid.*).

Contrary to many expectations, then, the Islamic state did not ban women's employment outside the home. State legislation did encourage women to stay at home; but what proved more inhibiting to women's employment was male prejudice and negative attitudes operating at the local level. The state was more interested in imposing a particular gender division of labour at work than pushing women out of the labour force altogether. Even on this, however, the state was not united and the fierce debate about women's work between various factions of the Islamic elite resulted in *ad hoc* policies on female employment. Meanwhile, women continued to use the opportunities open to them for supporting themselves and their families and contributing to the economy.

10 Policing the family

Once the Islamic family was linked to the Islamic nation it had to be socially protected. The construction of women's double role at home and in society entailed both hope and danger for the survival of the Islamic Republic. Women's participation in national processes was encouraged as a means of sustaining the state's popular support, legitimising its Islamisation policies and counteracting the influence of what was defined as Western conceptions of women and family. However, women's social participation also entailed fear of breakdown of Islamic morality and disorder. For the Islamic state, Western society epitomised all that was wrong in a society which permitted free association between men and women: destruction of the family, low rates of marriage, high rates of divorce, low status of motherhood, adultery, illegitimate children, prostitution, homosexuality, AIDS, and so on (*Ettelaat*, 53).

If the survival of the Islamic Republic depended on the social and political participation of women, then its demise had to be prevented by protecting the Islamic family from the side effects of women's social integration. The Islamic state had to devise a strategy to keep women active in society while protecting the Islamic family. The recipe for the protection of women and the family included severe punishment for adultery, gender segregation in social activity and public space, strict dress codes for women, the introduction of gender division in education and employment, and adaptation of women's social participation to the requirements of the Islamic family. Some of these measures were discussed before in the previous chapters: we noted the implementation of sex segregation and gender division in education and employment, and how almost every aspect of women's activity outside the home was subjected to rules and codes which checked its effect upon the household. Other policies adopted to guard the family against 'social evils' were of a more direct and forceful nature. These included imposition of *hejab*, gender segregation of public space and punishment for adultery.

Gender segregation

Many forms of gender segregation, including *hejab*, were deeply rooted traditions in Iran. The Pahlavi era had by no means eradicated these practices totally, and the practice of *hejab*, in particular, had a cultural significance which went much deeper than state policy could ever go (Milani, 1992). Pre-revolutionary Iranian society was indeed still quite conservative in relation to the integration of the sexes. The mainstream education system was segregated and co-education was limited to a small number of private schools at nursery and primary levels, and universities. Although men and women could mix freely at work, in the streets and in other public spaces, women were often restricted by acceptable codes of behaviour, dress and speech.

However, at the same time, the practice of gender segregation was considered to be the hallmark of backwardness by most twentieth-century political ideologies. The Islamic Republic did not introduce gender segregation and *hejab* as new concepts to the Iranians. Using force to regulate women's clothes, too, was not a new phenomenon. Reza Shah's forceful removal of women's *hejab* in the 1930s was part of the contemporary history of gender relations, and folk stories of the removal of women's *hejab* (*kashf hejab*) were still being passed on to younger generations by women who had personal experience of it (see chapter 3). But what came as a surprise in post-revolutionary society, was the Islamic Republic's reversal of the twentieth-century trend of gender desegregation and its praise of gender segregation as a signifier of Islamic modernity. *Hejab* and public segregation of men and women were being constructed by the Islamic state as a superior form of gender relation on the ground that these practices made it possible for women to rock the cradle with one hand and build the nation with the other. The Islamic state's enforcement of *hejab* and male–female segregation was giving these traditional practices a new political dimension.

Imposition of hejab

The process of imposition of *hejab* was a long and difficult one. It took place in two stages. The first stage was targeting of the public sector and imposition of *hejab* on women employees and clients of government departments and public services. The second stage was imposition of *hejab* on women on a wider scale in public or private whenever they were in the presence of men other than their kinsmen.

The initial attempts of the Islamic leadership during the life time of the

Provisional Government to impose *hejab* on women were discussed earlier (see chapter 7). It started with Ayatollah Khomeini's advice to female state employees to wear *hejab* at work, which was later withdrawn as a result of enormous protests by women. The question of *hejab* continued to remain on the agenda and was drawn into the struggle for political power between different factions of the post-revolutionary leadership. The collapse of the Provisional Government, which increased the power of the hardline clergy within the state, prepared the political atmosphere for the further Islamisation of women's appearance. Ayatollah Khomeini's decree on 'administrative revolution' was followed by the enforcement of *hejab* on women employees of the state. The increasing suppression of freedom to express political dissent, the physical intimidation of peaceful protest gatherings by gangs of *hezbollahis*, and the increasing impotence of the moderates within the state, made the imposition of *hejab* possible at this time.

The first stage of the imposition of *hejab* was well on its way by the summer of 1980 when Ayatollah Ghoddusi, the Chief Revolutionary Prosecutor, issued instructions to the public sector warning them that they should 'either enforce *hejab* on their women employees or sack them ... The presence of women employees without *hejab* in offices will not be tolerated' (*Ettelaat*, 54). This was followed by the official definition of *hejab* given by the Council of the Revolution as 'covering of the head and all of the body except for the circle of the face and hands from the wrist' (*Bamdad*, 3). During the next year or so, the state concentrated on consolidating compulsory *hejab* for working women. Women employees who resisted compulsory *hejab* or did not comply fully with it were suspended or sacked. The 'administrative revolution' led to substantial short-term unemployment among middle-class professional women (*The Guardian*, 2).

The next step was to extend the imposition of *hejab* to female users of public services. Women not wearing Islamic clothing were refused entry to public premises; they were also banned from travelling with the national airline without *hejab* (*Ettelaat*, 55). The private sector was the next target and private offices and factories were instructed by the state to observe the Islamic *hejab* code for their female employees. The harassing of women without *hejab* by Islamic zealots continued in the streets and the government was forced every now and then to denounce 'those who take the law into their hands' (*Keyhan*, 65). But despite official discouragement of harassment, the IRP's organised mobs did the state's job for it and by the spring of 1981 it had become almost impossible for women to appear in public without a headscarf and not risk verbal abuse or physical attack.

The dismissal of President Banisadr in June 1981, which resulted in violent confrontation between his supporters and the revolutionary guards, was the final blow to coalition rule and freedom of political activity (see chapter 7). This prepared the scene for the hardline clergy to exercise their increased political power. The first stage of the imposition of *hejab* was almost completed and state policy on *hejab* was entering its second phase. In the run up to the events of June 1981, the IRP organised a massive women's rally on the occasion of the birthday of the Prophet's daughter, Fatemeh (which had become the official women's day) which issued a resolution asking for 'total and complete adherence to Islamic values by all sections of Iranian women'. It condemned those 'who dishonour the blood of the martyrs of Islam by adhering to the corrupt values of the previous regime' (*Ettelaat*, 56). The IRP also spread rumours that the Majles was planning to pass a law on Islamic *hejab* to make it a punishable offence for women to appear outside their homes without *hejab*. This was strongly denied by Azam Taleghani, the moderate woman deputy (*Ettelaat*, 57). This created an impression of popular support for *hejab* and legitimised the labelling of opponents of *hejab* as 'counter-revolutionaries' (*Iran Times*, 2).

The Bureau for Combating Corruption stepped up its activities in response to 'popular demand' for *hejab* by closing down a number of parks in Tehran for 'lack of observance of Islamic code of conduct by some women'. It warned the 'sisters who intend to use the parks to observe Islamic *hejab* or be prevented from entering the parks' (*Keyhan*, 66). The authorities announced that women without *hejab* were banned from entering or leaving the airports (*Keyhan*, 67) and the national airline, Iran Air, asked women employees in its offices overseas to wear *hejab* (*Keyhan*, 68). It also announced that the import of all types of make up and fashion products were banned (*Keyhan*, 69). The beginning of the school year was an opportunity for the authorities to design an Islamic uniform for school girls. This included a large headscarf, a long and loose grey overall and trousers. The Ministry of Education made it compulsory for school girls to wear this uniform (*Keyhan*, 70). The anti-corruption court issued instructions to private companies, threatening them with prosecution if their female employees did not observe *hejab*. It defined *hejab* much more strictly, and for the first time officially asked women to wear a strict Islamic *hejab* (*Ettelaat*, 58). From then on the large headscarf and long thick loose overalls and trousers became the order of the day for women in the office or the street. Those who did not comply risked abuse, attack or arrest. By the end of 1981, the Islamic state had managed fully to impose the Islamic *hejab* on women.

Segregation of public space

The policy of Islamisation of women's clothes developed in parallel with public segregation of the sexes. Public segregation covered two broad areas: first, the sexual segregation of public space; and second, the segregation of social activities. With regard to the mixing of sexes in public, the Islamic Republic concentrated its efforts on a number of areas. Some of the first public spaces to be segregated were the beaches. The way was opened for the revolutionary guards and local fanatics to enforce segregation of public beaches which was called upon by the Ayatollah Khomeini.

Public resistance and protest did not get far with the Islamic regime. Public beaches were divided up by wooden and cloth panels and the best and largest beaches were allocated to men. Women were gradually forced to give up wearing swimming costumes and swim in their Islamic uniforms comprising of headscarves and loose thick overalls. Every summer newspapers reported women being drowned for shortage of female life guards. There were also constant reports of the flogging of men and women who breached the segregation code. Many of these were families, relatives or friends using a mixed beach in a private villa (*Keyhan Havai*, 46). Segregation was rapidly extended to other areas. Hairdressers were the next target, and those not acting quickly enough to segregate were threatened with confiscation of income (*Bamdad*, 4).

But the Islamic Republic did not succeed in segregating public transport. Many attempts were made to segregate the bus and mini-bus services but none proved long-lasting. The segregation of bus services in Shiraz had to be abandoned due to strong public protest. Newspapers were inundated by protest calls from the public: couples had been forced to take separate buses when going shopping, a mother accompanying her sick son to hospital had been forced to travel on a separate bus, and so on (*Keyhan*, 71). The government, however, did not give up the idea and experimental projects on segregation were regularly put into practice (*Zan Ruz*, 57). On the other hand, the segregation of public places for political meetings and rallies, conferences, lectures and exhibitions was easily achieved and pictures of separate rows of men and women sitting in conference halls became commonplace. Parties, celebrations, wedding ceremonies and funerals, too, had to have separate sections for men and women. In short, the physical presence of men and women in the same space was strictly controlled, and except for limited professional, educational and political reasons, and under strictly supervised conditions, mixing of men and women became a matter for investigation and punishment.

Segregation of social activities was another aspect of state policy on gender segregation. It was applied to employment, education, services and sport. With regard to sport, segregation led to the near annihilation of women's sport (*Keyhan*, 72). The negative official attitude towards women's sport resulted in an unbalanced allocation of resources to women's sports in comparison with men's. Women, who had been banned from practising in open air sports grounds, were not allocated a sufficient number of covered grounds in which to practice and maintain standards. The most sophisticated and well-resourced stadiums were allocated to men. A shortage of female instructors was another problem. Women who had been largely coached by men before, now had to go without a coach or be instructed by less experienced female instructors. Women were banned from 'masculine' sports such as wrestling and weight lifting on the grounds that 'they spoil women's figures and change their natural state' (*Keyhan*, 73). Mountain climbing, a favourite sport among young women, was banned for women by the Federation of Mountain Climbing (*Keyhan*, 74). Segregation of skiing created many obstacles and hazards for the keen women skiers of north Tehran.

In short, women's sport was drained of life by lack of attention and resources because, as stated by Davud Mirshams, head of the Physical Education Organisation,

> In the Islamic Republic, women don't have time for sport. Women's main responsibility is housekeeping and child rearing and they can get a lot of exercise from doing these. The circumstances in our society at the moment do not allow women to spend their time on sport or on campaigning for it. The country has other priorities than spending money on women's sport facilities. (*Keyhan London*, 7)

Women's resistance to hejab *and segregation*

But the full imposition of *hejab* and sex segregation was not the end of the matter. Total control of male–female liaison was not an issue that could be dealt with once and for all and even though the Islamic uniform had been fully imposed, individual taste and pursuit of fashion could not be fully suppressed. Those women who had been forced into segregation and *hejab* used every opportunity to defy it. Young men and women were still appearing in public together. Some were even beating the Islamic regime at its own game by claiming that they were engaged in *sigheh*. Many women mocked their imposed *hejab* by showing strings of hair or leaving traces of make up on their faces.

The state policy on *hejab* and the forceful method of its imposition was opposed by sections of the Islamic women's movement from the start.

One of their main objections to it was women's negative psychological reaction to the forceful imposition of *hejab*. Although the problems caused by the forceful imposition of *hejab* affected women across all classes and categories, albeit to different degrees, nevertheless it was the upper and middle-class urban woman whose 'negative psychological reaction' to imposed *hejab* was articulated into a power relationship with the Islamic state (Najmabadi, 1989). The imposition of *hejab* signified a battle between women and the state over the control of the individual's body and personal space. This battle was taken up by those women who did not identify with the Islamic cause. It was these women and this power struggle which presented the most serious threat to the legitimacy of the Islamic Republic's policy of *hejab* as the protector of the Islamic family. The fashionable shapes and colours of their Islamic uniforms and their mildly made-up faces and thin tights, made the upper and middle-class women of the large cities a distinguishable cast. This group of women were identified by the authorities as violators of the spirit of segregation rules and were targeted for re-education and punishment. The rest of the 1980s was spent on combating the individualistic appearance of middle-class women and breaking their resistance to join the ranks of millions of anonymous Iranian women clad head to toe in black *chador* or covered by grey loose uniforms. The new term of 'bad-*hejab* women' was invented to describe women whose *hejab* did not adequately cover them and make them anonymous enough.

To maintain the imposition of gender segregation and deal with 'bad-*hejab* women', the state employed a number of methods. One of these was creating an atmosphere of fear of the '*hezbollah*' in the 'bad-*hejab* women'. Periodically, mobs of *hezbollahis* invaded the shopping parades of wealthy Tehran districts and attacked women who were wearing fashionable overalls and men wearing short sleeve shirts or ties. (*Keyhan*, 75). These attacks frightened women and prevented them from making a liberal interpretation of *hejab* rules. Every now and then, women were threatened and told either to tighten up *hejab* or face the wrath of the populace (*Keyhan*, 76). On the whole, however, the authorities preferred to keep control over punishment of 'bad-*hejab* women' and they discouraged mob attacks (*Keyhan*, 77). The issue of *hejab* was kept alive by demonstrations against 'bad-*hejab* women'. Such demonstrations, on a scale worth reporting by newspapers, took place on many occasions including March 1982, August 1984 and November 1985. But the main method of keeping control of *hejab* and public segregation was through law and the deployment of special patrols on the streets. Women's *hejab* became legally compulsory in 1983 when the Majles passed the Islamic Punishment Law (Flogging) 1983. This law specified seventy-four lashes as punishment for lack of strict observance of Islamic *hejab* by women (*Keyhan*, 78).

Furthermore, after the ratification of a new anti-corruption programme by the High Council of Judiciary in the summer of 1984, a special patrol was organised to deal with violations of *hejab* and the segregation rule in public (*Keyhan*, 79). The Anti-Corruption Patrol, which consisted of contingents of two men and two women, patrolled the streets stopping women who did not look anonymous enough, to either give them a lecture on how to improve their *hejab* or to arrest them. There were a variety of methods of prosecution for those who defied *hejab* and segregation. Local revolutionary committees and the Public Prosecutor's Office were both involved in punishing the offenders, who were often treated in an arbitrary and summary manner. Victims were detained for short or long periods and only released after paying substantial amounts. Sometimes revolutionary guards and Anti-Corruption Patrol administered the punishment of flogging on the spot in public.

But despite their obsessive control of *hejab*, the authorities were still dissatisfied with their success in dealing with 'bad-*hejab* women'. In 1986, Ayatollah Khoiniha, the Chief Public Prosecutor, said in an interview:

> I believe that the question of *hejab* should be left to the people to deal with. We obviously have not solved the problem by patrolling the streets. How many patrols should we allocate to this? And how many arrests for *hejab* would the resources of the Public Prosecutor's Office allow to take place everyday? We should pass a law to allow people to deal with the problem themselves. (*Ettelaat*, 59)

In 1987, Hojatoleslam Gohari, the head of the Public Prosecutor's Office in Tehran disclosed in an interview that there had been 165 arrests of 'bad-*hejab* women' in one week leading to punishments ranging from flogging to two years' imprisonment. He attributed this increase to the hot weather (*Ettelaat*, 60). Hojatoleslam Mohtashami, the Minister of Interior, raised the issue of 'increase in lack of strict observance of *hejab* in public and private (*Zan Ruz*, 58). Hojatoleslam Rafsanjani proposed a new punishment for those who defied *hejab* and segregation. He alluded to the existence of a Majles bill which proposed the creation of special camps for the re-habilitation of 'bad-*hejab* women', saying that 'These people will be detained there for 2, 3, 5 months or even a year to be educated. They will have to work as well. They will be charged for their stay there since such people are from well-to-do classes' (*Ettelaat*, 61).

But it was later disclosed that this proposal did not gain support in the Majles. He also talked about a new government initiative on *hejab* which made employment difficult for people with previous *hejab*-related convictions (*Zan Ruz*, 58). In January 1988, the Ministry of the Interior announced that 'in order to co-ordinate the actions of those responsible for tackling the problem of *hejab*, the government has approved the appropriate regulation' (*Zan Ruz*, 59). The regulation, which was disclosed later, was based on the Islamic Punishment Law (Flogging) 1983. This law had made it a punishable offence (by seventy-four lashes) for women who did not observe strict *hejab* in public. The new regulation did not talk about women who did not wear *hejab* women, as the possibility of any women daring to appear in public without *hejab* was very remote indeed, but it addressed the 'bad-*hejab* women' and extended the punishment of seventy-four lashes to them. It also defined what made a woman's *hejab* a bad one.

The list included: uncovered head, showing of hair, make-up, uncovered arms and legs, thin and see-through clothes and tights, tight clothes such as trousers without an overall over them, and clothes bearing foreign words, signs or pictures. The importers and traders of the latter type of clothes were also threatened with fines, imprisonment and flogging. The clothes women could wear in public were limited to the standard Islamic uniform of long, thick and loose overall, trousers, thick stockings and large headscarves folded in the front to cover every string of hair. The preferred colours were also specified as dark blue, black, grey and brown (*Zan Ruz*, 60).

Towards the end of the first decade of the Islamic Republic, the latest upsurge of pro-*hejab* campaign elicited exceptional vocal opposition from some factions of the Islamic women's movement. *Zan Ruz* magazine wrote an editorial ridiculing the periodic attempts of the authorities to eliminate the 'bad-*hejab*': "It is as if we have solved every other problem and 'bad-*hejab* women' are the only problem left. As if the problem of *hejab* is even more fundamental than struggling against imperialism, zionism, combatting inflation, food hoarding, bribery and so on. ... the campaign for *hejab* is in fact no more than a ploy to obstruct the path of women's growth in society" (*Zan Ruz*, 61).

The first decade of the Islamic Republic's policy on *hejab* and sex segregation, then, ended as it began with divided opinions, disillusionment and resistance.

Islamic punishment of secular gender relations

While *hejab* and sex segregation were familiar concepts for Iranians, the Islamic Republic's anti-corruption measures and the concept of legal retribution, or *ghesas*, as legitimate methods of policing the family, were somewhat novel developments within twentieth-century Iranian political ideologies. The most extreme measure taken by the Islamic state to protect the Islamic family, was to make sex outside marriage an offence punishable by death. Adultery and homosexuality had always been considered punishable offences in the Iranian law. But the treatment of adultery and methods of punishment assumed new dimensions in the Islamic Republic. As the family was turned into a political institution, the violation of its sanctity became a political crime. The importance of Islamic gender relation to the establishment of Islamic society required heavy punishment for its offenders.

Anti-corruption measures

The process of development of the Islamic Republic's policy on sex-related crimes was started immediately after the Revolution by the newly formed revolutionary courts, and culminated in the ratification of the Retribution Law (Ghanun Ghesas) by the Majles three years later. The establishment of revolutionary committees and courts was discussed earlier (see chapter 7). These grass-roots institutions were created as a safeguard against the political and military counter-revolution. But soon the revolutionary courts, which had sprung up all over the country and were run by local clerics and their militia, extended their remit to protect the Revolution against the social and ideological 'counter-revolution'. The revolutionary courts began a crusade against the 'counter-revolutionary efforts of the superpowers to divert the course of the Islamic Revolution through the spread of corruption in society' (*Ettelaat*, 62).

The concept of 'Corruption' contained adultery, prostitution, homosexuality, drug trafficking, alcohol consumption, and common crimes such as murder and theft. The anti-corruption zeal of the revolutionary courts and their pioneering methods of punishment shocked the world when reports of executions, hanging, stoning and flogging of women and men for sex offences appeared in internal and foreign newspapers. By the summer of 1980, there were regular reports of such punishments by revolutionary courts in most provincial towns. In that period alone in the southern town of Kerman several married women were executed for adultery (*Zenaye Mohseneh*) and two women and two men were stoned to death on charges of prostitution and homosexuality. Seven men were sent to the firing squad in various parts of the country in the same period for drug trafficking, sexual offences and murder (*The Guardian*, 3).

As these practices spread to most provinces, revolutionary courts became the target of severe criticisms both by the moderate faction of the state and by the opposition. Ayatollah Khomeini's son, Ahmad, condemned the execution of prostitutes on the grounds that 'until society is fully Islamic and all women are secure and protected, Islamic punishment of prostitutes should not be implemented. . . . There may be a danger that an honourable mother is forced to turn to prostitution to feed her children' (*Bamdad*, 5).

Azam Taleghani protested that women should be given an opportunity to shed the corruption of the Pahlavi era from their minds and bodies before being punished for adultery and prostitution. She argued that women should themselves combat 'drug addiction, prostitution and helplessness which are the inheritance of the hated monarchist regime' (*Keyhan*, 80). Even Ayatollah Khalkhali, much feared for his summary executions of officials of the Shah's regime, did not condone the execution of adulterous women (*Keyhan*, 81). But the practice continued, since Ayatollah Khomeini remained sympathetic towards Islamic punishment of sex-related offences, and political expedience prevented the hardline clergy from curtailing the activities of the grass-roots organisations. Khomeini silenced Islamic objections by supporting the revolutionary courts which punished sex-offenders. With the establishment of the Bureau for Combatting Corruption, the definition of corruption was extended to cover a whole range of social and cultural activities such as gambling and games like chess and snooker, most types of entertainment, films, theatre, music, art, mixing of men and women, and wearing of un-Islamic clothes by men and women. The Bureau set out to cleanse the post-revolutionary society of the manifestations of 'Westernised' gender relations. In its inauguration statement the Bureau made the following statement:

> The internal and external agents of colonisation have encouraged sin and have spread corruption in our Islamic society. To implement its plans, imperialism has employed the female sex as its agent. It has transformed the highest beings on earth [women] who are the source of creation of prophets, *emaman*, martyrs and other men of knowledge and courage, into 'liberated' women who are the companions of men in passion and corruption. . . . Those Islamic societies which have fallen for this conspiracy have lost their politics, economy and most of all their social and familial principles to the West. (*Ettelaat*, 62)

It promised to do its best to eradicate 'free relationship between men and women', to prevent 'the violation of our girls who are the honour and the future mothers of the country' and combat 'the institution of prostitution, and rid society of all sinful manifestations of colonialism' (*ibid.*). The Bureau adopted a carrot and stick policy towards prostitution. It announced that prostitutes who chose to repent would be assisted to marry and 'return to the warm embrace of family life', or be provided with jobs in specially set up workshops. Those who chose to 'continue their wicked ways, causing perversion of the country's youth and betraying the blood of the martyrs of the Revolution, would be punished by revolutionary courts' (*Keyhan*, 82). The red light districts in cities were destroyed. In Tehran, this led to clashes in which a number of prostitutes were killed and many were injured. Social workers in Tehran's Welfare Centre for

Prostitutes were accused of assisting prostitutes and attacked. The efforts of the Association of Social Workers to obtain legal support came to nothing and the operations of the Welfare Centre came to a halt (*Ayandegan*, 5). In Hamedan, nineteen prostitutes married local men who volunteered to save them. In Tehran, four revolutionary guards married prostitutes arrested in a brothel (*Keyhan*, 83).

Other sites of purification by the Bureau included restaurants, clubs and hotels. Discotheques and bars were closed down. Scores of young people were arrested in restaurants for 'sinful socialising'. Hotels were warned and checks were made to prevent the admission of unmarried couples. Clubs were closed for being 'dens of corruption'. The next targets were private parties and weddings, which were raided at random. The hosts and guests were taken to local Committees, and often flogged or fined after being charged with consumption of alcohol, participating in mixed parties and wearing un-Islamic clothes. Occupants of cars were asked for marriage certificates and arrested if they could not give legitimate reasons for being in mixed company.

Soon it became too dangerous to mix with the opposite sex in public or private. Sexual and political 'corruption' were considered as dual dimensions of the imperialist conspiracy against Islam. Hojatoleslam Rafsanjani explained this philosophy and advised the revolutionaries that:

> Today in our country Marxists, monarchists, nationalists, liberals, hypocrites [Mojahedin Khalgh], prostitutes, sinners, corrupt capitalists, black marketeers and smugglers are all related and feed on each other. ... The revolutionary committees should be aware of the different aspects of corruption in our society to be able to annihilate it. (*Ettelaat*, 63)

'Sexual corruption', indecency, adultery and homosexuality were among the charges regularly attributed to both Islamic and secular political opponents (*Keyhan*, 84). Officials of the Pahlavi regime were charged with corruption. The charge of prostitution was brought against the Shah's 65-year-old minister of education, Mrs Farrokhru Parsa, who was later executed (*Bamdad*, 6). Female opponents caught after the June 1981 events (see chapter 7), faced hideous tortures of a sexual nature. The catalogue of the physical and mental torture of women political prisoners included molestation, gang rape, deflowering of virgins on the eve of their execution, execution of pregnant women and girls as young as 9 years old, and so on (*Women and Struggle in Iran*, 2, p. 2).

Although anti-corruption measures continued as official policy in the Islamic Republic, their implementation required rationalisation, a process which began after the hardline clergy consolidated their power in 1981. In May 1981, the revolutionary courts were prohibited from dealing with corruption cases. A special branch of the revolutionary courts was set up as anti-corruption courts (*dadgah monkarat*) to deal with offences related to sex, drugs and other corruption charges. They operated under the supervision of the High Council of Judiciary (*Keyhan*, 85). Furthermore, the activities of the Bureau were curtailed and anti-corruption activities were assigned to revolutionary guards who were issued with identity cards (*ibid.*). It was also announced that those who made wrongful accusations against others would be prosecuted (*Keyhan*, 86). In this way, the state attempted to bring the numerous revolutionary law enforcement agencies under some control, and be seen to respond to the accusations of lack of individual safety and security in the country.

The next step was taken in 1984, when the revolutionary courts were abolished. The anti-corruption courts were brought under the cover of the Ministry of Justice. This resulted in a decrease in the number of convictions on sex-related offences due to legal obstructions. The deputy public prosecutor, Hojatoleslam Tabatabai, complained that 'the courts are often unable to convict adulterers because public prosecution of such offences is not allowed under the present law, and unless the offenders are sued by an individual or individuals, the offence would go without punishment'. He demanded the passage of a law by the Majles which established the supremacy of the *shariat* over the penal law (*Keyhan*, 87).

The law of retribution

The appearance of the Retribution Law (Ghanun Ghesas) on the statute book, and the gradual eradication of the Pahlavi law of Public Punishment, further rationalised the Islamic treatment of sex-related offenses. The Retribution Law was first proposed in 1980, when Ayatollah Beheshti was the head of the Supreme Court, on the basis of Article 158 (b) of the Constitution which instructed 'preparation of bills on judicial matters appropriate to [the form of government of the] Islamic Republic'. But it was not fully ratified until July 1982 and it took at least another two years to remove legal impediments to its full implementation. Of course, different aspects of the Retribution Law had been put into practice for some time without a legal basis by revolutionary courts and later by the anti-corruption courts. But the application of the Retribution Law found its appropriate legal base only after it was passed by the Majles in 1982.

The Retribution Law replaced parts of the Public Punishment Law (1924). It differed from the latter in a number of ways. The Retribution Law concentrated on two main types of offences: murder and bodily harm caused by one person to another; and sex-related offences (*Enghelab Eslami*, 2). The first part of the Retribution Law which dealt with murder and bodily harm, was based on the concept of punishment by retaliation.

This was a fundamental departure from the secular laws it replaced. Contrary to the Public Punishment Law, the concept of punishment under the Retribution Law was no longer based on the notion of 'society' versus 'individual' but rather on that of 'individuals and families' versus other 'individuals and families'. The core of the Retribution Law consisted of the conception that murder and injury of one person by another should be punished by retaliation of exactly the same nature, administered by the injured person or the family of the injured or murdered person, or their representative. There should also take place an exchange of blood money (*diyeh*) between the family of the murder victim and the perpetrator, who is being killed in retaliation. The first part of the Retribution Law consisted of 80 articles which covered retribution of murder by men and women; retribution of injury by men and women; and testimony to murder or injury by men and women. The second part of the Retribution Law which dealt with crimes of a sexual nature, defined five types of sexual interaction as crime and set out the due Islamic punishment for them. These were *zena*, male homosexual act (*lavat*), female homosexual act (*mosahegheh*), pimping (*ghiadat*), and wrongful attribution of *zena* or lavat to a person (*ghazaf*). It also specified punishment for alcohol consumption (*moskerat*). The punishments included execution, stoning, flogging, exile and shaving of hair. The analysis of 199 Articles of the Retribution Law demonstrated the kind of gender relations it aimed to reinforce in Islamic society. At least seven main observations can be made. First, the body of a woman was worth half that of a man as reflected in the clauses dealing with murder:

Article 5: If a Muslim man wilfully murders a Muslim woman, he will be sentenced to *ghesas* but the woman's guardian must pay the murderer one half of his blood money before he receives *ghesas*.

Article 6: If a Muslim woman wilfully murders a Muslim man, she will be sentenced only to *ghesas* and will not be entitled to blood money.

Article 46: If a man murders a woman, the guardians of the blood [the family of the victim] has the choice of either carrying out the *ghesas* and paying the murderer one half of the full amount of the blood money, or to refrain from *ghesas* and instead demand the woman's blood money from the murderer.

Second, the judgement of a woman was valued as half that of a man as reflected in the clauses dealing with testimony:

Article 33: (a) A case of wilful murder is proved only on the basis of testimony by two righteous men; (b) A case of semi-wilful or unintentional murder is proved on the basis of testimony by two righteous men, or [testimony] of one righteous man and two righteous women, or that of one righteous man and the plaintiff's oath.

Article 91: Adultery is proved on the basis of testimony by four righteous men, or three righteous men and two righteous women, whether it leads to flogging or stoning.

Article 92: In cases where adultery would lead to flogging, it could also be proven on the basis of the testimony by two righteous men or four righteous women.

Article 128: Women's testimony by itself or accompanied by one man's testimony does not lead to punishment for consumption of alcoholic drink.

Article 167: Pimping [*ghiadat*] is proven by testimony of two righteous men.

Third, a woman's reproductive function took priority over her life:

Article 50: A pregnant woman who is sentenced to *ghesas* must not receive it before she has given birth. After the delivery, if *ghesas* could lead to the child's death, then it must be postponed until the danger is over.

Article 90: If a woman who does not have a husband becomes pregnant, she shall not be subjected to punishment because of pregnancy unless her having committed adultery is proved by one of the methods stipulated in this law.

Article 103: The punishment of stoning shall not be enforced on a woman during pregnancy or labour, nor shall it be enforced after the delivery if the infant has not a guardian and there is fear of his [perishing]. However, if a guardian is found then the punishment shall be enforced on her.

Article 104: If the enforcing of punishment of the lash on a pregnant or nursing woman could cause damage to the fetus or to suckling, then the enforcing of the punishment shall be delayed.

Fourth, while the woman was totally associated with her unborn child, the total control of the life of the child when born belonged to the father and paternal grandfather:

Article 16: If an offspring is murdered by the father or paternal grandfather, *ghesas* is not due, but blood money should be paid to the child's inheritors.

Fifth, adultery by married men and women attracted the harshest of all punishments:

Article 100: Adultery leads to death by hanging in the following cases: (1) adultery with consanguineous kin with whom marriage is not permitted; (2) adultery with a step-mother; (3) adultery between a non-Muslim [man] and a Muslim woman; (4) rape and adultery by force leads to the killing of the adulterer who has forcefully committed it.

Adultery leads to death by stoning in following cases: (1) adultery by a *mohseneh* woman [a young woman who has a permanent husband with whom copulation has occurred and whose husband regularly sleeps with her] with an adult man. Note 1: A *mohseneh* woman's adultery with an underage man would lead to lashing and not stoning. Note 2: Adultery by a man or woman who has a permanent spouse, but does not have access to his [or her] spouse because of travelling, imprisonment or other valid excuses, would not lead to stoning. Note 3: A revocable divorce does not free the man or the woman from wedlock before the days of *eddeh* are over, but an irrevocable divorce does free them from wedlock.

Sixth, although men and women received the same punishment for adultery, nevertheless, the man's control of the woman's sexuality was established:

Article 23: Murder does not require *ghesas* if the victim religiously deserved to be killed. Religiously sanctioned killings include ... someone who insults the Great Prophet ... or at the Chaste *emaman* and *hazrat* [saint] Zahra ... someone who violates one's bounds and could not be repulsed but by murder; the husband who sees someone committing adultery with his wife in which case it is only permissible for the husband to kill both of them.

Seventh, the punishment for male homosexuality was much harsher than for female homosexuality:

Article 140: The punishment for *lavat* [male homosexuality] is death.

Article 159: The punishment for *mosahegheh* [female homosexuality] is 100 lashes.

The conditions for proving male homosexuality were easier and exemptions from punishment were more limited than those for lesbianism (Articles 138: 164). This was the case while adultery attracted similar punishment for men and women. Men were granted more freedom for sexual gratification within the confines of the polygamous family than women, and in practice, despite the equal rejection of male and female adultery by the letter of the law, men got away with adultery more easily. But they paid a heavier price than women for breaching the code of heterosexuality because of their crucial functions within the Islamic family in relation to reproduction and the gratification of women's sexual needs.

Islamic discourse of sex, sin and violence

The anti-corruption campaign and its legal backbone, the Retribution Law, aimed to guard the Islamic family against the evil influences of illegitimate sex. What this resulted in was the creation of a horrifying atmosphere of violence and revenge which claimed many female victims. It would require a separate study to examine the ways in which gender relations have been affected by the Islamic discourse of sex, sin and violence, and how women in particular suffered from its dominance. It will suffice here to conclude by citing some examples of the operation of the Islamic Republic's anti-corruption policies in relation to women. Although there were no systematic data or research available, newspapers documented numerous harrowing examples of *ghesas*. By 1983, it was reported, at least 100 acts of retribution had taken place in the Islamic Republic (*Iranshahr*, 5). A report on the work of the penal courts in Mashad indicated that damages paid by women to men for causing injury was more than double the amount due to the woman if a man caused the injury (*Keyhan (London)*, 8). Some newspapers printed the gruesome details of retribution. The case of a woman who had been blinded in one eye by her husband created widespread disgust. The court verdict was that she could choose to either forgive her husband or get retribution for her injury by blinding him in both eyes. She chose to blind him in one eye with a pair of scissors (*Keyhan (London)*, 9).

Newspaper accounts of domestic violence also demonstrated the extent to which men were taking the law into their own hands to decide and administer Islamic justice on women. According to research conducted in Tehran on divorce and its causes, 75 per cent of women who were involved in divorce disputes said that they had been physically attacked by their husbands (*Keyhan* (London), 5). The rate of domestic violence was reported to be as high as 72 per cent (*ibid.*). Many incidents of domestic violence ended with a woman's death or serious injury. A woman's menfolk tried her in a 'family court' on the charge of adultery and carried out the death penalty themselves (*Guardian*, 2).

A 28-year-old woman was knifed thirty-five times by a group of men who were her brothers and cousins. They confessed to having killed her because 'she kept leaving the house without permission and eventually when we saw her with a strange man, we decided to kill her' (*Ettelaat*, 64). A young pregnant woman was killed by her brother 'for being raped by an American hostage' (*Keyhan*, 88). Another woman who was pregnant was set on fire by her husband and father-in-law who punished her for disobeying them. The neighbours came to her rescue but were stopped by her father-in-law who protested that the neighbours were interfering with his right. He believed that according to Islamic law every Muslim man had the right to kill up to two women without facing punishment (*Iranshahr*, 6).

Summary

Part 3 attempted to demonstrate that the Islamic Republic did not inherit a ready-made Islamic policy on gender. The dominant conceptions of gender were constructed as events developed in post-revolutionary society. Historical conceptions of gender were drawn into the context of immediate social and political relations, and reformulations of relevance to the present emerged. Some of the historical conceptions inherited by the Islamic Republic were discussed in previous chapters.

These included the conception propagated by the radical movement of Moslem Brotherhood in the 1950s; the conception of gender relations presented in traditional religious instruction texts such as Ayatollah Khomeini's *towziholmasael* in the 1960s; the modernising approach to Islamic gender relations by Ayatollah Motahhari; and the revolutionary Shii conception of women propagated by Ali Shariati in the 1970s. These concepts were drawn upon to construct the Islamic Republic's gender policy. Political debate and power struggle between various Islamic factions led to the dominance of some of these conceptions in the Islamic Republic as opposed to others. The post-revolutionary power relations and radical political culture defined what was or was not accepted as Islamic in relation to gender.

The analysis of the gender policies of the Islamic Republic also demonstrated the main characteristics of the discourse of Islamisation in relation to women. To begin with, the discourse of Islamisation did not develop in a unified manner. Although it was formed within a particular framework of opposition to the Pahlavi system and what were defined as alien Western conceptions of gender relations, nevertheless it was formulated in a heterogeneous manner by a variety of sources with different and sometimes conflicting interests arising from political rivalries and ideological differences. Policies were made through Majles debates, *fatavi* of influential clerics, Friday Prayer Sermons, practices of grass-roots organisations and personal interventions of Shii leaders and state officials.

Moreover, the policies and practices adopted by the different agents of policy and law enforcement were based on particular political interests and concrete issues. The multiplicity of definitions and sources of Islamic policy created a situation in which different aspects of gender policy did not necessarily correspond with each other. As a result, state policy on gender remained heterogeneous and often contradictory in purpose and effect. Many examples of different policies undermining each other were cited. The policy of universalisation of marriage and encouragement of polygamy conflicted with that of population control, increasing divorce rates and the rising number of single women. The *ad hoc* manner in which education and employment policies were constructed provided other examples of the heterogeneous nature of the discourse of Islamisation. The disparity of purpose and effect was also evident in many state policies. The policy on *sigheh* aimed to control free sexual relations which were considered as a serious threat to the Islamic nation. But, on the other hand, it enabled men and women to overcome the strict sex segregation rules and to associate with each other in a variety of contexts. Women's *hejab*, too, despite its restrictive intentions, facilitated the sharing of public space between men and women.

The discourse of Islamisation faced a serious crisis not only in setting up policies but also in implementing them. It was noted how power struggles, political repression and economic stagnation affected the ability of the state to set coherent policies and ensure their effective implementation. The policy of encouraging marriage had to be abandoned in all but words due to economic impediments. Effective implementation of the policy on family planning was prevented by economic problems. The oppressive measures taken to enforce *hejab* and segregation created resistance amongst the middle-class urban target groups and resulted in a perpetual crisis in the implementation of gender segregation. Cultural stigmatisation of the practice of *sigheh* was another example of the way in which the Islamic Republic's policies fell short of securing unreserved enthusiasm of the 'Islamic nation'.

It was also noted that despite predictions, the discourse of Islamisation did not exclude women from participation in society. Women remained active in the social sphere and participated in even greater numbers in educational, welfare, economic and political activities. The state's enforced Islamisation, however, attempted to engineer a particular gender division of labour in the family and society, in which men and women preferred their 'natural' and Islamic roles. Women's active presence in society was needed by the Islamic Republic. Women were considered as the nurturers of the Islamic nation because of their role as creators of the family. But strategies such as *hejab* and segregation were adopted to preserve the sanctity of the Islamic family. The family and the segregated nation constituted the core of the Islamic discourse on gender relations. Woman as wife, mother and citizen was offered a bargain. She was to receive economic and legal protection by the Islamic state and its representative at home, the male head of the family. In return, she had to prove her credentials as an obedient wife, self-sacrificing mother and active citizen. However, after a decade of the Islamic Republic, the verdict of the Islamic women's movement was that the Islamic state had failed to keep its side of the bargain. In the process of defending women's side of the Islamic bargain, the women's movement extended the boundaries of the Islamic conception of women and bridged the dichotomy of Islamic and secular definitions of women's rights.

The Islamic Republic may have given its female supporters the opportunity for popular political participation and a sense of righteousness and self-worth for the sacrifices they were called upon to make for Islam. But it certainly did not improve their individual rights. Indeed, state policy on the family adversely affected the very women whose mass support contributed to the creation of the Islamic Republic as we know it today. A female supporter of the Islamic regime, poor and illiterate, reflected on her individual gains from the Islamic Republic. Roghiyeh Zibatalab was divorced and abandoned by her husband against her will after thirty-five years of marriage. Two of her six children were still teenagers and financially dependent on her. She complained bitterly about the indifference shown to her plight by the family courts. She said to a reporter from a women's magazine: 'Tell the authorities that women like me were those who responded to your calls for street demonstrations. When you asked us to march, we did. When you called upon us to join the Construction Corps, we turned up in the front line. But why, now that we need help, the courts mock our misery and laugh in our faces' (*Zan Ruz*, 62).

Conclusion Summary of themes and issues

By tracing the development of the position of women in twentieth-century Iran through the evolutionary and revolutionary transformations of political discourses, the preceding chapters established a number of general and specific points.

First, far from being marginal, the position of women was central to the political discourses of twentieth-century Iran. We noted how the political discourses under consideration linked women's social and familial positions to the status of the nation: the discourse of modernity in its first phase during the era of Constitutionalism considered women's emancipation as a precondition for modernity and progress; during the second phase of the discourse of modernity in the era of nation building, women's activities in the social sphere were regarded as vital to the establishment of the nation state; in the third phase of the discourse of modernity when nationalism became dominant, the position of women became a major issue of contention between the state and the opposition but nationalism failed to gain the initiative on women's issues; the era of modernisation which constituted the fourth phase of the discourse of modernity aimed to bring the familial and social position of women in line with the image of a great-civilisation-in-the-making; the discourse of revolution attempted to revolutionise society by revolutionising gender relations; and the discourse of Islamisation regarded the establishment of an Islamic nation as dependent on the Islamisation of the position of women.

It was also argued that the centrality of gender to the political discourses of twentieth-century Iran was intertwined with the preoccupation of these discourses with the issue of modernity, defined in its broad sense to encompass economic prosperity, social justice, political freedom and national independence. The periodical revision and reconstruction of the concepts and processes associated with modernity resulted in an evolving definition of women's subordination and emancipation. The 'modern' woman of the early twentieth century was seen to be an essential element of national progress; the 'Westernised' woman in the mid-twentieth century was regarded as a 'sex-object'; the 'revolutionary' woman of the late 1970s was associated with rejection of Western-style modernisation; and the 'Muslim militant' woman of the late twentieth century was regarded as signifying cultural authenticity and Islamic modernity.

Second, it was argued that the link between gender and nation in Iran was built around the central issue of Iran's relationship with the West. Iran had witnessed two major revolutions in this century, both of which revolved around the redefinition of Iran's relationship with the West. In the Constitutional Revolution of 1905–11, the redefinition involved coming to terms with the dilemma of how to preserve national independence in the face of the threat by Western dominating powers. The answer was sought in the construction of a modern nation state and adoption of Western social progress and technological strength. More than half a century later, during the Revolution of 1977–9, the redefinition of Iran's relationship with the West entailed a rejection of 'cultural imperialism' in favour of an 'indigenous' and 'authentic' Islamic model of modernity and progress. Both responses placed women at the core of the new relationship with the West. The modern secular woman of the mid-twentieth century signified a different relationship with the West than the modern militant Muslim woman of the late twentieth century.

Third, within the context of association between gender and nation and the central role assigned to relations with the West in this, the political discourses under consideration constructed women in a variety of ways. Women were constructed as citizens in the interest of nation building, but they were also defined in relation to their special roles within society and community. Women were defined as biological reproducers of the community and nation and assigned roles on this basis. Contrary to the common assumption, this was not confined to Islamic movements. Indeed, the construction of women as mothers and wives was shared by political movements, state policies and women's movements right across the spectrum. It was a widely shared conception that the family constituted the basis of the society and within it women played the most important role as mothers. Women were regarded as transmitters of communal and national values to the next generation. As a result, both preservation of the status quo and change were linked with the position of women. Women were constructed as reproducers of communal, national, cultural and religious identity. Women's behaviour, clothing, patterns of reproduction, life-style and ways of thinking were all regarded as symbols of communal identity and markers of national boundaries.

Fourth, the state played an important role in establishing and maintaining the link between gender and nation. The emergence of the state as instrument of public policy affected women. Despite their differing political projects, Iranian states have throughout this century attempted to engineer particular sets of legal and social positions for women by selecting certain aspects of women's lives for explicit or implicit intervention and certain others for non-intervention. With the growth of the state, women were increasingly targeted in state policies as a special category for health, education and employment programmes. Women's position within the family was also subjected to state intervention. State intervention, however, did not result in substantial and consistent improvement in the position of all women as the state often claimed. The policies of the Pahlavi state on the family were described as a modernisation of patriarchy rather than its fundamental revision. The efforts of the Islamic Republic to reverse Pahlavi modernisation of the family was gauged to be both unworkable and inhumane.

State policies on the family were complemented by the mobilisation of women in relation to political and developmental goals. It was noted that under the Pahlavi state, this double aim gave rise to a certain tension between women's social and familial roles. A variety of factors, including the role of the autonomous institution of Shiism *vis-à-vis* the state, resulted in tension over women's roles, with the state asserting authority over women's social role and the clergy claiming jurisdiction over their familial roles. The Islamic state aimed to overcome this tension by at least two means. First, by reversing the history of clerical opposition to women's political and social participation; and second, by constructing women as creators of the family and nurturers of the nation. Both states jealously guarded their authority and initiative over their gender policies and controlled the organisational form and gender demands of the women's movements. By destroying the independence of the women's movement through cooption and coercion, both secular and Islamic states aimed to protect the nation against what they considered as the negative side-effects of women's social emancipation. The state's interest in encouraging and controlling women's social participation arose from the importance of women in the context of twentieth-century society both to the family and the nation, and the conflicting priorities that this created for both secular and Islamic states. The wider implications of granting women real power and independence within the family and their independent presence in the social sphere prompted the states to preserve male dominance at home and create state-controlled women's organisations to ensure that women's lives inside and outside the home remained under the control of male guardians. In defining the nature of state policy, it was argued that neither of these states inherited a ready-made secular or Islamic policy on gender. Both the Pahlavi state and the Islamic Republic constructed the position of women in response to immediate indigenous and exogenous factors and events. Furthermore, neither sets of modernising and Islamising policies on gender were unitary policies. On the contrary, both had a heterogeneous nature and were at times contradictory in intention and effect. Far from being the result of the will of the Shah or Ayatollah Khomeini as the pillars of the modernising and Islamising states, gender policies of these states were the product of their respective social contexts and the outcome of negotiations between a variety of political and social forces.

The fifth thread which ran through the preceding chapters was the development of Shiism as a political force in Iran in this century. This refuted essentialist conceptions of Islam which defined it as an ahistorical and inflexible doctrine and the main determinant of the position of Muslim women in Iranian society. This study placed Shiism firmly within the political relations of its time and examined its role *vis-à-vis* the state and other political forces in various historical conjunctures. The analysis of political discourses demonstrated that contrary to the above conceptions, Shiism underwent a series of transformations in relation to its place within the political system and its construction of women. It was argued that far from being fixed and pre-determined, the political agenda of Islamic forces was set throughout this century in response to and as part of an interaction with other political forces. This was why Islamic gender policies put forward within various historical conjunctures were indeed heterogenous and at times contradictory. An example of this was the way in which some of the gender policies of the Islamic Republic, such as women's right to vote, contradicted previous positions adopted by Shii clergy under the Qajar and Pahlavi regimes.

Another issue in relation to the historical development of Shiism was the way in which Islamic views and policies on women were linked to the perceived relationship with the West. The clergy, as a political force, adopted two opposing stances on this during the Revolutions of 1905–11 and 1977–9. In the former, the clergy was part of a constitutional movement which considered the West as providing the best solution to the problem of national development. Within constitutionalism, the clergy resorted to those indigenous traditions and practices which allowed some reform on the position of women along the secular route. In the later Revolution, however, the clergy resorted to a particularly anti-Western Islamic ideology when confronted with Western support for a corrupt autocratic state, a powerless civil society and a failing national development strategy. The adoption of Islamic ideology by the revolutionary leadership was very much linked to the question of Iran's relationship with the West and its internal manifestations, and was not, as has sometimes been argued, the result of a desire to return to traditional

Islam. In this context, it was argued that the role of Shii modernism and radicalism in revolutionary mobilisation was an essential one. By problematising 'cultural imperialism' , a new 'revolutionary' and 'authentic' Muslim culture was constructed which appealed to wide sectors of the urban population. Women and the family were situated at the heart of this new Muslim identity.

Sixth, it was also demonstrated that nationalism occupied an important place in the political discourses of twentieth-century Iran, particularly in relation to women. Nationalism constituted the main vehicle for both secular and religious political action in Iran, and played an important and varied role in all major political developments in Iran since the turn of the century. Iranian nationalism adopted multiple forms: the spontaneous nationalism of the constitutional period was transformed into statist nationalism under Reza Shah; liberal nationalism gained momentum and seized political power in the 1950s; cultural nationalism gained ascendance as the authentic vehicle for political action in the 1960s; and the 1970s witnessed replacement of nationalism with Islam as the oppositional force capable of mobilising mass political action. This history demonstrated the way in which boundaries of nationalism, Marxism and Islam shifted in different political contexts and what implication this had for political construction of women. Secular nationalism as an independent oppositional force tended to play a supportive role in relation to the women's movement. Indeed it was the liberal and socialist nationalism of the turn of the century which first put forward women's cause within the constitutional movement. But once in power, the secular nationalism of Reza Shah's state aimed to co-opt and lead rather than support and respond to women's demands.

Later in the 1940s and 1950s, the left proved a much more vigorous force in raising women's demands and mobilising female support. When in power, the nationalist government of Mosaddeq failed to articulate and present nationalist policies on women, while Tudeh Majles deputies raised women's issues in the Majles and mobilised middle and lower-class women. Indeed, the assessment of the debate over women's political rights in the post-Mosaddeq era of the 1950s and 1960s demonstrated that nationalists of all shade and form did not have an alternative 'nationalist' gender policy to the one presented by the Pahlavi state. The rise of cultural nationalism and its closer association with Islamic modernism in the late 1960s and 1970s, however, changed this. This was the era in which the modern Islamic family and militant Muslim woman were constructed as the dominant alternatives to secular conceptions of women. The position of nationalists on women became an issue once again after the Revolution of 1977–9, when the nationalist-led Provisional

Government failed to prevent forcible Islamisation of women's position because of its inability to present alternative policies to those of the Pahlavi state and the Islamic hardliners.

The link between nationalism and Islam was crucial in determining the gender policies of the Islamic Republic. After the Islamic Republic settled into a theocracy, nationalism as a mobilising force was squeezed out of the political scene. The state attempted this by constructing nationalism as synonymous with anti-imperialism on the one hand, and replacing nationalism with Islam as the main mass mobilisation force, on the other. The new alliance between Islam and anti-imperialism constituted the cornerstone of the Islamisation policies of the state. The context of revolutionary populism, anti-imperialism and power struggle determined which concepts and ideas on women were defined as 'Islamic' and which as 'un-Islamic'.

Seventh, another important issue to raise here is women's own participation in the process of construction and modification. The foregoing analysis of women's activities and movements demonstrated that far from being passive recipients of their roles and despite their invisibility within the mainstream version of Iranian and other Middle Eastern histories, women have affected national processes as much as they are affected by them. The involvement of Iranian women in society took many forms. The focus here was on those aspects of women's social, political and economic roles which became political issues within the dominant political discourses in this century. In relation to women's participation in politics, despite their exclusion from formal public politics, as is the case for women in most of the world, Iranian women did involve themselves in politics in one way or another. The extent of this involvement differed from one context to another. Sometimes it was confined to small numbers of elite women taking up limited political action as was noted during certain periods during the Pahlavi era. In other times, large groups of women from different classes were mobilised in pursuit of nationalist, Islamic and gender goals as was the case during the Constitutional Revolution, the nationalist movement of 1950s, the Revolution of 1977–9 and the post-revolutionary protests against Islamisation of women's rights.

The political objectives pursued by women, too, differed contextually. Women defined their subordination and emancipation differently in accordance with the terms of the political discourse within which they operated. The contrast in the objectives of women's movements within the discourses of modernisation and Islamisation can be described as one obvious example. Moreover, it was demonstrated that women did not act as a homogeneous category with unified political objectives. It was not possible to identify separate and unified male and female interests within the processes of national development and political change in twentieth-century Iran. While some men supported women's emancipation and made alliances with women for the advancement of their cause, other men and women took up political action against the change in the status quo on women. This was not because women did not recognise their 'interests' as a result of their 'false consciousness'. It was because they saw their interest in different things and for them, political differences cut across gender divisions. Women's subordinate legal status has indeed been interlocked with a series of privileges and protection within the family around the role of motherhood. Iranian women's movements have continuously tried to retain and improve positive aspects of the family while eliminating its excesses and abuses of women's rights. Furthermore, women's political differences did not automatically arise from class differences. The pattern of women's participation in the Revolution of 1977–9 and the nature of their gender demands was given as an example, where it was not possible to draw a straight line between class origin and political standpoints on women without resorting to reductionism.

Throughout the twentieth century, women have relentlessly organised and reorganised themselves into political groups and women's movements to campaign for change or defend their rights. Despite their initial dependence, during the Constitutional Revolution, on male supporters for organising and mobilising, women soon situated themselves in the forefront of their movement which developed into a motivated and active, independent women's movement in the early decades of the century. However, what proved to be the main determinant of women's ability to influence their fate was not their motivation and skills, but the state's political manipulation and repression. Consecutive governments attempted to bring spontaneous women's movements under their wing and turn them into cheer leaders of state policy. Despite this, women adjusted and continued to play as many roles as they were politically allowed to in determining women's reproductive and productive roles and individual rights. In this final decade of the twentieth century, the end result of this historical process is an Iranian women's movement which has branched out in many political and ideological directions in Iran and in exile.

A final and related point to raise is the extent to which political discourses, including state policy, legal change and political mobilisation, have affected the living conditions and life experiences of ordinary women. Contrary to general theories which determine women's position with reference to a single cause, be it Islam (Orientalism), state policy (modernisation theory), integration into the world capitalist system (dependency theory), cultural imperialism (Islamists), and so on, the present study of political discourses demonstrates that no general and pre-determined relationships have necessarily existed between political discourses and women's actual living conditions. More often than not, political discourses have affected women's lives in unpredictable and contradictory ways, and the ways in which they have constructed women has depended on the immediate issues and priorities of the time. The failure of both modernisation and Islamisation policies to affect women in a coherent and consistent way despite the determination of the state, illustrated this. The problem with the debate within the literature on the effect of state policy, legal change, or Islamic doctrine on women is that a straight causal relationship is often drawn between politics, law or ideology and women's 'real' life experiences.

It has been the contention here that Muslim women's living conditions, like those of women in any other society, are constructed within a wider context of social relations and through interaction between a variety of discourses and practices which include both political and discursive ones. This refutes the inference that Muslim women are oppressed because of their low legal status and exclusion from formal political decision-making processes. This inference is no more than a reductionist generalisation, because it relies on an outmoded definition of power which is based purely on access to formal power structures. It fails to recognise power within both formal and informal socio-political networks, and as a result, women's other spheres of power, authority, influence and control within the wider social and gender relations are ignored.

How concrete life experiences of different categories of women are affected by political processes can only be determined within the wider context of social relations. This is where specific state policies or legal changes can be juxtaposed with other discourses and discursive practices which may be relevant to women's life experiences. This task is clearly beyond the confines of this book. The aim here was to examine the ways in which political discourses constructed women and their life choices, and how certain categories of women perceived political change and reacted to it. We are still a long way away from fully understanding the ways in which politics converges with other diverse and complex experiences of various categories of Middle Eastern women. For this, we must turn to future research.

Glossary

Akhund Low-ranking priest and preacher. Women can be *akhund*. Another name for a preacher is *molla*.

Alem Singular of *olama*.

Andarun Women's dwelling in the affluent polygamous households of the old days. It was a *haram* on a smaller scale.

Chador Literally means a tent. It is a full-length loose cover worn by women, which envelopes the body from head to toe. It is normally held in place by a hand under the chin or, if the woman is very strict, under the eyes.

Eddeh (Idda) A period of celibacy immediately after divorce or the death of a husband during which the woman may not remarry. This is normally for three menstrual cycles, and its purpose is to determine whether the woman is bearing a child from her previous husband.

Ejtehad (Ijtihad) The Shii practice of forming a religiously binding opinion which can only be exercised by a limited number of high-ranking clerics in every generation; those who have risen to the position of a *mojtahed*. *Ejtehad* is exercised in the absence of the last Shii *emam* Mehdi, who is believed to be in occultation.

Emam (Imam) Literally means leader. Shii *emaman* are twelve descendants of Prophet Mohammad, starting with his son-in-law Ali, and ending with Mehdi (or Mahdi), the twelfth *emam*, who is considered to have gone into hiding and is expected to come out in the future to fill the world with justice. Ayatollah Khomeini is the only Shii *mojtahed* who has been given the title of *emam*. Shii use of the title *emam* is much stricter than the Sunni one. In the latter, *emam* refers to a religious leader recognised by a local or national Muslim community to lead its congregations.

Emaman Plural of *emam*.

Faqih High-ranking cleric who is expert on *feqh*. Commonly used synonymously with *mojtahed*.

Farsi The official and dominant language in Iran.

Fatva Religious edict. Opinion exerted by a *mojtahed* or *faqih* on any matter. It is a Shii practice that in case of doubt, followers of a *mojtahed* ask for his opinion or *fatva*, which is normally the final say on the matter.

Fatavi Plural of *fatva*.

Feqh (Fiqh) Islamic jurisprudence.

Foqaha Plural of *faqih*.

Gharbzadegi Westoxication; being influenced by Western culture. The term is used to describe those Iranians who embrace Western culture without reservation. *Gharbzadeh* is the person who is Westoxicated.

Ghesas (Qisas) Retribution for killing or injuring. The law of *Ghesas* is the penal law of the Islamic Republic and is based on the idea of the victim or victim's family having the right to retribution against the perpetrator of a crime against them.

Hadith The collected record of sayings and actions of the Prophet and Shii *emaman*. The importance of *hadith* is second to that of the *Qoran* as the basis of Islamic *feqh*.

Haram (Harem) or *(Harim)* The special quarter in old palaces where the king or Caliph's many wives and children lived segregated and out of sight.

Hejab (Hijab) Literally means a partition or curtain. It describes a type of women's clothing which protects her body from the eyes of men who are forbidden to her. The exact form of *hejab* varies, but it is regarded in its current usage to include a headscarf, a loose and long dress which is high at the neck and has long sleeves, and a pair of trousers under it to cover the legs; *chador*, or veil, is a more strict form of *hejab*.

Hezbollahi Partisan of God. Fanatical supporters of Ayatollah Khomeini described themselves as such, conveying the meaning that they do not belong to earthly political parties and only follow God's word by following their leader Khomeini.

Jahad (Jihad) Islamic holy war against infidels, or to spread Islam. It is a duty of every Muslim man to participate in *jahad* if called upon. Women can play a role in a defensive *jahad* but not in an offensive one. Its current usage in the Islamic Republic also refers to the endeavour and sacrifices of the people for various Islamic and national causes.

Karbala A centre of Shii worship in Iraq, which is the original site of a fatal battle between the followers of the third Shii *emam*, Hosein, and the army of the Sunni caliph Yazid which led to the defeat of the Shiis. The date, a very important one in the Shii calendar, is commemorated annually with special processions, flagellations and religious plays.

Majles (Majlis) The Iranian national assembly or parliament.

Maktabkhaneh Religious schools where the *Qoran* was taught before the establishment of state education.

Marjae Taghlid Literally means the source of emulation. It refers to the *mojtahed* whose words and actions must be emulated by his followers.

Mehrieh (Mahr) Bride price agreed between the families of the bride and groom and written into the marriage contract. It is supposed to be paid by the husband to the wife on demand after consummation of the marriage. But the normal practice is for it to be paid on divorce.

Moharram The month in the Islamic calendar in which the battle of *Karbala* took place.

Mojtahed (Mojtahid) A Shii cleric who has reached the height of religious knowledge and expertise and is hence able to practise *ejtehad*. Each *mojtahed* has his own followers and his opinion or *fatva* is religiously binding for his followers. Women cannot become *mojtahed*.

Mojtahedin Plural of *mojtahed*.

Molla (Mulla) A low-ranking cleric who is normally the local link between the mosque and the people.

Mostazaf The disinherited. The singular of *mostazafin*. This term became prevalent in the Islamic Republic for describing the lower classes.

Nafagheh Alimony, payable after divorce by a man to a woman if she has child custody.

Olama (Ulama) Islamic religious scholars. Other descriptions include *mojtahedin* and *foqaha*.

Rowzeh A religious gathering in mosques and private houses. The ritual that goes with it is that a male or female *molla* or *akhund* recites the tragedy of *Karbala* and sufferings and martyrdom of Shii *emaman* and their family and followers in the hands of Sunni rulers, while the audience cry and pray.

Shariat (Sharia) Islamic canonical law. Refers to the totality of Islamic rules, encompassing all affairs of the Muslim community.

Shiism A branch of Islam whose founders were partisans and followers of Ali, the Prophet's son-in-law. Shiis believe that after the Prophet's death the leadership of Islam should have gone to Ali, his son-in-law. There are many branches of Shiism, but the largest one is Twelver Shiism which follows the teachings of twelve Shii *emaman*, starting with Ali and ending with Mehdi who is believed to be in occultation and will one day emerge to fill the world with justice. Twelver Shiism has been the official religion in Iran since 1501.

Sigheh (or Muta) Used as both name and verb for temporary marriage. It is a practice which is confined to the Shii branch of Islam, in which every man is entitled to have as many *sigheh* wives as he wishes. It is a form of marriage based on a contract, which is bound by a time limit of between one hour to ninety-nine years. Its aim is satisfaction of sexual urges, but children born in *sigheh* marriages are legitimate. *Muta* is the Arabic term for it is.

Sofreh A religious ceremony which is held in private houses by women, to give thanks for a wish come true. It involves a *rowzeh* and a feast of special food at the end.

Taghut A phrase coined by Ayatollah Khomeini to refer to the pre-revolutionary Pahlavi regime and Westernised society. It means the era of idolism or demonism.

Taghuti Idol worshipper; demonic; Westernised person.

Taghlid Religious emulation. Every faithful in Shiism has the obligation to choose a *marjae taghlid* to emulate in all earthly and other worldly matters.

Touziholmasael The book of religious instructions issued by each *marjae taghlid* to guide his followers on all earthly matters.

Velayat Faqih The guardianship of the Islamic jurisprudence. It refers to Ayatollah Khomeini's thesis about the guardianship of the *faqih* as the head of state, which constitutes the basis of the Constitution of the Islamic Republic.

Zena (Zina) Fornication; adultery, sexual intercourse between men and women who are not married to each other. In the Islamic Republic *Zena* is a crime punishable by flogging or stoning to death.

References

BOOKS AND ARTICLES

Abadi, Shole (1993): 'Mirza Fath Ali Akhundzadeh Va Masaleh Znan' [Akhundzadeh on the question of women]. In *Nimeye Digar*, no. 17, Winter 1371.

Abdel-Kader, Soha (1984): 'A Survey of Trends in Social Sciences Research on Women in the Arab Region, 1960–1980'. In *Social Science Research and Women in the Arab World*. Paris: UNESCO.

Abdu-Lughod, Janet (1981): 'Book Review'. In *Arab Studies Quarterly*, vol. 1, no. 4.

Abrahamian, Ervand (1968): 'The Crowd in Iranian Politics: 1905–1953'. In *Past and Present*, no. 41.

(1978): 'Iran: the Political Challenge'. In *Middle East Report*, no. 69, July–August.

(1980a): 'The Guerrilla Movements in Iran 1963–1977'. In *Middle East Report*, no. 6, March–April.

(1980b): 'Structural Causes of the Iranian Revolution'. In *Middle East Report*, no. 87, May.

(1982): *Iran Between Two Revolutions*. Princeton: Princeton University Press.

(1989): *Radical Islam: The Iranian Mojahedin*. London: I.B. Tauris.

Abu Odeh, Loma (1993): 'Post-colonial Feminism and the Veil: Thinking the Difference'. In *Feminist Review*, no. 43.

Adamiyat, Fereydun (1967): *Andishehaye Mirza Agha Khan Kermani* [The reflections of Kermani]. Tehran: Tahuri, 1346.

(1970): *Andishehaye Mirza Fathali Akhundzadeh* [The reflections of Akhundzadeh]. Tehran: Khwarazmi, 1349.

(1975): *Fekr Democracy Ejtemai Dar Nehzat Mashrutiat Iran* [The idea of social democracy in the constitutional movement of Iran]. Tehran: Entesharat Payam, 1354.

(1978): *Ideology Nehzat Mashrutiat Iran* [The ideology of the constitutional movement of Iran]. Tehran: Entesharat Payam, 1357.

(1980): *Andisheh Taraghi va Hokumat Ghanun Dar Asr Sepahsalar* [The ideas of progress and rule of law in the era of Sepahsalar]. Tehran: Khwarazmi, 1359.

Adamiyat, Fereydun and Nategh, Homa (1978): *Afkar Ejtemai, Siasi va Eghtesadi Dar Asar Montasher Nashodeh Doran Qajar* [The social, political and economic thoughts of Qajar period in unpublished documents]. Tehran: Entesharat Agah, 1356.

Afari, Janet (1993): 'Taamoli Dar Tafakor Ejtemai-Siasi Dar Enghelab Mashruteh' [Women's socio-political thought in the Constitutional Revolution]. In *Nimeye Digar*, no. 17, Winter 1371.

Afkhami, Mahnaz (1984): 'A Future in the Past – The Pre-Revolutionary Women's Movement'. In R. Morgan (ed.): *Sisterhood is Global*. Garden City: Anchor Books.

Afshar, Iraj (1972): *Maghalat Taqizadeh* [Collection of articles by Taqizadeh], III. Tehran: Chapkhaneh Bist-Panjom Shahrivar, 1351.

(1977): *Seyyed Hasan Taqizadeh: Ruznameh Kaveh* [Taqizadeh: *Kaveh* newspaper]. Tehran: Chapkhaneh Bist-Panjom Shahrivar, 1356.

(1979): *Mosaddeq va Masael Hoghugh va Siasat* [Mosaddeq and the questions of law and politics]. Tehran: Entesharat Zamineh, 1358.

Afshar, Haleh (1981): 'The Position of Women in an Iranian Village'. In *Feminist Review*, no. 9.

(1982): 'Khomeini's Teachings and Their Implications for Iranian Women'. In A. Tabari and N. Yeganeh (eds.): *In the Shadow of Islam.*

(1985): *Women, Work, and Ideology in the Third World.* London: Tavistock.

(1988): 'Behind the Veil: The Public and Private Faces of Khomeini's Policies on Iranian Women'. In B. Agarwal (ed.): *Structures of Patriarchy.*

Agarwal, Bina (ed.) (1988): *Structures of Patriarchy: the State, the Community and the Household.* London: Zed Books.

Aghajanian, Akbar (1988): 'Post-Revolutionary Demographic Trends in Iran'. In H. Amirahmadi and M. Parvin (eds.): *Post-Revolutionary Iran.*

Ahmadi, Ashraf (1964): *Twelve Years in Constructing a new Iran: 1953–1964.* Tehran: Central Council.

Ahmed, Leila (1982): 'Western Ethnocentrism and Perceptions of the Harem'. In *Feminist Studies*, vol. 8, no. 3, Fall.

Akhavi, Shahrough (1980): *Religion and Politics in Contemporary Iran: Clergy–State Relations in the Pahlavi Period.* Albany: State University of New York Press.

Al-Ahmad, Jalal (1981): *Plagued by the West.* Translated by Paul Sprachman. New York: Caravan Books.

Albert, D. H. (ed.) (1980): *Tell the American People: Perspectives on the Iranian Revolution.* Philadelphia: Movement for New Society.

Algar, Hamid (1973): *Mirza Malkom Khan: A Study in the History of Iranian Modernism.* Berkeley: University of California Press.

(1980): 'Ayatollah Khomeini: The Embodiment of a Tradition'. In K. Siddiqui (ed.): *The Islamic Revolution in Iran.*

(1983): *The Roots of the Islamic Revolution.* London: The Open Press.

Al-Hibri, Azizah (ed.) (1982): *Women and Islam: Special Issue of Women's Studies International Forum.* New York: Pergamon Press.

Allaghi, Farida and Almana, Aisha (1984): 'Survey of Research on Women in the Arab Gulf Region'. In *Social Science Research and Women in the Arab World.* Paris: UNESCO.

Al-Qazzaz, Ayad (1977): *Women in the Middle East and North Africa: An Annotated Bibliography.* Austin: University of Texas.

Al-Sayyid Marsot, Afaf Lutfi (1978): 'The Revolutionary Gentlewomen in Egypt'. In: L. Beck and N. Keddie (eds.): *Women in the Muslim World.*

Althusser, Louis (1971): *Lenin and Philosophy and Other Essays*. London: New Left Books.

Amanat, Abbas (1989): *Resurrection and Renewal: The Making of the Babi Movement in Iran 1844–1850*. Ithaca: Cornell University Press.

Amin, S. (1976): *Unequal Development: An Essay on the Social Formulation of Peripheral Capitalism*. Hassocks: Harvester.

Amirahmadi, Hooshang (1990): *Revolution and Economic Transition: The Iranian Experience*. Albany: State University of New York Press.

Amirahmadi, Hooshang and Parvin, Manouchehr (eds.) (1988): *Post-Revolutionary Iran*. Boulder: Westview Press.

Amnesty International (1987): *Iran: Violations of Human Rights*. London: Amnesty International Publications.

Anderson, Benedict (1983): *Imagined Communities: Reflections on the Origin and Spread of Nationalism*. London: Verso.

Arasteh, Reza (1964a): 'The Struggle for Equality in Iran'. In *Middle East Journal*, vol. 18.

(1964b): *Man and Society in Iran*. Leiden: E. J. Brill.

(1969): *Education and Social Awakening in Iran, 1850–1968*. Leiden: E. J. Brill.

Arbery, Arthur John (1955): *The Koran Interpreted*, 2 vols., London: Allen and Unwin.

Arjomand, Said Amir (1988): *The Turban for the Crown*. Oxford: Oxford University Press.

Asadipour, Bijan (1977): *Tanz Khanegi* [Domestic humour]. Tehran: Entesharat Morvarid, 2537.

Atkinson, James (1832): *Customs and Manners of the Women of Persia and Their Domestic Superstitions*. London: The Oriental Translation Fund of Great Britain and Ireland.

Azari, Farah (1983): *Women of Iran: The Conflict with Fundamentalist Islam*. London: Ittaca Press.

(1984): 'Goftegui Ba Do Zan Irani' [A conversation with two Iranian women]. In *Nimeye Digar*, no. 1, Spring.

Baffoun, Alya (1984): 'Research in the Social Sciences on North African Women's Problems, Trends and Needs'. In *Social Science Research and Women in the Arab World*. Paris: UNESCO.

Bagley, E. R. C. (1971): 'The Iranian Family Protection Law of 1967: A Milestone in the Advance of Women's Rights'. In C. E. Bosworth (ed.): *Iran and Islam*. Edinburgh University Press.

Bahai, Sheykh Muhammad Ebn Hosein al-Ameli (1905): *Jamee Abbasi*. Completed by Nizam Ebn Hosein Savaji. np., 1248.

Bahar, Malek ol-Shoara (1944): *Tarikh Mokhtasar Ahzab Siasi Iran* [A short history of Iranian political parties], I. Tehran: Rangin Press, 1323.

Bahrami, Abdollah (1965): *Tarikh Ejtemai va Siasi Iran Az Zaman Naser od-Din Shah Ta Akhar Selseleh Qajar* [The social and political history of Iran from Naser od-Din Shah to the end of Qajar dynasty]. Tehran: Sanai, 1344.

Bakhash, Shaul (1984): *The Reign of Ayatollahs: Iran and the Islamic Revolution*. New York: Basic Books.

Bamdad, Badr ol-Moluk (1977): *From Darkness into Light: Women's Emancipa-*

tion in Iran. Edited and translated by F. R. C. Bagley. New York: Exposition Press.

Banisadr, Abolhasan (1980): *Khanevadeh Dar Eslam, Masaleh Hejab, Sytemhaye Ettelaati* [The family in Islam, the issue of hejab and information systems]. Tehran: Entesharat Payman Azadi, 1358.

(1982a): *Khianat Be Omid* [The betrayal of hope]. Paris: Entesharat Enghelab Eslami, 1361.

(1982b): Unpublished interview, conducted by Nahid Yeganeh. Paris.

Baraka, Iqbal (1988): 'The Influence of Contemporary Arab Thought on the Women's Movement'. In N. Toubia (ed.): *Women of the Arab World.*

Baran, Paul (1975): *The Political Economy of Growth.* New York: Monthly Review Press.

Baron, Beth (1982): 'Images of Middle Eastern Women in the Accounts of British Women Travellers'. Unpublished MA Dissertation. School of Oriental and African Studies, London University.

Basari, Talat (1967): *Zandokht: Pishahang Nehzat Azadi Banovan Iran* [Zandokht: the pioneer of the Iranian women's emancipation movement]. Tehran: Ketabkhaneh Tahuri, 1346.

Bauer, Janet (1983): 'Poor Women and Social Consciousness in Revolutionary Iran'. In G. Nashat (ed.): *Women and Revolution in Iran.*

Bauer, Janet (1985): 'Demographical Change, Women and Family in Migrant Neighbourhood of Tehran'. In A. Fathi (ed.): *Women and the Family in Iran.*

Bayat-Philipp, Mangol (1978): 'Women and Revolution in Iran, 1905–1911'. In L. Beck and N. Keddie (eds.): *Women in the Muslim World.*

(1981): 'Tradition and Change in Iranian Socio-Religious Thought'. In M. bonine and N. Keddie (eds.): *Continuity and change in Modern Iran.*

Baykan, Aysegul (1990): 'Women between Fundamentalism and Modernity'. In B. S. Turner (ed.): *Theories of Modernity and Postmodernity.* London: Sage Publications.

Beck, Lois (1980): 'The Religious Lives of Muslim Women'. In J. Smith (ed.): *Women in Contemporary Muslim Societies.*

(1992): 'Qashqa'i Nomads and the Islamic Republic'. In *Middle East Report*, no. 177, vol. 22 (4), July–August.

Beck, Lois and Keddie, Nikki (eds.) (1978): *Women in the Muslim World.* Cambridge: Harvard University Press.

Benard, Cheryl (1980): 'Islam and Women: Some Reflections on the Experience of Iran'. In *Journal of South Asia and Middle East Studies*, vol. 4, no. 2, Winter.

Benard, Cheryl and Khalilzad, Zalmay (1984): *The Government of God: Iran's Islamic Republic.* New York: Columbia University Press.

Berman, Marshal (1982): *All that is Solid Melts into Air: The Experience of Modernity.* London: Verso.

Betteridge, Anne H. (1980): 'The Controversial Vows of Urban Muslim Women in Iran'. In N. A. Falk and R. Gross (eds.): *Unspoken Words, Women's Religious Lives in Non-Western Culture*. San Francisco: Harper and Row.

(1983): 'To Veil or Notto Veil: A MatterofProtest'. In G. Nashat (ed.): *Women and Revolution in Iran.*

Bhabha, Homi K. (ed.) (1990): *Nation and Narration*. London and New York: Routledge.

Binder, Leonard (1962): *Iran: Political Development in a Changing Society*. Berkeley: University of California Press.

Blanch, Lesley (1978): *Farah: Shahbanu of Iran, Queen of Persia*. London: Collins.

Bonine, Michael and Keddie, Nikki (eds.) (1981): *Continuity and Change in Modern Iran*. Albany: State University of New York Press.

Boyce, Annies (1930): 'Muslim Women in the Capital of Persia'. In *Moslem World*, no. 20, July.

Boyne, Roy and Rattansi, Ali (eds.) (1990): *Postmodernism and Society*. London: Macmillan.

Chehabi, Houchang E. (1990): Iranian Politics and Religious Modernism: *The Liberation Movement of Iran under the Shah and Khomeini*. London: I. B. Tauris.

Cole, Juan R. (1981): 'Feminism, Class and Islam in Turn-of-the-Century Egypt'. In *International Journal of Middle East Studies*, vol. 13.

Cole, Juan and Keddie, Nikki (eds.) (1986): *Shiism and Social Protest*. New Haven: Yale University Press.

Committee For Women's Liberation in Iran (1978): *Do Maghaleh Darbareh Setamkeshidegi Zan Dar Iran* [Two articles on women's oppression in Iran]. London, 1357.

Confederation of Iranian Students Abroad (1976): *Nameh Parsi*. Special Issue on International Women's Day, vol. 15, no. 1. West Berlin, 1355.

(1978): *Roshangar*, no. 3. West Berlin, 1357.

Constitution of the Islamic Republic (1980). Translated by Hamid Algar. Berkeley: Mizan Press.

Dallalfar, Arlene (1987): 'Jaye Khali Zanan Dar Mohasebat Amari' [The under-estimation of women's economic activities in the subsistence economy]. In *Nimeye Digar*, no. 5, Winter 1366.

Democratic Organisation of Iranian Women (DOIW) (1982a): My Struggle is My Life. West Germany.

(1982b): *Women in Iran*. West Germany.

Dhalla, Manekji Nasarvanji (1922): *Zoroastrian Civilization From the Earliest Time to the Downfall of the Last Zoroastrian Empire*. New York.

Doulatabadi, Yahya (1947): *Tarikh Moaser* (Contemporary History), II. Tehran: Chapkhaneh Chehr, 1326.

Ebrahimi, Irandokht (1967): *Enghelab Octobr va Iran* [The October Revolution and Iran]. Tehran: Hezb Tudeh, 1346.

El Saadawi, Nawal (1980): *The Hidden Face of Eve: Women in the Arab World*. London: Zed Press.

(1982): 'Woman and Islam'. In A. al-Hibri (ed.): *Women and Islam*.

Elwell-Sutton, L. P. (1941): *Modern Iran*. London: George Routledge and Sons.

Emami, Seyyed Hasan (1960): *Hoghugh Madani* [The Civil Code], II. Tehran: Entesharat Daneshgah Tehran, 1339.

Ettehadiyeh, Mansureh et al. (1982): *Khaterat Taj ol-Saltaneh* [The memoirs of Taj ol-Saltaneh]. Tehran: Nashr Tarikh Iran, 1361.

Fadaiyan Eslam (1950): *Rahnamaye Haghaegh* [The guide to the truths]. Qom: 1339. In Adele K. Ferdows (1967): *Religion in Iranian Nationalism: The Study of the Fadaiyan-i Islam*. Ph.D. Dissertation. Indiana University.

Fadaiyan Khalgh (1977): *Elamiyeh Be Monasebat Enfejar Anjoman Iran va Amrica Be Monasebat Safar Toteehgaraneh Carter Namayandeh Gharatgaran Amrica*. Leaflet about President Carter's visit to Iran. 1356

(1978a): *Har Sazeshi Ba Regime Khianat Be Arman Mordom Ast*. Leaflet against compromise with the Shah's regime. Azar 1357.

(1978b): *Masael Konuni ffonbesh Va Maraje*. Leaflet about the religious leadership of the antiShah movement. 1357.

(1979a): 'People's Fedayi Open Letter to Khomeini'. In *Middle East Report*, no. 7576, March–April.

(1979b): *The New Conspiracy of World Imperialism Against the Iranian Masses*. Leaflet. January.

Fallaci, Oriana (1973): 'The Shah of Iran'. In *New Republic*, no. 1, December.

(1976): *Interview with History*. Boston: Houghton Mifflin.

Farman Farmaian, Sattareh (1992): *Daughter of Persia*. New York: Crown Publishers.

Farrokhzad, Forough (1985): *A Re-birth*. Translated and introduced by David Martin. USA: Mazda Publishers.

Fathi, Asghar (ed.) (1985): *Women and the Family in Iran*, Leiden: J. Brill.

Fazai, Yusof (nd): *Tahghigh Dar Tarikh va Falsafeh Babigari* [Research about the history and philosophy of Babism]. Tehran: Moaseseh Matbuati.

Ferdows, Adele (1983): 'Women and the Islamic Revolution'. In *International Journal of Middle East Studies* no. 5.

Ferdows, Adele and Ferdows, Amir H. (1983): 'Women in Shii Fiqh: Images Through Hadith'. In G. Nashat (ed.): *Women and Revolution in Iran*.

Fernea, Elizabeth Warnock (ed.) (1985): *Women and the Family in the Middle East: New Voices of Change*. Austin: University of Texas Press.

Fernea, Elizabeth Warnock and Ferena, Robert A. (1978): 'Variations in Religious Observance Among Islamic Women'. In N. Keddie (ed.): *Scholars, Saints and Sufis*. Berkeley: University of California Press.

Fernea, Elizabeth Warnock and Bezigan, Basima Qattan (eds.) (1977): *Middle Eastern Muslim Women Speak*. Texas: University of Texas Press.

Fischer, Michael M. J. (1978): 'On Changing the Concept and Position of Persian Women'. In L. Beck and N. Keddie (eds.): *Women in the Muslim World*.

(1980): *Iran: From Religious Dispute to Revolution*. Cambridge, MA: Harvard University Press.

Fischer, Michael and Abedi, Mehdi (1989): 'Revolutionary Posters and Cultural Signs'. In *Middle East Report*, no. 159, vol. 19 (4), July–August.

Floor, Willem M. (1983): 'The Revolutionary Character of the Ulama: Wishful Thinking or Reality? In N. Keddie (ed.): *Religion and Politics in Iran*.

Fluer-Lobban, Carolyn (1980): 'The Political Mobilization of Women in the Arab World'. In J. Smith (ed.): *Women in Contemporary Muslim Societies*.

Foran, John (1989): 'The Concept of Dependent Development as a Key to thePolitical Economy of Qajar Iran (1800–1925)' In *Iranian Studies*, vol. 22 no. 2–3.

Fozuni-Siasi, Shahnaz (1976): *Self and Role Perception Among Young Employed Iranian Women of Lower Class Origin*. Ph.D. Dissertation. University of Pittsburgh.

Frank, A. G. (1969): *Latin America: Underdevelopment or Revolution?*. New York and London: Monthly Review Press.

Friedl, Erika (1981): 'Women and the Division of Labour in an Iranian Village'. In *Middle East Report*, no. 95, March–April.

(1992): 'The Dynamics of Women's Spheres of Action in Rural Iran'. In N. Keddie and B. Baron (eds.): *Women in Middle Eastern History*

Friesen, John K. and Moore, Richard V. (1977): 'Iran'. In D. Momeni (ed.): *The Population of Iran.*

Ghaemmaghami, J. (1967): *Asnad Tarikhi Vaghayee Mashrutiat Iran* [Historical documents about the events of the Constitutional movement in Iran]. Tehran: Zaban va Farhang Iran, 1346.

Ghahreman, Sahar (1988): 'Siasat Hokumt Eslami Piramun Dastrasi Zanan be Amuzesh Ali Va Asarat An Dar Mogheiat Ejtemai-Eghtesadi Zanan' [The Islamic state's policy towards women's access to higher education and its effects on women's socio-economic position]. In *Nimeye Digar*, no. 7, Summer 1367.

(1989): 'Zan Dar Arseh Siasat Va Jang: Tajrobeh Kordestan' [Women in politics and war: the case of Kordestan]. In *Nimeye Digar*, no. 9, Spring 1368.

Ghavimi, Fakhri (1973): *Karnameh Zanan Mashhur Iran* [The profile of famous Iranian women]. Tehran: Entesharat Vezarat Amuzesh va Parvaresh, 1352.

Ghorbani, Farajollah (1989): *Khanevadeh: Majmueh Kamel Ghavanin Va Mogharart* [Family: the complete collection of laws and regulations]. Tehran: Entesharat Ferdowsi, 1368.

Ghoussoub, Mai (1987): 'Feminism – or the Eternal Masculine – in the Arab World'. In *New Left Review*, no. 61.

Golbon, Mohammad (1975): *Naghd Va Siahat: Majmueh Maghalat Va Taghrirat Fatemeh Sayyah* [The collection of writings of Fatemeh Sayyah]. Tehran: Entesharat Tus, 1354.

Gran, Judith (1977): 'Impact of the World Market on Egyptian Women'. In *Middle East Report*, no. 58.

Gulick, Margaret and Gulick, John (1976): 'Migrant and Native Married Women in the Iranian City of Isfahan'. In *Anthropology Quarterly*, vol. 49, no. 1.

(1978): 'The Domestic Social Environment of Women and Girls in Isfahan, Iran'. In L. Beck and N. Keddie (eds.): *Women in the Muslim World.*

Gurney, J. D. (1983): 'A Qajar Household and its Estates'. In *Iranian Studies*, vol. 16, no. 3–4, Summer–Autumn.

Habibi, Nader (1989): 'Allocation of Educational and Occupational Opportunities in the Islamic Republic of Iran: A case study in the political screening of human capital'. In *Iranian Studies*, vol. 22, no. 4.

Haeri, Shahla (1981): 'Women, Law and Social Change in Iran'. In J. Smith (ed.): *Women in Contemporary Muslim Societies.*

(1989): *The Law of Desire.* London: I. B. Tauris.

Haines, Pamela (1980): 'Women in Today's Iran'. In D. H. Albert (ed.): *Tell the American People.*

Hairi, Abdolhadi (1977): Shiism and Constitutionalism in Iran. Leiden: Brill.

Halliday, Fred (1979): *Iran: Dictatorship and Development.* Harmondsworth: Penguin Books.

(1989): 'The Revolution's First Decade'. In *Middle East Report*, no. 156, vol. 19 (1), March–April.

Hammam, Mona (1981): 'Labour Migration and the Sexual Division of Work'. In *Middle East Report*, no. 95, March–April.

Harrison, David (1988): *The Sociology of Modernisation and Development.* London: Unwin Hyman.

Hashemi, Fereshteh (1981a): 'Women in an Islamic Versus Women in a Muslim View'. In A. Tabari and N. Yeganeh (eds.) (1982): *In the Shadow of Islam.*

(1981b): 'Proposal for the Legal Revival of the Rights of Women'. In A. Tabari and N. Yeganeh (eds.) (1982): *In the Shadow of Islam.*

Hegland, Mary (1983a): 'Aliabad Women: Revolution as Religious Activity'. In G. Nashat (ed.): *Women and Revolution in Iran.*

(1983b): 'Two Images of Husain: Accommodation and Revolution in an Iranian Village'. In N. Keddie (ed.): *Religion and politics in Iran.*

(1986): 'Political Roles of Iranian Village Women'. In *Middle East Report*, no. 138, vol. 16 (1), January–February.

(1992): 'Political Roles of Aliabad Women: The Public–Private Dichotomy Transcended'. In N. Keddie and B. Baron (eds.): *Women in Middle Eastern History.*

Hendessi, Mandana (1990): *Armed Angels: Women in Iran.* Report no. 16. London: Change.

Hijab, Nadia (1988): *Womanpower: The Arab Debate on Women at Work.* Cambridge: Cambridge University Press.

Hinchcliffe, Doreen (1968): 'The Iranian Family Protection Act'. In *International and Comparative Law Quarterly*, no. 5, April.

Historical Documents (1974–9): *Asnad Tarikhi Jonbesh Kargari Social Democracy Va Komonisty Iran* [Historical documents of social democratics, communists and workers' movements]. Italy: Mazdak, 1358. Tehran: Elm, 1358.

Hooglund, Eric (1989): 'The Islamic Republic at War and Peace'. In *Middle East Report*, no. 156, vol. 19 (1), March–April.

Ioannides, Christos (1984): *America's Iran.* Lanham: University Press of America.

Iran Almanac: Book of Facts (1962–77): Tehran: Echo of Iran.

Iranian Women's Independent Movement Abroad(1980): *Jonbesh Zanan Va Masaleh Hejab* [Women's movement and the question of *hejab*]. West Germany: Jonbesh Mostaghel Zanan Irani Dar Kharej Az Keshvar, 1359.

Jalali, G. H. and Payman, H. and Majd, A. (1977): 'Study of Abortion at Farah Maternity Hospital, Tehran'. In D. Momeni (ed.): *The Population of Iran* (1977).

Jamalzadeh, Seyyed Mohammad Ali (1978): *Tasvir Zan Dar Farhang Irani* [Women's image in Iranian culture]. Tehran: Amir Kabir, 1357

Javadi, Hasan (1985): 'Women in Persian Literature: An Explanatory Study'. In A. Fathi (ed.): *Women and the Family in Iran* (1985).

Jayawardena, Kumari (1986): *Feminism and Nationalism in The Third World*. London: Zed Books.

Jeffery, Patricia (1979): *Frogs in a Well: Indian Women in Purdah*. London: Zed Books.

Kamarehi, Khalil (1941): *Zan Dar Eslam* [Women in Islam]. Tehran: 1320.

Kambakhsh, Abdolsamad (1972): *Nazari Be Jonbesh Kargari Va Komonisti Dar Iran* [A look at the communist and workers' movements in Iran]. N.p: Entesharat Hezb Tudeh Iran, 1351.

Kandiyoti, Deniz (1987): 'Emancipated but Unliberated? Reflections on the Turkish Case'. In *Feminist Studies*, vol. 13, no. 2, Summer.

Kandiyoti, Deniz (ed.) (1991a): *Women, Islam and State*. London: Macmillan Press.

(1991b): 'Islam and Patriarchy: A Comparative Perspective'. In N. Keddie and B. Baron (eds.): *Women in Middle Eastern History*.

Kanun Banovan (1935): *Khatabehaye Kanun Banovan Dar Sal 1314* [Collection of Speeches given in the Ladies' Centre in 1925]. Tehran: Entesharat Kanun Banovan, 1314.

Kasravi, Ahmad (1974): *Khaharan Va Dokhtran Ma* [Our sisters and daughters]. Tehran: Nashr Va Pakhsh Ketab, 1353.

(1978): *Tarikh Mashruteh Iran* [The history of the Constitutional Revolution], 2 vols. Tehran: Amir Kabir, 2537.

Kazemi, Farhad (1980): *Poverty and Revolution in Iran*. New York: New York University Press.

Kazemzadeh Iranshahr, Hosein (1971): *Asar Va Ahval Kazemzadeh Iranshahr* [The life and works of Kazemzadeh Iranshahr]. Tehran: Eqbal, 1350.

Keddie, Nikki (1968): *An Islamic Response to Imperialism: Political and Religious Writings of Sayyid Jamal od-Din al-Afghani*. Berkeley: University of California Press.

(1978): 'Class Structure and Political Power in Iran Since 1796'. In *Iranian Studies*, vol. 11.

(1979): 'Problems in the Study of Middle Eastern Women'. In *International Journal of Middle East Studies*, vol. 10.

(1980): *Iran, Religion, Politics*. London: Frank Cass.

(1981): *Roots of Revolution*. New Haven and London: Yale University Press.

Keddie, Nikki (ed.) (1983): *Religion and Politics in Iran: Shiism From Quietism to Revolution*. New Haven: Yale University Press.

Keddie, Nikki and Baron, Beth (eds.) (1991): *Women in Middle Eastern History: Shifting Boundaries in Sex and Gender*. New Haven: Yale University Press.

Keller, James and Mendelson, Lloyd (1971): 'Changing Family Patterns in Iran: A Comparative Study'. In *International Journal of Sociology of the Family*, March.

Kermani, Mirza Agha Khan (1990): 'Bakhshhayi Az Sad Khatabeh'. In *Nimeye Digar*, no. 9, Spring 1368.

Kermani, Nazemoleslam (1982): *Tarikh Bidari Iranian* [The history of awakening of Iranians], 2 vols. Tehran: Entesharat Agah, 1361.

Khaleghi, Ruhollah (1974): *Sargozasht Musighi Irani* [The story of Iranian music]. Tehran: Vezarat Farhang va Honar, 1353.

Khamsin (1973): *Women in the Middle East*. London: Zed Books.

Khomeini, Ruhollah (n.d. a): *Kashf ol-Asrar* [The discovery of secrets]. First published in 1971. Qom.

(n.d. b): *Resaleh Towziholmasael* [The book of religious instructions]. Qom: Ganjaneh Publication.

(n.d. c): *Hokumat Eslami* [The Islamic Government]. First published in 1971. Qom.

Kramer, Martin (1987): *Shi'ism, Resistance, Revolution*. Boulder: Westview Press.

Lerner, Daniel (1958): *The Passing of Traditional Society*. New York: Free Press.

Liberation Movement of Iran (1983): *Asnad Nehzat Azadi Iran: 1340–1344* [Documents of the Liberation Movement of Iran 1961–1965], 2 vols. Tehran: Nehzat Azadi, 1361.

Madelung, Wilfred (1979): 'Shii Attitudes Towards Women as Reflected in Fiqh'. In A. L. Al-Sayyid Marsot (ed.): *Society and Sexes in Medieval Islam*. Malibu, CA: Undena Publications.

Mahallati, Zabihollah (1955): *Riahin ol-Shariat: Dar Tarjomeh Daneshmandan Banovan Shii* [The history of Shii Women Scholars], 5 vols. Tehran: Darolketab Al-Eslamiyeh, 1334.

Mahdavi, Shireen (1985): 'The Position of Women in Shii Iran: Views of the Olama'. In E. W. Fernea (ed.): *Women and the Family in the Middle East*.

Majlesi, Allameh Mohammad Bagher (1951): *Helliayt ol-Mottaghin* [The ornaments of the pious]. Tehran: Elmi Bookshop, 1330.

Maki, Hosein (1979): *Tarikh Bistsaleh Iran* [The twenty-year history of Iran], 4 vols. Tehran: Amir Kabir, 1358.

Malek, Farnaz (1984): 'Nedai As Diar Tajrobehhaye Aqim Eshq' [On Forugh Farrokhzad's poetry of love]. In *Nimeye Digar*, vol. 1, no. 1, Spring 1363.

Malekzadeh, Mehdi (1949): *Tarikh Enghelab Mashrutiat Iran* [The history of the Constitutional Revolution], 7 vols. Tehran: Ebn Sina, 1328.

Malkom Khan, Mirza: *see* Nategh, Homa.

Mansur, Roshanak (1984): 'Chehreye Zan Dar Jaraid Mashrutiat' [Women's image in the constitutional literature]. In *Nimeye Digar*, vol. 1, no. 1, Spring 1363.

Martin, Vanessa (1989): *Islam and Modernism: The Iranian Revolution of 1906*. New York: Syracuse University Press.

Marxists and Women's Question [Marxistha va masaleh zanan] (1975): Author(s) unknown. New York: Mazdak, 1354.

Massell, Gregory J. (1974): *The Surrogate Proletariat*. Princeton: Princeton University Press.

Matindaftari, Hedayatollah (1982): Unpublished interview, conducted by Nahid Yeganeh. London.

Mehran, Golnar (1989): 'Socialisation of School Children in the Islamic Republic of Iran'. In *Iranian Studies*, vol. 22, no. 1.

Mehrpour, Hosein (1989): *Barrasi Miras Zojeh Dar Hoghugh Eslam Va Iran* [Analysis of a wife's inheritance rights in the laws of Islam and Iran]. Tehran: Entesharat Ettelaat, 1368.

Mernissi, Fatima (1975): *Beyond the Veil: Male–Female Dynamics in a Modern*

Muslim Society. Cambridge: Schenkman Publishing Company.
(1988): 'Democracy as Moral Disintegration'. In N. Toubia (ed.): *Women of the Arab World.*

Mies, Maria (1986): *Patriarchy and Accumulation of a World Scale: Women in the International Division of Labour*. London: Zed Books.

Milani, Farzaneh (1992): *Veils and Words: The Emerging Voices of Iranian Women Writers*. Syracuse: Syracuse University Press.

Milani, Mohsen M. (1988): *The Making of Iran's Islamic Revolution: From Monarchy to Islamic Republic*. Boulder: Westview Press.

Millet, Kate (1982): *Going to Iran*. New York: Coward, McCann and Geoghegan.

Minces, Juliette (1980): *The House of Obedience: Women in Arab Society*. London: Zed Books.

Mirani, Kaveh S. (1983): 'Social and Economic Change in the Role of Women: 1956–1978'. In G. Nashat (ed.): *Women and Revolution in Iran.*

Mirvahabi, F. (1975): 'The Status of Women in Iran'. In *Journal of Family Law*, no. 14, 1975–6.

Moaser, Hasan (1973): *Tarikh Esteghrar Mashrutiat Dar Iran* [The history of the establishment of constitutionalism in Iran]. Tehran: Entesharat Ebn Sina, 1352.

Moazen, Naser (ed.) (1978): *Dah Shab* (Ten evening meetings by poets and writers in the Iran–German Cultural Association). Tehran: Amir Kabir, 1357.

Moghadam, Valentine B. (1988): 'Women, Work and Ideology in the Islamic Republic'. In *International Journal of Middle East Studies*, vol. 20.

Moghadam, Valentine B. (ed.) (1993): *Modernising Women: Gender and Social Change in the Middle East*. Boulder: Lynne Rienner Publishers.

Mohaqeq-Damad, Seyyed Mostafa (1986): *Barrasi Feqhi Hoghugh Khanevadeh: Nekah Va Enelal An* [A jurisprudent assessment of family rights]. Tehran: Nashr Olum Eslami, 1365.

Mohebbi, Manuchehr Khodayar (1946): *Sharik Mard* [The man's partner]. Tehran: 1325.

Mojab, Shahrzad (1991): 'Kontrol Dolat Va Moqavemat Zanan Dar Arseh Daneshgahhaye Iran' [State control and women's resistance in Iranian universities]. In *Nimeye Digar*, no. 14, Spring 1370.

Mojahedin Khalgh (1978): *Payam Sazeman Be Kolliyeh Niruhaye Enghelabi Mihan: Democrathaye Enghelabi Va Enghelabiyun Komonist* (A message to the revolutionary and reformist forces). Tehran: 1356.
(1979a): 'On the Question of Hejab'. In A. Tabari and N. Yeganeh (eds.) (1982): *In the Shadow of Islam.*
(1979b): *Women in the Path of Liberation*. Tehran: Sazeman Mojahedin Khalgh Iran, 1358.
(1979c): *Entezarat Maghtai Az Jomhuri Eslami*. Leaflet on conjunctural expectations from the Islamic Republic. Tehran: Sazeman Mojahedin Khalgh Iran, 1357.
(1980a): *Majmueh Elamiyeha Va Mozegirihaye Siasi Mojahedin Khalgh: Dey-Bahman 1357* (Collection of declarations and announcements of the Mojahedin during January–February 1979). Tehran: Sazeman Mojahedin Khalgh Iran, 1359.

(1980b): *Didgahhaye Mojahedin Khalgh Darbareh Ghanun Asasi.* Leaflet on the Mojahedin's views about the Constitution of the Islamic Republic. Tehran: Sazeman Mojahedin Khalgh Iran, 1359.

(1981): *Ayatollah Kashani Va Nehzat Melli Be Rahbari Doctor Mosaddeq* (Leaflet about Ayatollah Kashani and Mosaddeq). Italy: Anjoman Danesh-juyan Mosalman, 1360.

Molyneux, Maxine (1981): 'Women and Revolution in the People's Republic of Yemen'. In *Feminist Review*, no. 1.

Momen, Moojan (1985): *An Introduction to Shii Islam.* New Haven: Yale University Press.

Momeni, Djamshid (1972): 'The Difficulties of Changing the Age of Marriage in Iran'. In *Journal of Marriage and the Family*. August.

(1975): 'Polygamy in Iran'. In *Journal of Marriage and the Family*. May.

Momeni, Djamshid A. (ed.) (1977): *The Population of Iran: A Selection of Reading*. Honolulu and Shiraz: East-West Population Institute and Pahlavi University.

Moslem World (1911): 'The New Women in Persia', no. 1, April.

Mossavar-Rahmani, Yasmin (1983): 'Family Planning in Post-Revolutionary Iran'. In G. Nashat (ed.): *Women and Revolution in Iran.*

Motahhari, Morteza (1974): *Masaleh Hejab* [The question of *hejab*]. Qom: Entesharat Sadra, 1353.

(1978): *Nezam Hoghugh Zan Dar Eslam* [The system of women's rights in Islam]. Qom: Entesharat Sadra, 1357.

Nafisi, Said (1965): *Tarikh Ejtemai Va Siasi Iran Dar Doreh Moaser* [The social and political history of Iran in the contemporary period], I. Tehran: Entesharat Bonyad, 1344.

Nahavandian, Mohammad (1978): *Peykar Priuz Tanbaku* [The victorious tobacco struggle]. Tehran: Parto, 1357.

Nahid, Abdolhosein (1981): *Zanan Iran Dar Jonbesh Mashruteh* [Iranian Women in the constitutional movement]. West Germany: Jonbesh Mostaghel Zanan Irani Dar Kharej Az Keshvar, 1361.

Najmabadi, Afsaneh (1987a): 'Depoliticisation of a Rentier State: The Case of Pahlavi Iran'. In H. Beblawi and G. Lucian (eds.): *The Rentier State.* London: Croom Helm.

(1987b): *Land Reform and Social Change in Iran.* Salt Lake City: University of Utah Press.

(1987c): 'Iran's Turn to Islam: From Modernism to a Moral Order'. In *Middle East Journal*, vol. 41, no. 2, Spring.

(1989): 'Power, Morality and the New Muslim Womanhood'. Paper presented to the MIT Centre for International Studies, 20 March 1989.

(1991): 'Hazards of Modernity and Morality: Women, State and Ideology in Contemporary Iran'. In D. Kandiyoti (ed.): *Women, Islam and State.*

Najmabadi, Afsaneh (ed.) (1992): *Ma'ayib al-rijal: Vices of Men* (translation of and introduction to the text by Bibi Khanum Astarabadi). Chicago: Midland Press.

Najmabadi, Afsaneh (1993): 'Zanh-yi Millat: Women or Wives of the Nation'. In *Iranian Studies.* Forthcoming.

Naqvi, Ali Reza (1967): 'The Family Laws of Iran', 4 parts. In *Islamic Studies*,

vols. 6 and 7, no. 2–4, June 1967–September 1968.
Nashat, Guity (1980): 'Women in the Islamic Republic of Iran'. In *Iranian Studies*, vol. 13, no. 1–4.
Nashat, Guity (ed.) (1983): *Women and Revolution in Iran*. Boulder: Westview Press.
Nategh, Homa (1976): *Mirza Malkom Khan: Ruznameh Ghanun* (Collected editions of *Ghanun* newspaper, edited by Malkom Khan, compiled and introduced, H. Nategh.). Tehran: Sepehr, 2535.
(1979): *Mosibat Vaba Va Balaye Hokumat* [The calamity of cholera and the pain of government]. Tehran: Nashr Gostaresh, 1358.
(1980): 'Negahi Be Barkhi Neveshtehha Va Mobarezat Zanan Dar Doran Mashrutiat' [A look at some of the writings and women's movements in the constitutional period]. In *Ketab Jomeh*, no. 30, 1358.
(1983a): 'Jang Fergheha Dar Enghelab Mashrutiat' [The battle of factions in the constitutional movement]. In *Alefba*, vol. 3, Summer 1362.
(1983b): 'Masaleh Zan Dar Barkhi Az Modavenat Chap Az Nehzat Mashrutiat Ta Asr Reza Khan' [The question of women in some of the publications of the left from the constitutional period to Reza Shah's era]. In *Zaman Now*, no. 1, November 1362.
National Union of Women (NUW) (1979a): 'An Analysis of the Socio-Economic Situation of Women in Iran'. In A. Tabari and N. Yeganeh (eds.) (1982): *In the Shadow of Islam*.
(1979b): 'Message to the Solidarity Conference'. In A. Tabari and N. Yeganeh (eds.) (1982): *In the Shadow of Islam*.
(1979c): 'Darbareh Laghv Ghanun Hemayat Khanevadeh [About the abrogation of the family protection law]. In *Barabari*. Issue 21.6.79/ 31.3.58.
Navai, Abdolhosein (1976): *Dolathaye Iran Az Aghaz Mashrutiat Ta Oltimatom* [The governments of Iran from the beginning of constitutionalism until the Russian ultimatum]. Tehran: Entesharat Babak, 2535.
Nirumand, Bahman (1969): *Iran: The New Imperialism in Action*. Translated by Leonard Mins. New York: Monthly Review Press.
Nobari, Ali Reza (ed.) (1978): *Iran Erupts*. Stanford: Stanford University, Iran America Documentation Group.
Nourai, Fereshteh (1973): *Tahghigh Dar Afkar Mirza Malkom Khan* [Research on Mirza Malkom Khan's ideas]. Tehran: Ketabhaye Jibi, 1351.
(1975): 'The Constitutional Ideas of a Shi'ite Mujtehed: Muhammad Husayn Naini'. In *Iranian Studies*, vol. 3, 1975.
Nurbakhsh, Javad (1983): *Sufi Women*. New York: Khaniqahi Nimatullahi Publications.
On the Oppression of Women in Iran [Darbareh Setam keshidegi zan dar Iran] (1972). Author(s) unknown. New York: Entesharat Fanus, 1351.
On the Question of Women [Darbareh Masaleh zan] (1971). Author(s) unknown. New York: Entesharat Fanus, 1350.
Organisation of Women's Emancipation (OWE) (1979a): 'Women in the Eyes of Clerics of Islamic Revolution'. In A. Tabari and N. Yeganeh (eds.) (1982): *In the Shadow of Islam*.
(1979b): *Rahai*, no. 12.

(1980): 'The Veil and the Question of Women in Iran'. In A. Tabari and N. Yeganeh (eds.) (1982): *In the Shadow of Islam*.

Pahlavi, Ashraf (1980): *Faces in the Mirror*. Englewood: Prentice Hall.

Pahlavi, Mohammad Reza Shah (1960): *Mission For My Country*. London: Hutchinson.

(1967): *Enghelab Sefid* [The white revolution]. Tehran: Ketabkhaneh Saltanati, 1346.

(1975): *Be Suye Tamadon Bozorg* [Towards the great civilisation]. Tehran: Markaz Pajouhesh va Nashr Farhang Siasi Doran Pahlavi, 1354.

(1980): *Answer to History*. New York: Stein and Day.

Pakizegi, Behnaz (1978): 'Legal and Social Positions of Iranian Women'. In L. Beck and N. Keddie (eds.): *Women in the Muslim World*.

Parliamentary Proceedings of the First Majles (1946): In *Ruznameh Rasmi Keshvar Shahanshahi*. Issue 12 Mordad, 1325.

Parvin, Manuchehr and Taghavi, Majid (1988): 'A Comparison of Land in Iran under Monarchy and under the Islamic Republic'. In H. Amirahmadi and M. Parvin (eds.): *Post-Revolutionary Iran*.

Patai, Raphael (1967): *Women in the Modern World*. New York: Free Press.

Paydarfar, Ali (1975): 'The Modernisation Process and Household Size: A Provincial Comparison in Iran'. In *Journal of Marriage and the Family*. May.

Paydarfar, Ali and Sarram, Mahmud (1970): 'Differential Fertility and Socio-Economic Status of Shirazi Women: A Pilot Study'. In *Journal of Marriage and the Family*. November.

Pazargad, Bahaeddin (1966): *Chronology of the History of Iran: 2850 B.C. to 1963 A.D.* Tehran: Eshraghi Bookshop, 1345.

Peykar Organisation (1978): *Elamieh Darbareh Khatarat Liberalism* [Leaflet about the dangers of liberalism]. 1357.

Rafii, Mansureh (1983): *Anjoman: Organ Anjoman Velayati Azarbayjan* [About *Anjoman* newspaper]. Tehran: Nashr Tarikh Iran, 1362.

Rahnavard, Zahra (1978): *Payam Hejab Zan Mosalman* [The message of Muslim women's *hejab*]. Tehran: Nashr Mahbubeh, 1357.

(1979): *Tolue Zan Mosalman* [The dawn of the Muslim Woman]. Tehran: Nashr Mahbubeh, 1358.

Rain, Esmail (1976): *Anjomanhaye Serri Dar Enghelab Mashrutiat* [Secret societies in the Constitutional Revolution]. Tehran: Javidan, 2535.

Rajavi, Masoud (1982): Unpublished interview, conducted by Nahid Yeganeh. Paris.

Ramazani, R. K. (1988): 'Intellectual Trends in the Politics and History of the Musaddiq Era'. In J. Bill and R. Louis (eds.): *Musaddiq, Iranian Nationalism, and Oil*. Austin: University of Texas Press.

Ramy, Nima (1983): *The Wrath of Allah*. London: Pluto Press.

Rassam, Amal (1984): 'Arab Women: the Status of Research in the Social Sciences and the Status of Women', and 'Toward a Theoretical Framework for the Study of Women in the Arab World'. In *Social Science Research and Women in the Arab World*. Paris: UNESCO.

Ravandi, Morteza (1978): *Tarikh Ejtemai Iran* [The social history of Iran], 3 vols. Tehran: Amir Kabir, 1357.

Reeves, Minou (1989): *Female Warriors of Allah: Women and the Islamic Revolution*. New York: E. P. Dutton.

Rezvani, Maryam (1985): 'Zan Mojahed Cheguneh Tavallod Yaft?' [How was the Mojahed woman born?]. In *Mojahed*. Issue 3.5.85/14.2.63.

Rice, Colliver C. (1923): *Persian Women and Their Ways*. London: Seeley, Service and Co.

Rostow, W. W. (1960): *The Stages of Economic Growth: A Non-Communist Manifesto*. Cambridge: Cambridge University Press.

Royanian, Simin (1979): 'A History of Iranian Women's Struggles'. In *The Review of Iranian Political Economy and History*, vol. 3, no. 1, Spring.

Rubin, Barry (1980): *Paved with Good Intentions: The American Experience and Iran*. Oxford: Oxford University Press.

Sabbah, Fatna A. (1984a): *Woman in the Muslim Unconscious*. Translated by Mary Jo Lakeland. New York: Pergamon Press.

Sabban, Rima (1988): 'Lebanese Women and Capitalist Cataclysm'. In N. Toubia (ed.): *Women of the Arab World*.

Sadeghipour, A. R. (ed.) (1968): *Yadegar Gozashteh* [Collection of Speeches by Reza Shah]. Tehran: Javidan, 1346.

Sadigh, Javad (1973): *Melliyat Va Enghelab Dar Iran* [Nationalism and revolution in Iran]. New York: Entesharat Fanus, 1352.

Sadowski, Yahya (1993): 'The New Orientalism and the Democracy Debate'. In *Middle East Report*, no. 183, vol. 23 (4), July–August.

Sadr-Hashemi, Mohammad (1984): *Tarikh Jaraed Va Majallat Iran* [The history of the press in Iran], 2 vols. First published in 1948. Tehran: Entesharat Kamal, 1363.

Safa-Esfahani, Kaveh (1980): 'Female-Centred World Views in Iranian Culture: Symbolic Representations of Sexuality in Dramatic Games'. In *Signs: Journal of Women in Culture and Society*, vol. 6, no. 1, Autumn.

Said, Edward (1978): *Orientalism*. London: Routledge and Kegan Paul.

Salehian-Farnoodymehr, Nezhat (1975): 'Psychological Survey Attitudes toward Equal Rights for Women (Iran)'. Ph.D. Dissertation. United States International University.

Salman, Majida (1978): 'Arab Women'. In *Khamsin*, no. 6. London: Pluto Press.

Sanasarian, Eliz (1982): *The Women's Rights Movement in Iran*. New York: Praeger.

Sanati, Mahdokht (1993): 'Sedigheh Doulatabadi: Zendeginameh' [Doulatabadi's life]. In *Nimeye Digar*, no. 17, Winter 1371.

Sayigh, Rosemary (1981): 'Orientalism and Arab Women'. In *Arab Studies Quarterly*, vol. 3, no. 3.

Sayyah, Leyla (1990): 'Tehran-e Shast Hasht' [Tehran of 1968]. In *Nimeye Digar*, no. 11, Spring 1369.

Schimmel, Annemarie (1982): 'Women in Mystical Islam'. In Al-Hibri (ed.): *Women and Islam*.

Sedghi, Hamideh (1980): 'An Assessment of Works in Farsi and English on Iran and Iranian Women: 1900–1970'. In *The Review of Radical Political Economies*, vol. 12, no. 2, Summer.

Sedghi, Hamideh and Ashraf, Ahmad (1976): 'The Role of Women In Iranian

Development'. In J. W. Jacqz (ed.) (1976): *Iran: Past, Present and Future.* New York: Aspen Institute for Humanistic Studies.

Shariati, Ali (1975): *Entezar Asr Hazer Az Zan Moslaman* [The expectations of the present era from Muslim women]. Tehran: 1354.

(1976): *Zan Dar Cheshm Va Del Mohammad* [Woman in the eye and heart of Mohammad]. Tehran: 1355.

(1978): *Ommat Va Emamat* [Islamic community and leadership]. Tehran: Entesharat Ghalam, 1357.

(1979): *On the Sociology of Islam.* Berkley: Mizan Press.

(1980): *Fatima is Fatima.* Translated by Laleh Bakhtiar. Tehran: Hamdami Foundation.

Shaw, S. and Shaw, E. (1977): *History of the Ottoman Empire and Modern Turkey.* Cambridge: Cambridge University Press.

Shekholeslami, Pari (1972): *Zanan Ruznamehnegar Va Andishmand Iran* [Women journalist and free-thinkers of Iran]. Tehran: Chapkhaneh Mazgraphic, 1351.

Shuster, Morgan (1968): *The Strangling of Persia.* New York: Greenwood Press.

Siavoshi, Sussan (1990): *Liberal Nationalism in Iran: The Failure of a Movement.* Boulder: Westview Press.

Siddiqui, Kalim (ed.) (1980): *The Islamic Revolution in Iran.* London: The Muslim Institute.

S. J. R. (1978): *Barrasi Va Tahlil Nehzat Emam Khomeini* [The assessment and analysis of *emam* Khomeini's movement]. Tehran: Nashr Ahrar, 1357.

Smart, Barry (1990): 'Modernity, postmodernity and the present'. In B. S. Turner (ed.): *Theories of Modernity and Postmodernity.* London: Sage Publications.

Smith, Jane (ed.) (1981): *Women in Contemporary Muslim Societies.* Lewisburg: Bucknell University Press.

Soltanzadeh, Avtis (1922): 'Mogheiat Zan Irani' [The position of Iranian women]. In *Historical Documents*, vol. 4, 1974.

Statistical Centre of Iran, Plan and Budget Organisation (1976): *Statistical Yearbook of Iran: March 1973–March 1974.* Tehran, 1355.

(1980): *Sarshomari Omumi Nofus Va Maskan Aban Mah 1355* [Census of population and housing of November 1976]. Tehran, 1359.

(1985): *Iran Dar Ayeneh Amar* [Iran in the mirror of statistics]. Tehran, 1364.

(1987): *Salnameh Amari 1365* [Statistical Yearbook of 1986]. Tehran, 1366.

(1988a): *Nashrieh Shomareh 13: Khanevadeh* (Periodical no. 13: Family). Tehran, 1367.

(1988b): *Sarshomari Omumi Nofus Va Maskan Mehr Mah 1365* [Census of population and housing of October 1986]. Tehran, 1367.

(1988c): *Salnameh Amari 1367* (Statistical Yearbook of 1988). Tehran, 1367.

(1988d): *A Statistical Reflection of the Islamic Republic of Iran*, no. 4. Tehran, 1367.

(1989): *A Statistical Reflection of the Islamic Republic of Iran*, no. 5. Tehran, 1368.

(1990): *A Statistical Reflection of the Islamic Republic of Iran*, no. 6. Tehran, 1369.

Suratgar, Olive Hepburn (1951): *I Sing in the Wilderness: An Intimate Account of Persia and Persians*. London: Stanford Press.

Tabari, Azar (1980): 'The Enigma of Veiled Iranian Women'. In *Feminist Review*, no. 5.

(1982): 'Islam and the Struggle for Emancipation of Iranian Women'. In A. Tabari and N. Yeganeh (eds.) (1982): *In the Shadow of Islam*.

Tabari, Azar (1983): 'The Role of Shi'ite Clergy in Modern Iranian Politics'. In N. Keddie (ed.): *Religion and Politics in Iran*.

Tabari, Azar and Yeganeh, Nahid (eds.) (1982): In the Shadow of Islam: *The Women's Movement in Iran*. London: Zed Press.

Taleghani, Mahmud (1979): 'On Hejab'. In A. Tabari and N. Yeganeh (eds.) (1982): *In the Shadow of Islam*.

Teymouri, Ebrahim (1982): *Tahrim Tanbaku, Avalin Moghavemat Manfi Dar Iran* [Tobacco boycott: the first negative resistance in Iran]. Tehran: Ketabhaye Jibi, 1361.

Torkman, Mohammad (ed.) (1983): *Sheykh Shahid Fazlollah Nuri* [The writings of Fazlollah Nuri]. Tehran: Entesharat Farhangi, 1362.

Touba, Jacqueline R. (1972): 'The Relationship Between Urbanisation and the Changing Status of Women in Iran 1956–1966'. In *Iranian Studies*, Winter 1972.

(1975): 'Sex Role Differentiation in Iranian Families Living in Urban and Rural Areas of a Region Undergoing Planned Industrialisation in Iran (Arak Shahrestan)'. In *Journal of Marriage and the Family*. May 1975.

Toubia, Nahid (ed.) (1988): *Women of the Arab World*. London: Zed Books.

Touhidi, Nayereh (1990): 'Masaleh Zan Va Roshanfekran Teye Tahavolat Daheye Akhir' [The woman question and intellectuals over the past decade]. In *Nimeye Digar*, no. 10, Winter 1368.

Tucker, Judith (1978): *Women in Nineteenth-Century Egypt*. Cambridge: Cambridge University Press.

(1983): 'Problems in the Historiography of Women in the Middle East: The Case of Nineteenth Century Egypt'. In *International Journal of Middle East Studies*, vol. 15.

Tudeh Party (1944): 'Proposals for a New Electoral Law'. In *Parliamentary Proceedings of the Fourteenth Mailes*. Issue 24 Mordad. Tehran, 1323.

(1978a): 'Tudeh Party Calls For a United Front'. In *Middle East Report*, no. 71, October.

(1978b): 'Tudeh Leader on the Religious Movement: an Interview with Iraj Eskandari'. In *Middle East Report*, no. 7576, March–April 1979.

(1979): *Tajrobeh Tarikhi Rah Roshd Gheyr Sarmayedari* [The historical experience of the non-capitalist path to development], no. 2. Tehran: Entesharat Hezb Tudeh, 1358.

(1980): *Tarkhaye Pishnahadi Hezb Tudeh Iran Darbareye Degarguni Va Nosazi 3'ameeh Iran* [The proposals of the Tudeh Party on the reconstruction of Iranian society]. Tehran: Entesharat Hezb Tudeh, 1359.

Van Dusen, Roxann A. (1979): 'The Study of Women in the Middle East: Some Thoughts'. In *Middle East Studies Association Bulletin*, vol. Io, no. 2.

Vardasbi, Abuzar (1981): 'Zan Dar Eslam Hoghughi Nadarad?' [Don't women have rights in Islam?]. In *Mofahed.* Issue 29.9.81/7.7.62.

Vatandoust, Gholam Reza (1972): *Seyyed Hasan Taqizadeh and 'Kaveh': Modernism in Post-Constitutional Iran (1916–1921)*. Ph.D. Dissertation. University of Washington.

Vatandoust, Gholam Reza (1985): 'The Status of Iranian Women During the Pahlavi Regime'. In A. Fathi (ed.): *Women and the Family in Iran.*

Vieille, Paul (1988): 'The State of the Periphery and its Heritage'. In *Economy and Society*, vol. 17, no. 1, February.

Wallerstein, I. (1979): *The Capitalist Werld Economy.* Cambridge: Cambridge University Press.

Wilber, Donald N. (1975): *Riza Shah Pahlavi: The Resurrection and Reconstruction of Iran.* New York: Exposition Press.

Women's Organisation of Iran (1975): *The Employment of Women.* Tehran: Women's Organisation of Iran.

Women's Section of the National Front (1979): 'Protest Letter'. In A. Tabari and N. Yeganeh (eds.) (1982): *In the Shadow of Islam.*

Women's Solidarity Committee (1979): 'Conference Report'. In A. Tabari and N. Yeganeh (eds.) (1982): *In the Shadow of Islam.*

Woodman Stocking, Annie (1912): 'The New Woman in Persia'. In *Moslem World*, no. 2, October.

Woodsmall, Ruth (1936): *Moslem Women Enter A New World.* London: Allen and Unwin.

(1960): *Women and the New East.* Washington DC: The Middle East Institute.

Yankachena, M. (1959): 'The Feminist Movement in Persia' (in Russian). In *Central Asian Review*, no. 7.

Yeganeh, Nahid (1982): 'Women's Struggles in the Islamic Republic of Iran'. In A. Tabari and N. Yeganeh (eds.): *In the Shadow of Islam.*

(1984): 'Jonbeshhaye Zanan Dar Iran' [Women's movements in Iran]. In *Nimeye Digar*, no. 2, Autumn 1363.

(1992): 'Zan va Zananegi Dar Farhang Siasi, Dini va Donyavi Iran' [Womanhood in religious and secular political culture in Iran]. In *Nshriyeh Bonyad Pajukeshhaye Zanan Iran*, no. 3.

(1993a): 'Women, Nationalism and Islam in Contemporary Political Discourse in Iran'. In *Feminist Review*, no. 44.

(1993b): 'Feminism and Islam in Iran'. In *Middle East Studies Review.* Forthcoming.

Yeganeh, Nahid and Keddie, Nikki (1986): 'Sexuality and Shii Social Protest in Iran'. In J. Cole and N. Keddie (eds.): *Shiism and Social Protest.* New Haven: Yale University Press.

Youssef, Nadia (1974): *Women and Work in Developing Societies.* Berkeley: California University Press.

YuvalDavis, Nira and Anthias, Floya (eds.) (1989): *Woman, Nation, State.* London: Macmillan Press.

Zubaida, Sami (1982): 'The Ideological Conditions for Khomeini's Doctrine of Government'. In *Economy and Society*, vol. 11, no. 2, May.

(1988): 'An Islamic State? The Case of Iran'. In *Middle East Report*, no. 153, July–August.

(1989): *Islam, the People and the State: Essays on Political Ideas and Movements in the Middle East.* London: Routledge.

(1989a): 'The Nation State in the Middle East'. In S. Zubaida (1989).
(1989b): 'Classes as Political Actors in the Iranian Revolution'. In S. Zubaida (1989).
(1989c): 'Components of Popular Culture in the Middle East'. In S. Zubaida (1989).

Zubaida, Sami and Stauth, George (1987): *Mass Culture, Popular Culture and Social Life in the Middle East*. Frankfurt: Campus Verlag. Colorado: Westview Press.

Zwemer, A. E. and S. M. (1926): *Moslem Women*. Cambridge, MA : Central Committee of the United Study of Foreign Missions.

NEWSPAPERS AND MAGAZINES

Ayandegan: Daily newspaper published in Tehran until August 1979.
1 (28.7.79/6.5.58) **2** (12.3.79/21.12.57) **3** (16.6.79/26.3.58)
4 (12.6.79/22.3.58) **5** (6.3.79/15.12.57) **6** (3.3.79/12.12.57)
7 (9.6.79/19.3.57)

Bamdad: Daily newspaper published in Tehran during 1979–81.
1 (20.1.80/30.10.58) **2** (6.3.80/15.12.58) **3** (8.7.80/15.4.59)
4 (14.6.80/27.3.59) **5** (22.9.80/31.6.58) **6** (23.4.80/3.2.59)

Enghelab Eslami: Newspaper of the followers of Abolhasan Banisadr, the first president of the Islamic Republic of Iran, published daily in Tehran and weekly abroad.
1 (5.7.80/27.9.59) **2** (12.3.81/21.12.59) and (3.4.81/13.2.60)

Ettehad Mardom: Newspaper of the Tudeh Party published abroad.
1 (22.3.82/3.12.60) **2** (22.2.86/3.12.64)

Ettelaat: Daily Newspaper published in Tehran since the 1940s.
1 (10.3.79/19.12.57) **2** (13.6.79/23.3.58) **3** (14.3.79/23.12.57)
4 (10.5.81/20.2.60) **5** (10.7.80/19.4.59) **6** (24.1.80/4.11.58)
7 (19.11.79/28.8.58) **8** (5.1.85/15.10.63) **9** (20.5.81/30.2.60)
10 (1.12.85/10.9.64) **11** (7.6.86/17.3.65) **12** (21.10.84/29.7.60) to
(17.11.84/26.8.63) **13** (21.11.85/11.8.64) **14** (20.5.86/30.2.65)
15 (19.5.86/29.2.65) **16** (6.2.85/17.11.64) **17** (12.10.85/20.7.64)
18 (5.11.85/14.8.64) **19** (2.11.85/11.8.64) **20** (10.9.79/19.6.58)
21 (5.4.86/15.2.65) **22** (29.3.83/9.1.62) **23** (17.1.85/27.10.63)
24 (23.10.85/31.6.64) **25** (13.2.82/24.11.60) **26** (20.4.81/30.2.60)
27 (4.11.85/13.9.64) **28** (23.1.85/3.11.63) **29** (4.11.85/13.9.64)
30 (2.11.85/11.8.64) **31** (27.1.86/7.11.64) **32** (3.3.86/12.12.64)
33 (12.2.86/21.12.64) **34** (15.3.86/24.12.64) **35** (7.5.86/17.2.65)
36 (23.4.86/3.2.65) **37** (6.10.86/14.7.64) **38** (14.3.85/23.12.63)
39 (21.5.79/31.2.58) **40** (21.7.86/30.4.65) **41** (26.9.79/4.7.58)
42 (29.1.80/8.10.58) **43** (8.10.85/16.7.64) **44** (31.3.81/11.1.60)
45 (30.5.82/9.3.61) **46** (6.10.86/14.7.64) **47** (17.11.83/26.8.62)
48 (9.7.80/18.4.59) **49** (24.10.87/2.8.66) **50** (8.4.85/19.1.64)
51 (5.2.85/16.11.63) **52** (7.4.81/ 18.1.60) **53** (2.11.85/11.8.64)

54 (6.7.80/15.4.59) **55** (8.9.81/17.6.60) **56** (25.4.81/5.2.60)
57 (11.5.81/21.2.60) **58** (30.11.81/9.9.60) **59** (23.4.86/3.2.65)
60 (25.4.87/5.2.66) **61** (27.4.86/7.2.65) **62** (13.5.80/ 23.2.59)
63 (16.2.85/27.11.63) **64** (12.6.79/22.3.58)

The Guardian London: **1** (1.11.78) **2** (18.6.79) **3** (4.7.80)

Iranshahr (Berlin): Iranian newspaper published in Berlin by Kazemzadeh Iranshahr in the early 1920s.
1 (July 1923, no. 12) **2** (May 1925, no. 7) **3** (August 1924, no. 11–12)

Iranshahr: Iranian weekly newspaper published in exile in London and New York during 1978–84.
1 (27.10.78/5.8.57) **2** (1.12.78/22.10.57) and (22.12.87/1.10.57)
3 (1.11.78/10.8.57) **4** (16.3.79/26.12.57) **5** (12.8.83/21.5.62)
6 (23.4.84/3.2.63)

Iran Times: Iranian newspaper published in the US in English.
1 (13.6.86) **2** (17.7.81)

Jahan Zanan: Magazine of the Democratic Organisation of Iranian Women, a branch of the Tudeh Party.
1 (2.2.80/11.12.58)

Javanan: Youth magazine published in Tehran.
1 (Nos. 1163, 1989)

Jomhuri Eslami: Daily newspaper published in Tehran since 1979 representing the views of the Islamic Republican Party.
1 (9.4.81/20.1.60) **2** (23.2.83/4.12.61) **3** (26.2.83/7.12.61)

Kar: Newspaper of the Fadaiyan Khalgh Organisation published in Tehran and abroad.
1 (15.7.80/24.4.59) **2** (8.3.81/17.12.59) **3** (2.7.80/11.4.59)
4 (12.10.81/18.7.60) **5** (26.2.81/17.12.59)

Kaveh: Iranian newspaper published in Berlin during 1916–22. In Seyyed Hasan Taqizadeh: *Kaveh*. Compiled and introduced by Iraj Afshar, Tehran:
1 (No. 12, 1920) **2** (No. 36, 1920) **3** (No. 6, 1920)
4 (No. 4–5, 1920) **5** (No. 8, 1920)

Ketab Jomeh: Literary/political periodical published in Tehran.
1 (No. 30, Esfand 1358/March 1980)

Keyhan: Daily newspaper published in Tehran since the 1940s.
1 (10.3.79/19.12.57) **2** (20.3.79/28.12.57) **3** (11.3.79/20.12.57)
4 (9.8.79/18.5.58) **5** (6.7.80/15.4.59) **6** (10.3.79/19.12.57)
7 (9.8.79/18.5.58) **8** (26.2.79/7.12.57) **9** (5.3.79/14.12.57)
10 (9.8.79/18.4.58) **11** (24.9.79/2.7.58) **12** (9.2.83/13.11.61)
13 (4.11.81/13.8.60) **14** (15.6.80/25.3.59) **15** (3.11.81/12.8.60)
16 (4.4.83/15.1.62) and (9.4.83/20.1.62) **17** (8.2.84/19.11.62)
18 (9.2.83/20.11.61) **19** (9.9.79/18.6.58) **20** (25.7.82/3.5.61)
21 (11.12.80/20.9.59) **22** (15.4.82/26.1.61) **23** (16.7.88/25.5.67)

24 (25.3.86/5.1.65) **25** (21.2.83/1.11.61) **26** (31.10.81/9.8.60)
27 (9.2.83/20.11.61) **28** (4.11.84/13.8.63) **29** (4.11.81/13.8.60)
30 (9.2.80/20.11.60) **31** (28.1.82/8.11.60) **32** (31.12.81/10.10.60)
33 (26.4.81/6.2.60) **34** (30.7.83/8.5.62) **35** (24.10.83/2.8.62)
36 (1.8.87/10.5.66) **37** (22.7.88/1.5.67) **38** (4.3.79/14,12,57)
39 (9.4.84/20.1.63) **40** (24.5.81/3.3.60) **41** (7.4.80/17.2.59)
42 (12.4.84/22.2.63) **43** (30.5.89/9.3.61) **44** (19.4.80/30.1.59)
45 (31.1.82/10.10.60) **46** (27.7.81/5.5.60) **47** (1.2.83/12.11.61)
48 (13.1.83/23.10.61) **49** (2.11.81/11.8.60) **50** (2.8.83/31.5.62)
51 (13.3.81/22.12.59) **52** (24.2.83/5.12.61) **53** (15.9.79/24.6.58)
54 (10.1.82/20.10.60) **55** (11.5.82/21.2.60) **56** (2.10.81/11.8.60)
57 (11.4.83/22.1.62) **58** (12.12.82/30.9.61) **59** (24.2.83/5.12.61)
60 (26.5.82/5.3.61) **61** (1.1.83/11.10.61) **62** (27.1.61/7.12.61)
63 (26.5.83/8.3.62) **64** (1.2.83/12.11.61) **65** (9.9.80/18.6.59)
66 (16.8.81/25.5.60) **67** (27.9.81/5.7.60) **68** (16.9.81/25.6.60)
69 (22.10.81/30.7.60) **70** (20.9.81/29.6.60) **71** (20.11.83/29.8.62)
72 (6.3.79/15.12.57) **73** (17.7.86/26.4.65) **74** (20.7.84/29.4.63)
75 (23.4.82/3.2.61) and (25.4.82/5.2.61) and (7.5.82/17.2.61)
76 (31.3.83/11.1.62) and (24.4.85/4.2.64)and (24.8.85/2.6.64)
and (18.7.85/27.4.64) **77** (23.4.85/3.2.64) and (8.12.85/17.9.64)
78 (9.9.83/18.6.62) **79** (19.7.84/28.4.63) **80** (5.2.80/16.12.58)
81 (7.1.79/17.10.57) **82** (20.2.80/1.12.58) **83** (31.5.80/10.3.58)
84 (27.7.81/5.5.60) **85** (11.8.82/20.5.61) **86** (3.6.82/13.3.61)
87 (6.4.84/17.1.63) **88** (8.4.80/19.1.59) **89** (26.1.84/6.11.62)

Keyhan Havai: Weekly summary of *Keyhan* for airmail, published in Tehran since 1960s.

1 (7.6.78/17.3.57) **2** (5.1.77/15.10.56) and (9.3.77/19.12.56)
3 (2.2.77/13.11.56) **4** (26.7.78/4.5.57) and (1.11.78/10.7.57)
5 (2.8.78/10.5.57) and (25.10.78/3.8.57) **6** (2.6.78/12.3.57)
7 (28.6.78/7.7.57) **8** (25.10.78/3.8.57) **9** (11.10.78/19.7.57)
(18.10.78/25.7.57) **10** (2.8.78/10.5.57) **11** (7.6.78/17.357)
and (28.6.78/7.7.57) (26.7.78/4.5.57) **12** (28.6.78/7.7.57)
13 (5.7.78/14.5.57) **14** (13.9.78/22.6.57) **15** (30.8.78/8.6.57)
16 (11.5.77/21.2.56) **17** (30.8/8.6.57) **18** (28.6.78/7.7.57)
19 (5.7.78/14.5.57) **20** (16.8.78/24.5.57) **21** (14.6.78/24.3.57)
and (21.6.78/31.3.57) and (28.6.78/7.6.78) **22** (14.6.78/24.3.57)
23 (6.9.78/15.6.57) **24** (11.10.78/19.7.57) **25** (6.9.78/15.6.57)
26 (11.10.78/19.7.57) **27** (25.10.78/3.8.57) **28** (1.11.78/10.9.57)
29 (17.10.78/27.10.56) **30** (7.2.79/18.11.57) **31** (24.1.79/4.11.57)
32 (7.2.79/18.11.57) **33** (24.1.79/4.11.57) **34** (7.2.79/18.11.57)
35 (14.2.78/25.11.57) **36** (30.8.78/8.6.57) **37** (1.11.78/10.9.57)
38 (29.12.78/8.10.57) **39** (1.11.78/10.9.57) **40** (3.8.78/11.5.57)
41 (21.3.79/1.1.58) and (20.3.79/30.12.57) **42** (8.3.89/18.12.67)
43 (18.10.89/26.7.68) **44** (1.8.79/10.5.59) **45** (24.4.85/4.2.64)
46 (20.6.79/30.3.58)

Keyhan (London): Weekly newspaper published in London since 1984.
1 (8.11.84/17.8.63) **2** (7.7.88/16.4.67) **3** (19.10.89/27.7.68)
4 (2.7.89/11.4.68) **5** (16.7.88/25.4.68) **6** (19.6.86/29.3.65)
7 (20.1.85/30.10.63) **8** (7.9.85/18.11.64) **9** (3.7.86/12.4.65)

Mahjubeh: Islamic women's magazine in English published by the Iranian government.
1 (May 1981)

Middle East Report (1979). Nos. 75–76, March–April. Washington.

Middle East Report (1991). No. 173, vol. 21 (6), November–December. Washington.

Mizan: Newspaper of the Liberation Movement of Iran published in Tehran during 1979–81.
1 (8.3.79/16.12.57) **2** (28.4.81/6.2.60) **3** (26.9.79/4.7.58)
4 (24.5.81/3.3.60) **5** (26.4.81/6.2.60) **6** (8.3.81/17.12.59)
7 (7.3.81/16.12.59)

Nimeye Digar: Iranian feminist periodical published in UK and US.
1 (No. 1, Spring 1984) **2** (No. 6, Winter 1988)

Payam Jebheye Melli: Weekly newspaper of the National Front, published in Tehran and abroad.
1 (29.4.79/9.2.58) **2** (12.2.81/25.11.59)

Ghanun: Iranian newspaper published by Mirza Malkom Khan in London during 1889–90. In *Ghanun* (Law). Compiled and introduced by Homa Nategh (1976). Tehran: Sepehr, 2535.
1 (No. 7) **2** (No. 10) **3** (No. 15)
4 (No. 13) (No. 19)

Rah Zeinab: Islamic women's magazine published in Tehran during 1979–81.
1 (2.6.81/12.3.60) **2** (10.3.81/19.12.59)

Soroush: Magazine published by the Ministry of Islamic Guidance.
1 (3.4.83/4.1.62) **2** (6.1.82/17.11.60)

Women and Struggle in Iran: Women's magazine published in the 1980s by the 'Aghalliyat' faction of the Fadaiyan Khalgh Organisation.
1 (No 4, Spring 1985) **2** (No 2, September 1982)

Zaban Zanan: Women's newspaper published in the 1920s and 1940s.
1 (No 2, June 1945)

Zan Ruz: Weekly women's magazine published in Tehran since the 1960s.
1 (22.3.81/2.1.60) **2** (29.10.89/6.8.68) **3** (2.11.89 11.9.68)
4 (4.11.89/13.8.68) **5** (14.7.84/23.4.63) **6** (4.7.84/23.4.63)
7 (22.3.81/2.1.60) **8** (4.6.89/13.3.68) **9** (20.12.89/30.10.68)
10 (22.4.89/2.2.68) **11** (3.2.90/14.11.68) **12** (4.11.89/13.8.68)
13 (16.11.89/25.9.68) **14** (2.12.89/11.9.68) **15** (20.1.90/30.10.68)
16 (2.11.89/11.9.68) **17** (17.6.89/27.3.68) **18** (18.7.89/28.3.88)

19 (2.6.89/12.3.69)
20 (3.10.81/11.7.60)
21 (5.8.89/14.5.68)
22 (19.9.81/28.6.60)
23 (14.4.84/24.2.62)
24 (18.3.84/27.12.62)
25 (31.10.81/9.8.60)
26 (12.5.84/22.2.63)
27 (20.1.09/30.10.68)
28 (16.9.89/25.6.68)
29 (17.10.87/25.7.66)
30 (27.7.88/5.5.67)
31 (5.12.81/14.9.60)
32 (4.7.81/13.5.60)
33 (17.23.90/26.12.68)
34 (28.4.84/8.2.63)
35 (9.5.84/29.2.63)
36 (3.6.89/13.3.68)
37 (8.5.84/18.2.63)
38 (12.4.89/23.2.68)
39 (12.4.89/23.2.68)
40 (29.7.89/7.5.68)
41 (7.4.84/18.1.63)
42 (16.1.84/26.10.62)
43 (26.5.84/5.3.63)
44 (27.5.89/6.3.68)
45 (24.6.89/3.4.68)
46 (9.6.84/19.3.63)
47 (22.8.87/31.5.66)
48 (5.9.87/14.6.66)
49 (25.8.84/3.6.63)
50 (29.8.87/7.6.66)
51 (17.7.88/26.5.67)
52 (2.12.89/11.8.68)
53 (13.10.88/21.7.67)
54 (8.8.81/17.5.60)
55 (31.3.88/11.66)
56 (12.8.89/21.5.68)
57 (21.1.89/1.11.67)
58 (30.4.87/10.2.66)
59 (7.1.89/17.10.67)
60 (12.4.89/23.1.68)
61 (6.5.88/16.2.67)
62 (20.1.80/30.10.68)

Index

Printed in the United States
152745LV00002B/12/A

9 780521 595728